Applying Sociology

Making a Better World

WILLIAM DU BOIS

South Dakota State University

R. DEAN WRIGHT

Drake University

ALLYN AND BACON

Boston • London • Toronto • Sydney • Tokyo • Singapore

Series Editor: Jeff Lasser
Editorial Assistant: Susan Hutchinson
Marketing Manager: Judeth Hall
Production Editor: Christopher H. Rawlings
Editorial-Production Service: Omegatype Typography, Inc.
Composition and Prepress Buyer: Linda Cox
Manufacturing Buyer: Suzanne Lareau
Cover Administrator: Brian Gogolin
Electronic Composition: Omegatype Typography, Inc.

Library of Congress Cataloging-in-Publication Data

Du Bois, William D. (William David)
    Applying sociology : making a better world / William Du Bois, R. Dean Wright.
       p.   cm.
    Includes bibliographical references (p.   ).
    ISBN 0-205-30616-0 (alk. paper)
    1. Applied sociology. 2. Social problems. 3. Social institutions. I. Wright, R. Dean.
  II. Title.

   HN29.5 .D8   2001
   301—dc21

                                            00-044769

Printed in the United States of America

10 9 8 7 6 5 4 3 2 1   05 04 03 02 01 00

To our mothers,
who gave us life in so many ways

Contents

PREFACE

Dreams. Who are we, and what will we become? Watch the children. Who are they? And what will they become? Society is the stage on which we enact our dreams. As children we start the dream anew. What will we make? How do we make a better world? It is an ancient conversation. So many people come and go. What will we become?

We are both professional sociologists. Like so many others, we entered the field to make the world a better place. However, the legacy of sociology today seems filled with esoteric theories, obscure statistical analysis, market research, jury consultants, researchers selling their work to the highest bidder, and armchair theories. It is hardly a legacy of which we can be proud.

Today sociology is dominated more and more by people whose research and applications have little lasting value. For many of our colleagues, sociological facts seem to be reduced to a formula: a never-ending process of analyzing minute bits and pieces of information, all of which lack the potential of being applied to assist real people in real situations to solve the problems of everyday life. However, we believe the discipline of sociology does, in fact, deal with real situations. It provides knowledge that can be translated into social inventions, with the potential of solving many of our social problems.

We start and end the book by wedding art to sociology. Even though art and sociology are commonly thought of as very different forms, we have come to the conclusion that they are common partners. We believe, as Robert Henri said in his classic *The Spirit of Art* in 1923, that "Art when really understood is the province of every human being."[1] Humans need art more than most of us realize. Art is fundamental to life. At our core we are both social and artistic. We are most human when we combine the two. All attempts to solve problems involve the use of art in everyday life. Henri notes that art "is simply a question of doing things, anything, well. It is not an outside, extra thing."[2] How perfect this concept is when we think about inventing social programs to make the world a better place in which we can all live.

Henri went on to comment:

> *When the artist is alive in any person, whatever his kind of work may be, he becomes an inventive, searching, daring, self-expressive creature. He becomes interesting to other people. He disturbs, upsets, enlightens, and he opens ways for a better understanding. Where those who are not artists are trying to close the book, he opens it, shows there are still more pages possible.[3]*

It was this type of thinking that first led us to conceive of writing a book that could bring together people who share the philosophy that knowledge must be applied to make sense out of society, research, theory, and practice. Each of us has gone through the experience of "becoming an academic." We worked together for several years and knew we shared similar ideas about how the discipline has gone wrong and what direction it should take to become more meaningful both to the professionals who share the name "sociologists" and to the real world in which they need to be working. All too many times the "maturation process" of becoming a "professional sociologist" involves shedding passion and feeling, and taking on an "objective" and "scientific" stance that dehumanizes both us and our subjects. The founders of our discipline, from the start, shared the belief that sociology could be better taught with a style different from the objective, scientific one now used by so many teachers. We have all read articles in professional journals that leave us saying . . . so what? When we ask each other what works have stood the test of time, we answer with *Street Corner Society* and similar works and then turn to the Chicago school where many original theories and ideas emerged. The "saints" of the discipline had practical experiences in the community. Their students then did the same thing with their students, . . . but somewhere we seem to have lost that quest for practicality.

Currently academic sociology could be accused of being a con game—a chain letter or pyramid game that teaches people to become sociologists so they can teach others to become sociologists. Sociologists need to be able to do something besides research and teaching. The market is saturated. In an Internet discussion on this point, one woman with a doctorate wrote that she was lucky enough to find a faculty position but many friends who graduated with her were beginning to look for waitress positions. This is a scandal. We need to be educating people in real skills to change the world rather than just in methods of amassing piles of the esoteric trivia that so often masquerade as knowledge in theses and dissertations (not to mention journal articles). Sociology needs to *do* something. We need to create jobs, skills, and a better world.

We must outgrow the sophomoric version of sociology that dominates so many journals and textbooks. A true sociology lives precisely *between* the university and the real world. We must take our knowledge and apply it to the real world. We need tools rather than just textbooks and journal articles.

As Thomas Szasz[4] noted, if the first sin was eating from the tree of knowledge of good and evil, the second sin was trying to build a Tower of Babel up to the heavens. The tower was destroyed and people scattered across the earth with different languages. Academics have not been guilty of clear speech since.

A psychology professor recently told about teaching graduate students how to do a research paper. He took them to the library, showed them the journals, and said, "Now if you see an article that looks like it might be interesting, and you might enjoy reading it, then that isn't a scholarly article." When the laughter died down, he explained he wasn't joking.

It is customary in academic writing to use the third-person voice—objective, detached, and uninvolved. It is a symptom of our scientific, masculine culture that strips us of our personal voice. But sociology must be relevant to our personal lives or it has no meaning. James Hillman's critique of psychology is no less true of sociology:

> *By psychology's "mortal" sin, I mean the sin of deadening, the dead feeling that comes over us when we read professional psychology, hear its language, the voice with which it drones, the bulk of its textbooks, the serious pretensions and bearded proclamations of new "findings"*

that could hardly be more banal, its soothing anodynes for self-help, its decor, its fashion, its departmental meetings, and its tranquilizing consulting rooms, those stagnant waters where the soul goes to be restored, a last refuge of white-bread culture, stale, crustless, but ever spongy with rebounding hope.

Neglect of beauty neglects the Goddess, who then has to steal back into the departments as sexual harassment, into the laboratories as "research" experiments with sex and gender, and into the consulting rooms as seductive assignations. All the while psychology, without beauty, becomes victim of its own cognitive strictures, all passion spent in pushing for publication and position. Without beauty, there's little fun and less humor. Grand motivations are lost to psychological categories like grandiosity and inflation, while the adventure of ideas is cut to fit experimental designs. Whatever romance might still be left appears in the desire to help suffering people by entering a "training program" for therapists. But if helping is the calling, then better to apprentice with Mother Teresa than to expect a psychology without soul, beauty, or pleasure to train you to help the suffering. Psychology has no self-help manual for its own affliction.[5]

We must return love and the good to center stage. Our academic credibility might suffer if we placed beauty at the top of our research agenda. However, as the artist strives, we must strive to make a better life. We must create a society and organizations in which people flourish. To borrow Hillman's word, we must re-vision sociology.[6] What is at stake is nothing less than the soul of the discipline. We must return to the original vision and purpose of the discipline—making a better society. Sociology should have a foot in both worlds: the academy and everyday life. It is important to return to the blackboard to understand what is going on; to retreat, regroup, imagine bold new alternatives, and create. We must then apply what we know. This book was written by people struggling to apply their knowledge to make a better world. Many of the articles use a first-person voice as authors bridge between academic knowledge and everyday life.

We have argued that sociology should be halfway between the university and the streets. We have tried to make the language of this book reflect that perspective. We have sought to avoid the academic writing style of the ivory tower. At the same time, we have not tried to avoid sophisticated sociological thinking. Indeed, we have tried to translate it into everyday language and animate it with practical examples of how it can be applied. When jargon is necessary, we have sought to define its meaning promptly. We hope our writing style reflects our purpose: to hold an open informal conversation about what we are doing, how to do it, and what we should be doing. We have asked each contributor to "tell us everything you know. If you were passing on your knowledge to your children, what would you tell them?"

It is our desire in presenting this collection of articles, many original and others synthesized from existing works, to return to the tradition that once was shared by almost everyone in the discipline: using existing knowledge and expertise to address problems in society and thus make the world a better place in which to live.

The reader will find many different writing styles. Most of the articles are accessible to the intelligent layperson. In the introductory article, Bill Du Bois lays out a framework for doing applied sociology and he challenges us to return to the original vision of sociology. This is the one academic article in the book. The layperson who finds it too technical might want to skim to the synergy portion. The sociologist will find this article fertile ground for showing that applied work is real sociology.

Part One, "Designing the Culture," presents articles on the fundamental aspects of organizational culture, community, and society. These are the building blocks that the artist can use in creating a better society.

Part Two, "Applications to Specific Settings," presents applications to both social problems and specific social institutions.

In the first reading of the final section, Pat Sheehan presents the trials and tribulations of surviving as an applied sociologist. We then conclude the work with our vision. "The Sociologist as Artist" outlines our thesis: showing how the best sociology applies knowledge to construct programs that benefit people. We hope you will find these works interesting—and that they will spark you to creativity and invention.

Many of the articles were written especially for this book, whereas others were reprinted from other sources. Some of the articles were actually "manufactured" by the senior editor. They were pieced together from other writings, promotional materials, speeches, and even sermons. In a few cases, some sections were constructed by interviewing busy practitioners and turning their comments into prose.

ACKNOWLEDGMENTS

We would like to thank the following reviewers: Michael V. Miller, University of Texas at San Antonio; Elizabeth N. Nelson, California State University, Fresno; and Maliha Zulfacar, California Polytechnic State University–San Luis Obispo. On a more personal side, we would like to thank many people for the support and encouragement they provided as this book was maturing: colleagues, fellow sociological travelers from the humanist tradition, and friends without whom we would have called it quits many times. We especially want to thank Rita and Sue. Rita literally read every page of the manuscript as Bill was preparing it; she offered critique and added her artistic touch by drawing the images that appear at the top of the preface. Sue managed to keep her life as well as Dean's going during the final stages of this manuscript. We are forever in debt to the two of them.

—Bill Du Bois
dubois@itctel.com

—Dean Wright
dean.wright@drake.edu

NOTES_____

1. Robert Henri, *The Art Spirit* (New York: J. B. Lippincott Company, 1923), p. 15.
2. Ibid.
3. Ibid.
4. Thomas Szasz, *The Second Sin* (Garden City, NY: Anchor Books, 1974).
5. James Hillman, *The Soul's Code: In Search of Character and Calling* (New York: Random House, 1996), pp. 36–37.
6. James Hillman, *Re-Visioning Psychology* (New York: Harper and Row, 1975).

ABOUT THE CONTRIBUTORS

Darrol Bussler, Ph.D., says his experiences as a student in a one-room country school in central Minnesota provided the basis for his beliefs regarding learning and schooling. He is an educational reconstructionist serving as a faculty member at Minnesota State University, Mankato, where his research interests focus on democratizing education. After having been a victim of crime, he is working to develop restorative justice processes in communities, including partnerships with schools.

Mark Carey is currently Deputy Commissioner, Community and Juvenile Services Division, Minnesota Department of Corrections. Previously he was director of the Dakota County Community Corrections. He has more than twenty years of experience in the correctional field serving as a counselor, probation officer, planner, and consultant. He taught juvenile justice at Rochester Community College, and has written and published more than a dozen articles. He is currently on the American Probation and Parole Association (APPA) Board of Directors, and in 1993 was selected as the Corrections Person of the Year by the Minnesota Corrections Association.

Barbara Carson, Ph.D., is an associate professor at Minnesota State University, Mankato, in the Department of Sociology and Corrections. She received her doctorate in sociology from the University of New Hampshire. She conducts research on how society legitimates violence and teaches courses in the areas of violence, peace studies, and criminal justice.

Desmond M. Connor is a rural sociologist–applied anthropologist (Ph.D., Cornell, 1963) with an international practice in public participation; he is also the president of Connor Development Services, Ltd., in Victoria, British Columbia, Canada. During the past thirty years, he has completed more than 300 projects, mostly in Canada. The library of his website has an overview article, four case studies, publication reviews, and other papers; see www.connor.bc.ca/connor.

Corey Dolgon, Ph.D., is the chair of sociology at Worcester State College and has published widely on community-based research and political activism in the academy. As a graduate student, he worked on the Homeless Action Committee and wrote a dissertation on economic development and cultural politics in Ann Arbor, Michigan. Dolgon is on the Editorial Committee for Radical America and is currently working on a book about the post–World War II history and political economy of the Hamptons in Eastern Long Island called *Spending Time in the Hamptons.*

William Du Bois, Ph.D., currently teaches sociology at South Dakota State University. He has consulted with a wide variety of organizations and people including state government, school administrators, chambers of commerce, women's crisis centers, juvenile group homes, bars and nightclubs, managers, nursing home administrators, and medical staff.

Gary Gunderson, MDiv, D.Min., is director of the Interfaith Health Program at The Rollins School of Public Health of Emory University, having initiated it at Emory University nine years ago. He is an ordained American Baptist Minister and Fellow of the Center for Community Transformation, Chicago Theological Seminary. Gary is the author of *Deeply Woven Roots* and *Boundary Leaders,* and numerous articles and presentations dealing with the role of faith groups in advancing the health and wholeness of communities. He has extensive experience in Africa in economic and community development and has served as Honorary Consul for the country of Burkina Faso since 1988.

Bernie Jones has been a practitioner, researcher, evaluator, trainer, and teacher of community development over the last thirty-plus years, as well as a community leader. A community development and planning consultant, he is also coordinator for CRUNCH, a community development consortium in downtown Victoria, British Columbia. Formerly, he was associate professor of Urban and Regional Planning, and associate director of the Colorado Center for Community Development at the University of Colorado at Denver. He also served as associate professor in the Graduate School of Social Work, University of Denver. The American Planning Association published his *Neighborhood Planning: A Guide for Citizens and Planners.*

Sidney Jourard, Ph.D., was one of the founding voices of humanistic psychology. Until his premature death in 1975, he taught at the University of Florida. His books include *Personal Adjustment, The Transparent Self, Disclosing Man to Himself, Self-Disclosure: An Experimental Analysis of the Transparent Self,* and *Healthy Personality.*

Ken Kiser is a professor of sociology at Oklahoma State University. From 1988–1991, he was a visiting professor at Virginia Tech and associate director of the Virginia Productivity Center, which did research and development work with a variety of organizations including the U.S. Navy, Pennsylvania Power and Light, Bay State Gas Company, and Virginia Fiber Corporation. He is the coauthor of two books on Total Quality Management including *Putting TQM to Work* with Marshall Sasshin. His current interests include organizational change and especially the transition from old manufacturing systems to e-based commerce. He received his Ph.D. from Ohio State University.

Frank Lindenfeld, Ph.D., teaches sociology at Bloomsburg University. He is a former president of the Association for Humanist Sociology. He has written and co-edited several books on economic democracy including *When Workers Decide: Workplace Democracy Takes Root in North America.* He is co-founder of the Rural Enterprise Development Corporation, a technical assistance group that provides loans to small businesses and microenterprises in North Central Pennsylvania.

Lawrence Miller has been a management consultant to major corporations during the past twenty-five years, assisting in the creation of high performance–high involvement cultures. He founded and recently sold the Miller Howard Consulting Group and has authored several books including *Barbarians to Bureaucrats: Corporate Life Cycle Strategies,* as well as several practical manuals for implementing team management and redesigning organizations using a holistic process of systems redesign. He is currently serving nonprofit organizations focused on social and economic development.

Martin G. Miller, Ph.D., is a sociologist at Iowa State University. He conducts workshops on "Developmental Coaching: An Approach to Positive Youth Development in Sports" and has written several articles in the field of the sociology of youth sport. Closely tied to his writings in this book, he coaches youth softball and volleyball teams and has done so for eighteen years. He is the founder, program director, president of the Board of Directors, and a coach of the Iowa Heart Volleyball Association, Inc., a United States Volleyball affiliate (a mid-Iowa juniors volleyball program). He is currently the president of the Board of Directors of the Iowa Region USAV and the Iowa Region juniors program representative to the national governing board of USAV.

Hal Pepinsky, Ph.D., teaches criminal justice at Indiana University, and is the author of many books including *The Geometry of Violence and Democracy,* and co-editor with Richard Quinney of *Criminology as Peacemaking.*

Paul Rossler received his Ph.D. in Industrial and Systems Engineering from Virginia Polytechnical Institute. He is currently an associate professor at Oklahoma State University in industrial engineering. His research and teaching focus on organizational performance and improvement processes as well as information systems. He previously taught at Kettering University.

Pat Sheehan received her Ph.D. from Tulane University in 1997. She is currently an adult protective services investigator for the state of Indiana and teaches sociology part time at the southeastern campus of Indiana University.

Art Shostak has been an applied sociologist since earning his Ph.D. in 1961. His work with unions dates back earlier to his B.S. degree work in Industrial and Labor Relations (1954–1958). After six years with the Wharton School at the University of Pennsylvania, he joined the faculty at Drexel University in 1967. He began teaching as an adjunct for the AFL-CIO National Labor College in 1975. His nineteen books include such titles as *CyberUnion: Empowering Labor through Computer Technology; For Labor's Sake: Gains and Pains as Told by 28 Creative Inside Reformers; The Air Controller's Controversy: Lessons from the PATCO Strike; Blue-Collar Stress; Blue-Collar Life;* and *Blue-Collar World.* He consults with unions in the United States and Canada about using computers, futuristics, and industrial sociology.

William Wagner is chair of the Department of Sociology and Corrections at Minnesota State University, Mankato. His years of study and teaching in the area of juvenile delinquency brought him quite naturally to a focus on parenting. The art of critique combined with a genealogical method informs his research agenda, and he admits that he steps off the straight and narrow path to discover the many untried possibilities for self-creation. He considers the sociological enterprise too important to rest in the hands of a single paradigm. He is a "recovering scientist" who recognizes that human beings and human communities are too complex for the simplistic equations which describe the relationship between independent and dependent variables. His writing in the area of parenting has transformed his own relationship with his children and suggests that this is the greatest reward of the work.

William Foote Whyte, Ph.D., was professor emeritus in The School of Industrial and Labor Relations at Cornell University until his death in July 2000. He was the author or coauthor of twenty books. His best-known book is *Street Corner Society.* In 1994 he published an autobiography, *Participant Observer.*

R. Dean Wright, Ph.D., is professor of sociology at Drake University. He has been president and is currently treasurer of the Midwest Sociological Society, has been or is a member or chair of numerous community and state agencies and organizations, has consulted widely in the community, and specializes in crime, poverty, homelessness, and minorities of South Asia.

A Framework for
Doing Applied Sociology

WILLIAM DU BOIS

Editors' Note: This article lays the theoretical groundwork for an applied sociology. What we are doing in this book is not a new rendition. It is the very core of what sociology has been in the past and always should be. This article is by far the most academic in the book. The casual reader and layperson may wish to skip to the synergy section of the article, which is must reading for everyone.

I recently went to my first sociology convention in years. I remember now why I quit going. As I wandered from session to session, people were discussing all the right topics: women's rights, poverty, homelessness, racism, social change, organizational cultures. All the right topics were there. But somehow the participants weren't having the right conversation.

I doubt whether much came out of that convention besides more journal articles, more research proposals, more analysis, more hypotheses, and more theoretical musings. Sociology certainly did not seem to be threatening the world with social action. It certainly did not look like sociologists were about to *do* something. Sociology seemed content to remain merely academic.

Applied sociology requires an entirely different paradigm than does traditional scientific sociology. It focuses on action and social change. Applied sociol-

ogy asks different kinds of questions. It is a different kind of conversation. As Kenneth Boulding (1977) noted, the question for the social sciences is simply, What is better, and how do we get there?

What type of framework would be useful for applied sociologists? What concepts would help create viable social change and effective social action? What sort of theoretical framework and resources would be helpful for someone *doing* sociology? This article is a theoretical attempt to lay out some of the necessary ingredients for doing and making a sociology of social change and action.

THEORY IN APPLIED SOCIOLOGY

Applied sociology requires a different theoretical framework than does either grand theory, which tries to explain everything, or "abstract empiricism," which just collects data with no concern for generalization. Robert Merton's (1968) compromise concept of "middle range" theories with limited scope isn't very helpful, either. It retains the biases of both: the complete elaboration of grand theory and the detailed

Adapted with permission of the Association for Humanist Sociology from "A Model for Doing Applied Sociology: Insights and Strategies for an Activist Sociology," by William Du Bois, 1997, *Humanity and Society, 21*(1).

analysis of abstracted empiricism. What we need are not middle-range theories, but middle-range *goals* for theory.

We must examine the purpose of theory for an applied sociology. Scientific analysis aspires to complete dissection and total explanation. However, applied sociology is interested in viable action and solutions to social problems. Rather than seeking full dissection and total elaboration, we need a framework that organizes our understandings and provides direction for movement. Theory should be a participatory resource. We should know in advance that life cannot be reduced to the blackboard. Theories in sociology need not present full elaboration. We need a framework we can use to guide our action.

Marshall McLuhan's (1964) idea of cool and hot mediums is relevant here. A cool medium is vague and sketchy, with details needing to be filled in; a hot medium is sharply defined, with all details clearly distinguished. Theories should be cool mediums rather than hot ones. Science is a hot medium. It seeks full explanation, filling in every detail in grid-like fashion. Science dissects everything, leaving no room for involvement. The early scientists thought they would discover the truth and the truth would then tell us how to live. The fully defined findings of science would then be imprinted upon the world. A theory of action for applied sociology needs to be a cool medium. A cool medium may be vague: It frames the area, suggests a few significant landmarks, and invites details to be filled in in participatory fashion.

To be useful, a map need only organize our understandings, help us find our way when we are lost, and provide direction for our action. As Edmund Carpenter (1970) notes: "Columbus' maps were vague and sketchy, but they showed the right continent." So much of our grand theory and abstract empiricism provides maps of the wrong territory. If we opt for the wrong kind of conversation, we may never get to the new world.

THE CHANGE THE WORLD CONVERSATION

Sociology originated in the "change the world" conversation of August Comte and Karl Marx. It began at a time when a long line of philosophers were suggesting we move out of the armchair of philosophy and into the world of action. As Marx summarized: "The philosophers have described the world, it is now up to us to transform it." The early sociologists would have thought that to talk of an "applied sociology" was redundant. The very focus of the discipline was on social action. Sociologists sought to achieve social amelioration—to make things better, to improve the world.

According to Ernest Becker (1968, pp. 43–44), sociology is an "ideal-type science"; that is, it is involved in imagining a better world.

August Comte, who coined the word "sociology," . . . was to be the towering theorist of the "emerging" society. . . . His life's work is normally considered to fall into two distinct phases: the first work was a treatise on all sciences, putting forth the striking proposal that sociology followed logically in the history of the development of the sciences. . . . The second work enunciated the 'Religion of Humanity' based on love: in the new community, sociology would subserve the social order and be used to promote social interest instead of the private interest that was rampant. . . .

Admirers of Comte based their admiration on the first work, and considered that the second work was done in the grip of dementia or senility. Often, they explicitly indict Comte's love affair with Clotilde de Vaux. We shall return to the reasoned and necessary unity of Comte's system; suffice it to say for now that, contrary to the opinion of many superficial commentators, Comte was well aware of what he was doing—the two "phases" of his work were an integrated whole. The first period was a systematization that he undertook on a positivistic, scientific basis to avoid the charges of mysticism which he knew might be leveled against his guiding ideas. The second period was a frank predication of his life work on feeling, love, and morality, which he felt were the basis for his whole position.

Becker (1971, p. x) notes that sociology is "historically and by its very nature, a utopian science." Comte felt (Becker, 1968, p. 381) that

We needed a science which would help us "live the dream" better than it was lived in the Middle Ages, or in "primitive" society—a science that would seek to develop the conditions of life enhancement.

Gradually, however, sociology drifted away from action as it gained the legitimacy and safety of scientific status. As with classical philosophy, the question, "How do we make the good?" was replaced with the question, "How do we find the truth?" A direct moral intervention to address social ills seemed too audacious. Sociologists wrestled with causal analysis, theoretical abstractions, and surveys. Grant proposals replaced social action. Research findings became of paramount importance, and sociology climbed back into the armchairs of social philosophy and data analysis. Action was postponed.

Every generation has had critics who have questioned what sociologists are doing and asked that we return to the original "change the world" focus of the discipline. Robert Lynd (1939), having done the classic research on social class and having collected voluminous amounts of data, returned to ask the question: But *Knowledge for What?* What are we *doing?*

C. Wright Mills (1959) challenged a generation to move past the Power Elite and envision social solutions to everyday problems. Mills's *The Sociological Imagination* means integrating personal problems and social issues in a way that will provide creative social inventions to address problems experienced by individuals. The sociological imagination is not just a diversion for the Sunday newspaper magazine. The purpose of the sociological imagination is not armchair analysis and understanding. The purpose of the sociological imagination is to see the common threads so we can create common resources to help individual problems. The sociological imagination implied inventing social resources that bridge the space between the micro and the macro. The sociologist as artist creates participatory resources that individual actors can use in their own dramas to solve their own personal problems.

Peter Berger (1963) had it wrong in *Invitation to Sociology.* He invited people into the field on the premise that even if we can't change our conditions, we can use science to explain our situations. However, it is not enough for creatures caught in a trap to look up with some measure of understanding of their plight. The invitation that actually gets people involved in sociology is the invitation to change the world. Sociology is not just about analysis or descrip-

tion or even understanding. *Sociology is about transforming the world.*

The argument has been made that the immature social sciences will someday reach the stature of the mature physical sciences, and we have been taught to model sociology after physics and chemistry. We climb up a scientific Tower of Babel to discover God's Rule Book—the true laws of the universe. But it is such an exercise which is immature. Most of what we know about human behavior looks more like fundamental principles than like laws. And the attempt to find foolproof prescriptions for living looks more like folly than wisdom. A value-free science appears to be not only impossible, but dangerous.

Wanting to separate themselves from mere speculative social philosophy, early sociologists joined the scientific bandwagon that was proving so successful for the physical sciences. Insecure about the identity of their discipline, they sought the canopy of scientific status. But by the middle of the twentieth century, even the foundations of physical science were being reexamined. Polanyi (1958) showed scientific knowledge was ultimately personal knowledge; and Kuhn (1964) demonstrated that the scientific establishment functioned like any other inbred group, automatically excluding certain worldviews and operational styles from club membership. In *The Structure of Scientific Revolutions,* Kuhn showed that scientific laws are legislated just like any other laws—they are social agreements among the experts, arrived at by argument, persuasion, and popularity.

Butterfield (1957) argued in *The Origins of Modern Science* that intuition plays a far greater role in scientific discoveries than we have recognized. Cassirer (1944) argued that science deals not just with facts but with the *art* of organizing information into a *story.* In *The Uncertainty Principle* (1977) Heisenberg proposed that some things are forever unknowable because the very act of observing them alters their course. As Einstein had found with relativity, sociologists realized that we would never be able to determine one final truth by a scientific process. It was questioned whether the "immature" social sciences would ever ripen into "mature" sciences.

Many sociologists also began to question whether sociology really should model itself after physical science (Horowitz, 1964; Lee, 1973; Mills, 1959; Phillips, 1971). Are value-free methods really suitable for a study of humanity? Discontented with a scientific model that stressed objectivity, controlled experiments, and an absence of values (Hampden-Turner, 1970; Maslow, 1966; Matson, 1964; Mills, 1959; Phillips, 1971), these sociologists sought a more involved approach. Kenneth Burke (1945) argued science does not find the "truth": Scientific "truths" are only stories or metaphors providing a way to organize our information. Scientists do not passively *discover* a world; they selectively shape images to a particular view and *shape* the world in that image.

In *The Sociological Imagination,* C. Wright Mills argued we have confused rationality with thinking. Rationality is a method of thinking based on the scientific method. Yet the ability to think is not dependent on a predetermined method. Reason often demands that we form our judgments from our experience; we must not allow a method of thought to dictate our thinking. In our age we have mistaken rationality for reason, when in fact they are often opposites. To forgo allegiance to the scientific method does not mean we have abandoned thinking and reason. It may mean we that we have graduated to more mature thought.

Do we want a valueless sociology? Do we really not care how our findings are put to use? This is the question Alvin Gouldner addressed in *The Coming Crisis in Western Sociology* (1970). Gouldner asks if sociologists really want to be the handmaidens of government. Do we trust that value-free findings will somehow be used for good? Unfortunately, for most, Gouldner's crisis came, went, and died without a whimper. Most sociologists whored after grant money with little thought to whose interests sociology was serving. They remained unconcerned that the values had already been programmed into most research. They were content to sit musing over interesting insights. For many politicians, sociological research became a delaying tactic: money could be spent on more research with action postponed forever. And the question of whom sociology serves, which was so prominent in the 1960s, became muted in a modern world of government demographics, market research, political pollsters, and

jury consultants. Values were simply sold to the highest bidder.

B. F. Skinner wrote a novel about an ideal society called *Walden Two* (1961). Ironically, the coldly clinical Skinner impassioned people and launched a generation of social scientists who believed in creating the great society. Skinner's imagined new society was to be based on science. Science fiction writers warned that it took us toward a sinister Brave New World. But Skinner's key argument, which he makes in *Beyond Freedom and Dignity,* must be addressed: Science and technology have truly equipped us with awesome power. Abstaining from choices only abdicates the choice to someone else. We are left with value decisions that previously were reserved for the gods. When it comes to human nature and the social world, the question is not What is? The question is, What would you like? What do we want to make? We must function as artists making a world.

A PRAGMATIC MODEL

Sociology should be in a different theater from traditional science. Sociology grew up with the dream of being a *pragmatic* discipline. Moving beyond mere moral philosophy, it was to study behavior and consequences. Ironically, it was a psychologist, Erich Fromm, who succinctly summarized the sociological insight: We can do almost anything to people, but we can't do it without consequences (Fromm, 1968, pp. 63–64). If one buys this sociological understanding, each environment increases the likelihood of certain consequences. Strategies are not true or false, but they do have implications. We can change those consequences by creating resources in the environment.

The sociological model is probabilistic. When it comes to social policy, sociology has no need for a strict causal model. By way of example: Life insurance companies have done perfectly fine with an actuarial model. A prevention program involving exercise, good diet, stopping smoking, and no excessive drinking is associated with good health. It does not matter that a strict cause-and-effect chain has not been totally established. Correlational data work just fine. Everyone knows that such a prevention program can be effective; and indeed, life insurance companies have staked their financial security on these data.

Similarly, for a crime prevention strategy, correlational data would suit us. By introducing resources to promote meaning, empowerment, and community, we could significantly lower crime. The fact that a correlation might be only +.20 (accounting for only 4% of variation) does not mean that reflecting it in our prevention design will not reduce crime. Life insurance companies would love information on a variable of even this small magnitude. Paying attention to it would lower liability. With crime as with most social problems, the problem did not arise because of only one factor, and a one-factor solution will not work. Incorporating everything we know into our prevention design makes for success. A strict researcher will say that this contaminates our research design and makes it impossible to isolate variables for causal analysis. The action sociologist will reply simply: Who cares? Our goal is not causal dissection. It is inventing programs that work. Our evaluation will be our success. Success will be evidenced by lower crime rates.

By seeding resources in the environment, we can increase the likelihood of certain behaviors. To understand individual struggles and situations, we might ask the question, What resources would be helpful to individuals in such a situation? The sociologist should function as an artist inventing new resources and social forms.

The best sociology has always been *art* . . . or perhaps *social architecture*. It has been designing programs, imagining a new society, and inventing new social forms. Ernest Becker is right when he contends that sociology is and always has been an "ideal type" science. It is in the realm of imaging a better world.

Sociology should be about *inventing*. It should be about inventing social forms, social programs, social constructions, and participatory resources. The sociologist as artist creates resources that are offered up to the culture.

A POSITIVE CRITICAL THEORY

Critical theory seeks to critique social theories. Any knowledge claim has a particular bias and would shape the world to a particular image. Thus any social theory would place some version of the truth in control while neglecting others. Critical theory and postmodern theory examine these implications and what is wrong with any given perspective.

Critical theory is right in asserting that a science that will tell us how to live is an obsolete idea and must be discarded. However, it is an armchair luxury merely to condemn without beginning the hard work of deciding what to recommend.

The quest to find final truths is obsolete. When something is obsolete, it is taken to the junkyard. Having declared scientific sociology to be junk, we must not stop there. Critical theory has always been a "negative" theory, analyzing what is wrong with a perspective while examining motives and potential abuses. But we can construct a "positive critical theory" by sorting through theories for insights worth keeping. As anthropologist Edmund Carpenter (1970) notes, it is in the junkyard that artists can see true forms. Freed from their original purpose, ideas that are the junk of science and grand theory can be recycled. We must sort for meaningful theoretical insights and significant research findings. Amidst the junk, sociology has many valuable treasures worth recovering.

RECOVERING FORMALISM

We also need to recover the important sociological tradition of formalism. Sociologist Georg Simmel avoided most of the problems with science. While most early sociologists were laying a framework for discovering laws of the universe, Simmel (1950) focused on the study of social forms. Formalism is a different way of arranging all of sociology. Simmel sidestepped the search for final truths and gave us tools for action. Social forms are the resources that the sociologist as artist uses to create.

Despite some differences, there is a similarity between Simmel's idea of social forms and Marshall McLuhan's idea of media. Media are "extensions of the person." Social forms and media include language, laws, rules and policies, organizations, definitions of the situation, material artifacts, shared meanings, social arrangements, and indeed all social constructions, as well as mass media.

These are the tools we use to construct society. Social forms and media are the paints the sociologist as artist will use to paint the canvas of society. It is instructive that both Simmel and McLuhan felt it important that we study their dynamics. Rather than being lost in a debate over final scientific truths, they sought a rendition of sociology in which the artist would learn the peculiarities and nuances of each tool/form/medium. Simmel's formalism is radical because it avoids a scientific rendition of knowledge. Such an approach is the foundation for our being able to envision a version of sociology as art.

AN ACTIVE DRAMATURGY

All the definitions of society center upon *action*. Society is something that we *do*. It is a *lifestyle*. Culture, on the other hand, is a series of *resources* that we use to create the play. An organizational culture is a set of resources people bring to the situation. Society itself is the play—the action—the lifestyle. Culture is the stage, the props, the costumes, the plot, the roles, and the stage directions. Culture is a set of shared meanings. It includes the definitions of the situation, the vision, the stories, the folklore, the shared understandings, the language, the material artifacts, the rules and policies, the norms, the theme/mood, and the ethos.

An active dramaturgy would imply creating the play—providing resources and staging the dream. The passive dramaturgy of Erving Goffman (1961) and others is descriptive and narrative (Brisset and Edgley, 1961). It resembles a slow-motion, narrative journalism. For all its critique of science, traditional dramaturgy retains two central tenets of scientific ideology: It maintains both a detached, uninvolved objectivity and a value-free approach. A full dramaturgy would make the break with science and enter the business of creating the world. How do we create a better drama? As artists, we create resources that can be used to better stage the world.

The most important sociologist of our time has gone unnoticed or forgotten. Ernest Becker taught sociology at the University of California at Berkeley in the 1960s. His work won the Pulitzer Prize in the 1970s. And yet most sociologists aren't familiar with either his name or his work.

Becker's most important work for sociology is *The Structure of Evil* (1968). The work could just as easily have been called *Making the Good,* as it is the story of sociology's quest to change the world. In the late 1960s, however, a title such as *The Structure of Evil* was academically respectable, whereas *Making the Good* would not have been considered legitimate.

As artists, sociologists are called on to create a better world. Ernest Becker writes that it is a question of aesthetics: good art or bad art. Good art brings us to meaning. Bad art leaves us impoverished: feeling controlled, impotent, and empty. Evil is seen as a complex response to the coercion of human powers and to the restriction of human meanings. Translated into simple language, this means evil stems from powerlessness and a lack of meaning. A sterile environment empty of resources and devoid of opportunities for participation leads to a shallowness that restricts living and renders us alienated. It also means viewing human beings as objects for manipulation instead of as full people deserving respect and wonder. Becker (1968) writes:

> When science opted out of life and objectivized man, scientists of course lost the possibility of seeing any mystery at all in man, of seeing any heightening being, even in secular terms. (p. 267)

> . . . mostly people approach each other from the point of view of their roles, rather than as whole beings. . . . They have, in effect, subverted the possibilities of their total being to the narrow interest of action and uncritical survival. . . . The question posed by any cultural game is the question about higher and lower esthetics—about "good" art and "bad" art . . . whereas true esthetics should liberate man, develop his freedom, and further his whole self, "everyday" esthetics—sacrifices most of the total man to a mere part, to the part that must convey the sliver of conviction necessary to sustain the ongoing cultural game. . . .
> . . . "higher" esthetics is precisely that; it calls more of man's spirit into play, releases more of the inner personality and brings it to bear upon the world. (pp. 273–274)

Good art creates a social drama that respects the wholeness of the person. Rather than just being empty social roles, such an interhuman encounter gives us a feeling of connection to life. We become creative and expansive. Bad art simply reduces the human spirit for other purposes. People become objects to be used, manipulated, and controlled.

> . . . the degration of commercial advertising is a logical part of a particular kind of world view. . . . We have destroyed the interhuman in our time simply because we have refused to implement social forms which would liberate man. (Becker, 1968, pp. 274–275) [Non-Inclusive Language in Original]

We need to create participatory resources that empower people. We need to create resources people can use in their own daily dramas to create more meaningful lives. The sociologist as artist becomes an inventor of social forms.

In Becker's understanding, heroism is the heart of meaning. An effective environment provides opportunities for each of us to be a hero—to be a star. A culture without opportunities to be a star lacks meaning. This is not the version of being a star that relegates others to the sidelines watching the parade. A star is a person who is involved in an activity that concentrates his or her attention for a meaningful purpose. Interestingly, Tom Peters and Bob Waterman (1983) in their *In Search of Excellence: Lessons from America's Best Run Companies* used Ernest Becker's social psychology as their framework. They found that an excellent organization created opportunities for heroism, found ways to honor its heroes, and highlighted a vision so people felt part of a meaningful activity.

Fully using Becker's work would imply an action-oriented dramaturgy involved in providing people with resources to better live the dream. For example, creating meaningful opportunities to be a star is just as relevant to inner-city gang problems as it is to ending alienation in the workplace. What kinds of props, resources, and programs would actors in certain situations find valuable? Becker's perspective on life as theater would imply inventing participatory resources individual actors could then utilize in

their own personal dramas. The sociologist as an artist would seek to invent "good art"—creative social forms, programs, and resources that individuals could utilize to construct better lives.

ACTION SOCIOLOGY: AN EXTENSION MODEL OF SOCIOLOGY

Action sociology is, by its very nature, controversial. It was not an accident that the sociology department at Washington University in St. Louis, which had witnessed the rebirth of action sociology, was one of the first sociology departments to be abolished. Deans simply got tired of fistfights in the hall, front-page controversy, and political problems. The department of Alvin Gouldner and Irving Horowitz was abolished, and a retreat was made to the calm passivity of the ivory tower. People and their problems would now come into the university only as data.

In the physical sciences, action created no problem. Cloaked in the respectability of science, policy decisions could be disguised as value-free analysis. But when we move to community problems and the social sciences, everything changes.

Ernest Becker notes in *The Structure of Evil* (1968):

> The founding of a science is never a cognitive problem alone: it is always inseparably a moral problem, a problem of gaining broad agreement to act on the basis of a theory. . . .
>
> In the human sciences the problem of gaining wide loyalty to a paradigm is no different than in any other science. . . . Only, a subtle new factor magnifies the problem immensely, and gives it entirely new proportions: in the human sciences it is sharpened to an extreme degree, because the agreement cannot be disguised as an objective scientific problem . . . in the natural and physical sciences, paradigm agreement looks like a matter of option for an objectively compelling theory. . . . In the human sciences, the same kind of option for a compelling theory looks unashamedly like a wholly moral option, because of the frankly moral nature of its subject matter. . . .
>
> Paradigm choice, in sum, in the human sciences, differs in no way from that of the other sciences except

that the willful, moral nature of the option cannot be disguised. . . . (p. 362)

In other words, sociology (just like any other science) is about values and making the world in a certain image. However, when we move from the physical world into the social sphere, new problems emerge. This is nowhere more apparent than when we recommend that applied sociology embrace a true extension model of education. An extension model places sociology precisely *between* academia and the world. True action sociology integrates sociological knowledge into practical solutions. It utilizes an extension model of education, bringing research findings and theoretical insights to problems in the field, and community problems back to the university for the invention of solutions.

Unfortunately, two factors have prevented most cooperative extension services from being active as applied sociologists:

1. Extension services have realized that political controversy is intrinsic to action sociology and have retreated from this theater.
2. Rather than staying balanced at the fulcrum between the university and the field, extension sociologists have tended to tilt one way or the other. They do not stay firmly balanced with a foot equally in both worlds. Furthermore, those in the field are treated as more "profane," with higher status reserved for the researcher firmly entrenched at the university.

A true applied sociology is balanced permanently between both worlds—the blackboard and the problems. As diagrammed in Figure 1.1, this functions in two directions: (1) Problems are brought to the classroom, where solutions are invented and brought back to the field and implemented. (2) Sociologists seek to find creative new ways to apply research findings and theoretical insights in the world.

We cannot escape the question of values. Knowledge means we have the power to shape the world. What kind of world do we want to shape? Ironically, B. F. Skinner had it right in *Walden Two:* a scientific notion of human behavior means we must ask questions that previously only gods could answer. What

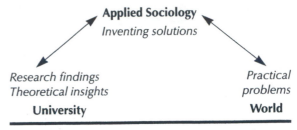

FIGURE 1.1   Extension Model of Applied Sociology

kind of world do we want to make? Becker (1968) continues:

> *To opt for a theory of human ills is not only to opt for the kind of person one is going to have to pay deference to professionally; it is also to opt potentially for the kind of world* one is going to wake up in, *the kind of human beings that one will have to* come across on the street. *To opt for a particular theory of human ills is very much like falling in love in the strictest sense: it is to opt for the presence of a certain kind of being in the world, and hence for a certain kind of world.* (p. 364)

When it comes to the social dimension, universities' cooperative extension services have chosen to *react* and to *follow.* They have waited for requests from constituencies to address whatever locals consider the problem to be. They have chosen to trail with an analysis of symptoms rather than to lead and treat the real underlying problems. This has been politically safe, but we cannot afford such a luxury. We must remember that the word *education* comes from the Latin word meaning "to lead forth." If extension programs react and follow the popular fad, then we have abdicated our responsibility and can hardly pretend that we are involved in "education." Again the question becomes one of values. To lead forth: where and how? What values do we recommend?

Aristotle recommended a "science of the polis"— a science of community—that would use knowledge to improve the community. A science of society is by its very nature political. The problem is that when it comes to social problems, everybody thinks they're an expert. In addition, many special interest groups purposely pollute our understanding by promoting their own agendas.

Yet when we review sociological knowledge, some understandings and agreements do emerge. A consensus of sociologists would conclude that a variety of social problems arise from the consequences of alienation and that the antidotes are meaning, opportunity, and community. The general public may clamor for more prisons and fewer programs for the poor, but any thoughtful review of sociological research will reveal the futility of such a strategy. And when we focus on the nature of the social bond that we call society, some natural conclusions emerge. Organizational and corporate consultants are beginning to teach that an effective organizational culture must start with values (Deming, 1986; Miller, 1984; Peters and Waterman, 1982). An effective society must also start with values. The question is, which values? How do we decide on values without confronting all the problems that first led to the separation of church and state—and, at the same historical time, to the enthronement of science as our method of deciding?

Erich Fromm (1968) notes that we can arrive at an agreement if we start with one basic idea: Social arrangements should function for the human.

> . . . one may arrive at objective norms if one starts with one premise: that it is desirable that a living system should grow and produce the maximum of vitality and intrinsic harmony, that is, subjectively, of well-being. (p. 96)
>
> The value system corresponding to the point of view presented in this book is based on the concept of what Albert Schweitzer called "reverence for life." Valuable or good is all that which contributes to the greater unfolding of man's specific faculties and furthers life. Negative or bad is everything that strangles life and paralyzes man's activeness. All the norms of the great humanist religions like Buddhism, Judaism, Christianity, or Islam or the great humanist philosophers from pre-Socratics to contemporary thinkers are the specific elaboration of this general principle of values. Overcoming of one's greed, love for neighbor, knowledge of the truth (different from the uncritical knowledge of the facts) are the goals common to all humanist philosphical and religious systems of the West and the East. [Non-Inclusive in Language Original] (pp. 93–94)

Many have felt Fromm was a "lightweight," because his argument covers such a broad range and uses such large strokes. But it is necessary to be just this bold if we are going to approach a synthesis.

A SCIENCE OF HUMAN BEHAVIOR

A different conception of science must emerge. Our means must mirror our purposes. Thomas Kuhn in *The Structure of Scientific Revolutions* (1964) demonstrated that science is simply an agreement between those who have studied a body of knowledge. Scientific laws are thus legislated like any other laws. They are agreements. The question for the social sciences becomes, Where do we want to stake our agreement?

In the social sciences, as Becker notes, we will never be able to totally explain a phenomenon before we act. Our subject is human life. We will never have all the answers. How much information must be in before we act? We need some orienting framework within which to act. How do we organize our understandings? We need a conversation that *begins* with values rather than forbids values. But which values? We are back in the old "change the world" conversation with all its subtle nuances, problems, and potential abuses.

Even the physical and biological sciences are realizing that even they are ultimately in a conversation about how to make the world. This realization brings us back to Aristotle's notion of a "science of the polis" in which values would be supreme and science would be but a tool in a conversation that gets us back to better living.

Lay people have a concept about conversation that is unencumbered by any possibility that talk will lead to action. The person on the street would call such talk "bullshit." Unfortunately, we don't have a similar concept in sociology. In academia, we are taught to mince our words. In real life, people wouldn't put up with such empty theories. Such conversation is perfectly all right provided we don't maintain a pretense that such talk will ever lead to action. However, we need to label theories for what they are. Too many theories postpone action forever.

There is a story about the famous writer Honoré de Balzac. Broke and badly in need of money, he convinced a wealthy benefactor to finance the production of a new play. Balzac entered into the production enthusiastically. He booked a hall for a play, did all the publicity, and hired actors. He realized only at the last minute that he had forgotten to write the play. He then got several friends together and proposed that they divide up the task, each writing one act. One friend begged him for the details of the plot: What was going to happen, and when? Balzac's reply: "If I have to tell you that, we'll never be finished in time." This is the perfect criticism of science. If we have to know the finished plot before we act, then we'll never be finished in time.

Ironically, social scientific research almost always *postpones* action. Even the most conservative politician can take an issue "under advisement" and defer it to wait on "further research." With life, all the facts will never be in.

We don't need a completed blueprint. Details will be filled in along the way. What we need is a direction and a way of traveling—a framework to recommend to legislators, policy makers, and managers.

DESIGNING THE GOOD SOCIETY

Rather than just waiting on all the facts to be in, what if we were to just leap ahead and imagine an ideal society? Such an adventure is not without precedent in sociology. Talcott Parsons (1951) imagined an ideal social system. He seemed to realize that sociology is in the business of doing just that.

It is not Parsons's method, but his vision with which we must find fault. His ideal focuses on the needs of the social system rather than the needs of the person and would lead to an authoritarian order. However, it is the boldness of Parsons's step that deserves our appreciation: He left behind merely describing the world *as it is* and sought to envision society *as it should be.* In doing so, he returned us to the business of sociology as envisioned by Comte, Marx, Spencer, Weber, and Ward. It is the business of making the world.

Parsons's theory of the ideal society was bad art if our goal is creating a society in which individuals thrive. However, his theory became a model for organizations and government. Sociological theories often have a great impact on the world. Witness the example of Nazi Germany which can be laid in the lap of sociologists who embraced Social Darwinism and provided a foundation and rationalization for many of Hitler's views. Theories can be very dangerous if we envision the wrong ideal.

The knowledge we produce *will be used.* The question is how: What kind of world will we make? If you refuse to have this conversation, then you are left with the very value-free world in which the modern scientific version of sociology thrives: consumer market research, government by public opinion polls, jury consultants, spin control, and the manufacturing of the common denominator television programs. This is hardly the legacy we should leave behind.

We choose what kind of society to make. What kind of model of an ideal society would be useful in actually making a better world? We are left with an age-old question: What is the Good?

SYNERGY AND THE GOOD SOCIETY

In ancient philosophy there was a debate over whether we should "find the truth" or "make the good." "Finding the truth" won out, and science was launched. The idea was that after we found the truth, then we could make the good. A large part of the reason "the good" lost had to do with problems in defining the good. Isn't the good just a matter of perspective? Anthropologist Ruth Benedict (1934, 1970) solved a 2,000-year-old philosophical problem. She provides us with an operational definition of the Good: The Good is synergy. Synergy is a win–win situation between individuals, between the person and the organization, and between the individual and the society.

Under some conditions people flourish. Under other conditions, although the spirit is willing, people atrophy. How do we create conditions under which people flourish? How do we design cultures and organizations in which people thrive? This should be the task of sociology.

Some social arrangements provide the context for healthy life. Abraham Maslow (1971) wrote:

> ... *a society or a culture can be either growth-fostering or growth-inhibiting. ... This makes possible a comparative sociology, transcending and including cultural relativity. The "better" culture gratifies all basic human needs and permits self-actualization. The "poorer" cultures do not. (p. 211)*

We must begin to entertain the idea that there is such a thing as a "good" culture. Synergy is the first concept that emerges after we leave behind the value relativity of a neutral science. Such a conversation bridges new territory which has been considered illegitimate.

Ruth Benedict had worked hard to establish the scientific status of the human sciences. Cultural relativity was both the foundation for the scientific status of anthropology and its banner of academic credibility. Benedict was afraid she would be misunderstood and accused of being value-laden if she presented her ideas concerning synergy (Maslow, 1971). Yet everything she knew as a trained observer of cultures suggested that the cultures she had studied could easily be separated into two clusters. In one cluster, the actors—the people involved themselves—defined life as good. And when we looked at social indices, life did appear to be good from a human standpoint. Murder rates, alcoholism rates, suicide rates were low. Divorce was infrequent. People said they were happy. Religion defined the world as a good place ruled by benevolent gods. Benedict herself said that the key intuition she had about these cultures was life was somehow "nice." (And she didn't feel the least bit comfortable with such a nonscientific notion.) *Yet from any human standpoint, life in these cultures did appear to be factually better.* Something about the cultural arrangements was such that people flourished. The people and the social data testified to the success of these social arrangements. What explains this?

In another cluster of cultures, individuals defined life as bad and deemed the world an unhappy place. Their religions held the world was an evil place ruled by jealous, vengeful gods. And social indices in these cultures seemed to bear out the actors' testimony:

Crime rates were high; aggression was high; suicide rates, divorce rates, alcoholism were all high. By both objective and subjective evaluations, individuals did not seem to thrive under these social arrangements.

Ruth Benedict's concern with cultural relativity is understandable. She had stumbled upon synergy, the first concept that emerges when we move past value neutrality and relativity as the supreme goal: past a value-free version of science and into a full science that respects and values human life. Cultural relativity and objectivity do not mean that we should not have values. They mean that we must set aside our values lenses long enough to see.

Erich Fromm (1956) says the core component of objectivity is actually respect. The word *respect* comes from the Latin meaning "to look at." Objectivity is a commitment to see things as they are—to not falsify data. It means to look at something as it is, not as you would like it to be or through your own particular values and biases. Objectivity is not a commitment not to have values, but a commitment to see the other as he/she/it is.

Fromm adds another important idea for a human science: that it differentiate between curiosity and interest. A human science should not be idly curious, unconcerned, and uncaring. It is then that science is dangerous. It is then that science can become mindless meddling or callous cruelty. Instead, as sociologists in a human science, we need to be interested in and concerned about what we are studying. Synergy recognizes that as human beings we do have a stake in the outcomes of sociological science. We are not idly curious but intimately involved in the human experiment.

It is interesting to note that a young graduate student of Benedict's was so impressed with her insights on synergy that he made a career out of identifying and studying people who reminded him of Ruth Benedict—whose interaction with other people encouraged and created a synergistic involvement. The student's name was Abraham Maslow. He called people like Ruth Benedict "self-actualized." She became his role model for psychological health (Maslow, 1971).

Synergy thus got smuggled into psychology through the back door, as it were. And sociology has still not gotten around to exploring the implications of Benedict's argument: the creation of social arrangements, social forms, and social context that encourage synergy. The psychological concept of self-actualization is incomplete without a companion sociology that focuses on synergy.

Synergy is an operational definition of the good. Synergy may be defined in at least five important ways:

1. The communal good = the individual good
2. A win–win situation
3. Alignment of organizational goals and individual interests
4. $1 + 1 > 2$
5. Higher-order synthesis

The Communal Good = The Individual Good

An age-old philosophical argument concerns what should happen if there is a conflict between the community and the individual. Traditionally, as noted earlier, philosophy solved this by deciding that if a conflict should occur between the individual good and the communal good, the communal good should have eminent domain.

> The communal good > the individual good.

Benedict found that in noneffective societies this arrangement had been followed. In this arrangement, the individual is left with a choice between personal or communal interests. This societal tension between the individual and society usually results in the individual taking turns between community interests and self interest. Complete sacrifice of self for community is impossible. The self can only be kept down for so long. People have human needs that must be met. Indeed, the work of Sigmund Freud and of all the psychologists who followed him testifies to the fact that if we deny self in one way, it resurfaces in another. The tension between self and society resurfaces as aggression, alcoholism, depression, suicide, compulsive shopping, marital discord, and all varieties of anomie. When obedience to societal rules does not function for the person, symptoms of social decay arise.

In contrast, Benedict found that in effective social arrangements, society had been arranged so the communal good and the individual good were identical. The same act accomplished both the individual good and the communal good.

> The communal good = the individual good.

Charles Cooley (1929) noted that "Self and Other are but two sides of the same coin." One can fulfill oneself only in the context of community; and community can thrive only if it is a context in which individuals can fully be themselves. Half a century later, survey researcher Daniel Yankelovich (1981) noted the same dynamics. He shows how the social ethic of self-denial got turned upside down into an ethic of self-fulfillment. Sacrificing the self for the sake of community is clearly "the communal good > the individual good." The self-fulfillment ethic is "the individual good > the communal good." However, self-fulfillment cannot take place in a vacuum. Yankelovich says that individuals who concentrate on themselves and withdraw from others do not grow; they shrink. Realistic self-fulfillment demands a context of community, supportive social resources, and supportive others. As Maslow notes, self-actualized people are outside themselves; immersed in community, purposes, and meaning; and able to be involved with others. The only realistic strategy is what Yankelovich terms an "ethic of commitment," in which commitment is made to both maximum self and maximum community.

Effective social arrangements create an environment in which people can get their needs met. A human system that does not meet human needs will produce all sorts of unwanted consequences.

Benedict had used the concept of synergy initially to explain why some societies are violent and others peaceful:

> *Is there any sociological condition that correlates with strong aggression and any that correlate with low aggression? . . . From all comparative material the conclusion that emerges is that societies where non-aggression is conspicuous have social orders in which the individual by the same act and at the same time serves his own advantage and that of the group. The problem is one of social engineering and depends*

upon how large the areas of mutual advantage are in any society. Non-aggression occurs not because people are unselfish and pursue social obligations above personal desire, but when social arrangements makes these two identical. (quoted in Maslow, 1971, p. 40)

Win–Win

Effective societies structure win–win social arrangements. Ineffective societies arrange life into win–lose situations. Benedict's synergistic societies (those with a win–win framework) have substantially lower rates of aggression than do nonsynergistic societies. This only makes sense. Aggression must abound if the only way a person can get ahead is at another person's expense.

The United States, with the highest murder rate of any modern industrial nation, illustrates the point. As sociologist Harry Edwards (1982) notes, the American Dream is structured on the existence of an underclass of losers. The losers mow yards, do laundry, wait tables, clean houses, and in other ways support the lifestyle of the winners. You know you are a winner when you have a group of losers to take care of you. Similarly, in business, politics, and sports, you know you are a winner because you beat someone else.

However, losers are dangerous. They are always waiting to get back at you next season. King of the Mountain is a dangerous game, whether it be in the corporation or international relations. The consequences can be as subtle as ulcers or as drastic as riots and revolution. Most historians cite the way we dealt with the Germans as losers following World War I as the breeding ground for World War II. The Harvard Negotiation Project and other peace efforts are beginning to teach that the only successful conflict resolution is a win–win agreement. Even neighborhood disputes must be solved in truly win–win fashion or their resolution won't last. The rush to anything else may seem expedient, but only the creative invention of win–win arrangements will lead to a lasting peace.

It also must be noted that the win–lose criterion for success is traditionally a masculine phenomenon. The traditional feminine worldview emphasizes co-operation rather than competition. The emphasis at home and in the family has been on win–win dynamics. In the family, you certainly can settle for nothing less than a win–win situation. If one child feels like a loser, you are in for a long afternoon. We are beginning to learn that in business and international relations, as in the family, win–win solutions are the only thing that is practical in the long run.

The Politics of Self-Esteem. The win–win framework can also be tied to social psychology. Psychologist Alfred Adler sees the key element in the formation of personality as the development of self-esteem. Win–win dynamics are essential for the successful formation of self-esteem. If a person has a superiority complex (the winner), it is actually a compensation mechanism to disguise an inferiority complex (the loser). Inferiority complexes are the product of a win–lose dynamic. People often try to overcome inferiority complexes at another's expense, but such is never practical. Only win–win resolutions will allow individuals to feel good about themselves.

Sociologist Erving Goffman also speaks of the social staging of self-esteem in terms that have traditionally been associated with etiquette. He talks of "saving face." Goffman notes that each social interaction has a public face. The only way either person can feel good is if this face is preserved and both people come out ahead. If one person establishes victory at another's expense, neither party comes away feeling permanently satisfied about the interaction. Goffman sees these "face-saving" rituals as key to successful social life (Becker, 1962).

Alignment of Organizational Goals and Individual Interests

In *Re-Inventing the Corporation* (1985) John Naisbett and Patricia Aburdene talk about synergy as *alignment*. These authors find the most effective companies have managed to align organizational goals and individual interests. Rather than merely ask the individual to sacrifice for the sake of the company, the best organizations find ways to benefit both individual and the organization.

Peters and Waterman's *In Search of Excellence* (1982) found that successful companies pay attention to the dynamics of human behavior. Harvard business professor Rosabeth Moss Kanter speaks of achieving synergies as the key for effective corporations. However, some of Kanter's clients in *When Giants Learn to Dance* (1989) seem to think synergy is only a matter of chemistry between individuals and the proper matchmaking. Synergy is not a matter of chemistry but of social design. Kanter's earlier work on communities and utopias recognized this. Successful social arrangements must be designed whereby the organization and person both thrive. The manager must become an inventor and an architect of new social arrangements and social forms. This is precisely the conception of Warren Bennis in *The Unconscious Conspiracy: Why Leaders Can't Lead* (1976). Bennis envisions the effective leader as a "social architect." A social architect must design organizational culture so as to align the interests of the individual and the organization. Without such alignment, the organization pays the price in employee alienation—manifested in absenteeism, turnover, employee theft, sabotage, sagging morale, declining productivity, poor quality control, and declining profits. We cannot afford to squander human resources.

1 + 1 > 2

Synergy may also be defined as a condition in which the whole is greater than the sum of its parts. The whole is greater than the "run of individual actions."

Sociology itself is founded on the notion that the whole is greater than the sum of its parts. Society is not just the sum of the individuals in it—such would be psychological reductionism.

We might contrast social arrangements in which 1 + 1 > 2 with arrangements in which 1 + 1 < 2. Jessie Bernard (1972) talks of how a woman often *dwindles* into becoming a wife. Here we have a picture of a social relationship where the partners are *less* as a couple than they were as two individuals. We can almost see the spouses lopping off parts of themselves to fit themselves into the relationship.

Higher-Order Synthesis

Synergy literally means a "synthesizing energy." The word was used by Lester Ward to denote a *creative synthesis*. Ultimately, synergy must be a matter of balancing the long term versus the short term.

In the short run some things are clearly a zero-sum game: a transaction in which someone has to lose. This Saturday night we can go to either the movie you want or the one I want. We can't go to both. However, if we view higher-order priorities, we may value spending time together. In the long run, we may both win.

Competing for scarce resources may mean a zero-sum game. For example, two neighboring communities may be competing for a new factory. Working together, however, they may bring the factory to the area and in the long run benefit the economy of both.

The zero-sum approach assumes a pie of a fixed size. If we divide the pie so one piece is bigger, then other pieces must be smaller. But synergy is a creative process in which the size of the pie actually grows. Although someone's proportion may shrink, the size of the pie may grow so that individual pieces are actually larger. We may all win by sharing a larger pie. In the long term, we can invent arrangements that allow the important needs of all to be met. Again, under some social arrangements, people flourish; under others, people atrophy.

Synergy is the cornerstone on which we can begin the work of sociology. It provides an ideal vision for the Good. Synergy should be our evaluative mechanism. If we have losers, then we must return to the drawing board.

DEFINING THE SITUATION: HUMAN NATURE

Human nature seems to be a self-fulfilling prophecy. If we treat people as if human nature is evil, that seems to be the case. If we act toward people as if human nature is good, then that seems to become true.

In many ways, synergy, too, is a self-fulfilling prophecy. Ruth Benedict talks about how synergistic societies never give up on an individual. Crime exists in these societies, but people believe that criminals will come around, repent, and eventually outgrow the behavior. And sure enough, in these societies, the self-fulfilling prophecy tends to be true.

Benedict (1970) writes that some cultures nourish the person who misbehaves:

> *People are apt to wait patiently for his growth in wisdom and discretion. The whole course of his experience has inculcated in him a faith in the rewards of acting with his fellows. He sees life as an area of mutual advantage where by joint activity he attains his own personal desires. (p. 55) [Non-Inclusive Language in Original]*

In other cultures, people who violate social norms are labeled as "no damn good," and society gives up on them. Labeling theory demonstrates the consequences of both positive and negative self-fulfilling prophecies. Correctly understood, labeling theory focuses on the *consequences* of defining a situation. It is not the label or the belief that creates the self-fulfilling prophecy. It is the willingness of people to *act* on the basis of a definition of the situation—to *treat* people differently. We define a person as bad, then act accordingly by putting the person in prison and treating him or her as a criminal. In synergistic societies, the definition of the situation is that people are basically good, and the society then acts in ways that create such a self-fulfilling prophecy.

The lesson of culture appears to be that scientific analysis of human nature will not do. It is not a matter of whether human nature is innately good or innately evil. As philosopher Jose Ortega y Gasset (1941) notes, the reason science has not been able to find human nature is that there is no such thing as human nature. He summarizes:

> *Man is not a thing, man has no nature. . . . [Science] was in no state to confront human problems. By its very constitution it could do no other than search for man's nature. And naturally, it did not find it . . . man has no nature. Man is not his body, which is a thing, nor his soul, psyche, conscience, or spirit which are also things.* Man is no thing, but a drama—*his life, a pure and universal happening . . . man, in a word, has no nature; what he has is . . . history. (pp. 185, 199–200, 17)*

> *. . . human life, it would appear then, is not a thing, has not a nature, and in consequence we must make up our minds to think of it in terms of categories and concepts that will be radically different from such as shed light on the phenomenon of matter. (p. 186) [Non-Inclusive Language in Original]*

The social sciences require a different methodology. There is no human nature. History shows the variable forms that human behavior can take. The question in the present and for the future is, What do we want to make?

SOCIAL ARCHITECTURE

We should be about *inventing*. The sociologist as an artist invents new social forms. We should be creating new resources, inventing programs, and designing demonstration projects. We should be offering up participatory resources that actors can bring to the situation to create their own meaning.

Most social engineering is simply bad art. A better metaphor for sociology is that of social architecture. Social *engineering* implies that we have total control of the environment in the first place and seek to manipulate from an all-knowing perspective. The ideal vision for the sociologist as artist is the metaphor of the social architect designing organizational cultures. Social architecture offers up resources that individuals can use in their own way.

Applied sociology can serve as an incubator for new ideas and model programs. A word of caution needs to be introduced here. As with architecture, a brilliant design is not always apparent at first. An act of creative genius may be moaned about at first, even though later we come to love it. A social resource can be evaluated only after it is lived in and interacted with and we can see how it works. It is the role of the architect to be able to anticipate how a design will function. Architects can be right and they can be wrong. True artists often create magic beyond what we initially see in the design.

The sociologist can help invent new solutions to social and organizational problems. Unfortunately, most social policy is bad art. Most of the people inventing new social forms and social policies have minimal sociological knowledge, and most sociologists have relegated themselves to the obscurity and irrelevance of science. We need a new kind of sociology. We must return to the roots of the discipline and create a bold new applied sociology.

CONCLUSION

Young people originally enter sociology eager to change the world. As older people retire from the field and pass the torch to the next generation, they once again point to the vision of making the world better. In between the hope of youth and the hope of the old, the midlife business of sociology takes place with little attention to changing the world.

We need to return the task of changing the world to the everyday work of sociology. Leaving behind the security of science, we must return to the "change the world" conversation with all its subtle nuances

and potential abuses. Rather than aspiring to capture life in theory, an applied framework need only be a participatory resource for organizing our understandings and our actions. We must function as artists to create a better world. The sociologist as artist would become an inventor of social forms, social constructions, and effective social arrangements. Synergy should be the evaluative standard for our efforts. We must fashion win–win situations between individuals, between persons and society, and between organizational goals and individual interests. We must create cultures in which people flourish.

Marshall McLuhan notes the study of human behavior "is based on making not matching." Sociology too often consists merely of "name-calling": matching behaviors to categories, labeling experiences, renaming the world with new concepts. Instead of labeling, defining, and analyzing, we must be about creating a better world. Sociology should be about making.

REFERENCES

Becker, Ernest. *The Birth and Death of Meaning.* New York: Free Press of Glencoe, 1962.

Becker, Ernest. *The Structure of Evil.* New York: Free Press, 1968.

Becker, Ernest. *The Lost Science of Man.* New York: George Braziller, 1971.

Becker, Ernest. *The Revolution in Psychiatry: The New Understanding of Man.* New York: Free Press, 1974.

Benedict, Ruth. *Patterns of Culture.* Boston and New York: Houghton Mifflin, 1934.

Benedict, Ruth. "Synergy: Patterns of the Good Culture." *The American Anthropologist,* Volume 72, No. 2, 1970.

Bennis, Warren. *The Unconscious Conspiracy: Why Leaders Can't Lead.* New York: AMACOM, 1976.

Berger, Peter. *Invitation to Sociology: A Humanistic Perspective.* Garden City, N.Y.: Doubleday, 1963.

Bernard, Jessie. *The Future of Marriage.* New York: World Publishing, 1972.

Boulding, Kenneth. Keynote Address, Southwest Sociological Association, Dallas, 1977.

Brisset, Dennis, and Charles Edgley. *Life as Theater: A Dramaturgical Sourcebook (Communication and Social Order).* New York: Aldine DeGruyter, 1990.

Burke, Kenneth. *A Grammar of Motives.* New York: Prentice-Hall, 1945.

Butterfield, Herbert. *The Origins of Modern Science.* New York: Harper and Row, 1957.

Carpenter, Edmund. *They Became What They Beheld.* New York: Outerbridge and Dienstfrey, 1970.

Carpenter, Edmund. *Oh, What a Blow That Phantom Gave Me.* New York: Holt, Rinehart, and Winston, 1973.

Carpenter, Edmund, and Marshall McLuhan. *Explorations in Communication: An Anthology.* Boston: Beacon Press, 1960.

Cassirer, Ernest. *An Essay on Man: An Introduction to a Philosophy of Human Culture.* New Haven: Yale University Press, 1944.

Comte, Auguste. *Cours de philosophie positive.* 6 Volumes (1830–1842). Paris: Schleicher edition, 1908.

Cooley, Charles H. *Human Nature and the Social Order* (1929). St. Louis: Transaction Books, 1982.

Culkin, John. "A School Master's Guide to Marshall McLuhan," in *McLuhan: Pro & Con,* edited and with an introduction by Raymond Rosenthal. New York: Funk & Wagnalls, 1968.

Deming, W. Edwards. *Out of the Crisis.* Cambridge, Mass.: Center for Advanced Engineering Study, Massachusetts Institute of Technology, 1986.

Durkheim, Emile. *Rules of Sociological Method.* New York: Free Press, 1950.

Edwards, Harry. Lecture Notes. University of California, Berkeley, 1982.

Feyerbend, P. K. "Against Method: Outlining of an Anarchistic Theory of Knowledge." *Minnesota Studies in the Philosophy of Science.* Minneapolis: University of Minnesota, 1970, pp. 17–130.

Fromm, Erich. *Man for Himself.* New York: Fawcett Premier Books, 1947.

Fromm, Erich. *The Art of Loving.* New York: Harper and Row, 1956.

Fromm, Erich. *The Revolution of Hope.* New York: Harper and Row, 1968.

Glass, John F., and John R. Staude. *Humanistic Society: Today's Challenge to Sociology.* Pacific Palisades: Goodyear Publishing, 1972.

Goffman, Erving. *Asylums: Essays on the Social Situation of Mental Patients and Other Inmates.* Garden City, N.Y.: Anchor Books, 1961.

Gouldner, Alvin W. *The Coming Crisis of Western Sociology.* New York: Basic Books, 1970.

Gouldner, Alvin W. *For Sociology: Renewal and Critique in Sociology Today.* New York: Basic Books, 1973.

Hampden-Turner, Charles. *Radical Man.* Cambridge, Mass.: Schenkman Publishing, 1970.

Harris, T. George. "About Ruth Benedict and Her Lost Manuscript." *Psychology Today,* June 1970, pp. 51–52.

Heisenberg, Werner. *The Uncertainty Principle and the Foundations of Quantum Mechanics.* New York: Wiley, 1977.

Horowitz, Irving Louis. *The New Sociology.* New York: Oxford University Press, 1964.

Kanter, Rosabeth Moss. *When Giants Learn to Dance.* New York: Simon and Schuster, 1989.

Kuhn, Thomas S. *The Structure of Scientific Revolutions.* Chicago: University of Chicago Press, 1964.

Lee, Alfred McClung. *Toward Humanist Sociology.* Englewood Cliffs, N.J.: Prentice-Hall, 1973.

Lynd, Robert S. *Knowledge for What?* Princeton: Princeton University Press, 1939.

Mannheim, Karl. *Ideology and Utopia: An Introduction to the Sociology of Knowledge.* New York: Harcourt Brace, 1936.

Maslow, Abraham. *The Psychology of Science: A Reconnaissance.* New York: Harper and Row, 1966.

Maslow, Abraham. *Toward a Psychology of Being.* New York: Van Nostrand, 1968.

Maslow, Abraham. *The Farthest Reaches of Human Nature.* New York: Viking, 1971.

Matson, Floyd. *The Broken Image.* New York: George Braziller, 1964.

McLuhan, Marshall. *Understanding Media.* New York: McGraw, 1964.

Mead, George Herbert. *Mind, Self, and Society.* Chicago: University of Chicago Press, 1938.

Merton, Robert. *Social Theory and Social Structure.* New York: Free Press, 1968.

Mills, C. Wright. *The Sociological Imagination.* New York: Oxford University Press, 1959.

Miller, Lawrence. *American Spirit: Visions of a New Corporate Culture.* New York: William Morrow and Company, 1984.

Naisbitt, John, and Patricia Aburdene. *Re-Inventing the Corporation: Transforming Your Job and Your Company for the New Information Society.* New York: Warner Books, 1985.

Oretga y Gasset, Jose. *History as a System.* New York: Norton, 1941.

Parsons, Talcott. *The Social System.* Glencoe, Ill.: Free Press, 1951.

Peters, Thomas J., and Robert H. Waterman. *In Search of Excellence.* New York: Harper & Row, 1982.

Phillips, Derek. *Knowledge from What?* Chicago: Rand McNally, 1971.

Polanyi, Michael. *Personal Knowledge.* Chicago: University of Chicago Press, 1958.

Rogers, Carl R. *On Personal Power.* New York: Dell Publishing, 1977.

Skinner, B. F. *Walden Two.* New York: Macmillan, 1961.

Skinner, B. F. *Beyond Freedom and Dignity.* New York: Knopf, 1971.

Simmel, Georg. *The Sociology of Georg Simmel.* Translated by Kurt H. Wolff. Glencoe, Ill.: The Free Press, 1950.

Sorokin, Pitirim. *Altruistic Love: A Study of American Good Neighbors and Christian Saints.* Boston: Beacon Press, 1950.

Sorokin, Pitirim. *Explorations in Altruistic Love and Behavior: A Symposium.* Boston: Beacon Press, 1950.

Sorokin, Pitirim. *Ways and Power of Love.* Boston: Beacon Press, 1951.

Weber, Max. *From Max Weber: Essays in Sociology.* Translated, edited, with introduction by H. H. Gerth and C. Wright Mills. New York: Oxford University Press, 1946.

Yankelovich, Daniel. *New Rules: Searching for Self-fulfillment in a World Turned Upside Down.* New York: Random House, 1981.

PART ONE

Designing the Culture

Pick up any management book and it will tell you that an effective manager manages the "organizational culture." Most people understand this to mean that we must manage the environment as well as the person. Human behavior takes place in a context. How do we manage the environment? What exactly is an organizational culture?

ORGANIZATIONAL CULTURE

An organizational culture is the set of resources people bring to the situation. Society itself is the play—the action—and the lifestyle. Culture is all the resources people have available to create the play.

Culture is a set of shared meanings. It is the plot, the vision, the stories, the folklore, the shared understandings, the language, and the rules and policies. It is also the stage itself: The physical environment where the play occurs. It is the props, the programs, and the participatory resources as well as the costumes and roles.

The Stage: The physical environment itself influences the nature of interaction. This includes physical dimensions, layout and design, circulation paths, definitions of the situation, and symbols.

Shared Meanings: A culture provides resources including language, vocabulary, shared understandings, definitions of the situation, folklore, humor, and stories.

Vision: Who are we and what are we doing? A vision is not a mission statement, but a clearcut purpose: a reason to get up in the morning and a reason to stay up.

Roles: The definitions, power structure, and themes are reflected in the roles provided in a culture. These roles again are resources which make it more likely a given type of interaction will occur.

Norms, Rules, and Policies: The formal and informal norms governing interaction in a social structure.

Props and Costumes: These influence the definition of the situation and make it more likely certain types of behavior will occur.

Ethos: The general mood characteristic of a culture.

STYLES OF ORGANIZATIONAL MANAGEMENT

Traditionally, managers used a *military style of management:* the general on the hill gives orders that are then passed down the chain of command to staff who implement the blueprint. The costs of this military style have been well documented. Sociologists note that there are always consequences to how we treat people. We *can* ignore human needs and treat people in an authoritarian way, but we can't do it without consequences. The organizational consequences of worker alienation include low motivation, low productivity, high worker turnover, high absenteeism, employee theft, industrial sabotage, poor communication, labor problems, and other conflicts.

In the industrial economy, the emphasis is on unskilled, cheap labor. People were considered a necessary nuisance. Ideally, people were replaced by machines whenever possible. A machine will work twenty-four hours a day—it doesn't need coffee breaks, sick days, or have family crosses. Creativity and human input are not welcome. On an assembly line, a surprise can mean only one thing—something broke.

The military model squanders human resources. Psychologists first convinced many managers to pay attention to workers, arguing that if human needs were not met, it may interfere with work. Management slowly began to focus on the dynamics of human behavior, but the emphasis was on individual needs and one-to-one communication between management and workers. The context of interaction was left unchanged. People were not allowed to change their environments, the nature of work, or the structure of their organizations. Although management cared more about people, decisions were still made by a "thinker" on top of the organization (management) and then carried out by workers (labor).

However, in 1957 the world changed for all time and no one noticed. This was the time the Soviets launched *Sputnik,* the first satellite, which was to transform communications and render the world into what Marshall McLuhan called a *global village.* But even more important, this year, for the first time in history, the majority of jobs were in service and information rather than industry. Today, more than 90 percent of all jobs are in service or managing information, with less than 10 percent directly involved with producing a product. We have moved from an industrial economy to an information economy.

In the information–service economy, management turned 180 degrees. The *human resources model* is sociological: It looks at the environment. Whereas in the military model people are a necessary nuisance, in the information–service economy, people and ideas are the source of wealth. Putting people together effectively is good business. The human resources model emphasizes creating effective social arangements to get the best from your human resources. The new manager functions as a social architect, designing and managing the organizational culture.

2

Doing Sociology with the Design Professions

BERNIE JONES

Editors' Note: Bernie Jones shows how sociological research methods can be applied in unique new ways to work with the social design process from start to follow-up evaluation. This classic article is addressed to professional sociologists and design professionals. The layperson and casual reader may wish to begin with the next article.

Winston Churchill is reported to have said, "We shape our buildings, and then they shape us." Sociologists have a vital role to play in that shaping process. This paper reviews the nature of and rationale for sociological practice with the design professions. Over the last two decades the design and planning professions have gone through an internal revolution as they introduced the systematic utilization of social and behavioral scientists into their work. Starting in the late 1960s, the author began consulting with designers and planners on such projects as comprehensive community plans, low-income housing developments, child-care facilities, educational facilities, and neighborhood parks.[1]

Working as a consultant to architects, planners, and users requires the clinical sociologist to modify standard research methods and techniques because many of them do not work effectively in field settings. A diagnostic approach to the planning process, incorporating analysis of the consequences of specific design decisions, marks the contribution of the clinical sociologist who is able to adapt research methods to the immediate needs of the situation, provide meaningful feedback to clients, and help facilitate constructive interaction among various participants in the process.

RATIONALE

As early as the 1920s, Park (1951) acknowledged that there is a rhyme and reason to the way people use the physical terrain of the city. The Chicago school of ecological sociology that emerged from his seminal work was very much attuned to the physical environment of the city. Significant early studies include McKenzie's (1923) observation of the urban milieu, Shaw's (1929) studies of delinquency in the city, and Wirth's (1928) classic study of the urban ghetto. Later, others moved to the micro level, studying how people interact with their immediate environment: Festinger, Schacter, and Back (1950), Hall (1966), Barker (1951, 1968, Barker and Gump 1964), and Fried (1972).

Interest in the interactive relationship between human behavior and physical settings is reflected in professional societies and journals devoted to the

Reprinted with permission of the Sociology Practice Association from "Doing Sociology with the Design Professions," by Bernie Jones, 1984, *Clinical Sociology Review, 2*, pp. 109–119.

subject (e.g., the Environmental Design Research Association, *Environment and Behavior*) and courses on such topics as social factors in urban design. Practitioners in these areas, variously calling themselves environmental sociologists, environmental psychologists, social psychologists, or design researchers, concur that physical settings and our ideas about them affect social interaction, and vice versa.

A corollary aspect of this reciprocal relationship between behavior and environment is that all physical designs emerge from social processes. Decision-making activities involve intensive interaction among designers, planners, architects, and others engaged in the design/planning process. Figure 2.1 shows the scope of concerns associated with the various design professionals involved. In addition, government officials, lending institutions, building contractors, landowners, and users play a variety of significant roles in shaping the process. The multiplicity of roles involved in the process makes it particularly amenable to sociological practice informed by knowledge of role expectations, cultural and occupational values, theories of community and urban ecology, and social research techniques.

THE SOCIOLOGICAL VIEW OF DESIGN AND PLANNING

Basically, design is a value-added process. Borrowed from economics, this term means that as raw material becomes a shaped, finished product, its value increases each step of the way. At the same time, however, the range of final forms the raw material can take grows increasingly narrow as the process nears completion. The design process is similar. The architect or planner begins with an idea; as design decisions are made about it, the idea becomes more real and more valuable, but the range of final designs contracts. Architects, for instance, start with a *program,* which is a verbal outline of needs the building or space should satisfy. During *conceptual design,* schematic or general design ideas are formulated, and the range of outcomes starts to narrow. Accepted conceptual designs are fleshed out during *design development,* further locking the designer into an evolving final form. During the *construction documents* phase, the final form is dictated in a set of instructions to the building contractor. Few significant changes are made during the last stage, *construction supervision.* Other designers and planners follow similar stages of work.

This aspect of design and planning holds import for the sociologist because it suggests that involvement of potential users of a facility in the design process must occur during the very first stage. *Once the design process gets under way, the possibilities for alterations, based on human needs expressed either directly by the users or indirectly by a sociologist, quickly shrink.* In addition, the further along the design process, the more specific and technical the

FIGURE 2.1   Concerns of the Design Professions

	DESIGN PROFESSIONS					
	Furniture Designer	Interior Designer	Architect	Landscape Architect	Urban Designer	Planner
Props	X	X				
Rooms		X		X		
Dwelling unit		X		X		
Building			X	X		
Site			X		X	X
Neighborhood			X	X		X
Community				X		X
Region						X

work becomes, making it harder for the layperson to contribute meaningfully.

Another sociologically relevant perspective on the design/planning process concerns the degree of role specialization involved in it. The built environment has not always been the product of people called architects, planners, landscape architects, and the like. "Architecture without architects has occurred throughout much of history" (Rudofsky 1964). Rapoport (1969) discusses the way that people in earlier times were able to plan, design, and build living environments that were well suited to their needs. No one stood between the user and the final product, which enabled the user to make sure that the building reflected his or her personal needs and culture.

With industrialization, bureaucratization, and specialization, however, the proliferation and professionalization of roles in the design process has expanded significantly (see Figure 2.2). All the activities current specialists handle were once the responsibility of the one-person or one-family designer–builders of earlier times.

As the cast of characters grows, the role of the ultimate user is proportionately reduced. Furthermore, the technical skills of other participants easily overshadow user contributions. As the number and variety of roles in the design process multiply, concern for user needs diminishes in its centrality. Competing considerations include the traditions of each professional, profit motives, competition and friction between professions, government regulations, and funding problems. However important these considerations may be to the various participants, they are not necessarily related to meeting the user's unique needs through good design.

THE POLITICS OF DESIGN AND PLANNING

Perhaps the most significant tangential considerations are political ones. I am defining "political" in the broadest sociological sense of decision making and the use of power. Design process decisions about whether something should be built, where it should be built, for whom it should be designed, are intensely political decisions often involving power struggles over such issues as zoning, land use, eminent domain, displacement, gentrification, accessibility to special populations, integration, segregation, social impact, and environmental protection.

If the design/planning process is political, entering into it constitutes taking sides, responding to an audience, and rendering oneself accountable to some party: playing the role of artist for a wealthy patron, methodologist for professional colleagues, or uncritical procurer for parties financing a project. Although all focus on an end product (judged in terms of cost effectiveness, artistic merit, or "monument value"), and all are to some extent accountable to a fee-paying client who has the power to make choices and pay for their realization, the products of these various roles differ. The artist may produce luxury homes; the methodologist "significant architectural statements"; and the procurer may produce oppressive, alienating office environments, prisonlike public housing, or may threaten neighborhoods.

On the other hand, a designer may be equally concerned with the process of decision making and

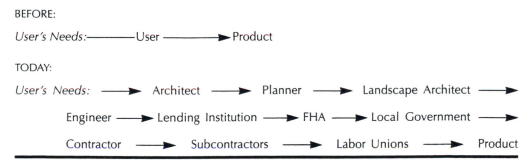

FIGURE 2.2   Specialization of Roles in the Design Process

the impact of certain decisions on the social context of the site and its immediate environs. This approach emphasizes accountability to those who will be directly affected by the design outcome, as well as to those who pay the fee (they are not always synonymous). In this case, the designer may serve as a social change agent whose audience is composed of the potential users and/or those people most directly affected by the designs. The designer joins in a cooperative, working relationship with the audience to bring about some improvement defined positively by the community in question.

Depending on the self-image of the designer or planner, he or she will be involved either in demystifying and democratizing the process, or in perpetuating the mystery of design and preserving a monopolistic control over the built environment. The role of the clinical sociologist is in improving communication between user and professional specialists, democratizing the decision-making process, and in defining the impact of specific plans on the community surrounding a site.

APPROACHES AND METHODS IN ENVIRONMENTAL SOCIOLOGY

Varieties of Practice

Practicing sociologists who refer to themselves as environmental sociologists or design researchers work at several levels, defined largely in terms of when during the design process they intervene. (I am excluding here pure research on person–environment relations, and focusing on applied work with design and planning professionals.)

1. Predesign Research.   In general, the most frequently occurring form of design research obtains information about potential users that will aid the designer or planner in turning out a product sensitive to user needs. The sociologist plays a translator role, interpreting the language of layperson and design professional to one another. The sociological expertise called for is in locating and communicating with the potential users, asking appropriate questions about their needs, or observing their lifestyles, then

translating that information into terms the designer/ planner can comprehend and utilize. For instance, one of my projects involved articulating the child-rearing practices of a low-income population to the architect so that he could design a culturally sensitive neighborhood child-care center. Another contract entailed translating student and faculty ideas regarding a new community college to the architects. The challenge was to communicate to the professionals various design concerns shared by the users (size, shape, color, safety, style, spirit, function) regarding particular spaces, buildings, and landscape.

2. Research on the Design Process.   Much less common is sociological research on the process itself. On the community college project, I was asked to monitor design team and user interactions, give the designers feedback about the effectiveness of their work, and identify the most productive interaction modes.

3. Postoccupancy Evaluation.   An increasingly popular form of design research consists of evaluating a finished, occupied, and utilized facility or space. The object is to determine whether it is working from the perspective of users. This represents a significant shift in the profession of design in which evaluation has tended to be based on visual and aesthetic factors, awards are often given before structures are built, and user satisfaction has been an afterthought at best.

In the postoccupancy evaluation of low-income housing, for example, I found residents' concerns focused, first, on functional aspects of the project (why a certain feature was omitted, whether the paint was washable, etc.); second, on sociological implications of design (issues of privacy or the image of the project in the surrounding neighborhood); and, third, on aesthetics (shape, color, line, and form). This is in marked contrast to the criteria often used in making professional awards.

The role of the clinical sociologist is in generating preoccupancy data, translating the needs of the user and the surrounding community to the design professionals and planners, facilitating interaction between them, democratizing the decision-making process, and evaluating the outcomes.

Specific Methods

When doing any kind of sociological research, the practitioner has to select carefully the methods best suited to the task. Determining the best methods for design process research depends on analyses of such factors as the ease of locating users, the ease of gaining access to them, their willingness to cooperate, educational level and life styles, frequency with which they have been previously studied, timing and costs of the study, and willingness of the designer/planner client to allow research and respond to findings as presented. Data gathering on such projects is most successful when the methods allow: (1) the greatest number of users to make some contribution; (2) stimulation of one person's thinking by another's to produce a rich flow of ideas; (3) open-ended discussion rather than forced, restrictive choices; (4) input from users before preliminary designs are completed, rather than reaction to designs already generated; (5) exploration of what should be and what could be, rather than rehashing of what is or has been; (6) continual participation throughout the design process, rather than a one-shot chance to make input; (7) direct input by users, rather than solely through the clinical sociologist.

Sociological research on design/planning projects, like other sociological research, takes one of two forms: asking people about their behavior or observing their behavior. Both Michelson (1975) and Zeisel (1981) describe various methods in detail and illustrate their use. The following are methods I have used, ranked roughly from the least effective to the most effective in terms of the criteria listed above.

1. Reactor Panel. In this method, a small but representative sample of intended users reacts to designs or plans in various stages of completion. This approach is inexpensive and quick but is limited by the small sample. In addition, even sketchy designs and plans rendered by professionals can intimidate the layperson into a reluctance to criticize. I have used this approach in gathering data from users of married student housing, but only in combination with other methods.

2. Observation of Existing Facilities or Sites. This method yields indirect data in the sense that the researcher observes users in a site similar to the one to be designed, but he or she does not interact with them directly. Although this method can be time efficient, the major drawback is that patterns of current usage and design dominate, as if culture were not dynamic. Direct observation can be done with the naked eye, or via photography, film, or videotape. An excellent example is Whyte's study of the use of urban open space (1980).

3. Questionnaires. While this time-honored social science tool allows the practitioner to tap a large sample of users, one cannot possibly anticipate every design consideration; thus the one-shot nature of questionnaires becomes a serious drawback. An additional problem is the inability most people have to be very articulate about their design preferences. The method does have greater applicability for less design-oriented, more planning-oriented projects, where the task might be to establish general goals for a comprehensive community plan.

4. Joint Tour of Existing or Proposed Facility or Site. This involves users, the design team, and the sociologists all going through facilities or sites, conversing along the way. It is especially good for stimulating questions by the design team or the sociologist for the user. On a married student housing project, such a tour of several existing student housing developments generated helpful comparisons and the pinpointing of many good and bad design features.

5. Individual Interviews. Formal or conversational open-ended interviews with users start to yield good results, but lack the interrespondent stimulation that some other methods allow. I found this approach useful in some neighborhoods where residents could not be brought together easily, or at a community college where students' time was limited.

6. Public Meetings. A great deal of interrespondent stimulation occurs in large public meetings as ideas are bounced back and forth. However, the size of the group may intimidate the shy, retiring person and spur on the already vocal person. I concluded after using neighborhood meetings during an urban renewal planning study that they are better suited for the discussion of broad policy issues as opposed to specific design ideas.

7. Small Meetings.   These meetings usually afford the same rich exchange of ideas as the larger ones, and have the added advantage of allowing more people to participate. In evaluating low-income housing, for example, I found small house meetings useful for producing lively discussion.

8. Design Workshops.   An even better version of the small meeting, the design workshop allows design professionals and sociologists, using models, drawings, maps, floor plans, games of trade-off, and so on, to try to elicit ideas and put them into graphic form. Users can then see their ideas actualized, elaborate on them, and revise them. This affords an active role for the user. On the married student project, users arranged Styrofoam blocks on a topographic map of the site to show their preferred site plan.

9. Communications–Response Cafeteria.   Each of the data-gathering approaches outlined above has strengths and weaknesses; sometimes a combination of them can be used effectively. The combination approach is built on some assumptions about the social research process as a communications act. First, the burden of good communications rests upon the party wanting to communicate in the first place (for our purposes, the researcher). Second, that burden should also be upon the party with the greater resources for communications (again, the researcher). Third, and finally, good data cannot flow through a poor researcher/respondent relationship. I interpret these assumptions, then, to mean that the sociologist must ensure that no one who wants to give input is shut out simply by the choice of information-gathering methods. These assumptions lead to a basic hypothesis: the more heterogeneous the population of users, the more varied the types of data-gathering approaches will be necessary for greatest and most creative input.

For example, on a feasibility study for an urban renewal project, my team offered residents of the area a number of ways for participating and responding. A neighborhood storefront was established where residents could drop in, talk informally, review maps and drawings, and offer their ideas. Telephone inquiries were turned into semistructured interviews. Three field workers spent time in the neighborhood, frequenting natural congregating places and talking with people about the project. Short questionnaires were left at the counters of neighborhood shops; on several days tables were placed in large supermarkets, complete with staff, maps, photographs, and questionnaires. Two dozen community meetings of different sizes were held throughout the study area. Different demographic groups (young, old, renters, owners, etc.) gravitated to different channels of communication, thus confirming the team's implicit hypothesis.

In a second study utilizing this combined approach, the task was to obtain data from faculty and students at an existing community college about the design of a proposed new campus. The fact that only two weeks were allowed for research made a powerful argument for opening as many communication channels as possible. The team set up a space in the existing student lounge featuring a central table where informal conversations about the project were taped anonymously and with permission. A continuous slide show about the site, complete with music, stimulated ideas which could be recorded on long sheets of paper at the table or on large newsprint pads hung on the walls. A site planning game, consisting of a topographic map, various small objects to use as buildings, and appropriate labels, allowed users to visualize their ideas for the new campus. A sign-up list encouraged people to accompany us on a walking tour of the building site. Large sheets of paper asking, What would you like the new campus to be like? were hung in conspicuous places throughout the existing campus.

CONCLUSION

The results of these approaches were summarized and used to generate a list of specific concerns and recommendations which were submitted for response to the architects and planners. This process stimulated an ongoing exchange of ideas beginning early enough in the design process to make a realistic and meaningful impact on the decision making. In some instances the clinical sociologist's role will end at the point of diagnostically evaluating the potential impact of the plan on users, and tailoring research methods to the characteristics of users. However, the role may continue throughout the planning and revising stage into evaluation. In either case, the clinical sociologist performs an important role in reducing the distance between user and design product.

NOTES

1. In the category of designers and planners I am including interior designers, architects, landscape architects, urban designers, and planners, each of whom deals with different but overlapping parts of the built environment.

REFERENCES

Barker, R. *One Boy's Day.* New York: Harper & Row, 1951.

Barker, R. *Ecological Psychology: Concepts and Methods for Studying the Environment of Human Behavior.* Stanford, Cal.: Stanford University Press, 1968.

Barker, R., and P. V. Gump. *Big School, Small School.* Stanford, Cal.: Stanford University Press, 1964.

Festinger, L., S. Schachter, and K. Back. *Social Pressure in Informal Groups.* New York: Harper & Row, 1950.

Fried, M. "Grieving for a lost home." In R. Gutman (ed.), *People and Buildings,* pp. 229–48. New York: Basic Books, 1972.

Hall, E. *The Hidden Dimension.* Garden City, N.Y.: Doubleday, 1966.

McKenzie, R. D. *The Neighborhood.* Chicago: University of Chicago Press, 1923.

Michelson, W., ed. *Behavioral Research Methods in Environmental Design.* Stroudsburg, Pa.: Hutchinson Ross, 1975.

Park, R. "The city: suggestions for the investigation of human behavior in the city environment," *American Journal of Sociology* 10, pp. 587–612, 1951.

Rapoport, A. *House Form and Culture.* Englewood Cliffs, N.J.: Prentice-Hall, 1969.

3

Design and Human Behavior
The Sociology of Architecture

WILLIAM DU BOIS

Author's Note: When I first got my Ph.D., I went to work consulting for bars and night-clubs to design effective social settings. I have always said that a sociologist ought to be able to design a good bar—or else shouldn't be allowed to fool around with the rest of society. Unfortunately, most sociologists couldn't design a good bar. They are not good at putting people together, and their theories would make people flee rather than flourish.

I designed nightclubs in both Iowa and northern California. In the first consultation, club sales went from $1,500 a week to $10,000. By designing to promote positive interaction and community, people stayed longer, returned more often, and told their friends. People met people. One of the "problems" that developed was that so many of the crowd were getting married to each other that we had to recruit new customers. I later applied these same social design principles to a nursing home to create a sense of community. Applications can also be made to almost any setting for human interaction, from offices to recreational facilities, from day-care centers to factories to apartment complexes. I am currently most interested in applying these principles to a community recreation center, a convention hotel, a teen bar, and maybe a miniature golf course.

I have always wanted to write an article on the unlikely humanism of B. F. Skinner. There is probably a larger research base on Skinner's work than on anything else in the social sciences. Yet Skinner continues to infuriate because he overstated his case in an effort to control and manipulate.

Skinner (1971) didn't understand "manipulatable variables." The word *manipulate* comes from the Latin *manus,* which means "hand." A manipulatable variable is something that is literally "in hand." People are not manipulatable variables. They are not "in hand," and we should not aspire to any science that seeks such control.[1] However, some variables are by their very nature manipulatable variables.

Furniture, for example, is a manipulatable variable. It is literally "in hand." The decision is not whether to manipulate or not to manipulate. A chair must be put somewhere. The only question is whether we are going to manipulate it intelligently or just throw the whole process up to chance. We can take a chair and fling it into the air, letting it land where it may. Or we can place the chair intelligently. The question is not whether to manipulate, but how. We can design with attention to how it influences human behavior, or we can just leave it to chance.

THE APPLICATION
OF SCIENTIFIC KNOWLEDGE

It takes only the smallest bit of knowledge to launch a viable invention. Some of our greatest scientific inventions were created from the smallest spark. It takes only a little understanding to develop something new. The automobile, for example, is based on a few elementary principles. A small spark creates a small explosion, releasing energy that is channeled through a series of gears—and before we know it, we're driving down the road. We understand much about the fundamentals of effective human dynamics. The gears for effective design are simply consistent application of these fundamentals to every decision in the design. The influence of any one detail may be subtle. When all the countless details are added together, we create a collage effectively influencing human interaction. We know a great deal if we will just creatively apply what we know. By applying the smallest principle creatively, we are soon driving down the road.

Psychologists and architects have made us familiar with how color, lighting, and music influence behavior. The original color scheme in Denny's restaurants was chosen because it was experimentally found to produce the fastest "turnaround" time. The colors were designed so customers wouldn't linger: As soon as they finished their coffee, they would leave, vacating the chair for the next customer. Offices also select colors to improve efficiency; factories, to increase productivity; police departments and jails, to soothe emotions. The Iowa football team has painted the visiting team's locker room bright pink to rattle opponents. Lighting has also been used to create moods. The Target chain and many other retail stores use full-spectrum fluorescent lights to make colors look their very best. This lighting increases sales by 2 percent. Supermarkets and shopping malls have shown the value of music while you shop.

However, color, lighting, and music only scratch the surface. *Every decision on design has consequences for behavior*. Each is an opportunity to influence interaction. We can either allow those consequences to happen by chance, or consciously design for human interaction. We can gear every design decision to how it will influence human actors. It costs no more to design with behavior in mind. Too many expensive decors just sit there. We can get a bonus for our design investment by paying attention to the implications for human interaction.

Each decision provides an opportunity to turn the physical environment into a silent partner actively working for us.

Companies spend thousands on motivational speakers but usually neglect the implications an effectively designed cafeteria or break room can have for team building. Design can be used to promote positive interaction and community. Environments can effectively mix and match people, whether they be singles in a nightclub looking to meet someone or conventioneers seeking that one idea. Community can be designed into housing subdivisions, thus increasing the real value of the property. Shopping centers currently pay designers millions to "design teenagers out of them" by eliminating hangout nooks and loitering places—and yet the positive benefits of "designing community in" go unexplored. Shopping complexes can be designed where customers enjoy shopping and spend more doing it.

A few years ago, 3M corporate headquarters eliminated elevators because they stifle interaction and the flow of ideas. In an elevator people greet their coworkers by staring straight ahead in awkward silence. 3M, a company dependent on creativity and innovation, installed escalators because they provide a kind of face-to-face contact. Employees passing on the escalator might be reminded of an idea they'd forgotten to talk about, and meet on the landing. That chance encounter might lead to a new product. Just one creative new product idea would more than pay for the whole exercise. While the 3M escalator is a bit expensive for my tastes, it gets the point across.

Every aspect of an environment has implications for behavior. The old-time bartenders seemed to understand this: The traditional cocktail napkin with a cartoon on it is a good example. A customer may laugh at the cartoon and share it with someone seated near them. Such an encounter may lead to a conversation, another drink, and perhaps a whole evening. The cocktail napkin illustrates that no detail is too small to pay attention to.[2]

Hundreds of thousands of decisions go into designing an environment. Most go unnoticed. They are made unthinkingly in traditional ways or follow a copycat approach. Many get pushed down the line to someone trying to get some other job done. Suppliers, janitors, and delivery people probably make as many design decisions as anyone else. Franchises usually make a few design innovations, which become their trademark, and then do everything else just like the competition. As often as not, the "innovations" are colors and decorative themes.

We might think that surely there would be good reasons for typical design decisions. But when we search behind the conventions, we find most had more to do with convenient lumber sizes than with effective human dynamics. The origins of many practices are lost in historical accommodations for machines and practices long since extinct. Managers assume someone must be thinking about these things and paying attention to important details. They aren't.

In one of my consultations with a nightclub in northern California, my client wanted an afternoon crowd and worried particularly why women didn't hang out at the bar. The answer was really obvious: they had a 46½-inch-high bar. I am 5 feet, 9 inches tall. The bar hit me right below the chest. That would mean that for a 5-foot, 2-inch woman, the bar would be practically at neck level. When I searched into the origins of this high bar, I discovered it had been built by two 6-foot, 4-inch carpenters. As long as the bar remained that height, it was never going to be the site of much interaction. Interestingly, although it would have cost only a thousand dollars to lower the height to 42 or 43 inches, that was an argument that I lost.

Many elegant restaurants buy elaborate tables that don't work, or expensive booths that are just about as comfortable as bleachers. Architects and interior designers are supposed to know about these things. Yet most are more conscious of visual appeal than attentive to human dynamics. They design for the eye. Frank Lloyd Wright houses are famous for their beautiful designs, but real estate agents will tell you they are also notorious for "creating divorces" among the people who buy them. They are often up for sale. They are great showpieces, but people can't live in them.

In fairness, designers focus on cosmetics partly because they normally lack the power to make significant design changes. Intensive access to top managers and staff is usually lacking. Managers are accustomed to commissioning an architect and then receiving a finished blueprint. They hire an expert so they don't have to think. Yet how people think about their physical environment is usually part of the problem. Organizational problems are often reflected in the physical design, and vice versa. Too often, a designer is commissioned to "finish the job" only after muddled thinking has already dictated an ineffective design. A designer must have access to top managers. Time must be found for rethinking parameters and fundamentals of an organization's needs.

Industrial psychologists like to talk about the "Hawthorne Effect." Researchers at the Western Electric plant found that any change they made in the physical environment temporarily increased worker productivity. Production then soon returned to previous levels. This effect is normally interpreted as evidence of "experimental bias"—the fact that people tend to react when they know they're being experimented upon. But this misses the point of one of the most significant findings in social psychology. For the armchair scientist, experimental bias may be an important issue. For business, the crucial finding is that the studies demonstrated that attention to a worker's environment produces results. The changes were real. Increases in production, however temporary, surely more than paid for the cost of lighting and paint. It might pay to repaint every week. The Hawthorne Effect shows conclusively that workers will respond when they feel management is interested in their working conditions. Imagine what the effects would have been if researchers had stumbled upon factors that actually do contribute to permanent increases in productivity.

Many of those factors are there for the asking. So ask. This does not mean appointing a committee or conducting a complicated needs assessment survey. It does mean carefully listening to participants and carefully addressing the concerns raised. It also means utilizing what we know from sociology and applying it artistically to an organization's particular problems.

PROXIMITY AND CIRCULATION PATHS

Atmosphere and physical design influence behavior in ways you may have never suspected. A distance of as little as 6 inches across a table can be the difference between whether you feel involved or isolated. Friendship formation in apartment complexes can be predicted on the basis of nothing more exotic than proximity and circulation paths. Even crime rates have been significantly reduced by paying attention to socially defensible space in neighborhoods.

The work of B. F. Skinner has been brought into sociology by George Homans. In *Social Behavior: Its Elementary Forms* (1974) Homans shows how friendships in neighborhoods are related to physical design. In studies of neighborhoods, as shown in Figure 3.1, the people with the most friends tend to be C and H.

On the other hand, neighbors at the end of the block, in contrast, tend to know the fewest people. Real estate agents will testify that houses at the ends of the block will also have a higher turnover rate than those in the middle. C and H are likely to be immersed in community. C probably knows B and D and, depending on the width of the street (or whether they have exploring children), probably knows H, G, and I. Residents at the end of the block, such as A, F, E, and J, are more isolated. For example, E probably knows D, and may know I or J. In other words, C and H are likely to know twice as many people as residents situated at the ends of the block.

This of course is all probabilistic. Personalities and many other factors certainly enter into it. However, if we look at hundreds of neighborhoods, the likelihood is that those positioned at C and H will have more friends.

The reason for this is proximity. The closer people are, the more likely they are to interact and become friends. Physical nearness (propinquity) has also been discovered to be a major factor in mate selection (Burgess and Wallin, 1954). Not only does physical closeness make it more likely that people will know each other; it also increases the probability they will become friends and even marry.

A similar dynamic takes place with circulation paths. Figure 3.2 is a side view of a married student apartment complex. Residents on the top floor must climb the stairs and enter their apartment from the outside balcony. In this arrangement, people who live in apartment number 3 are likely to have the most friends. Residents of apartment 8 are likely to have the fewest friends. What is occurring has to do with opportunities and the likelihood of repeated interaction. Both proximity and circulation paths are at work here. Number 3 is likely to know 2 and 4, and may take the stairs to pass 1 and 6 some days, and 5 and 10 other days. Number 8, on the other hand, is likely to know only 7 and 9. Residents of apartment 2 would typically use the stairs on the left and likely know 3, 1, and 6. As Figure 3.3 shows, residents of apartment 3 have twice as many opportunities to meet neighbors as residents of apartment 2 and three times as many as residents of apartment 8. Research showed the number of friendships people had actually mirrored these probabilities. There were certainly many exceptions. However, over many apartment complexes, people whose apartments were situated to create more opportunities tended to have more friends.

Homans sums this up in his Liking Proposition (Figure 3.4). Proximity makes it more likely that people will interact in the first place. When people see each other frequently they become familiar and feel

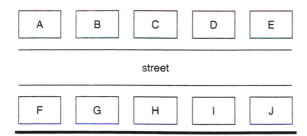

FIGURE 3.1　Friendships in Neighborhoods

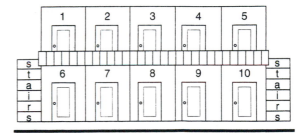

FIGURE 3.2　Friendships in Apartment Complex

Residents of Apartment	Number of Neighbors They Are Likely to Know
#3	6
#6, #10	4
#1, #2, #4, #5	3
#7, #8, #9	2

FIGURE 3.3   Opportunities for Friendship

like they almost know each other. This makes it more likely they will interact. Once they have interacted, it is more likely they will interact again. Having broken the ice and sat down at the same table with someone makes it easier to join them again. Repeated interaction, leads to positive interaction, which leads to liking and friendship.

One may wonder about repeated interaction leading to positive interaction. Would it not be just as likely to lead to negative interaction? This may happen, but not usually. Conflict is painful, and people generally seek to avoid it. When people interact, they tend to emphasize the positive. If people must interact, they shy away from areas of disagreement and cultivate areas of agreement and common interests. Thus, people who disagree on politics may avoid that topic and instead dwell on their shared allegiance to the local sports team. There also seems almost to be a social norm that people should get along. Repeated interaction has a tendency to be positive.

Homans's Liking Proposition can be used in design as a way to promote liking and friendships. The key is applying it consistently to every aspect of an environment. There is, however, one "limits proposi-

tion" that must be considered: the issue of personal space.

PERSONAL SPACE: GETTING THE DIMENSIONS RIGHT

Proximity leads to positive interaction up to a point, but people can be too close. When someone is right in your face, it can stifle interaction. Congestion and overcrowding can lead to anonymity and even aggression. In apartments, neighbors situated too closely ignore each other in an attempt to regain privacy. In nightclubs, fights tend to occur where circulation paths have created a bottleneck.

How close is too close? And what is just right? Comfortable dimensions for personal space vary from culture to culture, and within any culture there are going to be a few people who are exceptions. Most Americans feel most comfortable communicating at a distance of 30 inches nose to nose (Sommer, 1969). Moving even 2 inches closer unnerves people, making them feel their personal space has been invaded. A distance even a few inches farther away makes people feel remote.

Distributors sell all sizes of tables. For human interaction, however, only one size of square table makes sense for two to four people: 30 inches. When tables are larger, conversations tend to drift off and interaction stymies. Even lovers prefer this distance to talk comfortably face-to-face. For closeness, lovers tend to sit side by side. Side by side, all people can be much closer. In fact, most can be almost touching and still feel comfortable.

With several people seated around a circular table, another factor becomes important. A diameter of 30 inches is too small. People seated directly next to each other are too close for comfortable interaction: Most conversation thus gets directed to those

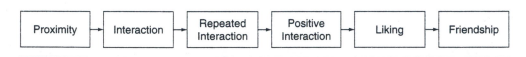

FIGURE 3.4   Homans's Liking Proposition

across the table. However, if the diameter of the table is too large, interaction tends to take place only *around* the circumference. The ideal size for a circular table is 42 inches. This allows interaction to take place both across and around the table. Sometimes this dimension can be stretched a little to accommodate more people around a table, but the dimension should never be so great as to prohibit normal interaction across the table.

Some dimensions can be scripted in advance. Many other dimensions need to be rehearsed. Several people can position themselves in an environment to discover the proper arrangements. What is too close? What is too distant? Does the width of an aisle or a hallway promote comfortable meeting, greeting, and a feeling of community, or do people pass as strangers? A little attention can go a long way toward creating a more successful environment.

Empowering the User

If one is designing a restaurant, it makes sense to sit in every seat. Every seat is either making you money or costing you profits. You need to know how a customer feels from each perspective and what arrangements or adjustments might be more effective. The only way you are going to discover small things that create problems is to try every single seat. Empowering the customer includes taking the time to see what it is like from every position customers might occupy.

Such an effort might take an afternoon, but it will pay for itself every night. You need to know what the customer feels like. When I consulted with a nursing home, the administrator and I immediately went on a wheelchair tour of the home to see what it was like from that perspective.

If we know the right dimensions, we can situate seating so the user maintains personal space and retains the power to make him- or herself accessible or inaccessible to others. I have done this with nightclubs to create social interaction. It could also be done to promote positive interaction and create community in convention hotels or teen social centers or hospital cafeterias.

If the dimensions are right, by simply moving their chair, people can control whether they are available to others or inaccessible. Dimensions at tables need to be perfect so a person can lean in for intimate conversation or scoot their chair back to remove themselves. Tables and seating can also be interrelated to provide occupants with the same power to allow access or make themselves unavailable with only a small movement of their chair.

In Figure 3.5, the person at Table A wants to make contact with a person at Table B, but that person is inaccessible. In Figure 3.6, the person at Table B moves back only a few inches, making himself or herself accessible to a potential conversation. Notice that the person at Table A can also choose to withdraw from interaction at any time by simply moving

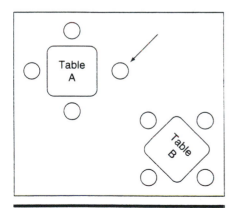

FIGURE 3.5 Privacy

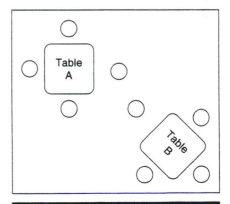

FIGURE 3.6 Accessibility

his or her own chair back up to the table. By interrelating the placement of tables, new friendships are likely to form. Many times two separate tables will get pushed together as groups join each other. Tables can be situated like this throughout an entire room. It may take a few hours to arrange every table so that it has access to others but retains personal space. Once the proper placement for each table and chair has been established, it can be marked on the floor in an inconspicuous manner so tables and chairs can be returned to their "home base" when customers leave.

Circulation paths may also be used to mix and match people. "Excuses for movement" can be situated to provide opportunities for people to pass each other as they are drawn to different areas. Many successful singles bars can attribute their success almost solely to this principle. There are only so many excuses for movement in a nightclub: rest rooms, bars, pool tables, video machines, cigarette machines, dance floor. Each needs to be strategically located to encourage interaction.

The old-time bartender introduced people to each other. An effective environment will introduce people by design even when the bartender is busy. Circulation paths, excuses for movement, and participatory resources are crucial in a singles club. Most people don't just see someone attractive across the room, walk over, and start a relationship. Approaching someone on the other side of the room involves too great a cost of rejection and a long walk back. It's easier to play a peekaboo ritual where you can gradually enter that space. As sociologist Lillian Rubin (1983) says, the mating dance is a "go away a little closer" ritual. An effective design provides opportunities for movement, excuses to enter the same territory, and areas to "homestead" close by. Many popular singles clubs flourish simply because of well-interrelated high cocktail tables that form an effective mingling area.

Social interaction takes place in what might be termed "acoustical" space. It doesn't take place in "visual" space. Visual space follows the eye. It is rational, thought out, planned. Things are neatly separated and intentionally either joined or disconnected. In visual space you would see something, plan an action, and do it. But social interaction doesn't usually happen that way. Acoustical space is quite different. Close your eyes. All things are sudden. They blend into each other. They collide and intrude. Things just happen. Meeting and interacting with someone is much more likely to happen in acoustical space, where people relax, forget themselves, and "bump into" someone. In visual space, I see someone across the room and I intentionally approach them, *causing* the interaction. In acoustical space, I forget myself and suddenly *discover* myself interacting with a person. Many times nightclubs will design spots where the occupants can see everything and be in control. But vision isolates. The occupants of such a booth discover themselves isolated and alone rather than in control. Interaction should just flow. There should not be disjointed junctures that require thought or planning. In an effective design, participants find that things just seem to happen.[3]

There must also be areas where people can retreat out of the flow.[4] There need to be places for couples and small groups that don't want strangers approaching.

Defensible Space, Approachable Space

The story is told that Old West cowboy Wild Bill Hickok always sat with his back to the wall. The one time he didn't, he was shot in the back and killed while playing poker. Like Wild Bill, most people like to sit with their backs to the wall. People like booths for that same feeling of security.

One of the reasons McDonald's does so much better than Wendy's is that Dave doesn't understand what business he is in. He thinks he's selling food. Most people actually prefer Wendy's food, but McDonald's understands they are selling atmosphere— as their slogan testifies, "food, folks, and fun." Interestingly, many McDonald's restaurants have booths where people can retreat and feel secure. Wendy's has only nice-looking but somewhat uncomfortable chairs, which are usually placed out in the open undefended.

Oscar Newman (1972, 1996) has shown how *defensible space* can be used to prevent crime. Much work with this concept involves creating visible open spaces, access to neighbors, and natural "blockades" to protect an environment. Recent Department of Justice approaches have applied these to housing projects, apartment complexes, and even parking garages with success (Fleissner and Heinzelmann, 1996; Smith, 1996; Taylor and Harrell, 1996).

Defensible space can be a double-edged sword, however. Many grocery stores put special displays in aisles, especially on weekends. Such a display can actually create a blockade and prevent the normal shopping that goes on in that aisle. Customers often hurry through the aisle so as not to intrude on another person's space. Although the particular featured item may sell more, the overall sales in that aisle may actually decrease.

In addition to defensible space, we can also create *approachable space* that invites people in. People seated at a table near the entrance to a room may effectively deter other people from entering. Ideally, in social settings, we want people to enter a room and proceed to the perimeters. This opens up the room, drawing people in, and allows occupancy to develop naturally. We can create resources that naturally draw people to the perimeters. Booths are one such resource. Most of the booths will usually get filled before many tables are occupied. Hangout nooks and drink shelves may attract people to previously underutilized areas. Rather than trying to *push* people to the perimeters, we must create resources that *pull* them.

Ways to attract people to the perimeters can be subtle. One way is to virtually shelve people against the wall with bench seating that "grabs" them: It is at a height such that leaning against it, people soon find themself seated. Aisles are thus opened up and freed for effective circulation paths.

A poor design often causes people to unintentionally blockade an area, making it unapproachable to all but the most intrusive individuals. Some restaurants have seating areas where the presence of even one or two customers makes others avoid sitting in that section. Benches in parks and on college campuses are often so poorly arranged that even one person effectively "confiscates" the area: Others wouldn't dream of invading that person's space.

It is fairly easy to predict which tables or seats will be occupied first, which will be taken next, and how the room will develop as more people enter. People usually seat themselves at a distance from other people. The area then fills in a predictable manner as each person sits a respectful distance from others. A well-planned design utilizes this knowledge so an area develops naturally without creating blockades.

DEFINITION OF THE SITUATION

Symbols allow us to define the situation, and that definition in turn tells us how to act.[5] When we enter an environment, we immediately search for clues to where we are. Once we have defined the situation, it is as if we have "packages of behavior" for each situation. Obviously, the package of behavior associated with a situation defined as a football game is quite different from the package for a library or a church. Even a small misreading of a situation can lead to great embarrassment.

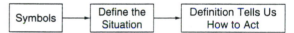

We all read situations almost unconsciously in order to determine the appropriate action for that setting. Top-ranking executives often arrange their offices complete with a "living-room" setting or a "kitchen table." This is more than a matter of just occupying space in a large office. Executives have learned such an atmosphere helps them do business better. People are apt to pull out behaviors associated with the more informal setting. It is easier to put clients at ease in the "living room" or to negotiate an important merger when participants are just sitting around the "kitchen table."

A club owner may want to create a spirit of "play" to encourage people to venture out. One chain creates the impression of a "carnival" definition of the situation as soon as one enters. Customers are more likely to pull out a playful package of behaviors. I am told of a downstairs bar in Illinois where customers can either enter via the stairs or take the slide. Customers can immediately leave the workaday world behind and enter a definition of play. The circular slide rumbles, so people hear whenever someone is coming down the slide. When the person arrives, everyone at the bar is looking at them and smiling.

Shopping malls may try to create a spirit of "adventure" and even of "vacation." They want people to explore and splurge. Other settings may wish to create definitions of "community." Some stores suggest just a "touch of class," posturing themselves one accessible status rung above their customers. Others, like the business executives, may strive to make their clients feel "at home." Seemingly inconsequential factors such as the design of women's rest rooms can have important ramifications about the "true" impression of a business.

Defining the situation is not a matter of decorating around a theme. It is setting the stage for the human drama. Subtle clues can be used to suggest different atmospheres and moods. These don't need to dominate, and many different moods can be interfaced together. Just a hint can provide a brief experience and define a mood. This is a far cry from theme restaurants that try to "trick" customers with a Mexican or Chinese decor. Defining a situation occurs within a theme. Thus, a Mexican restaurant might create elegance, a playful atmosphere, a community, or a bargain bazaar. Other appropriate definitions might help us feel at home, comfortable, and slightly (safely) adventurous.

In a nursing home consultation, I used definition of the situation to change the atmosphere. The word "home" was really a misnomer, because all the definitions in the facility shouted "hospital" rather than "home." Many of these could be changed without reducing effectiveness. The nurses' station was a case in point.

At first glance, the nurses' station in a nursing home looks very much like a hospital. There are charts, thermometers, foreboding medical apparatus, and nurses dressed in white. Typically, there are also residents stranded in disarray around the station with their wheelchairs facing in odd directions left where they have been abandoned. In this particular nursing home, the elevator opened right across from the station, which was centrally located in the middle of the floor. The first impression one received when exiting the elevator was depressing. This did not feel like a place to live.

The station was the center of communication for the floor. The residents congregated around the nurses' station in part because it was the hub of activity, close to the elevator, and in the middle of the floor. Other purposes also attracted them there. On the surface, the nurses' station looked very hospital-like: a clean, professional, efficient place to dispense medical needs. On the counter were all sorts of medical-looking things and professional records. However, tucked in drawers and cabinets under the counter was a whole other world: candy, magazines, playing cards, the residents' money, their cigarettes. Residents used the station much as we use a neighborhood convenience store. It was also where some would go to use the telephone.

It was but a small step to change the definition of the situation. Medications and hospital paraphernalia could easily go under the counter and in cabinets without decreasing the quality or efficiency of care. Out from the drawers came the candy, magazines, and other "neighborhood store" items. Since fast shopping is of no concern, a "convenience store" definition of the situation was not exactly appropriate. An old-time "general store" definition—a place where locals loiter and share gossip—made more sense. "General store" definitions can be highlighted with more magazines, old-fashioned stick candy in jars, and small grocery snacks such as apples and bakery items. In my consultation, I would even have put in an old time potbellied stove if the fire marshall would have allowed it.

In the new design (Figure 3.7) the counter facing the elevator is normal height, but the counter in the hangout nook is wheelchair height. This helps to bring residents into the alcove rather than leaving them blockading the hall.

Establishing the definition of the situation is sometimes subtle. I often advise clients to spend their money on a good carpet pad rather than on the carpet itself. It is the pad that gives you the feel and impression of being in a plush setting. Even the more expensive carpet pads are relatively inexpensive compared to the price of carpet.

Rest rooms are another crucial area that often gets neglected. All the atmosphere on the other side of the rest-room door can be ruined forever by a tacky rest room. Health codes limit some options, but one can still make an environment where people feel

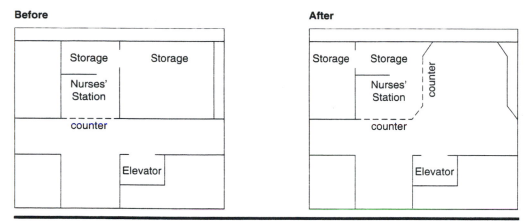

FIGURE 3.7   Nursing Home

at home. Bathroom stalls that don't lock are an atrocity. The money saved by only having a hand blow-dryer rather than paper towels can quickly be lost as customers feel less comfortable in your establishment. (One can make the argument that the blow-dryer is more sanitary, but actually most people end up wiping the last moisture from their hands on their clothes. We all know why businesses prefer these dryers: They are cheap. And that impression lingers as we return to shopping.) Women's bathrooms are particularly critical.

PARTICIPATORY RESOURCES

Participatory resources allow users to make the environment their own. Canned atmospheres turn people off. Every opportunity for involvement makes people feel at home. People resent canned environments addressed to an audience; after sampling such a setting once, they often don't return, as there is no room for participation and creating their own experience.

Marshall McLuhan (1964) spoke of hot and cold mediums. A hot medium is well defined: All the decisions have been made and life is predictable, sterile, with no room for participation. It is a gridlike picture where all the details have been filled in and spelled out. Conversely, a cold medium invites participation. It is vague and sketchy. It sets the frame but is incomplete, thus demanding participation to com-

plete the picture. A cold medium leaves openings for involvement.

This idea, which is conceptually sophisticated sociologically, may actually be utilized in a very simple manner. In one nightclub consultation, I turned the DJ stand into a voting booth to allow and encourage participation. Rather than being merely passive consumers of an environment directed at them, people became coproducers. I accomplished this in a very simple way: A chair-height step was built around the DJ stand. Anyone standing on the step was conspicuous across the room: People could see who was "voting." The step had multiple layers of padding beneath its carpet and felt very plush, elegant, and comfortable. The step was about the width of a chair, so it provided good balance; some people would actually pause to sit on it briefly. However, the DJ stand provided an uncomfortable back that ensured they wouldn't sit long. The height of the step not only made one visible throughout the room, but stepping up was a commitment and a statement in itself. The step was also not so high as to be prohibitive for anyone.

The first night the step was built I purposely "demonstrated" repeatedly how one could use it to talk to the disc jockey. After several of my quick trips to it, two young women ventured onto the step, and from that time forth there was never more than a few minutes that someone wasn't on the step. It now became impossible for even a new DJ to make a mistake reading the crowd's mood, because someone would immediately be there to correct and redirect choices.

It is important, when introducing something new, to make sure people know how to use it. *Design demonstrations* are essential. When building a drink shelf in a nightclub, for instance, I instruct that an empty glass or bottle be left on it. You want to show people what the shelf is for rather than trusting they'll discover it is there or have the courage to be the first to use it. In a concert dance hall, hooks were placed below a drink shelf adjacent to the dance floor so people could hang their coats and have an area to "homestead" as their own even while dancing. To get people to discover the hooks (actually wooden pegs), it was essential to have a couple of coats hanging there to demonstrate the idea. Surprisingly, people soon left not only their coats but their purses as well.

Similar to the step around the DJ stand, I have also seen three jukeboxes wired together function as a voting booth. This allowed patrons to choose among a wide range of songs without having to repeat. Each evening there would be an unspoken "debate" as people voted with their quarters, testifying to their own mood or predicament. Invariably the crowd would settle into a collective mood within a couple of hours and stay there for the night. Once this nonverbal consensus had been reached, people never seemed to violate it.

In setting up such a jukebox, it is essential to get the details right. Every song on the jukebox should be good. Too vast a selection of songs makes choices overwhelming; too small a selection means songs must be repeated often and the crowd can't agree to settle into a mood. Six hundred to a thousand selections is probably about right. The choices need to be displayed so all selections are visible at once— people shouldn't have to "turn pages" to discover what is on the jukebox. The area where song choices are displayed needs to be physically large enough that someone can approach the space, yet small enough to feel comfortable. The jukebox "voting" area should be large enough for more than just one or two people to congregate. It shouldn't be so large that it spoils the camaraderie of several people jointly making selections. It should be inviting and open to participation . . . possibly by someone you don't even know. The machine should also not take dollar bills. Selections should be one song for a quarter. We don't want anybody to confiscate the mood and destroy the participatory access. Of course, it is possible to put in several dollars in quarters, but this is less likely. A person stuffing 20 quarters into the machine would be apt to feel like they were being greedy and dominating the atmosphere.

Social designers can design resources that promote positive social interaction. Areas can be designed that people can "homestead" for their own intents and purposes. Opportunities to temporarily homestead areas allow people to create their own meanings and provide a feeling of place and ownership for the night. This can be accomplished by something as simple as a drink shelf or a hangout nook. Conversation pieces such as the cocktail napkins mentioned earlier are good examples of participatory resources. Participatory resources can be more elaborate, like the nurses' station. In nightclubs, it makes sense to design carefully tailored recreation areas where users feel at home and comfortable with every detail. For example, in a pool table area, every dimension has to be right, every drink shelf located perfectly, every bench situated so you lean against it and soon find yourself seated, comfortably relaxed. The area should promote a group identity for those in the area and should mingle people in ways that let them retain their personal power but facilitate easy interaction.

Designers can also take advantage of natural social resources and build on them. In office buildings, beverage machines are natural congregating areas. We should highlight any resource that attracts people and build on it to increase its social effectiveness. Snack machines or hallways may be the only occasion that many employees normally come into contact with one another. Mailboxes in apartment complexes or offices could offer important opportunities for meeting and greeting. Laundromats in apartments and dormitories are where you meet your neighbors. Shared resources that naturally draw people can be strategically located for improved interaction and circulation. Loitering areas outside of college classrooms should have benches and well designed hangout areas. We should anticipate different uses and the dramas that might occur in a setting, and design to improve them.

DESIGN FOR DIFFERENCE

Seemingly obvious considerations such as designing and integrating areas for different-sized groups, times of the day, moods, and situations are often neglected except for formally designated "multipurpose" rooms. Any time we take a situation or a person into account, we create a more effective design.

An environment should be designed for differences. We should imagine many types of people and situations. If you ignore these, customers will simply go somewhere else or not return as frequently. For example, in a nightclub, we might conceptualize several different areas: party, dance, conversation, mingling (singles), couples (retreat), bar, and recreation. From a schematic of the club, we can then decide where to situate each of these areas. Each area has different requirements and purposes. Acoustics and lighting should be tailored to the requirements of each of these areas.[6]

Areas should not only allow different usages and moods but also create a participatory framework. Designs can encourage participants to be creative in their use of the space. This provides a way for people to personalize the space and be more themselves. Many design decisions that could just as easily be left to participation are needlessly "bolted down." Participatory design does not mean throwing chairs in the corner and forcing people to arrange their own room. It does mean defining a frame that allows and suggests ways individuals might tailor their space to better suit their own needs and moods.

Often a preliminary framework can define the usage of an area while allowing details to be filled in by the residents. This is a different way of thinking about environments. Most designers are accustomed to dictating the usage of every last detail. This is not only often ineffective, but almost always needlessly expensive. Thus, a workshop in an apartment complex might be framed with nothing more elaborate than work tables and storage lockers for projects. The

participants can add tools and accessories to fit their needs and interests.

Canned environments make people feel like herded cattle.[7] A good design does not try to dictate behavior. It appreciates the diversity of human situations, anticipates details, and sets the stage for interaction. An effective environment is a series of props for the many different human dramas that will unfold in its setting. Canned environments tightly script the plot and anticipate only one given set of behaviors. Participatory resources allow people to stage the meaning of many different human dramas.

THE DESIGN PROCESS

The design process is a wonderful opportunity to get staff involved in and committed to their organization. One employee suggestion acted upon is probably worth more than thousands of dollars in motivational speakers. Once people learn they can change their physical environment, other organizational changes become easier to make.

Michael Brill (1984), in a study for Westinghouse, found that by paying attention to some simple design principles, the productivity of office workers increased by a factor of 15 percent their annual gross salaries. One of these principles was simply asking workers about what color to paint their offices. People enjoy choices.[8]

In any organization the people doing the work know more about the work than anyone else. A person using an environment is the expert on that setting. Time needs to be taken to carefully listen to the participants. Specific ideas may not be appropriate, but the rationale behind an idea is almost always right. An effective social design process synthesizes concerns into creative new ideas. It means understanding the needs, problems, and uses of a business both formally and informally. The needs assessment and idea generation phase is crucial. It is what architects refer to as the "programming" phase, although with most architects it usually consists of only slightly more than getting the contract. But it is here that the success and appropriateness of a design are usually predestined.

Designers must know how to listen. This often means separating the rationale from the idea—the grain from the chaff. Ideas are often wrong, but the rationale that generated them is usually right. In one nightclub consultation, people often recommended putting in couches. The club had once been a gym and had high wooden ceilings. Couches would have looked out of place. However, what I heard them identifying was a need for comfortable seating. Suggesting building comfortable booths satisfied everyone.

After the idea generation phase, the next step is sketching the parameters of a project: the amount of money committed to design changes, the things that can be changed as opposed to the things that are sacred, and the dimensions of the building itself. Once these factors are established, the design process can fill in the details within this frame. However, finding, testing, and stretching parameters are essential before significant work can occur. Without this initial work, designs can be haphazard, and later changes will prove expensive. How much would a client be willing to spend eventually over the next five years? Would the client be willing to move a wall? Starting with the parameters allows us later to evolve parts into a coherent whole.

An effective social design proceeds much like rubbing a coin against a scratch lottery ticket: One gradually reveals parts of the picture until the whole design emerges. Aspects of the design that are easy to see and we are sure of should be built first. As these become reality, they will help us discover other parts of the picture and to uncover a better design than if we had just blueprinted it all from the start. This means operating on many different fronts at once: sketching the parameters, involving people in all areas of an organization, and constructing resources and changes we are sure of; then noting how these changes may affect interaction in unanticipated ways before filling in the final details of a design. Thus a design slowly evolves into a whole.

We're not used to working this way. The mind is accustomed to issuing a final blueprint and then enforcing it. We can obtain a more effective design by evolving a whole rather than stamping out a preordained design in cookie-cutter fashion. The approach of evolving a design also has the added bonus of eliminating jealousies that occur, for example, when one department is redecorated and others neglected.

Finally, whenever possible, it is wise to "rehearse" a design with human actors and props. This will allow unanticipated subtleties to be ironed out before the plan is cast in stone. We cannot anticipate everything in advance at the drawing board.[9] Human actors need to be used to walk through potential designs and arrangements. (A word of caution here: Unless one does business with many professional athletes, one should strive to use normal-sized participants.)

There is a story told in architectural circles. I am never sure whether it is true or just a wonderful myth we should follow. Supposedly, when a college was being built in Minnesota, its president instructed the contractors not put in any sidewalks. Instead, students simply walked across the lawns, wearing down the grass on the frequently traveled paths. The president then ordered that the worndown paths be paved.

We have all witnessed grounds where the paved sidewalks take you out of your way. Paths run at right angles, often in an insane fashion. Grounds crews then battle to prevent the public from cutting across the grass. Hedges and even fences are erected to deter the natural flow of traffic. Instead, we should build on how people use an environment. There is also beauty in natural patterns. Right angles may be easy to draw, but interaction does not always fit the convenience of graph paper. Our designs should follow the flow of behavior rather than trying to restrict behavior to the confines of our designs.

LOW-SCALE SOLUTIONS

Another word of caution needs to be added. We are used to high-scale solutions. If there is a problem, we throw money at it. This often doesn't fix the problem. We dream of elaborate, high-technology solutions when often something subtle is more effective. The first idea that occurs to us is to build a wall, or tear down a wall, or buy a machine. Or we throw a tantrum and make a rule. However, low-scale solutions usually require more thinking, imagination, and appreciation of the problem. If we want people to occupy an area only for brief intervals, we can build seating "five-minute" comfortable. If we want people to occupy a neglected wall or space, we can construct a resource that invites them to it. Circulation paths can be changed by means of minimal clues, without signs or major partitions. Subtle low-scale solutions are often much more effective than major expensive solutions—which often serve only to announce that we have redecorated. Low-scale solutions require more creative problem solving. The actual physical manifestation may be as simple as the step around the DJ stand.

SUMMARY AND CONCLUSION

Physical design can be tailored to promote positive interaction and community. Design provides an effective way to increase motivation, communication, and team building. A design in which people enjoy themselves more can also be used to increase sales, repeat business, and word-of-mouth advertising (see Figure 3.8).

Every decision on design has consequences for behavior. Every decision should be geared to create behaviors that are right for your organization. Seating can be situated to promote positive interaction while retaining personal space. Circulation paths can mix and match people, providing opportunities for meeting, excuses for movement, and areas for retreat. Dimensions are critical factors determining whether participants feel comfortable, crowded, or isolated. Defensible space and approachable space can give users choices about their surroundings.

Definition of the situation can be used to create different moods and behaviors. Participatory resources can be created so people become coproducers rather than passive consumers of the environment. Designs can pay attention to patterns of use, highlight the spots people already like, provide areas to homestead, utilize unused areas, and leave room for participation.

FIGURE 3.8 Applications of Social Design

SETTINGS	BENEFITS OF SOCIAL DESIGN
Apartment complexes, neighborhoods, subdivisions, retirement communities	Improve occupancy and real estate values; create community and establish a preferred place to live
Teen clubs, senior centers, nightclubs, recreation facilities, amusement parks	Improve attendance, length of stay, frequency of visits, and word-of-mouth
Concert halls, sports complexes	Improve attendance, frequency of visits, and friendliness of atmosphere
Offices, factories, schools	Improve communication, teamwork, productivity; reduce conflict and turnover
Juvenile and criminal justice facilities	Reduce conflict and inmate problems; improve staff satisfaction and morale
Colleges and universities, day-care centers, nursing homes	Improve retention rates, recruiting, and word-of-mouth advertising
Medical facilities	Improve service, morale, healing, return business, word-of-mouth advertising
Hotels, resorts, convention hotels	Improve word-of-mouth advertising, repeat business, length of stay
Retail stores, shopping centers, restaurants	Increase per-customer sales and repeat business

Forcing people doesn't work: People can always leave or not come back. Successful designs set the stage for interaction. The framework presented here is for the artist wishing to provide resources for the human drama, not for the scientist who would engineer behavior. These principles pull together a diverse body of knowledge on staging social situations and effective props for human actors. The concepts can be expanded upon creatively. They are not formulas: They're more like a set of paintbrushes and colors. They should be utilized artistically.

This model of social design is probabilistic, not deterministic. It does not try to force and control. It enables and facilitates. It doesn't determine behavior but increases the chances something will happen. An effective design provides opportunities, arranges seating and circulation paths effectively, defines the situation, invents participatory resources, and pays attention to the effects of design decisions on behavior.

We wouldn't think of designing a chair that was 8 feet tall. Yet most human actors must climb into settings that aren't designed for the proportions of human interaction. Attention to detail works. Gearing every design decision to pay attention to human components can create an effective environment. Decisions that were previously a distracting chore can be turned into meaningful opportunities to set the stage for more successful interaction.

NOTES

1. Skinner's argument in *Beyond Freedom and Dignity* was that social scientists have entered territory previously reserved for gods. What he failed to understand was that manipulation should be applied only to things, not to people. Social engineering would turn people into objects for manipulation. A true social architecture would manipulate only things. A moral social science would agree in advance that people must not be treated as things. People are not things; life is a drama.

2. We certainly need a better class of jokes on cocktail napkins; sexist jokes tend to predominate. Perhaps the syndicators of Dilbert, Peanuts, and Cathy could be persuaded to put out a line of cocktail napkins.

3. The distinction between acoustical and visual space has another implication: Except for major events, television does not belong in bars. Watching this visual medium takes people out of the moment.

4. Corners work for a specific purpose: to isolate people and give them a sense of territory. Otherwise they interfere with interaction; they break it and prevent it from flowing.

5. There are two components of definition of the situation. One is that symbols define the situation which tells us how to act. The other is the self-fulfilling prophecy: "If people define a situation as real, it is real in its consequences." Together they are the foundation of the social construction of reality.

6. Acoustics are almost never considered, except possibly after the fact as an expensive "tack-on." Acoustics can be successfully tailored for better interaction at almost no additional expense if we know from the start that this is an important factor. Keeping in mind the different areas of the club, we can then do an acoustical chart designating volume levels and acoustics throughout the club. For convenience, volumes can be rated on a scale of 1 to 10. The dance floor would be a 10, while the conversation area would be a 1 or 2. (Dance area = 10, party area = 8, recreation area = 6, mingling area = 5 or 6, couples area = 5 or 6, bar area = 5 or 6, conversation area = 1 or 2.) Acoustics can then be tailored to provide the right sound level for each area. Similar charts can be constructed for times of the day, sizes of groups, purposes, moods, and situations. Sound at the bar area should bounce at short distances so people can be heard. Sound in conversation areas and in couples areas should also bounce, but a degree of privacy should be afforded beyond a short distance. These acoustic effects can be designed into the club. For an amateur rule of thumb, if a material is hard, it bounces sound. If it is soft, it insulates sound.

7. Many design an environment so customers will be forced to do different things. Instead, however customers often flee when given a chance. Wendy's provides a clear example by placing "cattle stockades" to herd customers up to the front counter. McDonald's, on the other hand, has the civility to realize that they just want customers to get to the counter and it will all work out.

8. Too many alternatives may be experienced as confusion rather than freedom, but a good designer can set the frame and get people involved.

9. Architects often say they can, but they can't. It is true they are often very good at anticipating and visualizing a design. However, no one can anticipate everything. A design is always better with a rehearsal.

REFERENCES

Brill, Michael, with Stephen T. Margulis and Ellen Konar. *Using Office Design to Increase Productivity.* Buffalo, N.Y.: Workplace Design and Productivity, 1984.

Burgess, Ernest W., and Paul Wallin, with Gladys Denny Shultz. *Courtship, Engagement, and Marriage.* Philadelphia: Lippincott, 1954.

Fleissner, Dan, and Fred Heinzelmann. *Crime Prevention through Environmental Design and Community Policing.* Washington, D.C.: National Institute of Justice Research in Action, 1996

Homans, George. *Social Behavior: Its Elementary Forms.* Under the general editorship of Robert K. Merton. Rev. ed. New York: Harcourt, Brace, Jovanovich, 1974.

McLuhan, Marshall. *Understanding Media.* New York: McGraw, 1964.

Newman, Oscar. *Defensible Space: Crime Prevention through Urban Design.* New York: Macmillan, 1972.

Newman, Oscar. *Creating Defensible Space.* Washington, D.C.: U.S. Dept. of Housing and Urban Development, Office of Policy Development and Research, 1996.

Rubin, Lillian. *Intimate Strangers: Men and Women Together.* New York: Harper & Row, 1983.

Skinner, B. F. *Beyond Freedom and Dignity.* New York: Knopf, 1971.

Smith, Mary S. *Crime Prevention through Environmental Design in Parking Facilities.* Washington, D.C.: National Institute of Justice Research in Brief, 1996.

Sommer, Robert. *Personal Space.* Englewood Cliffs, N.J.: Prentice-Hall, 1969.

Taylor, Ralph B., and Adele V. Harrell. *Physical Environment and Crime.* Washington, D.C.: National Institute of Justice Research Report, 1996.

4

Transforming Community
Attitudes and Morale

WILLIAM DU BOIS

Editors' Note: Bill Du Bois illustrates revitalizing a community following a major bank closing during the farm crisis. He shows how elementary sociological concepts can be applied and expanded in new ways. We can start anywhere. Consistently applying what we know can work miracles.

In September 1983 the Exchange Bank in Bloomfield, Iowa, closed. It was the first bank closing at the start of the farm crisis. Eventually, depositors would recover 60 cents on the dollar. Originally, things didn't look even that good. At one point national television news reported that 20 percent of the county was up for sale. People wondered whether their town would survive.

I remember a story a local administrator told of how he'd gotten his job. All the candidates for the job interviewed on the same day, then went down to the local cafe and heard the local residents talk. The other candidates all withdrew from consideration, saying they wouldn't move their families to such a negative community.

The local residents were well aware of this atmosphere. There were several efforts to stifle negativity. The Rotary Club went so far as to institute a campaign to fine residents $1 for each negative comment or discouraging word. But two negatives do not make a positive, and such a negative "smile campaign" was doomed from the start. I remember seeing a newspaper article about it and discussing with students the futility of a forced smile campaign. We wondered what a positive smile campaign might look like.

In September 1986 I got a job with the Bloomfield Area Chamber of Commerce. The mood of the town still hovered on the brink. As the president of a local bank confessed, they were out of ideas as to what to do. In this climate they were even willing to hire a sociologist. While I talked publicly in economic development terms, I privately defined my job as transforming community attitudes and morale. Such a strategy would have economic development consequences. Local businesspeople might dream all they wanted of economic development. But unless the general mood of the community changed, one trip to the local cafe would send any potential new company fleeing much like the administrator interviewees. Positive ideas would also not grow and thrive within the community unless the cloud of despair lifted.

PARTICIPATORY RESOURCES

Changing community attitudes and morale means getting people involved with their lives and their town. People need to know they can do something that makes a difference. Bloomfield had suffered a massive defeat. Anomie was more than just a concept.

The old rules people had been taught to trust didn't work anymore. Smiles couldn't just be painted on from the outside. New lives don't come preassembled.

All across the country, small towns waited for salvation. Each tried to outbid the others for the newest factory, but there weren't enough factories to go around. And the factories that did come to towns were smaller, with fewer jobs than in the past. In Iowa, economic development figures showed that 90 percent of all new jobs did not come from outsiders but from someone already in the community who opened a new business or expanded an existing business. Yet communities failed to put their economic development dollars where the job creation was. They chased instead after the elusive new plant, staking their hope on an economic development strategy that was very similar to buying a lotto ticket.

Marshall McLuhan says every crisis is a potential opportunity. Unfortunately, it seems organizations will only try something new when the wolf's at the door, just at the point when they usually have the least money available to do anything. McLuhan (1964) also notes the difference between hot mediums and cold mediums, as discussed in Reading 3. A hot medium is well defined. It is prepackaged and addressed to a passive consumer. In contrast, a cool medium is addressed to the coproducer—it demands participation.

> *A hot medium is . . . "high definition." High definition is the sense of being well filled with data. A photograph is, visually, "high definition." A cartoon is "low definition," simply because very little visual information is provided. Telephone is a cool medium, or one of low definition, because the ear is given a meager amount of information. And speech is a cool medium of low definition, because so little is given and so much must be filled in by the listener. On the other hand, hot media do not leave so much to be filled in or completed by the audience. Hot media are, therefore, low in participation, and cool media are high in participation or completion by the audience. . . . (pp. 22–23)*

From this concept of hot and cold mediums I invented the idea of *participatory resources*. Participatory resources are vague and sketchy. They demand participation. They loosely frame a situation, leaving room for participants to fill in the details. A participatory resource is a prop that people can utilitize for their own purposes. Sociology as art would use the sociological imagination to invent social resources that individuals can utilize in their own personal struggles. Participatory resources lend themselves to innovative uses. They encourage imagination and invite participation.

As community development coordinator for the Bloomfield Area Chamber of Commerce from September 1986 through December 1988, I invented a series of participatory resources to transform community attitudes and morale. One participatory resource was the organization itself. It was necessary to design a participatory organization that empowered people and got things done. The organizational development included creating new shared understandings, reorganizing the committee structure, and streamlining the approval process for ideas.

In this article I will also highlight two additional social inventions: a horse-drawn tour of the Christmas lights and a Christmas giveaway program sponsored by local merchants.

PARTICIPATORY ORGANIZATIONAL STRUCTURE

Meetings of the Board of Directors of the chamber of commerce were very much like a duck shoot. People lobbed ideas over the table and everyone sat back and tried to shoot them out of the air. The only way something would get done was if somebody succeeded in lobbing an idea over the table at least three meetings in a row without it getting shot down. Only one idea had survived that process in years: They had agreed on a "Welcome to Bloomfield" sign but still couldn't agree where to put it. The sign sat propped up beside a barn outside of town awaiting placement near a road.

The reason for this "pick the survivor" process was that people were afraid that if somebody else's idea was chosen, their own idea wouldn't get done. Such was not paranoia, because choosing one idea usually would in fact rule out consideration of other ideas, often for the rest of the year. Halfhearted commitments doomed many projects. Common-denominator compromises tend not to be very creative in the first place, and even an idea's originator tended to burn out from lack of support. Nevertheless, taking communal pot shots at new ideas was everybody's shared understanding of how business at meetings should be conducted.

Culture is a set of shared meanings. Changing a culture means changing shared meanings. I invented a new shared meaning: From now on, we do everything. The new shared understanding, which I repeated at every opportunity, was: "If an idea isn't terribly illegal, terribly immoral, or terribly fattening (or terribly expensive), we do it."

This shared understanding is funny and playful. Yet this simplistic-sounding slogan actually conveys a sophisticated organizational dynamic. It creates a participatory framework and prevents a rigid organizational structure from forming. It conveys a clear idea of what kinds of things aren't appropriate, and at the same time it keeps people from interfering in one another's business.

One year we actually accomplished every idea presented at a communitywide planning meeting.[1] People presented ideas and were recruited to help carry them out. It is fairly easy to canopy several ideas into one promotion or event. An idea that might not stand alone may work when combined with several other ideas. This approach also ensures that several people will have already bought into the event because of the inclusion of their ideas.

Even particularly troublesome members of an organization become a sight to behold when their pet idea is empowered. If an idea is not particularly harmful, it is often worth its weight in goodwill to do it. Doing a project gets the member not only to support this project but to buy into the organization and future projects as well. Criticism disappears. By doing the person's idea, he or she often stops being critical of other people's ideas.

Sociologist Rosabeth Moss Kanter (1983), former editor of the *Harvard Business Review,* notes that nothing gets done without a product champion. A product champion is someone who takes an idea to heart: "This is *my* idea," "This matters to me," "I

think this is important," or "I just think this is neat; I want to see it happen."

Every year organizations make up their wish lists of things to do, much like New Year's resolutions. But unless an idea has a product champion, it will show up again on next year's list, because it won't get done. Product champions are essential to making things happen. Effective managers find and recruit product champions.

The task of an organization is to get the holy water to good ideas, bless them, and get them on their way. Too often the holy water is tightly locked up behind closed doors and it is virtually impossible to get good ideas blessed. Streamlining the approval process is essential to getting things done.

An additional shared understanding was also introduced in Bloomfield with some success: "If you care enough about an issue, then you need to go to the committee meeting planning it. If it is not important enough for you to go to the meeting, then you don't have a right to criticize what gets planned." This shared understanding empowered committees. Members no longer felt they had wasted their time only to have their best efforts vetoed by the board. The board now became a coordinating body with the real work taking place on committees.

The shared understanding of "if it's not terribly illegal, terribly immoral, or terribly fattening" provided an easy guideline. Even if people did not like a particular idea, as long as it was not particularly harmful, we did it. The shared understanding kept people minding their own business and empowered people. A new idea was no longer threatening—because doing one idea no longer excluded other ideas. In fact, the reverse was true. Ideas would often dovetail into one another, or would provide the catalyst for more ideas. Furthermore, when people saw outrageous or even mediocre ideas put into action, they would think, "If they are going to do *that* idea, then maybe they'll do *mine.*" Even failures had a positive effect, because they decreased the risk for others. People were more likely to venture out with their own ideas. The shared understanding provided a participatory framework for getting people involved and ideas accomplished.

Some of the ideas accomplished included a "Corn on the Cob Festival" featuring fresh sweet corn and a variety of games, a street dance, an ice-cream social, a Halloween scarecrow contest, a Christmas lighting contest, and cooperation with local rodeo and tourism groups. Planned workshops focused on advertising; small business start-up; economic assessment; and "Main Street renovations," which featured downtown historic preservation and a tour of the downtown with specific recommendations for each building. A "Davis County" brochure and a "Physician Recruitment" brochure were designed. In conjunction with the County Extension Service, the chamber helped organize a consumer survey of local businesses, an expanded farmer's market, and an "Ag Diversification Conference" featuring 30 speakers on 40 topics.

In addition to the participatory organizational structure, I invented a variety of other participatory resources. Among them: "KIDS in Business Day," when elementary-aged kids worked in retail stores, banks, the police department, the mayor's office, and restaurants and other businesses; the "Water Festival," a Fourth of July combination of water games designed to get everyone wet; a "Community Price Scavenger Hunt" in which people tried to find which Bloomfield store had the lowest prices on different items, which were then compared with a rival town's prices; a Valentine contest called "What Do Men Say? / What Do Women Say?," in which men and women tried to predict how the opposite sex would answer a series of survey questions; and "Hello Young Lovers," another Valentine contest, in which people tried to identify old wedding pictures. The most successful participatory resources I invented, however, were the horse-drawn tour of lights and the Elf of Bloomfield.

HORSE-DRAWN TOUR OF
THE CHRISTMAS LIGHTS

Bloomfield is a small town of 2,849 people with a lovely Victorian courthouse in the middle of the town square. The square has always been decorated at Christmas time, and the courthouse is visible for miles around. The horse-drawn tour of the Christmas lights was a ride around town in horse-drawn vehicles originating at the courthouse.

The basic specifics of the project were vague and sketchy; a participatory resource can be used in a variety of ways. This event encouraged many different dynamics. Some of these I could have predicted and indeed had imagined: romantic couples, sing-alongs, family/company outings, drinking parties, entrepreneurs making their own horse-drawn rigs, houses getting decorated, and increased tourism resulting in more business. Some I could have never dreamed of in my wildest imagination: the distance many would travel to ride; the loyalty of seniors even on the coldest nights; free publicity from the area TV station.

The tour of lights ran 22 nights each December. Half-hour rides were scheduled from 6 P.M. until 9 P.M. (although the drivers often ran late, and the horses usually weren't off the street until after 10). Initially there were three wagons and one carriage. As Christmas approached, vehicles were added as the demand increased, with as many as 18 running in peak season.

The wagons held 10 adults. The carriages held 3 adults plus children on laps. By the second year, one driver had built a wagon that held 22 adults. Another driver bought a new carriage. The horses pulling the wagons were large Belgian draft horses; the carriages used a matched pair of elegant quarter horses. The wagons cost $2 a person, and the carriage $15 a load.[2]

The tour of lights ran a designated route originating and ending at the courthouse. The route was approximately 1¼ to 1½ miles long and changed each year. People along the route were notified in advance and encouraged to decorate their houses. Campfire Girls distributed fliers to each home on the route. Within a few nights of operation, most of the houses were decorated. Banks and service organizations offered to provide labor and materials for anyone unable to decorate. Only a few people took advantage of this offer. Most people decorated themselves.

The horse-drawn tour sparked a spontaneous community cleanup. People became involved in fixing up their neighborhoods, because visitors would be riding past. Even though residents now had horse manure to shovel from their streets, they took pride in showing off their community. The tour of lights also led to increased sales of decorations. Merchants reported having trouble keeping Christmas lights in stock. Indeed, at one time lights were sold out of every store in a 30-mile radius.

A participatory resource is designed to lend itself to a variety of different purposes. It is a prop for many different dramas. Couples found the carriage a perfect prop for a date, a romantic evening away from the kids, or even an anniversary. A wagon full of party-goers might smuggle a bottle under their blanket and discover that the wagon was a prop for their festivities. People found themselves singing carols together with neighbors and strangers as wagons wove down silent streets past houses in the night. Companies used the ride to conclude office Christmas parties. Children rode with all the glee of an amusement park. Families found the ride a perfect family outing. Santa himself would also ride from time to time, or meet a wagon en route. Church groups, teen groups, a delinquent group home, and the county home for seniors all booked special passages. Indeed, seniors would ride even on the coldest nights of the year as other horse-drawn rides flooded their memories.

There were many different experiences on the tour of lights. A participatory resource provides openings that people can plug into. A television station 40 miles away put their news team in a carriage and taped their on-air Christmas greeting from Bloomfield town square. One young couple brought their whole wedding party and got married out on the tour of lights. The group returned to the courthouse square in wagons and carriages with champagne flowing.

Each detail of the tour of lights was honed and developed as we went along. The wagons and carriages were decorated with Christmas lights rewired to run on car batteries. Recharging the batteries each night was quite a production and involved most of the hardware stores in town.

Choirs would be invited to come sing at the courthouse the first few nights. This created activity on the courthouse square, and most of the choir would end up taking a ride themselves. The first time this happened, it demonstrated to doubters that the project was going to be a success. Seeing people riding encouraged others to ride.

One of the nice touches was a box of donated gloves, mittens, caps, and scarves used to bundle up riders who weren't properly dressed. There were even extra blankets people could share. This all added a warm touch of tucking people in as they got ready for what could be a quite cold 30-minute trip. Hot chocolate and coffee were also available at a warming house specially constructed on the courthouse lawn for the season.

More than 10,000 people rode the tour of lights each year. Most of them came from more than 60 miles away. They came to get a glimpse of small-town life and to catch the spirit of Christmas. Locals who rode witnessed their town in a new light. It was like watching a movie or taking a tour of your own life. Time stopped when you were on the tour taking a new look at your life and your town. Life was good; there was much to appreciate here. Visitors said nice things. This spirit became contagious.

People decorated their houses more with each passing week. There was a new community spirit. Visitors constantly reinforced a positive image. The merchants who stayed open expanded hours reported better sales. We courted the news media and fed them stories, and they responded. The reputation of the town changed. It became a model that others then tried to copy.

THE ELF OF BLOOMFIELD

The most creative participatory resource I invented was the Secret Elf. The horse-drawn tour of the lights was a medium-level participatory resource. The Elf was a much more advanced application of the concept.

Every year since the bank closing, merchants had gotten together for a "Great Christmas Giveaway." This was a raffle drawing for which stores gave away tickets with each purchase. Businesses gave away approximately $5,000 this way each year and accomplished virtually nothing. The giveaway had originated as a way for businesses to give something back to the community. However, the money wasn't doing much. Customers didn't see the give-away as a gesture of goodwill. Many didn't want to be bothered checking numbers and refused to take the tickets. The random drawing didn't really increase shopping or contribute significantly to community morale.

Bloomfield's ill-fated "smile campaign" had attempted to force people into not saying negative things about the town. What would a positive smile campaign look like? How could the $5,000 in the Great Christmas Giveaway be recycled to get more bounce for the buck?

Social psychologists suggest that the best rewards are spontaneous, on-the-spot, and tied to a behavior. How could giving the money away improve community attitudes and morale? An old television show called *The Millionaire* had featured a character named Michael Anthony who would show up and present a chosen person with a million dollars from an anonymous benefactor. What would a cheaper version of *The Millionaire* look like in Bloomfield?

The Secret Elf was invented as a way of giving away money spontaneously, on-the-spot, and tied to a behavior. The Elf was simply a button that people would conceal on themselves, inside a lapel, in a pocket, or inside a purse. The only time these persons would ever reveal their identity and show the button was when they were giving away an envelope. The envelopes had a picture of the Elf and said: "Thanks for Being in Bloomfield— We're Glad You're Here." Inside the envelope was $20 in "Elf money." The coupons had the Elf's picture and were redeemable at any participating business, which meant virtually every business in town. The coupons had an expiration date of December 25, so they had to be spent.[3]

The person playing the Secret Elf was told to catch someone in the act of doing good, or to find someone who personifies the Christmas spirit or someone who just really is deserving. When a Secret Elf had identified a recipient, he or she would display the Elf button and give away the envelope, and both would sign a release form acknowledging the exchange. The names of recipients (but not of the Elves) were then published in the newspaper. The reason for the release was to simply have some control over the process. You could give the envelope to whomever you wanted. If you wanted to give it to your spouse, that was permissible. However, with the release we would know you had done that (and probably not ask you to be an Elf again).

The only rule was that you must give the envelope away either in a Bloomfield business or adjacent to a Bloomfield business. You could decide in advance whom you were going to give it to. That was perfectly legal. You just couldn't go to that person's home to give them the envelope. You would have to wait and catch them out in a Bloomfield business.

The envelopes normally contained $20 in Elf money. Just before Christmas I would take eight envelopes and stuff $50 in each. For these I would commission very special Secret Elves who were instructed to make sure they found someone especially deserving. Fifty dollars two days before Christmas in a poverty-stricken town is enough to make or break someone's Christmas.

At any one time, there were many secret elves on the street. At least 4 elves were commissioned for each day, with 10 or more each weekend day. But people might take several days to give the envelope away, so one could never be sure how many elves were actually afoot. One could also never be sure who was the Elf. The person in front of you in line at the grocery store might be the Elf, or the person behind you, or the clerk; or actually, every one of you might be an Elf.

As I had hoped, inside jokes developed. People would say, "Oh, you're just doing that because you think I'm the Secret Elf." The Elf reinforced positive behavior and community spirit. It also led to a mood of excitement and expectancy. Many people would stay in town and come downtown to shop because of the expectancy that something might happen.

Creating Win–Win Situations

The evaluative standard for social inventions should be their ability to create synergy. The Elf created a win–win situation. The person receiving, the person giving, and those watching were all winners. The person receiving the envelope certainly felt like a winner: How wonderful that someone would just walk up out of nowhere and give you $20. And certainly it is more blessed to give than to receive. At first it was very hard to recruit Secret Elves. People grudgingly agreed to do it almost as a favor. Once people had done it, however, they were standing in line wanting to do it again. Some people said that it wasn't Christmas unless they got to play the Secret Elf.

People would initially agree to be the Elf figuring they would go downtown and dispense with the task in a few minutes. However, people would get involved in it. They would end up wanting to savor the experience. Once you gave the envelope away, the exercise was over and you were no longer the Secret Elf. So people would often take two or three days to find exactly the right person.

The people witnessing the exchange got vicariously involved. Shopping was no longer the same when you got to see someone get a gift. People returned home feeling like they'd shared a special moment. Some stories were funny, such as the time when an entire store of people tried to convince a woman that she shouldn't persist with her claims of "I'm really not interested." It took the onlookers and the store clerks nearly an hour to persuade the poor woman that she should accept the gift and that there truly were no strings attached. Some of the stories brought us to tears: the woman who broke down, saying now she could afford Christmas dinner for her family, and bought a turkey; the man who broke down crying and said that now he could get his wife a present and bought a toaster.

The Secret Elf also created a win–win situation for the merchants. It brought more people downtown and led to an atmosphere of excitement in the stores. It provided the best word-of-mouth advertising in the world. Someone from out of town who received an envelope was going to go home and call everyone they had ever known and say: "You'll never guess what happened to me today in Bloomfield." They were going to be on the phone all night. For $20, the town was going to get advertising better than money could buy.

The Elf was an experiential exercise in giving. It was very much like a humanistic psychology exercise. It created community and trust; it opened people up to each other on new levels. Every time someone would show up in my office crying or laughing, I would know they had just played the Secret Elf. I remember stories of someone giving away the envelope and everyone in the entire store crying and hugging.

The exercise was very much a lesson in sharing. People almost seemed to follow the written instructions they were given when they received their button: "Take a Little Time to Share the Christmas Spirit. Your mission, should you decide to accept it, is to catch someone in the act of doing something good, find someone who personifies the Christmas spirit, or someone who is really deserving. Let the spirit of the Elf guide you. You will find exactly the right person." Magic may just be a myth we invoke. It seemed it had been there all the time and we had just been missing the dance.

The Costumed Elf

The Elf was a participatory resource of the highest order. Every aspect involved opportunities for people to plug in new ideas of their own. Once we had decided to have a Secret Elf, it was only a short step to decide that we might as well also have a costumed Elf. A local merchant designed and made the costume. A high school student was commissioned to draw a picture of the Elf mask, and this was put on the Secret Elf button. The picture was then turned into posters and advertising. Every Great Giveaway merchant displayed the Elf's picture in their window.

The costumed Elf became the foundation of community television promotions. The Elf appeared in everyone's Christmas television commercials—trying on clothes in a store, hobbling on crutches into the hospital, pushing a wheelbarrow full of money into a bank, sawing a board at the lumberyard, or perched on top of a grain truck, driving it with reins. A local radio announcer produced the Elf's voice for radio advertisements and community promotions.

The Elf became Santa's companion. The Elf rode on the tour of lights from time to time. He/she also received more invitations to parties than even Santa did, and often would ask to bring Santa along so as to not hurt his feelings.

As a participatory prop, the Elf became quite a production. Lots of people wanted to play the Elf. The costume itself was in great demand. Sometimes there was almost a tug of war as we choreographed it so the Elf could be at two places close to the same time. Many people wanted to know who the Elf was. The answer was everybody.

We actually used an official schedule to keep track of where the Elf was to be, when, and who would be wearing the costume. The Elf had a booking agent who kept track of such things. The mask was regularly sprayed with alcohol disinfectant after each use. The Elf also had regular dry cleaning appointments scheduled. The Elf's pant legs and sleeves could be rolled up or down depending on the Elf's height on each occasion.

Close to one hundred people were the Elf each season. The Elf who appeared in most of the TV commercials was my personal favorite. He was remarkably childlike and innovative once in costume. In his other life he was a local minister, who was quite concerned that his congregation might disapprove if they learned his identity. The Elf's identity was always a state secret. This led to more involvement and curiosity.

The Elf is an excellent example of how to invent a participatory resource, then tailor every aspect to improve community attitudes and morale. Business donations for the new version of the Great Christmas Giveaway doubled to more than $10,000. More than half of that money was given away by Secret Elves. A smaller amount was retained for a more traditional raffle drawing. Every aspect of this was played to the hilt. The Elf conducted public drawings at four different stores around town every hour on Saturday afternoons. The Elf was now transported from store to store by horse-drawn carriage. Santa and the Elf would ride into the courthouse square together; Santa would take up residence in his special house to greet children, and the Elf would set forth to do the drawings. The Elf would then return to pick up Santa at the end of the day, and the two would be transported away.

A large crowd would follow the Elf from store to store. Every drawing turned into a production. The Elf would joke and play at each drawing with children, merchants, and onlookers. This drew people into the stores, where they might see something they'd later purchase. The drawings were exciting events that attracted people to downtown Bloomfield.

The drawings were for Elf dollars that must be redeemed by Christmas.[4] The prizes ranged from $50 to $250. Businesses were also solicited to donate noncash prizes as part of the drawing. Some of these prizes were small, such as a $25 gift certificate at a particular store. Some were much more substantial, such as the use of a new Lincoln Continental for New Year's Eve weekend.

Raids on Other Communities

The Elf was also used in one more imaginative way. We made "raids" on other communities. Five days before Christmas (when it was too late for other communities to respond), the Elf appeared in every community within a 60-mile radius distributing envelopes containing special coupons. The envelopes had the Elf's picture, store hours, and the town slogan, and told of Great Christmas Giveaway drawings every Saturday. Inside all envelopes were 10 percent, 20 percent, and 30 percent discount coupons for Bloomfield stores and a schedule for the horse-drawn tour of lights. Many envelopes also contained one wagon ticket.[5] Some envelopes also contained coupons redeemable for merchandise from a particular store.[6] A few envelopes simply contained $5, $10, or even $20 in Elf money, which could be spent only in Bloomfield before Christmas.

The Elf money distributed in this way was specially marked so it could be tracked. Only about 10 percent of the $5 distributions brought people to town, whereas about 35 percent of the $10 distributions and nearly 70 percent of the $20 distributions were redeemed.

For two days someone was in the Elf costume 14 hours a day as we made a sweep of every town in the area. The Elf went from town to town waving at people and giving away envelopes. In downtown areas, the Elf would walk the streets. The Elf also actually distributed to several farmers as they worked their fields.

We returned one day to find our local police in hysterics: They said the police scanner had been abuzz all afternoon as police in one town tried to track the Elf. Merchants in that town had complained about whether the Elf had a peddling permit to distribute coupons. (We didn't.) Dispatchers and police from all over the area had joined in with comments on the pursuit in what were remembered as hilarious conversations. Unaware, the Elf had managed to stay one step ahead.

In truth, we were prepared for such dramatics and high theater. Should the Elf have been arrested, Santa and some volunteers had already been enlisted to march on the jail. Their picket signs would read "Free the Elf." We would have been on the national news by evening.

Those who begrudged the Elf coming to their towns didn't understand the dynamics of how the economy works. Keeping the Elf out of their communities was not the point. An imaginative town would have created their own mascot and also visited other towns. Of course, when they came to Bloomfield, the Elf would have come right out and welcomed them. One could picture a series of Christmas "critter wars" in which mascots of different towns might make raids on one another. It would have made the entire area an exciting place to shop and be at Christmas. Rather than creating losers, it would have led to a win–win situation for everyone. Regional sales would have increased. The "wars" between the Elf and other mascots would have helped keep people in small towns and away from the larger urban shopping centers in Des Moines a hundred miles away.

The Elf demonstrates how a participatory resource works. It is a participatory prop in an active drama. Each aspect could be expanded upon. Participatory resources lend themselves to creative uses. Some of these applications can be anticipated in advance by the artist inventing the resource. Others are discovered along the way. The ideal participatory resource is available for people to bring to their own particular dramas to use in new and inventive ways.

The Secret Elf itself was never publically promoted. We used a reverse advertising strategy. It was very much an inside joke. The Elf's picture was everywhere, but we never went public with the story. People could know about the Secret Elf only by participating in it. It was a word-of-mouth, folklore experience. Winners' names were published in the newspaper, but the way the promotion actually worked was never mentioned. This produced a community feeling and a secret in which people could be invited to participate. I can remember no mention ever being made of the fact that it wasn't being publically disclosed. It was just a secret that was shared by almost everyone in town. And that more people came to know about every day.

THE RESULTS

Creating participatory resources worked. Changing community attitudes and morale translated into economic development benefits. Sales figures show that Bloomfield sales stopped declining and leveled off (Figure 4.1), whereas comparable-sized towns continued to decrease. Similar-sized county seat towns in Iowa all experienced declines in retail sales between 1985 and 1989.[7] Bloomfield also was the only county seat town of its size to have an actual increase in number of firms in the county between 1980 and 1995[8] (Table 4.1). Within two years, 30 new businesses opened in a town of 2,849 people. Chamber of Commerce memberships increased 93 percent at the same time as dues were increased 25 percent. In winter 1987, a $2.99 million school bond received 53 percent of the votes. It needed 60 percent to pass. By July 1988 it received 56.7 percent countywide (with 72 percent yes in Bloomfield itself). In June 1989 it passed with 70.9 percent. A $610,000 bond issue for a new swimming pool fell five votes short of 60 percent in November 1989 but passed with 70 percent of the votes six months later. Bloomfield—an area where once 20 percent of the people had wanted to flee and had put their homes up for sale—voiced faith in the future. Attitudes had changed.

REFERENCES

Kanter, Rosabeth Moss. *The Changemasters: Innovation and Entrepreneurship in the American Corporation.* New York: Simon & Schuster, 1983.

McLuhan, Marshall. *Understanding Media.* New York: McGraw, 1964.

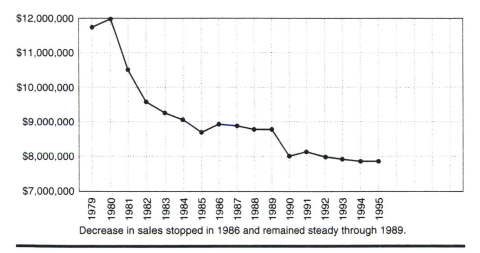

Decrease in sales stopped in 1986 and remained steady through 1989.

FIGURE 4.1   Bloomfield Retail Sales 1979–1995 (in constant 1971 dollars)

TABLE 4.1   Bloomfield and Comparable-Sized Iowa County Seat Towns

	BLOOMFIELD (Pop. 2,849) Davis County	**CLARION** (3,060) Wright County	**GARNER** (2,908) Hancock County	**GRUNDY CENTER** (2,880) Grundy County	**ONAWA** (3,283) Monona County	**ROCK RAPIDS** (2,693) Lyon County	**SAC CITY** (3,000) Sac County	**SIBLEY** (3,051) Osceola County
Change Number of Firms in County 1980–1995	+1.9%	–10.9%	–5.2%	–5.6%	–9.0%	–7.1%	–15.9%	–16.4%
Retail Sales Change 1985–1989 (in constant dollars)	–1.2%	–18.6	–5.1%	–24.1%	–10.5%	–2.0%	–12.9%	–12.2%

NOTES

1. Actually, we did every idea *except* for one that I "forgot" to write down on the newsprint on the wall. Retaining the pen at a community planning session also allows one to rephrase and reframe suggestions to avoid pitfalls. Writing up the minutes of a meeting can also become a device for communicating and highlighting some shared understandings while deemphasizing others.

2. By the third year prices changed to $3 a person for the wagon and $18 a load for the carriage. A large carriage holding up to 11 people was added and priced at $5 per person.

3. The Elf dollars had an intricate design and raised lettering so as to be difficult to counterfeit.

4. In actuality, the Elf dollars were also honored after Christmas, and the Chamber of Commerce would still redeem them into January or later.

5. The presumption was that no one would drive 20 miles to ride the wagon by themselves; they would bring someone with them. Even if they did ride alone, they were likely to spend some additional money while in town.

6. The most imaginative of these simply said, "Come in and pick up a $10 bill at Hamilton's Produce." The owner figured that anyone coming to collect would spend enough money in town so he'd get his money back. Either now or later, the goodwill would pay for itself.

7. Between 1985 and 1989 Bloomfield held its own with retail sales decreasing only 1.2 percent, whereas comparable towns experienced a 5 percent to 24 percent decline. All similar-sized towns had a 12.2 percent median drop in sales during this period.

8. Number of firms increased 1.9 percent while the other county seat towns had losses ranging from 5.2 to 16.4 percent with a mean loss of 10 percent.

5

Preventing and Resolving
Public Controversy
Concepts and Techniques of Public Participation

DESMOND M. CONNOR

Editors' Note: Des Connor, a consulting sociologist and president of Connor Development Services Ltd. of Victoria, British Columbia, has been making a living in sociological practice since 1965. His unique brand of sociology develops win–win situations between companies and the public. He has consulted across Canada from his home in Vancouver and more recently has expanded internationally, working in Mexico and Spain.

Many managers, engineers, and other professionals resent the fact that concerned citizens are increasingly trespassing on their territory. These intruders question professional judgments, demand public inquiries, and often delay or even defeat proposed projects. This article reviews the reasons for public controversy and outlines a process for constructive citizen participation. Since designing and managing my first public participation program in 1965 for the St. John River Basin in New Brunswick, I have completed some 300 projects across Canada from Labrador to Whitehorse.

WHY PUBLIC CONTROVERSY?

Public opposition to projects today stems from several different factors.

Decision makers used to be able to rely on a fairly slow rate of social change amongst their people, who respected authority and were fairly satisfied with life. Increasingly, change now happens more quickly; people often resist authority and are more dissatisfied with their living conditions. The old DAD (Decide-Announce-Defend) style works less well today. Today, people distrust authorities and experts, and many have high levels of generalized anxiety and hostility. Those who used to accept the negative side effects of projects as the price of progress now tend to stand and fight.

People resist change when they do not understand or agree with the goals, methods, sponsor, or timing of the proposed change. Keeping the public in the dark is often a recipe for disaster. Organizations resist change and become out of step with their various publics, who then become angry with them. The corporate culture needs to be understood and then renewed. Communication blocks may occur within organizations which prevent them from making a real-time response to their publics. Fortunately, there are practical steps which can be taken to remove these blocks.

Schizophrenic management is another factor in public controversy. On one hand, the technical side of a project is designed and managed in a rational, scientific, and professional manner; yet on the other hand, the problematic human side of the enterprise is often dealt with in a totally ad hoc, reactive, unplanned form of management by crisis.

CONSTRUCTIVE CITIZEN PARTICIPATION

During the 1960s there was a good deal of participation in the planning of highways, airports, and other projects—but most of it was destructive, negative, and imposed by angry citizen groups rather than planned positively by project managers. The concept of "constructive citizen participation" was therefore formulated as

> *a systematic process which provides an opportunity for citizens, planners, managers and elected representatives to share their experience, knowledge and goals and combine their energy to create a plan which is technically sound, economically attractive, generally understood and accepted by most of those affected by it and is thus politically viable. (Connor, 1972)*

The objective of a public participation program is to develop informed, visible, majority public understanding, acceptance, and support for a valid proposal. Since 1971 this concept has been applied productively to dealings with the public in regard to new highways, airports, transmission lines, mines, harbors, industrial plants, waste management facilities, and other projects.

A BASIC STRATEGY

When a project is announced, a relatively small number of people, who are often its immediate neighbors, voice their opposition. The project's proponent typically calls a public meeting in order to explain the project to the people involved, confident that their opposition will then disappear. In fact, the public meeting usually crystallizes a more informed, organized, and articulate opposition and generates widespread negative publicity for the proponent and the project.

Our strategy as consultants is first to obtain a comprehensive understanding of the community and the various publics that have or may have a stake in the project. We are particularly interested in the latent and secondary beneficiaries of the project (what we refer to as the 5-volt positive people, compared with the 220-volt negative opponents).

We then provide a variety of ways for the different kinds of people to obtain relevant information in an understandable form; next, we involve them in a joint problem-solving process. As people work together, informed peer group pressure usually results in workable compromise solutions—solutions that are not ideal from anyone's point of view but are acceptable to all or nearly all.

SOME CORE CONCEPTS

Underlying this approach are some core concepts.

Understanding the community—its history, organizations, leaders, values, communications, and knowledge of and attitudes to the proposal and proponent—is the essential foundation for effective public participation. Prepare a social profile of the community or region as soon as possible.

Mutual education is a process by which each party becomes aware of and understands the issues, costs, and benefits of a proposal from the point of each other party. As a result of mutual education, each participant is more willing and able to work toward a generally acceptable solution. Mutual trust between the proponent and the various publics is essential; build it systematically by fostering acceptance, understanding, shared goals, and cooperative management. Remember, trust is easily lost.

Publics: Your project has as many publics as there are different kinds of people who care about it, positively or negatively. There may be a dozen different kinds of people with a shared interest in a proposal. Identify each public and work with them appropriately. When any statement refers to "the public" in the singular, the statement is probably false in some important respects. Some publics are organized and may have their own means of communication. Important publics include employees, neighbors, clients, suppliers, shareholders, environmentalists, and citizens at large.

Informed public goodwill: Major organizations today cannot afford to have significant elements of their publics ignorant and angry about them. Effective managers monitor what their publics know and believe about their organizations and take appropriate steps quickly.

Spend no more than 20 percent of your time and effort trying to directly change the minds of the committed opponents of a valid proposal. Instead, work to interest, inform, and involve the usually silent majority, and encourage them to deal with those who oppose the proposal. This approach is much more likely to be productive than trying to directly change the minds of those who are already locked into a set of values, beliefs, and negative positions. Many people have deplored the way single-interest groups and PACs have hijacked the democratic process; activating the usually silent majority restores balance to the political scene. In one recent project, despite months of negative media publicity, a simple program (social profile, responsive publication, and an open house) lasting less than a month led two-thirds of those with an opinion on the subject to support a waste management proposal when called in a telephone survey. Of course, proponents have to earn community support by ensuring that their proposal responds to community concerns.

As politics becomes more populist, politicians are more sensitive to where their support lies as well as to the sources of opposition. The Edmund Burke–type politician ("Leave me alone to wheel and deal as I see fit, and throw me out at the end of my term if you wish") seems like a vanishing breed compared with the union-delegate kind, who wants to know what the public wants and will usually vote for it. This type of politician supports public participation programs.

Latent and secondary beneficiaries are the people who stand to benefit in small and indirect ways as a result of a project that may be seen as controversial by others. While they are often difficult to reach, it is vital to identify, interest, inform, and involve these "5-volt positive" people. Often there are thousands of them compared with a small number of opponents.

A proponent often has more potential support than media coverage suggests. When the third terminal was being proposed for the Toronto international airport, the airport general manager was fearful that a public participation program would enable antinoise protesters to overwhelm the proposal. When social profiles of the three adjacent municipalities were prepared, the latent support for the airport and its expansion became clear. Display newspaper advertisements and open houses resulted in some 4,000 written responses, and a clear majority supported the proposal; the antinoise people were a small minority. Steps were taken to control noise, which reduced, but did not eliminate, the protests.

Conflict: In many situations conflict is normal and useful. When it is not, there are systematic ways to prevent and resolve conflict that may arise in connection with a given project. These methods often include building acceptance, understanding, and trust among the various parties and involving them in a joint problem-solving process.

Consensus is a noble ideal, but be prepared to settle for informed, visible, majority public support as a more realistic and achievable goal. Consensus decision making and alternative dispute resolution enjoy widespread interest today—but although both have a part to play, neither is a panacea. Consensus building is fundamental to most public participation programs; but when consensus is established as a norm for group decision making, everyone is, in effect, given a veto. Single-interest groups are likely to use their veto and perhaps abuse it.

The classic labor–management environment, in which consensus decision making was born, is usually different in many important ways from a typical land-use proposal in a community—in which there may be up to a dozen parties, wide variations in participants' strength and sophistication, long-term effects to consider, and so on. A continuing issue is the validity and reliability of the linkage between the representatives at the table and their constituencies; there is a perception problem, in that many constituents don't believe they are being properly represented.

Equity: A proposed solution must be seen as fair to all involved. Often this means that "everyone must win something," though not all need to win equally. In designing a public participation program, one secret of success is to try to ensure that every public wins something, even if it is only recognition.

Once the various publics for a proposal have been identified and understood, a serious review with the project manager can enable each public to obtain something of value to it. In some cases the proposal must be modified. The modified plan may not be quite as efficient, effective, or profitable as it initially promised to be, but compromise may be necessary if it is to become politically viable. In a pulp mill project near Vancouver, the construction force was initially scheduled to peak in July. When the construction manager realized the implications of this for the community, he arranged for it to peak in February. As a result, operators of service establishments enjoyed summer-level business for 18 months in a row, and at no additional cost to the project. Public input to the Victoria Eaton Centre resulted in increased street retail space, a compatible character for the exterior, underground parking, the retention of Broad Street, a varied roofline, and other elements desired by the public.

Organization development is a field of management that assesses the effectiveness of an organization and works to improve it; this kind of development is often necessary before a traditional organization "goes public" with a major project. The level and quality of public participation will be no better than the level and quality of staff participation in the project proponent's organization. If public participation staff themselves are managed in a top-down, traditional way, they are likely to manage the public in the same fashion. In contrast, participatively managed staff are likely to work with the public more interactively, because participation is part of the organizational culture. Before an organization "goes public," some internal organization development work is often necessary. Organization development can help build the capacity of the organization to co-manage shared goals with the community. The development of a relevant public participation policy is often part of the advance work needed before staff launches a proactive program with the organization's external publics.

Social impact assessment is a process that seeks to predict, evaluate, and manage the social effects of a policy, program, or project before it is implemented. This assessment is often required as part of the approval process for major federal projects.

Social impact assessment needs a participative methodology and a focus on co-managing the impacts of a proposal, whether foreseen or not. When regulatory hearings drive social impact assessment studies, the usual focus is on preparing an impressive series of reports for review. I believe it is much more important to develop the joint capacity of the community and the proponent to manage the project's effects, whether or not they are predicted. In a northern mining community, one of the results of a participative social impact assessment program was the establishment of an advisory planning committee, which replaced a reliance on the chamber of commerce as the major decision-making body in this unincorporated community of 350 to 400 people.

TIMING

Issue management is a systematic method used to identify, analyze, and take action on public concerns before they become critical issues that might develop into major controversies.

Timing is a key factor. Start early; be cost-effective in the use of citizens' time; and respect periods that are important to the community, such as seasonal work, festivals, and so on. Provide continuity between program phases and between planning, decision making, and implementation. Provide continuous and diverse opportunities for feedback; for example, reply coupons in publications, exit checklists at open houses, a hotline telephone, and regular chats with key nodes in community grapevines. Be responsive to feedback—adjust your initial program as needed.

SOME TECHNIQUES

The following techniques are widely used to implement the issue management strategy. The remaining sections of this article will discuss the first three techniques in detail.

1. *Social Profile:* This is a summary of the main characteristics of a community and its publics, including people's knowledge of and attitudes toward your industry, organization, and project. This study is prepared quickly and unobtrusively to provide a social database on which to plan and manage the human aspects of the projects.

2. *Responsive Publication:* This consists of short, simple, direct, and clear information that recognizes the negative as well as the positive aspects of a project and includes an easy means of response such as a reply-paid postcard, tear-off coupon, or hotline telephone number. Publications may be brochures distributed by householder mail or display advertisements placed in local newspapers.

3. *Open Houses:* Open houses offer a positive opportunity for people associated with the project to converse with interested residents of the area it affects, usually in the afternoon and evening in a local library or church hall. Visitors review graphic panels describing the project, talk with project staff, and are asked to register their views about the project before leaving. The results are usually a considerable improvement on the traditional public meeting.

4. *Planning Workshop:* This technique enables people with a variety of views on an issue to work together to resolve differences. Typically, a mix of representatives from the project, broadly based citizen groups, special-interest organizations, and perhaps relevant government agencies meet together for a day to review a proposed project, its community effects, local concerns, alternative ways of resolving concerns, decision criteria, and so forth. The leadership of the workshop require credibility with all the participants, insights into personal and group dynamics, and a substantial understanding of the project and the disciplines involved with it.

THE SOCIAL PROFILE

Understanding your community is the essential foundation for an effective public participation process. In too many cases, organizations rush into print and start a "dialogue of the deaf" because they haven't taken the time to develop a systematic appreciation of the people and organizations in the community or region involved. Our social profile, developed in the mid-1970s, provides a simple but comprehensive format for a 25- to 30-page report that is usually completed in 10 working days. Organizational profiles of the client organization, regulatory bodies, and other important corporate actors can be equally valuable.

The social profile is a comprehensive summary of the key characteristics of the people of a community or study area. Its purpose is to orient planners, engineers, and administrators to the social and cultural realities they need to understand and take into account if a project, program, or policy is to be accepted. In a recent profile, for example, we identified a pervasive dissatisfaction with the location of the proponent's head office in Montreal, far from the local community on the West Coast. This led the client representative to declare: "That insight alone justifies the cost of the profile!" A few months later the parent company spun off a West Coast subsidiary with its head office in Vancouver as the locus of operational decisions.

Rationale

New policies and projects often generate hostile public reactions because the proponents fail to understand and respond to the values, goals, concerns, and views of the people affected. For key people to make sensitive decisions, they need a character sketch of the community so they can relate their responsibilities and proposals to it. From the social profile they should grasp how and why this community is different from others and how it is likely to respond to a new activity, just as a personal profile enables a manager to judge how an individual might respond to a new assignment.

Data Collection

First, review nonreactive sources of information, many of which will often be available outside the community. Examples include back issues of the weekly press; aerial photographs, preferably 10 years apart; local histories in the regional library; university theses and government reports on the community. Make a content analysis of this material, identifying information under key headings such as:

- community issues
- active organizations

- leaders
- attitudes to growth
- knowledge of and attitude to the client and/or the proposal

Second, identify any people knowledgeable about the community who live beyond it, such as civil servants now in a regional center or capital city who currently service the community or who used to live in it. Interview some of these people by telephone or face-to-face in an informal way; that is, have a list of issues and questions you want to explore, but allow the conversation to be flexible rather than following a structured questionnaire.

Next, visit the community and initially immerse yourself in it, observing its people and how they spend their time and effort. Experience a day in the life of the community as unobtrusively as possible, and reflect on how its residents view their world.

Now start to visit some key people and interview them informally. A conversation about the history of the community provides a comfortable starting point and usually yields many insights into leadership, issues, factions, and so forth. Through such a conversation you will often be introduced to the elders of the community.

Look for people who have had long residence in the community, have high contact with its residents, and are sufficiently secure in their positions that they can talk freely. Some of these are the public health nurse, leaders of voluntary associations, some businesspeople, bank managers, clergy, the staff of service agencies, the school principal (and the janitor). Save interviews with local government officials and elected representatives for later so you will be better able to interpret their positions and discuss them in depth.

In talking with people, explore subjects until you obtain a consistent position from at least three sources. For example, if a certain organization appears to be a key factor in community decision making *(a)* according to your analysis of the local weekly and *(b)* according to a knowledgeable official living outside the community, and if this is *(c)* corroborated by two of these conversations in the community, count this as a fact established. You don't need to raise it in subsequent interviews but can go on to focus on other subjects that are still unclear. Note: This approach employs the navigator's technique of triangulation to establish facts with reasonable accuracy.

In some cases the range of people you can interview is restricted by the fact that clients do not want their interest in the community to become public knowledge. However, there are usually some key people from whom valid information can be obtained and who are accustomed to working under these constraints, such as bank managers, clergy, government officials, and so on.

In my own practice, I usually allow a trained and experienced social researcher (typically with the equivalent of a master's degree in applied social science) 10 days to complete a social profile. This usually breaks down into 1 day on written sources, 5 days in the community, and the remainder to write the 20- to 30-page report. This timetable has proved workable with small rural communities, regional municipalities, and major cities.

Alternative Ways to Collect Data

It is important to note that the foregoing approach to data collection is always modified by the size and unique circumstances of each community. Many variations are possible; a few alternative tactics follow.

1. Informal, In-House Method. If an organization has several staff members who are familiar with a community or area, provide them with the detailed Report Chapters outline shown in Box 5.1 and invite them individually to make notes from their experience on each point. Later, have them share their observations. The items they all agree on are probably true; for items on which there is disagreement or no information, ask someone to find out the true situation. If someone with community experience but a quite different perspective will volunteer to contribute their knowledge, the quality of the data can be considerably improved. For example, if a social worker or a public health nurse joins in to work with a group of engineers or foresters to prepare a social profile. The results may be written up in a report or may be left as an informal collection of notes. This informal, in-house social profile can be assembled unobtrusively at little or no cost.

Box 5.1

The Social Profile: Report Chapters

1. LOCAL HISTORY

- Identify early settlement, key events, and past leaders.
- What are the trends in land use? Note population trends; e.g., age and sex distribution, migration, ethnic origin, occupations, education (see census or planning studies).
- How does the history of the community help to explain its present position and character?

2. INDUSTRIES AND OCCUPATIONS

- What are the main employers, markets, skills?
- How do these affect the community's behavior?

3. DEVELOPMENT ISSUES

- What issues arose in past 5 years? Who got involved, what happened, and how was each issue resolved?
- What are current issues, and what, if anything, is being done about them (e.g., planning studies, etc.)?
- Identify attitudes toward growth.
- What are the implications of the above for the agency and/or proposal?

4. ORGANIZATIONS AND LEADERSHIP

- List the principal groups, their activities and officers, their roles in the community, etc.
- Identify and give a brief description of community leaders and influentials; e.g., people who have followers and are respected for their opinions.
- What does this imply for the proponent and its plans?

5. COMMUNICATION CHANNELS

- Outline the formal media; e.g., geographic coverage, capacity, and credibility of each; circulation/audience of each.
- Describe the informal networks—key nodes on grapevines, strategic listening posts in the community.
- What relevance have these channels for the agency and/or proposal?

6. KNOWLEDGE OF AND ATTITUDES TOWARD INDUSTRY/CLIENT/PROJECT

- What valid information, myths, and areas of ignorance are evident in key people and groups?
- How does the above affect information and education requirements for the proposed activities?

7. PUBLICS AFFECTED

- Summarize the key characteristics of each public; e.g., language, education, media and grapevines appropriate, organizations and relevant leaders, etc.
- What implications has this for the formation of a citizens' advisory committee or other techniques?

8. OBSERVATIONS AND CONCLUSIONS

- Provide a succinct outline of how the characteristics of this community appear to affect the agency and/or proposal and their implications for a public participation program if required.

2. The Community-Based Researcher. In 1994, Yukon College, in northern Canada, wanted to involve representatives of its predominantly First Nations rural communities in developing and determining first principles for its Northern Human Service Worker/BSW program. College officials invited Yukon's First Nations to identify "community consultants," people with an appropriate background; those nominated were trained in a two-day workshop in participatory research methods. During the next six weeks, they gathered information from various residents who formed 10 percent of the population in each of seven demographic groups in each community. The researchers consolidated their findings in another workshop. The process generated a great deal of interest and support for the BSW program as well as vital information. This process could be used to develop a social profile of a community or area.[1]

3. *The Community Workshop.* In 1996, a mining company wished to prepare social profiles of more than 20 communities near a proposed mine in northern Costa Rica. To expedite this program, and to build better relationships with the communities, I proposed that the company hold a half-day workshop with 6 to 10 knowledgeable residents in each community, using the social profile chapter topics (Box 5.1) to guide the discussion. In fact, the company hired a group of facilitators in the region; for the first community, they invited some 50 residents to a Saturday community workshop. Groups of 8 to 10 people worked on each main subject and reported their observations in a plenary session, which also generated considerable enthusiasm and goodwill as well as a rich database. Further workshops were held in other communities with similar results.

The Report

The social profile is designed to provide a kind of charcoal sketch of the main features of the people of the area and how they view and manage their world. Subsequently, the profile can readily be updated and carried out in greater depth as may be needed; for example, as part of a social impact assessment. However, it is not a substitute for a standard sociological study using a random sample of the population. Should this methodology be required, a previously prepared social profile can be very helpful in the design of the research questionnaire.

The writing style of the report must be simple and direct so that a busy manager or engineer can grasp the main points quickly and easily. Start with a map; eliminate jargon; omit heavy footnoting; place any large tables in an appendix, but first question if they are necessary. A photograph or two is often a more informative use of space.

The introduction to the report should indicate the sources of data, the limitations on data collection, the level of effort invested, and a request for comments and suggestions.

Following the usual table of contents, executive summary, and map, the remaining chapters can follow the headings listed as Report Chapters in Box 5.1.

In addition to a written report, some organizations that have to orient numerous staffers to the community will find it worthwhile to develop an audiovisual presentation of the social profile. This can be a simple one-projector production with a pulsed soundtrack (or a video), running perhaps 10 minutes; portable equipment can provide instant orientation to visitors and new employees. For example, if a seismic crew knows ahead of time that a certain trapper they may come across is in fact the chief of the people in the area, this recognition can prevent serious problems in community–company relations.

I believe that the social profile is one of the most cost-effective investments an organization can make when it develops a new policy, program, or project. It can identify the invalid perceptions and assumptions held by senior decision makers and planners; it can ground perceptions firmly in the reality of the community and the people affected; it can also open up new options for solving problems and making the most of opportunities.

RESPONSIVE PUBLICATION

The media is a dubious ally with its own agenda. If you want something said clearly and well, publish your message yourself. A proponent often has more potential support than media coverage suggests. The media have their own agenda and will usually use yours to achieve theirs.

Traditionally, we recognize the vital role of the media in the life of a community and endeavour to present a proponent's proposal through it by preparing news releases, holding news conferences, and such. This positive relationship may still be possible, especially in rural communities and with proposals that have no negative aspects. More recently, however, with the rise of investigative reporters, a generally skeptical attitude seems to pervade the urban media. And of course, headline writers will always highlight the conflict element in any story, because this grabs readers' attention.

For these reasons I prefer to prepare a display newspaper advertisement in a Q&A format with a tear-off reply coupon and publish it without notifying reporters beforehand. Advertising departments will respect this strategy if asked. Later, I will provide reporters with additional background material and graphics in response to their interest. *This approach enables the proponent to "scoop" the story with a positive presentation instead of letting headline writers and reporters highlight its negative aspects.*

Therefore, following the preparation of the social profile, we typically plan three cycles of public activity at milestone points in the study. The first of these is the responsive publication, as detailed in Box 5.2. (Note: A preview of this publication is always provided to all elected representatives the day before it is distributed to the general public.) A week or so later, we hold one or more open houses, depending on the geography and level of interest. We invite politicians for a preview over lunch; the following day, we provide the media with a brief outline of the results. Finally, two weeks later we hold a planning workshop with group leaders to work on project issues and interpret the data received from the preceding events.

THE OPEN HOUSE

For many years, the open public meeting was a standard vehicle for conducting a community's affairs. More recently, the traditional public meeting has often become a forum for community controversy, generating more heat than light.

There are many reasons for this transition: Communities have increased in size, are less homogeneous,

---

Box 5.2

The Responsive Publication

In most public information and participation programs, the primary means of providing most people with basic information is print. Whether in the form of a brochure sent by householder mail, a display advertisement, a tabloid insert in a newspaper, a booklet of some kind, or a poster, print is typically the cheapest means of distributing information.

Unlike the electronic media, print messages are relatively long lasting. In contrast to the demands of public meetings, print reaches its readers in the comfort and security of their own homes, enabling its message to be absorbed with a minimum of anxiety and at the reader's convenience.

A simple and direct style of writing is important. A few tips: Words of one or two syllables have more impact than those with three or four; words ending in -*tion* are soporific. Use the active voice in verbs rather than the passive; minimize surplus adjectives and qualifiers; keep sentences under 12 to 15 words.

Compare the Fog Index (percentage of words with three or more syllables in a sample of text) of your proposed publication with that of material your public usually reads. For example, a rural weekly may have a Fog Index of 6, an urban newsmagazine 10, and a planning report 20. Ensure that the character of the material is informative rather than persuasive. In an introductory publication, the response element should be open-ended; for example, invite "comments, questions, and suggestions." Later in the program you may request weighing evaluation factors and ranking alternative policies or solutions.

The choice of distributing information through a newspaper or by householder mail depends a good deal on how the market area of the newspaper(s) coincides with the location of the publics for the program. If the two do coincide, using the newspaper will not only be cheaper, as a rule, but will encourage editorials, news stories, and letters to the editor. This recognizes and involves the natural forum of the community.

If newspaper coverage does not coincide with the distribution of the publics, a householder mailer enables precise delivery of a brochure to a specific area. An advantage is that the brochure can be printed on a card stock so that a detachable reply-paid postcard forms part of the brochure. This will result in a higher response rate than a tear-off coupon in a newspaper, for which the respondent must find an envelope and a stamp.

During the incubation period following the publication, people have an opportunity to follow media coverage of the issues, discuss the issues with neighbors, and become more prepared to make the best use of the open house.

and are changing more rapidly than before. In these circumstances, a speaker who tries to present a subject effectively to one segment of an audience almost automatically offends another. Indeed, after a particularly trying experience, one engineer declared: "Public meetings are the last of the blood sports and like the others they should be outlawed!" As public meetings became increasingly problematic, the open house was developed as a more constructive vehicle by which a diversity of interested people could obtain information and register their views.

Public Meeting versus Open House

A typical public meeting commences at 8 P.M. with a technical slide presentation that lasts 30 to 45 minutes. Later, when a question period commences, perhaps 20 of 200 persons step up to a microphone to voice their concerns. The meeting often lasts more than 3 hours and usually generates more opposition than support for the subject at hand. This is partly a function of the adversary statement made by the placing of rows of seats opposite a raised podium. Also, the halls where meetings are held often have been the site of previous hearings or other negative experiences.

The open house, by contrast, is usually located in some valued local space such as a room in a library, school, or church and runs from 2 to 9 P.M. so as to be accessible to persons with small children, teenagers returning from school, and adults before or after supper. (In some rural areas in winter, 1 to 6 P.M. works best.) Visitors may come at any time and stay for as much or as little time as they like.

A series of display panels arranged on easels in a rough circle present the purpose of the project, the study team, various aspects of the issues, evaluation criteria, and alternative solutions. Often a diagram on one panel is followed by a short text explanation on the next so the visitor can obtain a grasp of the whole project without being led by the hand and talked at.

An automatic slide presentation on a small cube with a 3- to 5-minute cycle (or a short video) is useful to present visual aspects of the subject. Note: If chairs are provided, occupants will inhibit the desired flow of people through the exhibit.

A table with handout material is usually provided. Coffee and doughnuts or sandwiches should be available, preferably by contracting with a local group such as a ladies' auxiliary.

The open house is a powerful learning and problem-solving device that is readily adapted to most planning projects and the characteristics of most participants. The primary character of an open house is a free-flowing conversation directed by the visitors. People can come whenever they wish, stay as long as they wish, and address whatever topics interest them in whatever order they choose. As a result, the staff talk with a larger number and broader cross-section of the population than happens in the typical public meeting. The quality of the exchanges is usually much higher; the participants pose second and third questions and wrestle with alternative solutions. In many cases problems can be not only raised but actually resolved, unlike what usually occurs in a public meeting.

Feedback

The systematic gathering of informed public response is a vital feature of the open house. Staff, wearing name tags which also indicate their area of responsibility, can carry pads of open house record forms on which to note individual comments, concerns, questions, and suggestions. Where staff cannot provide immediate answers, they write down the name, address, and phone number for later follow-up. Visitors are most appreciative when staff undertake to refer questions or concerns that are not part of their project to the relevant organizations.

Although an open house is free to enter, visitors must pay to get out—by completing a short exit checklist! This generates quantitative data, such as weights on evaluative factors or ranking of alternatives. Background data obtained, such as geographic location or occupation, enables cross-tabulation.

Staffing

Staffing of an open house can usually be lighter during the day than in the evening. It is important to manage so as to avoid overcrowding; for example, an open house held from 7 to 9 P.M. may readily deteriorate into a regular public meeting, in contrast to one held from 2 to 9 P.M., which is unlikely to do so.

In one recent case, 250 people attended an open house from 2 to 9 P.M. Two staff members were present from 2 to 6:30 and four for the evening. Some 30 open house record forms and 130 exit checklists were completed. The staffers were able to interpret the project appropriately to housewives, environmentalists, and businesspeople.

When staff are preparing open house display panels, it is important that these are informative rather than persuasive and informal rather than formal. These finished graphics convey a nonverbal message that additional suggestions are too late.

Staff Training and Follow-Up

As a minimum, staff should gather in advance to identify probable questions and establish brief, correct, and consistent responses to them. For example, before one set of open houses dealing with a very controversial project, the staff reviewed some 30 probable questions and role-played their responses as if each were asked by

- an interested housewife,
- a high school science teacher,
- an old farmer, and
- an angry environmentalist.

An assertiveness training film, *When I Say No I Feel Guilty* (International Telefilms), was also used with considerable value.

After one or more open houses, it is important to have a debriefing meeting with the staff to obtain their reactions, insights, and suggestions for improvements at future events. Analyze the response and make it available to the planning team, and provide a news release to the local media so residents will know the sentiments of the community at large. Get back answers to questions recorded at the open house, and forward requests for action by other organizations.

Preparing Yourself for an Open House

Preparation for an open house should be both factual and attitudinal.

Factual Preparation. Develop a list of probable questions and ensure you can provide basic answers to all of them. Identify specialists who will be at the open house, or available from it by telephone, to provide additional detail if needed. Don't insist on knowing everything—it's human and appealing to occasionally admit, "I don't know now but I'll find out and get back to you." Get a pad of open house record forms to write down people's concerns and questions; also a name tag.

Attitudinal Preparation. Realize that many visitors to the open house have other things on their mind besides this proposal—family concerns, work issues. Their reaction to your project will reflect all these anxieties, so don't take an emotional outburst personally. Reflect sincerely on what it means to be a public servant. Your attitudes will show nonverbally, and will sink in far more than your technical information. Is the citizen–taxpayer your ultimate client or a stupid ass? Are women's questions as important as men's?

Select dress appropriate for the setting and the people you will meet; for example, probably not a suit. Let your appearance suggest that here is someone who is comfortable, open, and practical.

Managing Yourself on the Floor

Remember your role—to reply to questions, but not to preach or sell; to record people's concerns, questions, and suggestions, but not to debate them; to come across as a concerned and responsive servant of the public, not as an impassive expert with total job security. Cultivate brief answers—those who want more will ask.

Accept people's anger: "I can see you are angry about this. If I were in your boots, I probably would be too!"

Get specific: "What exactly is it that you are concerned about?" Ask for solutions: "What do you think can be done about this?" Explore options and their implications: "What else do you think we could do to solve this problem?"

Forestall repetition: "Yes, I think you explained that well earlier, so I've noted your points on this sheet and will pass them on to the planning team. Please excuse me now—I really should talk with someone else over there. Perhaps you'd like to pick up some of our fact sheets before you go home. Thank you and goodbye for now."

Admit that your organization and its staff have made some mistakes in the past. If you don't have all the answers, explain why, and offer to get back to the person later, taking their name and phone number on your pad. Ensure that visitors record their views before leaving.

Don't let any one person monopolize you; circulate. Don't stand around with your colleagues; look open, interested, and available to someone with a question. If there are too many staff people for the number of visitors, take your briefcase into a corner and do something interesting and useful. (Surplus staff look like a waste of taxpayers' money; inactive staff become bored or anxious.)

If you must smoke, especially a pipe or a cigar, do it elsewhere—many people are sensitive to the atmosphere these days. Pace yourself: Arrange to take a break after a couple of hours to ensure you are as fresh as possible for the 7 to 9 P.M. period.

Follow-Up

After the open house, evaluate it, preferably with your colleagues. How did it go? What things helped it to go as well as it did? What things hindered it from being better? What should be done to improve the next open house? What do you need to learn to be more effective in this setting? What action is needed on the requests, suggestions, and questions you received from visitors? Don't expect to be able to do all of these things easily and well without training in the relevant behavioral skills, including particular applications of assertiveness training.

Combined Open House–Public Meeting

As stated earlier, we usually prefer to have open houses rather than public meetings. However when a government agency insisted on public meetings, we teamed the two techniques. During the afternoon open houses, many individuals with personal concerns visited with the proponent's staff, settled their issues, and did not return for the meeting, thus reducing the numbers. Others, who planned to speak against the proposal in the evening, came in the afternoon and obtained some information; it is always easier to deal with informed opposition than with the ignorant variety.

When the public meeting began in the evening, the project manager reported on the number who had come to the open house and the substantial support they showed for the proposal. This encouraged supporters to speak up against opponents during the meeting—something that rarely happens. And at all three locations, the meetings were over by 9 P.M.—another rarity. Combining these two techniques seemed to generate some positive synergy. Try it!

CONCLUSION

In the introductory phase of a public participation program, the main objective is to present the proposed project clearly and fairly, including its negative aspects, and to obtain public comments, questions, and suggestions: "We know we don't have all the answers, but we want to make sure we have all the questions."

Later, in the alternatives-generating phase, the main thrust is to present the currently known alternative solutions and proposed evaluation criteria and to solicit any additional alternatives, further criteria, and weights on these.

Once this material has been dealt with, the evaluation phase focuses on presenting the technically sound alternatives and the technical evaluation of each according to the criteria, and on discovering how the various public rank them: "We are prepared to build any one of them—which of them are you prepared to live with?"

Evaluation is the best way to learn from both your successes and your failures. In the early days of my practice, I would keep a field-worker on for another week after the end of the project and have him or her carry out face-to-face interviews with participants in a recently concluded public participation program. Later, a telephone survey was used. In the mid-1980s, I hired a psychologist to interview both client representatives and interest-group leaders to identify what they liked and didn't like about our programs. We routinely evaluate every planning and instructional workshop. The results are not only valuable for the workshop leader but, when anonymous verbatim replies are consolidated and fed back to participants, they are instructive for them as well. Regular evaluations are both an insurance policy for the practitioner and a safety valve for the participants.

The final report on each project contains a chapter on the public participation process,[2] including a matrix showing the rank order assigned by the various publics to the several alternatives. Elected representatives can endorse the public preference or, if they choose another of the options, can see whom they need to persuade and what the concerns are. The approach is economical in the use of citizen leaders' time and recognizes that they have other priorities to attend to besides this project.

This approach is no panacea. It is demanding on proponents and citizens alike. However, examine it for yourself and you may find, as others have done, that the alternatives are worse.

NOTES

1. With thanks to Ms. Vera Asp, Vice-President, First Nations, and Ms. Amanda Graham, Chair of Social Sciences and Humanities, Yukon College, Whitehorse, YT, Canada.
2. For further information see Desmond M. Connor, *Constructive Citizen Participation: A Resource Book,* Fourth Edition; Development Press, 5096 Catalina Tce., Victoria, B.C., V8Y 2A5; 220 pp.; 1992. Tel. 604-658-1323; fax 658-8110. Or see http://www.connor.bc.ca/connor.

REFERENCE

Connor, Desmond M., "From Partisans to Partners," *Community Planning Review,* 22(1) (1972).

6

Visions of a New Corporate Culture

LAWRENCE M. MILLER

Editors' Note: As sociologist Max Weber noted, the question, "Who am I?" always arises in the context, "What am I going to do?" Consultant Larry Miller shows how organizations have identities just like people. An organization also can have an identity crisis. Without a sense of who we are, we don't know what to do. Even though everything may initially look like business as usual, ignoring the sociological environment may mean the organization is in trouble. Miller has worked with some of the top companies in the country and gives us a new vision for business.

The distinction between the leader and the manager can be summarized by the word "purpose." Leaders have a noble vision of their purpose. Leaders create energy by instilling purpose in others.

The chilling winds of a New York winter provided little comfort as I approached the glass edifice that housed one of the world's most successful financial institutions. I was not entirely sure that my report would not be met by a response more piercing than the winds accelerating through the canyons of lower Manhattan. My finding seemed almost too simple and perhaps too challenging to the leadership of the chairman of the company. The revolving doors brought relief from the cold. And as I signed in with the stern-faced guard who was far too serious about his duties, I imagined my departure following a failed meeting, being refused permission to leave, trapped for discovering the wrong answer.

Reprinted with permission of Lawrence M. Miller from *American Spirit. Visions of a New Corporate Culture*, by Lawrence M. Miller, 1984, New York: Morrow.

The chairman had been concerned about the turnover among the senior executives. The firm was a headhunter's paradise. There was a general lack of *esprit de corps* and loyalty among the very best and most successful managers. I interviewed the twenty-five senior executives. I suspect that their average annual compensation was in the $200,000 range. They ran a worldwide multibillion-dollar organization that was held in very high esteem. I pursued my usual line of questions in interviewing, the ones that had always proved fruitful before: "If you could change one thing about the way that you are managed, what would it be?"; or "What do you like best about working for . . . ?" I also asked specific questions about objective setting, review of performance, feedback, recognition, rewards, decision making, etc. The more questions I asked, the more I became convinced that these managers managed each other very well. They understood the basics of good management technique and practiced them. They were very intelligent and hardworking. Throughout all my questioning only one consistent complaint was voiced.

These executives were not sure what business they were in. They were unsure of their purpose. Yes, they understood very well that they were in the business of financial services, and that they were excellent at providing them. But recently their firm had made several acquisitions that had nothing to do with financial services. Why? What was the plan? How would this affect their careers? Was the ladder to the top through the well-established financial services, or would it be through these new ventures? The truth is that no one had the answers to these questions. The acquisitions had been made because the parent firm had a lot of cash, saw the opportunity to acquire high-growth, high-potential profit companies and improve their return on assets. These were financial decisions made by financial managers. However, the managers below them, who might very well have made the same decisions if they had been in a position to do so, experienced the acquisitions in quite a different way. These new ventures upset their cosmos. The managers had now lost that consolidated sense of business and social purpose that had served as a primary source of motivation.

The senior executives felt no great loyalty to this firm despite its success and prestige and the rewards it had bestowed upon them. The executives were highly trained and skilled, and they were in demand. They would be well paid and would obtain positions that satisfied their essential needs here or elsewhere. It was something else they wanted, and perhaps because all their other needs were so well met they knew what it was. It was a sense of mission. They wanted to know what they were working for. What was the strategy? where was the firm headed and why? and what were their roles in that strategy? Their inability to understand the mission of the corporation and their roles in the fulfillment of it was a source of substantial dissatisfaction.

My encounter with the chairman increased my respect for him. He listened to my explanation thoughtfully and understood. He agreed. He felt it himself. His sincere desire to do what was best for the business and for his fellow executives was his dominant motive, and he took pleasure in considering the alternatives. When I departed, the guard had changed. He was a she. Young and attractive this time, almost flirtatious. As I left the building I noticed that the wind had ceased its attack.

A THEORY OF THE BUSINESS

How can such a successful corporation lose its sense of purpose? This firm is by no means the worst offender. It has become common in our age of conglomerate corporate politics in which movement up the *Fortune* 500 ladder appears to be of greater significance than providing quality goods and services. The devotion to product or service has become less prevalent than the devotion to financial success. The mystery is that the devotion to the former is most likely to produce the latter, while devotion to financial success is less likely to produce either. We can blame the business schools and consulting firms who have promoted a type of strategic planning that mistakes financial manipulation for the more noble activity of creating wealth. Many of our corporations' executives do not understand the difference between the organization and the consolidation of wealth and the creation of wealth. Mergers and acquisitions give rise to a new organization of wealth, one firm now having greater assets than before; however, no new wealth has been created in the process.

Peter Drucker has been writing about the importance of business purpose for many years. Perhaps the idea is too simple for this age of complex analysis. "Every one of the great business builders we know of—from the Medici and the founders of the Bank of England down to IBM's Thomas Watson in our day—had a definite idea, had, indeed, a clear theory of the business which informed his actions and decisions. A clear, simple, and penetrating theory of the business rather than intuition characterizes the truly successful entrepreneur, the man who not just amasses a large fortune but builds an organization that can endure and grow long after he is gone".[1] A "theory of the business," as Drucker refers to it; or "superordinate goals," as Richard T. Pascale and Anthony G. Athos discuss in *The Art of Japanese Management;*[2] or a basic philosophy or beliefs, as Thomas Watson, Sr., so successfully instilled within

IBM. Tom Watson, Jr., clearly credited IBM's success to these beliefs: "I firmly believe that any organization, in order to survive and achieve success, must have a sound set of beliefs. Next I believe that the most important factor in corporate success is faithful adherence to those beliefs."[3]

Unfortunately, many of our most senior corporation executives have only the most shallow understanding of the purpose of their businesses. Too many of them will tell you that this purpose is to maximize return to stockholders. This says nothing at all. It is indicative of a manager who has been trained in technical skills but has no loyalties, no loves, and no business of his own. To maximize return on investments, assets, or profits is an inadequate statement of purpose. It is inadequate for two reasons: First, it completely fails to accomplish the paramount responsibility of leadership—to provide meaning and inspiration to those who are expected to follow. Those who do the work of the corporation must focus their energies on either product or customers. They must be motivated toward producing or creating the best possible product, or providing the best possible response to the needs of their customers. It is the responsibility of the executive to motivate employees toward this purpose. They are not and should not be focused on "return on assets." This result will follow if employees focus on that which they can influence and in which they can find personal meaning and reward.

Second, financial objectives are an inadequate statement of purpose because they fail to recognize the social justification for the existence of the corporation. This justification is a creative one. The purpose of the corporation is the creation of wealth, those goods and services that enhance our standards of living. When the corporation increases its productivity, it produces more goods and services at lower cost and thereby increases that which is available for consumption. This is an increase in the aggregate wealth of society. When the corporation produces a new technology or reduces the cost of technology, such as was done with the microcomputer, again it makes available a higher standard of living.

The creation of genuine wealth, goods, and services for consumers must be the primary purpose of the corporation. Achieving financial results is necessary, but secondary in purpose. Financial results will follow as the corporation and its stockholders succeed in their primary aim. To focus on financial results first detracts from the firm's ability to achieve those results because it fails to mobilize human energy.

Wealth is not money. Wealth is that which may be bought with money. Throughout the world there are many economies producing more money and less wealth. They are faced with this dilemma precisely because their productive institutions are inadequate to fulfill the primary purpose of producing the goods and services that comprise true wealth. The government can produce money; it does not produce wealth. This is the social purpose, the noble purpose, of our business institutions.

Robert B. Reich has articulated the problem deriving from the inadequacies of purpose and the failure to distinguish between the creation of wealth and its reorganization: "Managers have indeed adapted by innovating. But innovations have not been technological or institutional. Rather, they have been based on accounting, tax avoidance, financial management, mergers, acquisitions, and litigation. They have been innovations on paper. Gradually, over the past fifteen years, America's professional managers have become paper entrepreneurs."[4] "The problem is that paper entrepreneurialism is supplanting product entrepreneurialism as the most dynamic and innovative business in the American economy. Paper entrepreneurialism provides nothing of tangible use. For an economy to maintain its health, entrepreneurial rewards should flow primarily to products, not to paper."[5]

Andrew Carnegie understood the difference between the creation of genuine wealth and the manipulation of finances. In his later years, when he formed the Carnegie Steel Company, he pursued a very deliberate policy of creating a more productive enterprise while avoiding the financial manipulations that were very much the common practice of the day. His success was largely attributable to his devotion to the business of making steel rather than to reorganizing the symbols of wealth, stocks, bonds, and legal documents. A congressional committee later described his battle with the steel trusts as "a contest between fabricators of steel and fabricators of securities; between makers of billets and makers of bonds." Carnegie described one of the competing steel trusts as "the greatest concern the world ever saw for manufacturing stock certificates.... But, they will fail sadly in steel."[6] He was right, they did! While his competitors focused their energies on the manipulation of wealth's symbols, Carnegie devoted his attention to making steel at the lowest cost. Carnegie built not only one of the nation's largest and most productive enterprises, but one of the largest fortunes of the day which later he dedicated almost entirely to philanthropy.

LEADERS VERSUS MANAGERS

America has too many managers and not enough leaders. If we had more leaders we could do without half of the managers. The distinction between the leader and the manager can be summarized by the word "purpose." Leaders create energy by instilling purpose. Managers control and direct energy. Leaders define success in terms of the accomplishment of a business achievement, the success of a product or service. Managers define success according to measures that are derived from the process of business independent of the content of the business. Leaders appeal to the higher values, the long-term potential of the individual to feel a part of, a contributor to achievements of mankind. The manager appeals to the immediate needs for income, status, and security. Leadership brings out the creativity of the individual and inspires courage. Management without leadership produces conformity.

Our civilizations were built on the vision, the inspiration, the spirit of a religious leader. Western civilization emerged driven by the spirit of Christ. The Islamic civilization was founded and flourished because of the inspiration of Mohammed. So, too, have many of our major business organizations come into being, driven by the vision and the spirit of their founders. General Electric eventually emerged as a result of the creative genius and inventiveness of Thomas Edison. The Ford Motor Company emerged from Henry Ford's deep belief that there was a need and a mass market for cheap and dependable transportation. His mission was to create a manufacturing process that would make this transportation available at an affordable price. Such visions instill an energy not only in the individual entrepreneur who creates them, but also in those who follow in pursuit of the visions.

At this point in history, it is not the norm for individuals to find fulfillment of a higher purpose through their work. However, it is also not the norm to be highly dedicated and energized by work. If asked why they work, few would answer that they are fulfilling a mission. However, when asked, most will acknowledge that they would like to feel that they are accomplishing a purpose, a social good through their work.

A few years ago I was working with a manufacturer of metal products.[7] The culture of this company was in crisis. It had been very successful and was still successful. It had become a large conglomerate, with the metal business now representing only one of several businesses. The Boston Consulting Group had been hired by the corporation to assist in strategic planning. The metal company met the criteria for a "cash cow" almost perfectly, and the corporation followed the prescribed scenario of taking cash out of the metal company and buying higher-growth, potentially more profitable businesses. Money was not put back into the company for technical development, new equipment, or expenditures on the development of people. At the same time, overcapacity in the industry resulted in price erosion and subsequent plant closings. The company was not helped by its highly adversarial relationship with its unions. The managers were fine examples of a macho style of authoritarian management; they were uncreative and fearful for their jobs, and they intimidated their subordinates.

I was leading a one-day self-assessment session with a group of about twenty middle-level managers in this metal company. After giving the managers a model for assessing their culture, I asked them to form into small groups for about forty-five minutes to define some characteristics of their firm that they found attractive and some that they would like to change. Each of the four or five small groups nominated someone to report to the larger group the characteristics they had identified. When the last reporter spoke, he presented his impressions of the culture in a way that must not have been the result of the group's consensus.

"I remember ten or fifteen years ago, I used to work twelve hours every day, usually six days and sometimes seven days a week. I remember how I couldn't wait until I got to work in the morning. I would have done anything for this company. We were 'The Metal Company,' and we were proud of it. We were the best and we knew it. Now it's different. Now I come to work and I do my job because I'm a professional. But it is no secret that there are people at the top of this company who are ashamed of the word 'metal.' Now you have to search through the annual report to find it. We all know that they have no interest in this business except for the money they can drain out of it. Now all I hear people talking about is how long they have to go until they retire." He stopped, and everyone knew he had tears in his eyes. There was a long, quiet pause and he was not contradicted.

PRODUCTS, PEOPLE, AND CUSTOMERS

Purpose comes in many forms. It need not be the salvation of mankind. Being "The Metal Company," the best in the industry, is purpose enough for most people. Many managers and employees working in the personal computer business believe that they are the vanguard of a new day that will see our lives radically changed by easy access to computer technology. This is their purpose. Once, I visited a meat-packing plant that made sausages. I listened in awe as the manager of the plant explained to me how more people in the South woke up each morning to eat that company's brand of sausages than any other kind. He actually described for me his conviction that the quality of their sausages helped all those people enjoy the rest of the day. He truly believed it. He believed that the work he was doing was for a noble purpose. He was helping millions of people have a good day! All of these managers and workers are motivated by their own thoughts. They think about the good they are doing, the pride in being the best, the satisfaction of leading a change in lifestyle or making the best sausages in the world. They have purpose, and this purpose leads to productivity and satisfaction.

During recent decades there has arisen a cadre of executives at the top of our corporations who have served more to destroy purpose than to create it. These antileaders have put together some of the largest conglomerates in the nation. They have done so not by building a business but by the organization of finances. Many of them have never made an item, delivered a service, or sold a product to an actual customer. They know numbers. They do not know products, services, or customers. Success to them is found solely in the numbers. They have increased the size of their fiefdoms while understanding nothing of the businesses within them or of the motivations and fears of their employees. The managers who must run the businesses within these fiefdoms understand that they are judged now only on financial criteria, not on the merits of advancing the state of a technology, producing the highest-quality goods, or being respected by customers. These criteria are meaningful only to someone who loves and cares for the business of making clothes, fasteners, or furniture. If a manager's energies are directed more on the resulting numbers and less on the business itself, the business deteriorates. This scenario has been repeated a hundred times during the past decade.

The executives of our corporations did not go to leadership school. They went to management school. I recently spoke to a group of students at the Wharton Business School. Afterward, I chatted with four students who were obviously job hunting. I asked them, by the time they graduated with their MBAs, how many courses in managing, motivating, or leading people would they have had? They agreed without apology that the right answer was NONE! When they spoke about business they spoke about strategic planning models and quantitative theory. These students left me with the impression that they knew everything about numbers, models, and theoretic strategy but nothing about the substance of business or what business managers actually spend their time doing. They were prepared to enter the world of number manipulation. But when I asked them what type of business they would like to be in, they agreed that it didn't matter as long as it was one of growth potential. When I asked whether they were interested more in sales management or manufacturing management, they reacted with some disdain. They had no interest in these activities, they were interested in finance and strategic planning. They were not interested in spending time where actual business is conducted—in producing and selling—they wanted to ascend immediately to the high post of condescension, planning strategically in complete ignorance of the business.

This total deemphasis on the management of product, people, and customers in our supposedly best business schools is one of the most frightening facts of American education. Leading large groups of people and resources without a purpose more significant than that derived from playing a game of Monopoly is only one part of the problem of the way we are producing technical and financial managers.

Business strategy follows from a business purpose. If our business purpose is "to make available information processing and management technology to every home in America," then strategies of technical research, product development, marketing, and manufacturing must follow, and they can follow only from an understanding of and enthusiasm for the business purpose. None will follow a purely financial objective of increasing return on equity. The purely financial objective causes one to make decisions that lead away from a coordinated business purpose. This is not to say that financial objectives are undesirable. Of course, a business must achieve financial objectives, and these can motivate and direct performance constructively. However, those monetary goals should not be the primary motive forces in the creation of a business; they are a secondary method of measuring one aspect of its success.

THE SEED OF MOTIVATION

Understanding that the business serves a higher purpose not only results in sound and creative strategy, it also results in the willingness of individuals to sacrifice. We will sacrifice, in our personal lives and in our businesses, if we have a valued vision of the future. I remember listening to managers at Honeywell's Aerospace and Defense Group talk about the time when they were working on the Apollo program. They worked insanely long hours and with

total dedication. They worked as if they were at war. They felt that they were responsible for landing a man on the moon and that this nation's pride and prestige were in their hands. They made personal sacrifices that no manager could ask or demand. They were not motivated by the financial aspects of their project. They were not responding to management techniques or evident self-interest. They were responding to what they felt was a noble purpose, and through sacrificing to that purpose they achieved self-esteem.

Our need to motivate through purpose, to lead, is not only present within our corporations. It exists as a dilemma of our democratic capitalist society. We believe that our system of democracy and capitalism is the vehicle for achieving the highest living standard and the highest order of individual and collective freedom ever attained by mankind. Yet this system is failing to inspire others. Masses of people, particularly in those parts of the world which most need the productive impetus, are inspired not by our system, which has proved successful, but by one that has repeatedly failed to produce wealth or freedom. Why? Because in those areas of the world, they speak of freedom and power for the peasants while we speak of investments and acquisitions. Talk of "freedom and power for the downtrodden people" does inspire action. Our talk of investments and acquisitions is without meaning. Why are *we* not the revolutionaries leading the poor to freedom and ownership of the means of production when we have more experience with freedom and the ownership of the means of production than any people on earth? Because we have forgotten how to lead. We have forgotten how to inspire. We are consumed by our knowledge and love of techniques when knowledge and techniques have little meaning for those who need inspiration and will respond only to a higher purpose.

We who are the leaders of the institutions of free enterprise have a nearly sacred responsibility to make a connection between the effectiveness of those institutions and the human soul. "Throughout the world, capitalism evokes hatred. The word is associated with selfishness, exploitation, inequality, imperialism, war. Even at home, within the United States, a shrewd observer cannot fail to note a relatively low morale among business executives, workers, and publicists. Democratic capitalism seems to have lost its spirit. To invoke loyalty to it because it brings prosperity seems to some merely materialistic. The Achilles' heel of democratic capitalism is that for two centuries now it has appealed so little to the human spirit."[8] The financially oriented are satisfied with the proof of financial success. Unfortunately, the mass of people, within our society or within our corporations, are not primarily motivated by what is rational. It is the emotional—the appeal to the self-esteem, the spirit—that is the prime mover.

We must learn to create and utilize purpose in the management of our business and our nation. Business enterprises do have a noble purpose and we should recognize and proclaim it. The purpose of business is the creation of wealth—not for a few, but for all. Wealth is not money. It is the goods and services that business provides. It is we who are able to produce wealth who will eliminate poverty, disease, and ultimately war, who will free humanity from the chains of mindless toil so that we can pursue and utilize our higher capacities of mind and soul. Peter Drucker made a similar observation a number of years ago: "The achievement of business management enables us today to promise—perhaps prematurely (and certainly rashly)—the abolition of the grinding poverty that has been mankind's lot through the ages. It is largely the achievement of business management that advanced societies today can afford mass higher education. Business both produces the economic means to support this expensive undertaking and offers the jobs in which knowledge can become productive and can be paid for. That we today consider it a social flaw and an imperfection of society for people to be fixed in their opportunities and jobs by class and birth—where only yesterday this was the natural and apparently inescapable condition of mankind—is a result of our economic performance, that is, of the performance of business management. In a world that is politically increasingly fragmented and obsessed by nationalism, business management is one of the very few institutions capable of transcending national boundaries."[9]

Each business in our society, whether making steel, farming potatoes, producing cars, or processing

information, each in its own way contributes to this collective purpose. We who have the opportunity to choose must meditate on our purpose, communicate it to our managers and workers so that they may have the satisfaction of sacrificing their energies toward that which enhances their own dignity. This is the first priority of business leadership in the new age.

HOW WE BEHAVE—DEFINING OUR CULTURE

Managers need a framework and a language for articulating what features characterize their existing cultures and what behaviors they would like to see in the future. The current culture of the corporation is the sum of the habits of its members.

What is lacking in the frenzy to find new management practices is an examination of the soul and spirit of management, the foundation upon which management's right to manage rests. After fourteen years of assisting America's best corporations in their efforts to improve productivity, I had full confidence in our management techniques but decreasing confidence that any management technique alone was sufficient to the task. My colleagues and I had implemented performance improvement efforts in manufacturing and sales organizations of 3M, American Express, Ford Motor Company, and about a hundred other firms. We knew that by increasing involvement, positive reinforcement, and feedback we could better productivity in most organizations. However, those techniques, as much as they improved performance in the operations, were not adequate to address the more fundamental questions facing American management. Managers were facing a crisis of self-confidence, a questioning of the basic beliefs upon which their right to manage was founded.

As I spoke to growing numbers of executives about productivity and quality, I became increasingly convinced that a new statement of beliefs about management's role in the American corporation was needed.

My own discussions with executives about their management began to change. When I asked them about their own values, and about the values that they wished to see instilled in their firms, I found they were giving a great deal of thought to the culture of their corporations and to the cultures that would be required in the future. Out of these sessions I was able to start defining the values of the future corporate culture.

There is a new corporate culture emerging in American business. The decline of the old business culture and the struggle to establish a new one can be observed in almost every major corporation in America. Its motive forces are the financial necessity of improved productivity and quality and the demands made by employees for a more satisfying work environment. But new cultures are not built upon material necessity alone, they result from the creation and acceptance of new values, new visions, a new spirit. New cultures emerge when leaders proclaim and demonstrate those values through their own behavior.

The current anxiety about the American corporation and its productivity has resulted in a furious investigation of management techniques. Experimentation has never been greater, and it is clearly the result of the new economics of world competition. However, while this experimentation is healthy and encouraging, it is focused primarily on technique or structure. New techniques or structures succeed because they are an expression of an accepted value or spirit. The Catholic Church represented the creation of a new organization, a new structure. It could not have evolved in the absence of the spirit of Christianity that was its motivating force. Any explanation of its creation that ignores the values upon which it was built is inadequate. This motivating spirit created a willingness to sacrifice personal well-being for a higher purpose, a vision of the future. The American government as a structure similarly did not emerge simply because a technician perceived that the separation of powers, checks and balances, and representative democratic process were superior to other preceding forms of government. On the contrary, there was again a new ideal, a new vision of the future, a new spirit, articulated in the Declaration of Independence. The soul of a new nation was born.

We must examine the new values, visions, and spirit that are arising in the American corporation.

We must be concerned not merely with the techniques of the new management, but with its soul. There are values and a spirit at the foundation of how we organize and manage our corporations. These values are the deeply held beliefs, often unarticulated, that are the product of the culture's conditioning, its heroes, myths, and fears. These beliefs have emerged over the course of our nation's development, silent partners in the management of America's business. The answer to improved productivity, the remotivation of the business corporation, will not be found in simple management techniques. It will be found in the acceptance of and action upon new values. What is lacking is an examination of the soul and spirit of management, the foundation upon which management's right to manage rests.

The acceptance of new values has the power to create new cultures. Western culture has its roots in the Judeo–Christian tradition. American culture was created by the values of freedom of speech, religion, and the press. The culture of American commerce was founded on the ideas of free enterprise, free trade, and the novel notion that any individual could, with wit and work, attain wealth. The Marxist idea of the distribution of wealth according to need was sufficiently powerful, albeit flawed, to create revolutions. Thus, simple ideas can possess enormous power—the power to create a new society and to achieve a new standard of living. They can be the catalyst for the release of human potential. If we are to create new cultures within our corporations, we must determine upon which values we will build those cultures.

We take values for granted. The managers of our corporations are largely unaware of the cultural forces upon which their actions are based and cannot therefore question or alter those forces. How many managers understand the cultural roots of the command leadership that they habitually practice? How many realize they are operating in blind obedience to the conditioning of years of movies and television that proclaimed models that led to victory in ages now past? These managers act on assumptions that are likely to be of little benefit to the corporation of the future. What are the values, the spirit of management upon which the future corporation must be built? What are the values that will promote competitive success in the new world in which the corporation must compete on a global scale?

I have identified primary values which I believe will lay the foundation for a new competitive American corporate culture. The values are labeled "primary values" because they are applicable to the management of all organizations, and indeed many successful companies are already acting on them. I have selected these because my colleagues and I have observed they are the ones most related to high innovation, loyalty, and productivity. In brief, here they are:

The Purpose Principle

We all have a need to confirm our self-worth. Self-worth cannot be achieved in the absence of a sense of contribution to some higher purpose. Leaders fulfill this need. They communicate purpose to those who follow. The ability to communicate a valued purpose is a rare art among corporate managers. Achieving return on equity does not, as a goal, mobilize the most noble forces in our souls. The most successful companies have defined their aims in terms of product or service and benefits to customers in a manner that can inspire and motivate their employees. Most corporations do serve a worthy purpose. Individuals seek to identify with it. The competitive leader will make the connection between our souls and our work, and will benefit from the energies released.

The Consensus Principle

Managers are stuck in the culture of command. They feel an excitement, an exhilaration when they are able to command. Unfortunately, command behavior is what was successful in the crisis climate of battle. The leader of old marched ahead of his troops because he was the strongest and the most brave. He exemplified the values that were important to that organization. The future corporation will not march into battle. It will succeed by its ability to bring ideas together, to stimulate the employees and managers to think creatively. The employee will not be asked to risk life and limb for his superior. He will be asked to risk sharing his thoughts and feelings. He will be asked to focus not his physical energies, but his men-

tal energies. This change in task necessitates a change from command to consensus.

The Unity Principle

Our corporations maintain the traditions of a class society. We maintain the distinctions of management–labor, salary–hourly wage, exempt–nonexempt. thinker–doer. They are all false distinctions, the old, useless baggage of a deceased society, carried forward into a new world. We live in an age of unity, of integration, when distinctions that disunite and limit people are inherently counterproductive. There are other traditions from our past to which management must return. There was a time when ownership and identity with the job were a source of pride. The industrial age, with the anonymity of mass production, swung the pendulum from ownership to alienation. The electronic age, with its emphasis on information, the flexibility of information technologies, and the psychological needs for community, identity, and a source of personal worth, will swing the pendulum back toward ownership. The competitive corporation will accept the value of fully involving the individual in its workings and decision making so that he or she again feels in unity with and ownership for the work.

The Performance Principle

In Western society the corporation is the agency that metes out more rewards and punishments than any other. The prevalent principle by which it distributes its rewards is power. Those who organize, those who are in short supply, those who can control have power and are rewarded in proportion to that power. The distribution of rewards according to power is as old as our civilization. However, this system contains within itself the seeds of its own destruction. When rewards are granted without regard to performance, productivity suffers. When they are tied to performance, individual and corporate performances improve. If the corporation is to succeed in the new era we are entering, it must reevaluate the values by which it distributes its rewards. In the future rewards must be granted according to the value of performance, a value not currently exhibited at the level of the chief executive or the union apprentice.

The Intimacy Principle

The military model of management was necessarily impersonal. In battle the cost of personal involvement in the psychological world of another individual presented too great a risk to the emotional well-being of the leader. This is our tradition. Strength is represented as a detached, masculine absence of emotion and intimacy with fellow human beings. Management style will inevitably change because the future corporation is faced with a different challenge. The new challenge will be to tap not the physical labor of the individual, but his inner thoughts, his emotional and spiritual energies. This will require an intimate culture. Tasks will be accomplished when individuals are able to share openly without risk of emotional punishment, when managers have intimate knowledge of their subordinates' thoughts, feelings, and needs. But intimacy requires a strength and security that are not promoted in most American corporate cultures.

The Integrity Principle

Decision making in our organizations has become dominated by a concern for legalisms, regulations, and precedents. Integrity is the foundation upon which must be built all other values, and upon which rest the trust and relationship between individual and corporation. The ability to discriminate between what is honest and what lacks honesty is a skill that is critical to the establishment of the new corporate culture. We live in a society of law and legalism in which the lawyer has become the corporate high priest of right and wrong. That which is honest has become confused with that which is permissible by

law. Our managers and corporations generally adhere to what is legal. However, the law does not specify what is right, and it is a poor guide to making the decisions that will establish trust and unity between individuals and organizations, between customers and suppliers. These relationships have deteriorated to the point where they represent a drag not only on productivity within major corporations but also on their ability to market their products in this country. When managers are able to discern and act on that which is honest in spirit, trustful business relationships will be reestablished.

The American corporation is not dearly loved by the populace. The corporation is viewed as an impersonal edifice of materialism. It neither inspires man to achieve his highest aspirations nor inspires the loyalty and devotion that would contribute to its own purpose. American managers have a tradition of pragmatism which is a traditional source of strength. However, this pragmatism may require the balance of new values that are lofty, that do inspire the imagination, engage the loyalty and devotion of the common man.

The search for meaning and significance is a central characteristic of the human soul. Every person would like to find meaning and significance in his or her work. How many corporations provide this opportunity? The degree to which an organization is perceived to be in pursuit of and is acting consistent with noble ideals is the degree to which it is possible for the individual to believe that his or her efforts on behalf of that organization will be personally meaningful and significant. It is this spiritual deficiency in the culture of our corporations that we must address.

NOTES

1. Drucker, Peter. *Management: Tasks, Practices, Responsibilities.* New York: Harper & Row, 1974, p. 74.
2. Pascale, Richard Tanner, and Anthony G. Athos. *The Art of Japanese Management.* New York: Simon & Schuster, 1981, pp. 177–188.
3. Ibid, p. 184.
4. Reich, Robert B. *The Next American Frontier.* New York: Times Books, 1983, pp. 140–141.
5. Ibid. p. 157.

6. Livesay, Harold C. *American Made: Men Who Shaped the American Economy.* Boston: Little, Brown & Company, 1979, p. 123.
7. Note: The term "The Metal Company" is used to protect the anonymity of the actual firm.
8. Novak, Michael. *The Spirit of Democratic Capitalism.* New York: Simon & Shuster, 1982, p. 31.
9. Drucker, pp. 9–10.

Solving the Hotel's Human Problems

WILLIAM FOOTE WHYTE

Editors' Note: This article was written by William Foote Whyte in 1947. It anticipates much of what would later be called Total Quality Management. As the Japanese would show in the 1980s and effective U.S. companies would show in the 1990s, putting people together effectively is good business. Whyte's article is not just an important historical article—he writes about the very best of what we can do today. Paying attention to the people process can yield large benefits for an organization.

THE PEOPLE MAKE THE ORGANIZATION

"Unless you can build up good, stable, and cooperative relations among people, you don't have an organization which will continue to function and make a profit."

That point of view is steadily gaining ground in American management. Forward looking executives are now casting about to develop better ways of handling the human problems of their organizations. This effort has led to a great expansion in personnel departments.

In general, the hotel industry has lagged behind other industries in the development of personnel work, and many hotels are now seeking to move ahead in this area. This is a healthy sign, but I suggest that the hotel industry would be making a grave mistake if it simply tried to catch up with what other people are doing.

There is valuable work being done in some of industry's personnel departments. There is also much time, effort, and money being expended in activities which are either useless or of very limited value because they fail to grapple with basic problems. Therefore the hotel which is now launching its own personnel program should not seek to imitate established practices but should rather try to develop a program tailor-made to its own needs.

NO MAGIC FORMULAS IN PERSONNEL WORK

What does the executive or department head need to know in order to manage his organization effectively? There are many answers to this question, but I suggest that if he can answer the following two questions, he can then get all the other answers he needs to have. Here are the questions:

1. How can I get accurate information on the functioning of my organization?
2. How can I act on such information so as to improve the functioning of my organization?

The efficient hotel management today keeps elaborate records of the financial aspects of its business, and these serve as one sort of measure of the functioning of the organization, but behind the figures stand the people—workers, supervisors, and de-

Reprinted with permission of William Foote Whyte from "Solving the Hotel's Human Problems," by William Foote Whyte, 1947, *Hotel Monthly*.

partment heads. If their relations with each other are not organized effectively, costs go up. If there is friction among workers, between workers and supervisors, or between departments, it is impossible to give cheerful, thoughtful, and efficient service, and sooner or later the loss of guests will show up in the balance sheet.

We have found in our research that a company may have good systems for employee selection and training, for merit rating and job evaluation; it may pay good wages and provide insurance and other benefits, and still it will suffer from low employee morale, from absenteeism and labor turnover, from internal friction and low efficiency—unless the human relations of workers, supervisors, and department heads are organized with skill and understanding. On the other hand, as an effective organization is built up, it becomes easy to develop whatever personnel systems are helpful in improving efficiency and job satisfaction.

The moral is: there are no magic formulas in personnel work that produce a good organization. The first principle for effective action is: *Know your organization.*

HOTEL RADISSON SCENE OF EXPERIMENT IN BETTER PERSONNEL RELATIONS

It is one of the aims of the Committee on Human Relations in Industry to provide executives with the information they need for effective action. However, we feel that in the long run the business should not have to rely upon a university for such a vital function. It should be possible to develop the function within the organization itself. To learn how this might be done, it was necessary for us to experiment.

I am happy to say that the first opportunity for such an experiment was offered us by the hotel industry by the Hotel Radisson in Minneapolis, owned by Thomas J. Moore and Byron E. Calhoun, the latter until recently in active charge of the Radisson. Mr. Calhoun was seriously concerned over labor turnover and other human relations problems. In his two years as vice-president and general manager, he had not been able to find a personnel manager who was effective in this field. We agreed to provide him with a

man trained in our human relations research on condition that he set up the project on an experimental basis, making provision for research within the personnel department.

In mid-July of 1945, the project got under way with the following personnel:

Meredith Wiley, who had a year's training in our field research and an M. A. degree in Business Administration, became personnel manager of the hotel.

Edith Lentz, who had a year of research on the human problems of the restaurant industry, went in as a research assistant. While the whole project was financed by the hotel, Miss Lentz was on the payroll of the university being directly responsible to the Committee on Human Relations in Industry. She worked closely with Mr. Wiley throughout the project, spending full time in the hotel. She had no administrative responsibilities so her time was entirely devoted to research.

So that we would have a full record of the experiment, we arranged to have the work supervised by the Committee on Human Relations in Industry. Copies of all interviews and other data typed out by Miss Lentz or Mr. Wiley came in to the university, and it was my job, representing the Committee, to keep fully informed on developments at the Radisson and help Mr. Wiley and Miss Lentz to interpret the research findings. I spent something more than one day each month at the Radisson for this purpose and to discuss strategies of action with Mr. Wiley and Miss Lentz. I also conferred regularly with Mr. Calhoun and other hotel executives to interpret to them the development of the personnel program and get their ideas upon problems that needed attention.

CLEARED WITH UNIONS FIRST

On our first day at the Radisson, we sat down with officials of unions having contracts with the hotel and explained our intentions to them at some length. They pledged their cooperation, and there has never been any difficulty in our relationships from the first day on.

We were also formally introduced to department heads and supervisors of the hotel in a first day meeting. Here our reception was, if not hostile, at least reserved. People wondered what changes we were to bring about and quite sensibly withheld judgment until they should have a chance to see how the new program would affect them.

The first three months served as an adjustment period. Mr. Wiley's first job was to fit himself into the organization. While he tried to become familiar with people and problems, he consciously avoided bringing in any changes. While some people concluded from this slowness that nothing at all was going to happen, the period did serve to allay anxieties and build relationships between personnel manager and executives which were essential to all future actions.

Miss Lentz began her research at once. She was free to move about the organization and interview workers, supervisors, and department heads upon the human problems they faced. In her approach, she avoided interruptions, argumentation, and moral judgments and made every effort to draw full expression of problems not limited to the answering of specific questions. The problem was to get people to talk out their thoughts and feelings about their work situation.

Miss Lentz also fitted herself in through helping out with the work of certain departments at rush times. Since she had served as a waitress for three months in our restaurant study, it was easy for her to take on this role.

Before the end of the first three months, we had, through the observations of Mr. Wiley, and through Miss Lentz' research, a general picture of the human problems of the hotel, with detailed information on two departments. It was time to begin to act.

THE PROBLEMS OF THE ORGANIZATION

The actions of Mr. Wiley must be seen against the background of the problems that became evident in the first three months. This is the picture as we saw it.

1. Interdependence of Departments—Pressure of Customers.   The hotel was functioning at capacity, with a tremendous demand for rooms and for food and drinks. Even so the customer demand was highly variable, running from the occasional slack day to the peak of activity of large banquets and the sustained

pressures of market weeks. Within a single day, especially in the food departments, the tempo of activity was highly cyclical so that neither workers nor supervisors had the emotional security of a steady routine.

All organizations are made up of parts which are interdependent at least in the sense that one part cannot cease functioning without affecting other parts, but the interdependence of departments in a large hotel is much greater than this minimum. There the activities of many of the departments must be synchronized from hour to hour, from minute to minute, and, in some cases, even from second to second. To serve customers well in the dining rooms requires skillful timing of activities of employees in kitchen and dining rooms. To move guests in and out of rooms efficiently requires close cooperation between front office and housekeeping department and between housekeeping and laundry departments.

At some points, departments mesh so closely together that it is difficult to tell where one leaves off and the other begins. This gives rise to confusions in authority and responsibility. When this is added to the pressures of customers reacting through the highly interdependent parts of the organization, the human relations problems become acute.

2. Autocratic Supervision!   To meet the demands for quick action, the hotel tends to develop an autocratic structure in which orders are communicated rapidly from the top down but there is little effective communication from the bottom up.

3. Unclarified Personnel Policies.   The hotel had been under its present management for only two years, and that period had been one of great expansion of personnel and organizational change in order to meet the war boom volume of business. In such a situation, it was inevitable that there should be some confusion and uncertainty remaining on certain items of personnel policy.

4. Union Management Friction.   While the hotel had signed union shop contracts, and the top executives wished to get along with the unions, no adequate grievance procedure had been developed. Cases were taken up outside of the hotel with a representative of the hotel association. Since he repre-sented a large number of hotels, this often meant seri-ous delays in handling grievances. And it meant also that he did not have an intimate knowledge of the in-ternal problems of the Radisson.

RESEARCH AND ACTION

We got into action first upon problems of communi-cation in the organization. The discussion was opened in a meeting of department heads, which I was asked to address. Bringing in research materials from outside of the hotel, I pointed out the human relations difficulties which arose in organizations where communication was channeled predomi-nantly in one direction, from the top down. I empha-sized the importance of the interviewing approach and the holding of group meetings to build up two-way communication.

Department heads participated in the discussion with apparent interest, but the general reaction seemed to be that these were nice theories which would never be worked out at the Radisson in practice. At this point, Mr. Calhoun came into the discussion and gave his emphatic endorsement to our point of view. As he made it clear in this and in subsequent meetings that it was the policy of management to ease downward pres-sures and build upward communication, he made pos-sible the important changes which were to follow.

TROUBLE SPOTS UNCOVERED
IN COFFEE SHOP

At about this time (three months from the beginning of the project), Miss Lentz had completed her study of the coffee shop, and Mr. Wiley was prepared to act on this. The study showed that waitresses and first line supervisors were working under heavy pressures from above and felt that they did not have sufficient oppor-tunities to bring their problems to the attention of higher authorities. In addition to the pressures of cus-tomers, the waitresses were troubled by friction with kitchen personnel and food checkers. There were also several problems of physical conditions, the chief one involving the water spigot. At this time the waitresses had to walk the entire length of the large kitchen to fill

their water pitchers. This added appreciably to their work load, but, more important than that, it seemed to symbolize management's lack of concern for the em-ployees, as they had complained about the condition without getting any action.

For some months previous to the beginning of the study, this had been a major trouble spot in the or-ganization. Turnover figures had been the highest of any department in the house, averaging close to 50% a month, which meant, of course, that no stable work group was being built up.

The easing of pressures from above, which fol-lowed the discussions described earlier, was particu-larly noticed in this department. The waitresses were soon heard to comment upon the relaxing of emo-tional tensions. Miss Belliveau, the department head, also reacted favorably to this change and was able to handle her supervision with the quiet confidence so important for stabilizing the department.

After conferring with Mr. Wiley, Miss Belliveau began holding meetings of all members of her depart-ment to discuss dining room service problems. The waitresses spoke freely in these discussions and af-terwards spoke enthusiastically about the meetings.

The meeting approach was also used to handle problems of dining room–kitchen relations. Miss Belliveau suggested to Mr. Wiley that it might be a good idea to ask chef Bernatsky (now food and bev-erage manager) to sit in on one of the discussions. Mr. Wiley agreed and went to the chef to explain the developments and issue the invitation.

Thanks to skillful handling by Mr. Bernatsky and Miss Belliveau, the meeting brought about a remark-able change in the kitchen–dining room relations. The waitresses began by expressing their complaints against kitchen employees and the organization of work in the kitchen. Mr. Bernatsky encouraged them to speak freely, and it was evident that they were get-ting many long-standing complaints off their chests. Mr. Bernatsky was able to meet some of the com-plaints by promising to make specific changes in the kitchen. Where he was not able to make changes, he explained his problems thoroughly to the waitresses, and they seemed satisfied to let these complaints drop. When all the waitress complaints had found expres-sion, the direction of the meeting underwent a striking change, and the waitresses began asking Mr. Bernatsky for his advice on how they should handle certain problems they faced in getting service from the kitchen. Under these circumstances, Mr. Bernatsky was able to get across advice and direction which would never have been acted upon had he presented them in lecture form.

Removing the Trouble Spots

The meeting led to action by the chef on a number of counts. The waitresses complained that Sunday morning was the worst time for kitchen–dining room relations, and Mr. Bernatsky agreed to give particular attention to this problem. They suggested a more convenient arrangement of fruit juices so that they could be served without delay. This was worked out. They complained particularly against one cook whose station seemed to be a major friction point. This man was transferred to another station, so that he would not be in direct contact with the waitresses.

Other examples of action growing out of the meeting could be cited, but the list itself is not the important thing. As Mr. Bernatsky himself pointed out to us, once before he had tried to improve the arrangement of work for waitresses by changing the position of cups and saucers at one station. The waitresses had greeted the change with indignant protests. On the other hand, the changes growing out of the meeting were greeted with enthusiasm. As one waitress said,

> Honest, it's like a miracle. That kitchen's a different place. It's almost a pleasure to go out there, no fooling!

The moral here is simple. When changes are made without the consultation of people affected by them, the people generally oppose the changes. Only when changes grow out of such consultation do they make a contribution to employee morale as well as to efficiency.

The spigot problem was taken to Mr. Calhoun by Mr. Wiley. We found that the same plea had come up a year earlier and had been turned down on the grounds that a completely new set of dining rooms and kitchen were to be built as soon as materials and labor were available. But in the course of that year

the volume of restaurant business had doubled and it was still impossible to say when the new construction could begin. Under these circumstances, minor physical adjustments were certainly in order, Mr. Calhoun felt, and he ordered the change made. Placing the spigot inside the dining room meant a great saving of work for the waitresses, but, more important than that, it served to demonstrate to the girls that they could make their needs felt and that management was genuinely concerned with their problems.

In Four Months Labor Turnover Dropped to 7.7%

By the end of the year, the departmental labor turnover which had been running between 35% and 50% a month up to July had dropped steadily and was down to 8.0% in November and 7.7% in December. There had been no similar trend in figures for the whole hotel where the figures ran steadily close to 20% a month. From having the highest turnover record, the department dropped to where it had become one of the most stable in the organization.

To add to these statistics, we can cite the judgment of Mr. Calhoun, Mr. Bernatsky, and Miss Belliveau that the work was running much more smoothly. And Mr. Calhoun emphasized that this meant the dining room was meeting a much higher standard of service to the customers than had been the case some months before. He added the impression that the whole "atmosphere" of the dining room had changed for the better.

HOUSEKEEPING DEPARTMENT TACKLED NEXT

The next efforts were made in the housekeeping department where Mr. Wiley worked closely with Mr. Hale, the department executive, and Mrs. Grogan, the assistant department head. Here, as in the following case, I will not attempt to describe all developments but will limit myself to points which illustrate new possibilities in this approach to personnel work.

The group meetings which had proven so successful in the dining room were instituted here also, under the leadership of Mr. Hale and Mrs. Grogan.

Miss Lentz was invited to sit in on all meetings and keep a detailed record of their progress. She had already done considerable interviewing in the department, so she was by that time well known to the employees. Following the third weekly meeting, she made a quick canvass of employee sentiment, asking more than 25 of the maids (more than half of the total in the department) how they felt about the meetings. In general, she found that the maids welcomed the meetings and felt they were exceedingly helpful, but a few of the women expressed certain criticisms and reservations. Some mentioned points in the conduct of the meetings which made them uneasy and hesitant about expressing their thoughts and feelings.

Miss Lentz turned over these data to Mr. Wiley and discussed them with him. Mr. Wiley then laid out before Mr. Hale and Mrs. Grogan both the favorable and unfavorable reactions. On the basis of this discussion, Mr. Hale and Mrs. Grogan agreed as to how the future meetings should be conducted so as to improve their effectiveness. Miss Lentz's subsequent observations showed that they were following through on the revised plan of procedure with skill and understanding. And when she later checked employee sentiment again, she found that the former criticisms were no longer being expressed.

In this case, the personnel department provided not only advice and consultation but also a testing of results so that the department heads were able to increase their effectiveness on the basis of analyzed experience.

FOOD CHECKERS HAVE PROBLEMS, TOO

Miss Lentz next took up a study of the problems of the food checkers, who are stationed in the kitchen to total the checks of waiters and waitresses and to see that the food is served according to specifications. She found here serious problems in supervision and interdepartmental relations, which were worked on by Mr. Wiley. Since these problems did not involve any new applications of our personnel approach, they will not be discussed here.

In her work with the checkers, Miss Lentz developed an interesting combination of efficiency engineering with human relations research. She found

that the women complained that the work load was too heavy, that too many things had to be done at the same time. Specifically, they had difficulty in handling the room service phone at the same time as they were checking the trays of waiters and waitresses serving three different dining rooms through the single food checking stand.

On the basis of her observations and interviews, Miss Lentz made up a work flow chart which clearly illustrated the existing difficulties. Mr. Wiley set this before the executives of the restaurant section and also presented Miss Lentz's other data. After a lengthy discussion, they worked out two major changes.

Redistribute the Work Load

The room service phone was taken away from the checker stand, thus relieving the checkers of considerable work pressure. The work flow was then rechanneled. To serve two of the dining rooms, waiters and waitresses walked in the same direction. No change was made here. But waitresses serving the third dining room had to cut across the traffic. That dining room had its own checker's stand which, up to that point, had been used only to check beverages. Food checking was combined with beverage checking at this stand so that the food checking facilities were doubled. This redistribution of the work load was accomplished with the addition of just one employee.

The checkers reacted to the changes enthusiastically. One of them expressed the common view in this way:

Honestly you have no idea how different it is. It's just a new job altogether, that's all. It isn't only that the work is cut almost in half, either, but the confusion is so much less.

You see, when all the dining rooms were busy at once, before this new stand opened, half the waitresses would go in one direction when they left the stand, and the others would want to go the other way. They were forever getting into each other's way, and we were always afraid of trays upsetting or food splashing over the dishes. Not only that, but we didn't have time to be polite to people.

The room service phone would ring all the time, and we were just too busy to be courteous. I admit it, I know myself. I just had to be short with people. We

*tried to cut out every unnecessary work to save time.
Now—oh, I feel swell today. It is like heaven, really
it is.*

The waitresses and waiters noted the difference
and were particularly appreciative of the new checker
stand. As one of them said,

*Say, that new checker's stand is swell, isn't it? That
certainly made a big difference in our service. Gee, we
used to have to stand around and all the food would
get cold while we waited. Then the customers would
gripe. It wasn't our fault, it was just that we had to
wait out at that checker's desk. I'm sure glad this new
desk is in operation.*

In the course of the year, Miss Lentz also did research in the front office, the laundry, the service department (bellmen), and one of the other dining
rooms, and, of course, her contacts through the organization brought in scattered data on departments not
specifically studied. Since my emphasis here is on
outlining a new role for the personnel man, it is not
necessary to go into details on this research.

DEVELOP WAY TO GET QUICK
ACTION ON GRIEVANCES

In the course of developing his work with management, Mr. Wiley worked out a new relationship between management and the unions. This was not
done according to a prearranged plan. We would have
preferred to have line supervisors and executives act
for management on grievances, but at the time our
work began grievances were not being handled inside
the hotel at all. Recognizing the well-established
principle that grievances should be handled quickly
and in well-defined organizational terms, Mr. Wiley
became increasingly active in this field. Union stew-
ards and business agents would come to him with
grievances. He would then go to the appropriate department head to discuss ways of handling the problem. As Mr. Wiley had more experience in handling
grievances than the department heads, this naturally
resulted sometimes in the personnel manager steering
the executive toward the solution which he felt was
required by the union contract and by good industrial
relations practices.

In many cases there was ready agreement on the
disposition of the grievance. In some cases, the department heads accepted Mr. Wiley's opinion with
reluctance. They were, of course, free to stand on
their own opinion and appeal to Mr. Calhoun for support, but in all cases so far grievances have been settled without appeal to the top.

According to all our evidence, the personnel
manager's handling of grievances has not given rise
to any serious problems in his relations with supervisors and executives. On the other hand, we find the
union leaders very pleased with the new arrangement. They can get quick action on grievances, and
they are now dealing with a coherent management
policy in this area, so they know much better what to
expect. Nor does this mean that all of the cases are
settled in favor of the unions. On a number of occasions Mr. Wiley has told them that, on the basis of his
investigations, he feels the grievance is not justified.
So far they have accepted his judgment in these
cases. They seem to be convinced that he will bring
in a favorable decision for the union, when the facts
warrant it, and therefore they are willing to trust his
honesty and his judgment when the decision goes the
other way.

We do not look upon this present arrangement as
the ideal way of handling grievances. However. in
working out human relations problems, we always
have to start from where we are and measure progress
from that point. The present system is clearly a great
improvement over the former situation in which
grievances were not handled within the hotel at all. In
this field, as in others, it is Mr. Wiley's aim to build
up a situation in which department heads make the
decisions upon problems arising in their own departments. In the future it is likely that the department
heads will play an increasingly active part in the settlement of grievances.

DEFINING THE PERSONNEL MAN'S ROLE

As we worked on the problems of the Radisson, we
clarified our ideas on the personnel man's new role.
We present here what seem to us the principles of effective action that can be applied in developing this
work in other organizations.

1. Keep People's Confidences. In the course of time, if they do their jobs skillfully, the personnel man and especially his research assistant will be entrusted with much highly confidential information: how the individual feels about his superiors, his anxieties about his own job performance, his reactions to management rules, the personal problems he faces outside of the organization, and so on. Such data are essential for the understanding of human relations, and yet, if allowed to leak out, they can be highly damaging to the informants. Personnel men and research assistants must set for themselves a high standard of professional ethics on this point. They must promise to keep confidences, and they must keep their promises. People will naturally be suspicious in the beginning, but when they find that the things they have allowed to slip out when under emotional pressures do not come back at them from other sources, they learn to trust the personnel man and the research assistant.

2. Don't Ask Who Is to Blame for the Problems You Find. Try Instead to Explain Why People Act as They Do. In industry, as in other social structures, it is customary for those in positions of responsibility to try to determine who is to blame for the problems discovered and then to fix upon an appropriate form of punishment. At its worst, this approach leads to the punishment of innocent scapegoats. At best, the approach may fix responsibility for mistakes in a manner which will generally be thought fair, *but* it does not tell us why the individual made the mistake or what actions should be taken to help him function better in the future. We often find people handling their problems badly because they are under heavy pressure from superiors, they are facing conflicting demands, or they are otherwise bound by conditions beyond their control. In such cases, criticisms from superiors or from other people only accentuate the problems. On the other hand, an analysis of human relations will often point to changes that will relieve pressures and solve problems.

Furthermore, if the personnel man seeks to lay the blame, he gets involved in the politics of the organization. He is known to be *for* some people and *against* others, and all his actions are discounted on

this basis. Only if he casts aside moral judgments and analyzes behavior in terms of human relations can he gain a reputation as a disinterested technician of organization.

3. Work with the Man Most Directly Concerned with the Problem. For example, if a study of a department brings out certain problems involving the relations of the department head with his subordinates, every effort should be made to work these out through consultation between personnel man and department head. The department head will naturally fear that all his failings will be reported over his head and that he will then be subjected to increased pressure from his boss. Such fears will further disturb his performance and make him hostile toward the personnel man. On the other hand, if the department head gets help in the analysis of his problems and in the improvement of his performance, he can add to his sense of confidence and security.

We should not give the impression that this result is easily obtained. The problems of changing the behavior of supervisors are exceedingly complex and difficult, and we still have much to learn on this score. In some cases it may prove impossible to change behavior through working only with the man most directly concerned, and we have found it necessary to take problems up at higher levels (which involves us in problems to be discussed below). However, Mr. Wiley has always made every effort to solve each problem at the lowest possible level and thus to avoid suspicion that his job is to carry tales to the boss. We feel that this has been an important factor in building confidence in the program.

4. Work with the Man at the Top to Help Him Understand His Impact upon the Organization. I have already noted the key importance of the top executive in setting the pattern in human relations for his organization. This means that, unless the boss is willing and able to examine his own behavior, the personnel program will be seriously handicapped. It takes a big man to be able to do this. At the Radisson, we were extremely fortunate in this respect. In making arrangements for the project, Mr. Calhoun told us that he was chiefly interested in getting help for himself. He recognized that he sometimes failed to gain his ends through mistakes in the field of human relations. He hoped to improve his own social skills and understanding. Mr. Wiley and I found in the course of our work that we were indeed able to make suggestions to Mr. Calhoun involving his own activities and have them acted upon with skill and understanding. At the same time, we learned a great deal about problems at the executive level through our discussions with Mr. Calhoun.

At first we were reluctant to take up lower-level problems with the top executive even when they could not be worked out below him because we were not sure how Mr. Calhoun would handle these situations. However, we found that this was not as serious a problem as we had first anticipated. In the first place, the personnel man does not present the only channel through which the executive can become aware of human relations problems. He may learn that "something is wrong somewhere" through checking figures for labor turnover, through receiving union complaints, through a drop in production figures, or in still other ways. The personnel man then does not become involved in bringing an unsuspected problem to the attention of the executive and thereby perhaps exposing one of his subordinates to criticism. In all cases so far in our experience, it has been possible to start with discussion of problems whose existence is already recognized by the executive and, on the basis of research, to clarify the nature of the problem and to outline possibilities for effective action.

As time went on, we were able to present Mr. Calhoun with an increasingly full picture of the human relations problems of his organization. We could do this without jeopardizing the positions of his subordinates because discussions were not pitched on the level of laying the blame and "reading the riot act." Mr. Calhoun asked two general questions: What is the nature of the problem? And what can I do to help solve the problem? Discussions in this area led to greater social understanding and the development of more effective executive leadership.

5. *Present Facts and Interpretations, but, as Much as Possible, Let the Man Who Must Act Decide for Himself upon His Course of Action.* We do not believe that the personnel man should take it upon himself to solve all human relations problems for supervisors and executives. If he proceeds in that way, they will either rebel against his "interference" or else become so dependent upon his judgment that their own capacities are seriously weakened. Instead, it should be the function of the personnel man to build a problem-solving organization. That means that he should present supervisors and executives with the facts and interpretations which he feels are necessary in reaching sound decisions, but the actual decision-making process should be left to those in positions of line responsibility. While this may lead to mistakes in judgment which could be avoided by following the personnel man, the procedure seems to us essential in building up the long-run effectiveness of the organization. The supervisor or executive cannot learn to handle his human problems with skill and understanding unless he works out his own decisions.

6. *Develop Personal Influence, but Avoid the Use of Authority.* We feel that the personnel man should function in a strictly advisory capacity. As he learns to help the line officials toward the solution of their human problems, he will gain a constructive influence in the organization. But if he tries to exert authority—to tell line officials what they must and must not do within their departments—then he only confuses the structure of the organization and creates friction.

We have heard some personnel men say they could do a better job if they only had more authority. This is, we feel, an illusion. In general, we find that people cannot effectively serve two bosses. The only person who is in a position to lead and direct them is the line official who has the full-time responsibility for this job. The personnel man can be much more effective if he serves as advisor and aid to the line than if he tries to direct activities himself.

7. *Leave Rewards and Punishments in the Hands of the Line.* This means that promotions and salary increases, demotions and firings should all be handled by the executives. It means that reprimands for poor performance should be given by line officials and not by the personnel man, and the personnel man should avoid giving the impression that he is putting people "on the spot" with the boss. While he may compliment people for doing a good job, the really important recognition must come from line executives. While not handling rewards and punishments himself, the personnel man can work with supervisors and executives to improve their performance so that they may win top management's approval and avoid adverse criticism. The administration of these incentives should remain with the executives.

CONCLUSIONS

Our new approach to personnel work may be summed up in this way:

1. The personnel man, in this project, had command over a body of scientific knowledge. While we fully recognize the relatively undeveloped state of the science of human relations, the personnel man had been trained in this field through course work, and, more importantly, through a year of field research. On human problems, therefore, he based his judgment on this background of knowledge and was less likely to be led astray by his personal reactions to the individuals involved.

2. The personnel man had access to human relations research dealing directly with the problems of his own organization. When problems came to his attention, he did not need to guess at their origin or solution. His judgment was based upon past studies made by his research assistant or upon studies specifically designed to bring in data upon the problem in hand.

There are certain other aspects of human relations research that deserve special mention here. When the research interviewing program is skillfully carried out, that in itself tends to relieve tensions and have a generally favorable effect upon human relations. However, the interviewing approach alone cannot be counted on to solve many human relations problems. For example, in one department the first month of interviewing was accompanied by a striking drop in labor turnover. We hoped that this favorable result could be capitalized upon by prompt action upon the problems the interviews brought to light. Unfortunately, due to problems which need not be discussed here, the necessary changes did not take place until six months later. In the meantime,

turnover figures had jumped back to their former high level. According to our interpretation, the drop in turnover was due only in part to the feeling of relief on the part of the employees who had a chance to get their problems off their chests. They also felt, though no promises had been made to them, that the interviews would bring favorable changes in human relations. When these changes did not follow, the morale profit from the interviewing was dissipated. Therefore, if the employees are given to understand that there is a relationship between interviewing and action, the benefits from the interviewing program can only be preserved if there is a follow-through.

In the course of our research, we tied in certain aspects of management engineering (studies of the flow and organization of work) with our human relations approach. I feel that this is a necessary development. Too many managements look upon efficiency and human relations as two sharply separated subjects. To build up efficiency, they call upon their best engineering talent to conduct time and motion studies, to set up incentive pay systems, and so on. In all too many cases, these elaborately worked-out programs fail to achieve management's objectives because they meet resistance from informal groups of workers or from unions themselves. This resistance is clearly a problem in human relations. We feel that the long-run efficiency of industry can be served best by a skillful integration of engineering and human relations programs so that any engineering changes are carried through on the basis of the best human relations knowledge available.

A personnel research program, we feel, should not end with recommendations for action. Just as the chemist and the engineer must test their plans in the laboratory, so the personnel department should be so organized that it is able to follow very carefully any action which takes place as a result of its recommendations. At the Radisson Hotel, we were able to make such follow-up studies.

My emphasis upon interviewing for relieving tensions, upon efficiency engineering and human relations, and upon the importance of testing results should not obscure the main stream of our personnel research program, which involves the detailed study and analysis of the total social system of the relations of workers to workers, workers to supervisors,

supervisors to supervisors, supervisors to department heads, union business agents to department heads, and so on. It is this study of the structure of the organization of human relations which provides the framework for all our thinking and action in this field.

3. The personnel man was not limited to bottom-level problems. He was free to operate upon problems at all levels in the organization. The results obtained were made possible only by the changes in human relations which were brought about at high levels in the organization. Had Mr. Wiley been confined to bottom-level programs, the whole program would have broken down.

4. The personnel man was given high status in the organization. He reported directly to Mr. Calhoun, the operating executive of the hotel. In the beginning, the university connection no doubt served to give status to the personnel program, but, as Mr. Wiley developed his relationships with the hotel personnel and began to bring about favorable changes, his high position became more secure, and he was listened to with increasing respect.

This report should not give the impression that the changes in human relations were entirely due to the efforts of University of Chicago–trained people. It is the essence of such a personnel program that it rests ultimately upon the social skill and understanding of the line executives and supervisors. The personnel man can serve to provide a sounder basis for executive action, but unless key people in the organization take an interest in working out human problems, nothing will be accomplished. We were fortunate that the executives came to take a keen interest in the development of the program. And here, of course, the key man was Mr. Calhoun. His intelligent interest and solid support set the tone for the entire organization. It would have been impossible for us to move forward in this experimental direction had he been hostile or even indifferent to the program. That emphasizes once more the point that a personnel program designed to meet the needs of this critical age can only be developed if it has the support and lively interest of top management.

We still have much to learn in this field, but even now we feel that the initial experiment has shown such possibilities as to give us hope that the personnel man may at last come into his own as a scientist of organization so equipped and placed that he will be able to meet the pressing human relations problems of our industrial society.

8

Why Organizational Change Fails
Unspoken Truths about Change

PAUL E. ROSSLER AND KENNETH J. KISER

Editors' Note: In working with real-life organizations, Paul Rossler and Ken Kiser find organizational change is often like so many other New Year's resolutions. Managers who hire consultants for quick fixes may do more harm than good. In this article, the authors reveal the unspoken truths most consultants refuse to tell and most managers don't want to hear.

Most change consultants have reputations that far outstrip the proven effectiveness of their advice. This article questions that advice, states unspoken truths about change, and suggests new directions.

INTRODUCTION

Frederick Winslow Taylor, one of the first modern management consultants and an early industrial engineer, gave the following change advice in his 1911 book, *The Principles of Scientific Management.*

• Organizational change requires a change in values, beliefs, attitudes.

> . . . the really great problem involved in a change . . . to scientific management . . . consists in a complete revolution in the mental attitude and the habits of all those engaged in the management, as well as of the workmen. And this change can be brought about only gradually and through the presentation of many object lessons. (pp. 130–131)

• Don't attempt the change without top management understanding; and

> . . . in no case should the managers of an establishment . . . undertake to change from the old to the new type unless the directors of the company fully under-

stand and believe in the fundamental principles of scientific management and unless they appreciate all that is involved in making this change, particularly the time required, and unless they want scientific management greatly. . . . (p. 135)

• Get expert help.

> . . . companies are indeed fortunate who can secure the services of experts who have had the necessary experience in introducing scientific management, and who have made a special study of its principles. (p. 132)

• Start slowly.

> The first few changes which affect the workman should be made exceedingly slow, and only one workman should be dealt with at the start. . . . After passing the point at which one-fourth to one-third of the men . . . have been changed from the old to the new, very rapid progress can be made, because at about this time there is, generally, a complete revolution in the public opinion of the whole establishment. . . . (pp. 131–132).

• It will take two to five years.

> It is impossible to hurry it beyond a certain speed . . . even in a simple establishment, of from two to three years, and that in some cases it requires from four to five years. (p. 131)

- Don't rush it.

> *They were . . . warned by the writer, before starting, that they must go exceedingly slowly, and that the work of making the change in this establishment could not be done in less than from three to five years. This warning they entirely disregarded. They evidently believed . . . that they could do, in a year or two, what had been proved in the past to require at least double this time. (p. 133)*

All the above should sound familiar, repeated ever since Taylor's time by organizational change consultants. Unfortunately, Taylor didn't follow his own advice and never achieved the organizational change sought to the degree hoped for. Taylor's biographies tell us the following:

- Taylor's management methods were fairly well adopted at Midvale Steel Works (before he left the company in 1890) in large part because his boss was a longtime family friend.
- He then joined the Manufacturing and Investment Company, a new paper-making venture. He failed in his job, primarily due to conflicts with the owners.
- From 1893 until 1896 Taylor worked on and off as an independent consultant on shop management. He wasn't too successful, but his professional reputation continued to grow because of publications and speaking engagements.
- In late 1896 he took over the Simonds Company of Fitchburg, Pennsylvania. His approach failed to bring the desired results, and in 1898 the plant closed. Taylor suffered a "nervous breakdown."
- While recovering, Taylor was invited to join the Bethlehem Steel Company. A little more than two years later, he was fired
- From 1901 until his death 14 years later, he spent his time primarily in promoting scientific management.

Like Taylor, most modern-day organizational change consultants and gurus have reputations that far outstrip the proven efficacy of their advice . . . and have rhetoric that far outstrips reality. Failure with purposeful, organizational change tends to be the norm—and limited, short-term success the exception.

Yet conventional wisdom, ideology, and organizational politics stifle critical examination of the very foundation on which change advice is based and change is attempted. This article conducts such a critical examination and states the unspoken truths about organizational change.

UNSPOKEN TRUTHS: WHAT NO ONE WANTS TO HEAR

Truth 1: Lasting organizational change, while being dependent on the power and influence of top management, is even more dependent on the reaction and response to the change by the value-adding employees in any system.

Much of the discussion found in both books and seminars about organizational change emphasizes persistently the importance of leadership and leader power in successful change processes. Rarely does one find mentioned the more critical influence of followers (read employees) and their power in determining the degree of success or failure of organizational change attempts, both large and small. If one reads carefully much of the current literature on "leadership" it would appear that "followers" either are nonexistent or are generally characterized by such sheeplike compliant behavior that their reactions to any change processes are irrelevant. In reality, what is known is that most employees, and even most managers for that matter, don't readily welcome and embrace change processes in their work environments.

Rarely in much of the recent literature on new workplaces, or new paradigms, or the "new organization" is even the slightest mention given to the possibility that for many if not most people, desire for stability, predictability, and certainty will be significant obstacles to overcome in any change initiatives. What compounds this challenge is the fact that top management in most U.S. organizational settings has demonstrated in the last 20 years an unfortunate tendency—we would even call it an addiction—to jump on the latest organizational change and improvement fad. As a result of this top management addiction, the majority of U.S. workers have developed a deep-seated but legitimately understood degree of cynicism toward the latest change process being touted by management and their most recent change gurus and consultants. This cynicism makes most employees at best indifferent or passively compliant and at worst hostile to proposed changes, especially if they discover what their organizations are paying the change management consultants.

In addition, often ignored in the design of most organizational change processes is the basic fact that *most Americans do not view their work or their work roles as the central aspect of their lives.* While they may see work as a necessary economic activity in a consumption-based economy such as ours, they assign much higher priority to such other dimensions of their lives as family, church, or social or recreational activities. It is to these non-work-related areas that most working people are ready and willing to devote most of their social, mental, and physical energies, rather than to their actual work roles. Understanding this would seem to suggest that the additional level of involvement and effort asked of workers in the latest change initiative thought up by top management simply exceeds what many people are willing or able to give. The concept of "commitment to change" has a nice ring to it; but in reality the active enthusiastic involvement, let alone the commitment, of large numbers of value-adding employees over the long period of time necessary for most change efforts to successfully impact or improve an organization's performance may be a very low-probability event.

In recognizing the unlikelihood that most value-adding employees will enthusiastically embrace many change efforts designed, bought, or borrowed by their organization's top management, the proponents of any organizational change initiatives must be prepared to answer (and follow through on their answer to) a question commonly asked by employees in work environments where such initiatives are about to begin: What is in this for me and my fellow employees?"

Given that the success of any number of organizational improvement approaches currently in fashion—TQM, CI, CQI, TSM, reengineering, benchmarking, and so on—appears to be ultimately more dependent on the followers' buy-in and commitment than on

the leader's (or leaders') commitment, it would seem both prudent and wise for those leaders to be prepared to answer that question promptly, candidly, and honestly.

Additionally, because work is not the central dimension of most working people's lives, many people remain mentally healthy only because they don't let themselves become overly involved in their work. Increasingly, most employees find themselves either single with children or in two-paycheck marriages with children. For these employees, striking a balance between work and family proves far more difficult, demanding, and stressful than it ever was for Ozzie and Harriet. Commitment has a nice ring to it, but in reality it is unlikely to occur in large numbers of employees to any significant degree.

Finally, given the present economic context, the rewards that could get more employees actively involved in change—better pay and job security—are the rewards management seems least willing and least likely to give today. Instead, management opts for providing recognition, job enrichment (often in the form of job enlargement), team participation, and empowerment: rewards more appropriate in a context in which jobs are plentiful and pay increases steady. (Paradoxically, when jobs were plentiful and pay increases were steady, most employees desired recognition and job enrichment; management opted to provide more security and pay.)

Truth 2: Those targeted for change differ in regard to where they are with respect to change, their readiness to change, and the paths they may take to change.

Table 8.1 portrays a realistic model of how people and organizations change and all the messiness that implies. Such a model suggests that clients (i.e., individuals, groups, or whole organizational systems) differ as to where they are in the change process; that clients can move through any number of phases in no particular order; and that once a client has moved through a phase, no guarantee exists that the client won't revisit that phase time and time again. The model explicitly acknowledges the labor-intensive nature of change. Any change agent who desires to facilitate successful change must embed himself or herself into the system and gain the client's trust. The

TABLE 8.1   The Significant Differences between a Realistic Change Model and the Typical Change Model

REALISTIC MODEL	TYPICAL CHANGE MODEL
Clients differ as to where they are in the change process.	All clients are at the same starting point with respect to change.
These phases are not necessarily well defined or distinct.	Well-defined and distinct phases take place, each with a specified set of activities and tools.
Nor do all clients move through all the phases.	All clients move through all the phases.
Nor is there a particular order in which the phases occur.	Linear, progressive movement takes place from one phase to the next subsequent phase: step 1 then step 2 then . . . step N.
Nor is there any guarantee that once a client has moved through a phase, the client will not revisit that phase time and time again.	Arrows point one way, from start to finish.
Labor-intensive nature of change is acknowledged.	Labor-intensive nature of change is not discussed.

change agent must be much more than a technician who facilitates structured, linear change processes.

Table 8.1 compares a realistic model to the typical change model offered by organizational change consultants. Although consultants advocate tailoring their change process to a client's specific needs and circumstances, they don't appear to follow their own advice, especially during pilot project implementations. The typical approach employed is to select a project that both fits the particular change process advocated and provides an early success, then to choose participants carefully and hold their hand while guiding them through the process so as to produce an early and visible success. Such an approach ensures that little will be learned and no widespread applicability will result. In addition, consultants tend to label as "bad clients" those clients who fail to achieve change through their (the consultants') change process. In this traditional model there are few, if any, bad clients—only bad consultants. We need to recognize where clients are with respect to change, the type and degree of change possible with those clients, and the possible paths those clients will move through.

Truth 3: Effective implementation, not elegant design, forms the crux of the change problem; effective implementation is a low-probability event.

The change models designed and presented on flip-chart paper or overheads by consultants, managers, and staff personnel tend to be rational and elegant in design, manageable in terms of pilot project logistics, and ostensibly tightly linked to results (see Figure 8.1). Unfortunately, organizational systems have a way of mutating and rendering ineffective the very best of intentions. A great many variables—some known, some unknown; some controllable, some uncontrollable; some isolated, some interactive—determine an intervention's success or failure. Regardless of the intervention attempted, the causal chain between design and intended outcomes can break down in any number of places, and the more sophisticated the planned intervention, the more places that it can break down.

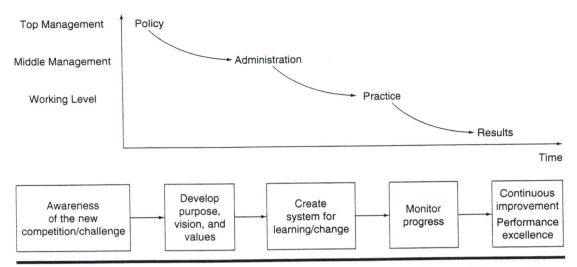

FIGURE 8.1   An Example of the Diagrams Drawn on Flip-Chart Paper by Consultants and Managers

In addition, slippage almost always occurs between design and implementation, for several reasons. First, it often isn't clear to managers and employees what the proposed change suggests they should now do. In the end, they must develop their own interpretations of what is wanted and expected of them. Second, most change is designed by senior managers, and those managers tend to push implementation details down, especially the messy ones. As a result, the proposed change is often based on unrealistic assumptions about what can be accomplished at the working level. In addition, conflicts among intended objectives often appear at the working level and must be resolved. Third, organizational inertia causes slippage: Managers and employees sometimes go on doing what they did before in the way they grew accustomed to doing it. From the point of view of change advocates, such behavior usually looks like deliberate resistance (which it sometimes is), if not sabotage. Fourth and last, the thick characteristics of organizational systems—personalities, power relationships, politics—have a way of mutating the very best of intentions. The end result: Implementation that achieves the hoped-for results in the way predicted is a low-probability event. Even in cases in which top management behaves in a way 100 percent consistent with the proposed change and the consistency between management's wishes and employees' understanding is relatively high, substantial slippage results. And oftentimes the point at which the slippage becomes most visible is the point at which the change attempt is abandoned—just where impact should occur.

Truth 4: Change tends to be incredibly labor intensive.

The belief that managers can get people (including themselves) interested in continually improving their own performance is dubious at best, false at worst. As William Morris points out in *Implementation Strategies for Industrial Engineers*, self-directed change is a low-probability event for many reasons:

- Clients, working by themselves, are seldom able to find and marshal the time, resources, knowledge, and sustained motivation to create and put into practice new ways of doing things.
- Attempts at unassisted and unsupported self-change suffer from numerous difficulties: Efforts can be simply forgotten after a while or get displaced on the client's agenda; they can get stalled by minor frustrations; they can be overcome by inertia.

- Despite the increasing presence of management conferences and training programs, change seldom occurs as a result of experts writing about or telling about or showing new methods.
- It is seldom helpful to say to a client, either directly or by implication, "If you really wanted to change, you could," or "If change is not occurring, you're not really trying."

Several of Morris's points are worth elaborating on. First, in any workplace there are a variety of working styles and preferences; the discipline and energy required to continually work smarter runs counter to many people's working styles and preferences. Even Taylor found that workers failed to follow prescribed methods over time, even when those methods resulted in higher pay for them; a supervisor or industrial engineer would have to continually provide guidance and training. Second, and perhaps more important, change requires time be spent on the part of employees; and time tends to be the one commodity that most employees perceive themselves as having very little of, especially given today's lean and mean staffing strategies. Consider, for example, that managers can be sent to short courses and conferences on change in large part because they, unlike most frontline employees, do not have to be replaced by someone while they are away from the job. And regardless of whether employees have much or little discretionary time, many seem unwilling to spend that time in pursuit of abstract organizational goals like continuous improvement, or even on more specific goals such as process improvement or reengineering. People who desire change in their personal life in such areas as lifestyle or role behavior spend enormous amounts of time and energy trying to achieve that change . . . and tend to fail more than they succeed. What can be expected with people for whom change in their work environment is someone else's agenda?

The nature of the change process itself suggests that the very efforts employed to gain organizational effectiveness tend to be, by their very nature, inefficient and labor intensive. In many of Taylor's work studies, more people were studying the work than were working. And once changes were made, super-

visors or industrial engineers would have to be continually sent to workers to reinstruct them in the proper methods. Even the famous Hawthorne experiments conducted in the plant's Relay Assembly Test Room had a direct-to-indirect ratio of 1:1, ensuring that the changes implemented in the test room could not be implemented plantwide unless top management was willing and able to substantially increase the number of skilled staff necessary to support and sustain the changes that occurred in the controlled experiment. Top management wasn't willing.

NEW DIRECTIONS

The above unspoken truths suggest the following. First, in many contexts, followers are more critical to effective implementation than are leaders. The more compatible the proposed change is with a client's past history, present culture, and present circumstances, the greater the likelihood of effective change. Change processes, therefore, *need to be designed around the needs, wants, and desires of followers* rather than the needs, wants, and desires of leaders, managers, staff personnel, and consultants. Despite Total Quality Management's emphasis on customer focus, the training that accompanies it tends to be driven by management and consultant agendas and not by the agenda of those targeted for training (i.e., the clients).

Second, because those targeted for change vary in terms of where they are with respect to change and in terms of their readiness to change, no single change model or implementation strategy can be used organizationwide. Accept pilot projects for what they are: rigged experiments conducted under ideal conditions in order to show limited success, where success gets to be defined by those in management who have a vested interest in demonstrating success. There is nothing overtly wrong with pilot projects, but resist the temptation to make them what they rarely, if ever, can be: models for broader or deeper change. The leap from pilot project to organizationwide implementation is enormous, regardless of the size or complexity of the organization.

Third, the unique needs and circumstances of clients almost guarantee that the change process will be inefficient and labor intensive. The reason most consultants propose up-front formal training—and why it is appealing to top management—is that training gives the appearance, and reinforces the impression, that change is occurring and that change can be done in an efficient way. However, few training sessions allocate time for dialogue on the legitimacy and practicality of what is being taught, let alone on some of the challenges of implementing the change (or tools or training) in a particular and unique system. When time is allocated for such dialogue, its purpose is to let people vent frustrations so the trainer can then move without interruption through the day's agenda. Changing course never seems to be an option. Because legitimacy and practicality issues are not addressed, and because past training programs have had little efficacy, most participants' bodies are present to a greater degree than their minds. And even when you have someone's mind to a great degree, no guarantee exists that what is taught is learned or, if learned, has any chance of being applied to any significant degree in the actual work setting. Again: Change seldom occurs as a result of people's reading new methods or expert's telling about or showing new methods. To get people interested in working harder, while difficult, is possible; to get them interested in working smarter is much more difficult and has seldom been done. Encouraging and helping people to work smarter is a labor-intensive and inefficient process.

Fourth, the ideal of a highly committed, high-performing workforce may sound good in boardrooms, academic journals, and conference presentations, but it is an unrealistic goal in almost any workplace. Again, work is not now, nor will it ever be, the central dimension of most working people's lives. Employees have minds of their own and control those minds. They struggle with making meaning in their lives, not only in relation to their self-presentation in personal contexts, but also through defining their self and maintaining the boundaries of that self, however defined, in an organizational context. There may be a significant number of employees who resent management's attempts to make them into management's version of a better person. The assumption that crafting a culture will automatically compel commitment to it doesn't automatically hold true. To the contrary, rhetoric, jargon, and acronyms probably do more to feed employee cynicism than they do to quell it.

Fifth and last, organizations should lower and realistically manage expectations for change. Expect change to cost much more than imagined, require much more time than expected, and produce very little in the way of long-term, systemic results. Taylor worked hard to communicate his ideas in such a way as to gain their acceptance and use by others (oftentimes not being his own best friend while doing so!). Yet Taylor, who worked in, managed, and consulted in factories, was unable to implement his philosophy organizationwide, meeting with failure more often than not. Because people, politics, personalities, and power relationships determine much of what goes on in organizations, the old cliché, "easier said than done," seems appropriate here. The world of work finds itself operating more in shades of "reality gray" than it does in the theoretical black and white of the design world. Significant individual and organizational differences make improvement phenomena not readily or easily generalized from one setting to the next. People don't leave human frailties and failings at the workplace door, to be picked up at shift's end. Shared views of the world seem unlikely anytime soon in most workplaces, as does behavior consistent with any single philosophy. Bottom line: Don't chase elusive perfection, don't embark upon any change process that has perfection as its goal, and don't hire any consultant who suggests otherwise.

REFERENCE

Morris, William Thomas. *Implementation Strategies for Industrial Engineers.* Columbus, OH: Grid, 1979.

9

Worker Cooperatives

A Democratic Alternative
to Capitalist Corporations

FRANK LINDENFELD

Editors' Note: Management graduate schools are suggesting the best companies pay attention to the people process including both its workers and its customers. Ironically, at the same time business schools are teaching a reckless renegade business philosophy of hostile takeovers, megamergers, and attention to nothing except bottom-line profit. Two major corporations often merge and lay off a large number of workers, resulting in lost jobs, desolated communities, and a quick profit for the corporation.

Where are our obligations? What is the purpose of a company? Is it just to make a profit for its stockholders? Or are there other purposes? Does a company have an obligation to its workers, the community in which it is located, the environment, and even the nation?

Many small towns face economic collapse when the major factory in town decides to close. Frank Lindenfeld offers another model. Rather than spending money with tax breaks, free rent, and other incentives to entice a new owner to buy the company, maybe the town might buy the factory and let the workers operate it themselves.

INTRODUCTION

One of the reasons I became a sociologist was to help build a better world. I have believed for a long time that oppressive structures such as giant corporations should be replaced through a process of building new, parallel, democratically organized institutions. I see the task of the sociologist as not just to describe the world, but to help change it by challenging dominating and promoting social justice. This I have tried to do through social activism, research, and teaching.

I have been particularly interested in the potential of worker cooperatives as building blocks of a more equitable economy. Worker cooperatives are enterprises that are locally rooted and democratically managed by their workforce. They are owned by their worker/members, who share their profits. Cooperatives actually have a long history, going back to the early days of the Industrial Revolution and socialist critiques of capitalism. The first worker cooperatives in North America were a by-product of wage-earners' strikes. Worker co-ops, co-op warehouses, and consumer co-ops were an integral part of the early U.S. labor movement. A major goal of the Knights of

Some parts of this article have been adapted from Frank Lindenfeld, "The Cooperative Commonwealth: An Alternative to Corporate Capitalism and State Socialism," *Humanity and Society* 21, 1 (1997), which was originally presented as his presidential address to the Association for Humanist Sociology.

Labor, founded during the 1870s, was to "establish cooperative institutions such as will tend to supercede the wage-system by the introduction of a cooperative industrial system." By the 1880s, the Knights had opened 50 or 60 consumer cooperative stores and helped form 185 to 200 worker cooperatives, including mines and various types of factories (see Curl, 1980).

Cooperative networks exist today in various countries, including the Seikatsu federation of consumer and worker co-ops in Japan, the kibbutzim in Israel, and the Lega co-ops in northern Italy. One especially vigorous model is the regional cooperative network in the Basque region of Spain in and around the town of Mondragon. Today, there are perhaps 500 to 1,000 worker co-ops in the United States and an equal number in Canada, many of them in Quebec. In the Atlantic Provinces, the Co-op Atlantic federation unites several hundred consumer and worker co-ops within a common network.[1]

Similar to the worker co-op is the democratic employee stock ownership plan, in which workers control the organization through their ownership of a majority of its stock. An estimated 10 million U.S. workers own a substantial share of company stock, and employees own a majority of hundreds of large companies. Most were set up primarily for their tax advantages and have not led to workplace democratization. However, majority ownership of company stock by employees has been accompanied by a substantial degree of worker participation in some of them. Another variation is the locally owned business in which a majority of the stock is held by community members. For example, the well-known football team, the Green Bay Packers, is owned mostly by residents of Green Bay, Wisconsin (see Shuman, 1998). While other cities must either cave in to demands for tax concessions or lose their teams to other cities, the Green Bay Packers will stay put.

Could employee-owned or locally owned, democratically managed companies and regional cooperative financial and business networks replace the existing system of transnational corporations and global investment banks? This seems an almost impossible dream, given the momentum of the present global corporate system and the immense resources of the transnationals and the wealthy few who are their main beneficiaries. Nevertheless, this task needs to be attempted. It may well succeed, as the inability of the corporate system to meet the needs of the great majority of workers and their communities becomes ever more apparent (see Korten, 1999).

One reason for my optimism is the example of the thriving Mondragon cooperative network. Part of that system's success can be traced to its beginnings in a technical school founded by a local priest, and the development of a cooperative bank providing funding and technical assistance to the fledgling co-ops (see MacLeod, 1997, and my discussion of Mondragon below).

Inspired by the example of Mondragon and other co-ops, a number of groups have been organized in the United States to raise public consciousness about the potential of worker cooperatives. They provide education, training, technical assistance, and financing for cooperative businesses. During the late 1970s I helped organize such a group in the Delaware Valley that was linked with other groups through a national federation. Though the federation did not survive long, two of its local constituent groups continued. One was the ICA Group in Boston, and the other evolved into PACE of Philadelphia.

One of PACE's accomplishments was to work with the United Food and Commercial Workers union to help workers idled by massive A&P supermarket closings to organize several worker-owned and-operated groceries, known as the O&O markets.[2] The worker-owned markets continued for some years, though only one was able to continue into the 1990s (Lindenfeld, 1992).

My interest in worker co-ops led me to Jamaica in the early 1980s, when I learned about the network of sugar worker cooperatives organized there while Michael Manley was prime minister. I teamed up with anthropologist Monica Frolander-Ulf to study these cooperatives (Frolander-Ulf and Lindenfeld, 1985). The purpose of the study was to spread knowledge about the struggles of sugar workers whose 5,000 members were organized into 23 cooperative farms. It was also to assist the co-ops with their educational program and share our observations with the organization's leadership.

To popularize the idea of workplace democracy, I have also helped to found and edit two publications, *Changing Work* and the *Grassroots Economic Organizing (GEO) Newsletter.* The bimonthly *GEO Newsletter,* in its 8th year of publication in 2000, has its own Web site, www.geonewsletter.org.

COOPERATIVE PRINCIPLES

How are worker co-ops similar to and different from capitalist companies? They are similar in that they are businesses that need to operate efficiently and earn some profit. However, they do not necessarily strive for profit maximization. Their main goals are to provide useful goods and services, benefit the local community, and retain good jobs for their members. Small cooperatives with fewer than 10 members are often organized as collectives with minimal division of labor. Larger co-ops usually hire managers who are responsible to a democratically elected governing board. Members of some co-ops actually belong to trade unions, which may set industrywide wage standards and help resolve grievances between workers and managers.

Though there are many varieties of worker co-ops, they generally share 10 basic principles.

1. Democratic Ownership and Control: One Person, One Vote.   Co-ops are controlled by their members, who participate in decisions at all levels. Policy decisions and elections to the governing board are based on one person, one vote. The resources of the organization are owned by its worker–members or by the community. In contrast to corporations, in which capital hires labor, in worker co-ops labor hires capital, paying interest for borrowed funds. Some cooperatives expect each member to invest money in the business. For example, the O&O markets required each worker–owner to put up $5,000, most of it borrowed from an employee credit union. Member investments are generally equal and do not give any extra vote or say in the business to those who invest more than the minimum.

2. Balancing Profit and Community Welfare. Whereas corporations try to maximize profits, worker co-ops strive to balance profit with worker and community welfare. Co-ops embody diverse social goals including:

- generating community employment, maintaining existing jobs, and creating good new jobs
- sustainable production of high-quality, safe, durable, and healthy goods and services without unnecessary damage to the environment
- reasonable prices to the consumer
- empowering worker–members by encouraging their education, personal growth, and learning of new skills
- maximize member participation in the organizational decision-making process

3. Equitable Compensation and Job Security.   A major goal of worker cooperatives is to provide members with adequate pay, as well as with steady, interesting, and challenging work, a positive work environment, and generous benefits and pensions. In good times, members share overtime, higher pay, or longer vacations. When business is slow, co-ops may reduce hours of work or pay rates for all, instead of laying off some members. Co-op pay scales maintain more modest differences between managers, professionals, and other workers than do capitalist companies. Some co-ops pay all members the same, regardless of the type of work they do. This was the case in some of the plywood manufacturing cooperatives in the Pacific Northwest. The Mondragon co-ops at first set a ratio of 1:3 between the lowest-paid members and the highest-paid managers; this was subsequently increased to 1:6. This contrasts to large capitalistic corporations, in which the ratio is usually 1:300. At Microsoft, Bill Gates earns more than 100,000 times the lowest paid employees, or more.

4. Profits Belong to the Worker-Owners.   In contrast with capitalist corporations, in which profits are divided among rich stock owners in proportion to their investment, worker co-op members share profits equally or in proportion to pay and hours worked. A portion of the profits may be used to support member education, or to provide health and welfare benefits such as day care or medical services; and some may be retained by the business to provide for replacing equipment or future expansion. *All the remaining profits belong to the worker–members.* They may be distributed in cash or retained in retirement accounts.

5. *Democratic Management.* Worker co-ops delegate responsibility and employ managers to help plan and coordinate the business. Worker co-ops do need middle managers and foremen, whose job it is to make sure employees are not goofing off or stealing from the company. But in worker co-ops, managers are responsible to a democratically elected board, and ultimately to the membership. Worker–members or their elected delegates have a say at all levels of the organization, from the work group level all the way up to the board of directors. To handle the inevitable disagreements between managers and workers, many co-ops have special grievance committees.

Worker co-ops strive to create a system of mutual cooperation. Managers do not impose their will but work with members to build an organization based upon mutual respect, trust, and democratic participation.[3] Many ideas are typically suggested by work groups "from the bottom up." As MacLeod (1997) points out:

> *Democratic control means participation in management and the ongoing development of the skills needed for self-management. There must be clear information available on the co-op's operations, systematic training of owner–workers, internal promotion for management positions, and consultations and negotiations with all cooperators in organizational decisions that affect them.*

6. *Limited Size.* Democratically organized workplaces often limit their size to 500 employees or fewer. If there is a need for more employees, they are usually spun off into two or more organizations. The optimum size is probably closer to 150 to 200 members, simply because organizations this size are better able to facilitate high member participation in decision making. Very large cooperatives may also be more prone to internal conflict. The only strike in the Mondragon co-ops occurred at ULGOR at a time when it had about 3,000 members (Whyte and Whyte, 1988).

7. *Safeguards and Grievance Procedures.* Although worker co-ops are democratic, there may nevertheless be conflicts and misunderstandings between managers and members. Even democratically chosen managers sometimes engage in arbitrary actions. To protect against this, some worker co-ops incorporate a union structure with a grievance procedure, providing for fair and impartial hearings and arbitration for certain kinds of disputes. Others set up special committees such as audit, watchdog, and grievance committees, which are elected by the membership and separate from the governing board.

8. *Emphasis on Education.* Worker co-ops empower their members by encouraging continuing education, personal growth, and the learning of new job skills. They educate their members to understand cooperative principles, maintain internal democracy, and help spread the cooperative movement. Many co-ops regularly allocate a portion of their budget for education and training to help develop members' skills and their commitment to the cooperative ethos.

9. *Cooperation among Cooperatives.* Worker co-ops collaborate with other cooperatives informally and as members of formal networks. They buy from and sell to other co-ops; share resources; develop plans for joint marketing; and support co-op banks, community development financial institutions, and technical assistance organizations. Isolated co-ops may find it difficult to survive in a capitalist environment. Cooperative networks like the one at Mondragon provide collective economic and political strength to spread the cooperative movement.

10. *Dedication to Social Transformation.* Cooperatives are dedicated to creating a better world. As MacLeod (1997) explains in writing about Mondragon:

> *The Mondragon co-ops reinvest the major portion of their surpluses in the Basque community. A significant portion goes toward new job development, to community development, to a social security system based on mutual solidarity and responsibility, to cooperation with other institutions (such as unions) advancing the cause of Basque workers, and to collaborative efforts to develop Basque language and culture. The co-ops proclaim their solidarity with all who labor for economic democracy, peace, justice, human dignity, and development in Europe and elsewhere, particularly with the peoples of the Third World.*

LEARNING FROM MONDRAGON

In addition to adhering to the principles I have just outlined, the Mondragon cooperatives adopted two important innovations. One is the internal capital account. A second is the development of a cooperative bank as the nucleus for a spreading network of first- and second-order co-ops. These two innovations significantly enhanced the viability of the Mondragon co-ops and deserve widespread emulation by other cooperatives.[4]

The Mondragon co-ops, for example, allocate 10 percent of their profits to education; 20 percent is reinvested in the business, and the rest kept in the form of internal capital accounts held for each worker–member. These accounts, which can grow to $50,000 or more, are refunded to members as an extra bonus on retirement. In this way, the co-ops were able to reinvest 90% of their profits, while each worker-member built up a sizeable account, providing them with an additional benefit over and above their regular pension, to be paid on retirement.

Internal capital accounts also help shield successful cooperatives against takeover by outside shareholders. In the Mondragon co-ops there are no shares that can be purchased by outsiders. Each worker has a vote in the company based on a share that has no monetary value and cannot be sold to non-members, any more than a citizen can sell his or her right to participate in national elections to a citizen of another country (see Ellerman, 1990).

Mondragon has a conscious policy of encouraging the development of other cooperatives and sharing resources with them. As new co-ops were formed, they formed an umbrella network of second-order co-ops and cooperative service organizations. Chief among these was the co-op bank, the Caja Laboral Popular. Member co-ops deposited their funds in the Caja, which was then able to extend loans to new cooperatives. The co-op bank also formed a technical assistance group that provided new co-ops with feasibility studies, market analyses, and other help.

By the 1970s this organizational effort had led to the emergence of a cooperative network that included several dozen manufacturing firms joined in an umbrella organization that subsequently evolved into the Mondragon Cooperative Corporation (MCC). The MCC also includes educational organizations, a social security system with its own medical staff serving co-op members, a research group, and a large network of associated worker and consumer co-ops. The cooperative network strengthens member co-ops and facilitates the sharing of resources. The MCC is currently organized into three major divisions, consisting of the industrial co-ops, the bank and related financial co-ops, and the consumer co-ops. By 1999, the MCC provided employment for some 30,000 persons, with annual sales of several billion dollars. The Caja Laboral Popular has accumulated substantial assets and about a million individual depositors.

The very size and scale of the MCC and its associated cooperative bank helped it to survive and meet the challenges of Spain's integration into the European Union. Though it has been financially successful and has not had to lay off workers, the MCC has been criticized for retreating from cooperative principles.[5] Critics point to overcentralization, too much power in the hands of the directors of the Caja, and investments in outside capitalist operations. Whatever the validity of these criticisms, Mondragon and other cooperative networks have a number of advantages over their capitalist competitors.

ADVANTAGES OF WORKER COOPERATIVES

Well-organized cooperatives are efficient and effective. They can save jobs, protect existing jobs, create good new jobs, and contribute to community prosperity and well-being. Above all, they enable members to control their work.

Worker cooperatives do not need as many supervisors as capitalist companies. Supervisors in a typical corporation look over workers' shoulders to make sure they are working hard and fast enough, that they are not goofing off or stealing tools. Worker cooperatives minimize such supervision and replace it with peer pressure. After all, a co-op member who provides shoddy service or makes defective products is stealing from co-workers as well as from himself or herself.

Members of worker co-ops are motivated to do a good job because they know it is their company and they will benefit from its profits. This leads to more effective customer service as well as greater worker ingenuity in coming up with suggestions to cut costs and improve operations. In addition, co-ops can reinvest profits back into the business to maintain competitiveness, modernize, and take advantage of new opportunities.

Democratic work organizations are more likely to implement policies favorable to employees than are capitalist corporations. The greater the degree of democratic participation, the greater the pressures to provide pleasant working conditions and variety in work, maximize use of members' skills and talents, and make all jobs in the organization good jobs with adequate pay and benefits.[6] Worker co-ops also tend to respect local communities and the environment, because their members live and work locally.

Workers need to feel a sense of control over their work. The biggest single gripe of corporate and government employees is that their bosses don't give them enough respect: Their ideas are not heard, and they are treated as though they cannot think. In worker co-ops members participate in decision making at both the work group level and the policy-setting level. Cooperative work groups often have considerable leeway in scheduling, hiring, and how to do their work. Decisions that affect the entire workforce cannot be implemented without the ratification and consent of a majority.

Democratically organized workplaces are effective in maintaining and saving jobs as well as in generating new jobs. Moreover, co-ops avoid laying off members during economic downturns. Instead, they cut back hours for all workers and even temporarily reduce member compensation, which is then made up when business conditions are better. When demand for the company's existing products or services diminishes, co-op worker–members have a strong incentive to suggest and help implement development of new products or services. Where there is a strong cooperative network, workers redundant in one co-op can be retrained and hired by another. During the recession of the 1980s, when other companies in Spain were laying off workers, the Mondragon co-ops were able to maintain their workforce intact.

Worker co-ops can save jobs through employee buyouts to avoid plant closings. In the United States, factory and office operations have been closed and

workers laid off as corporate executives have automated or shifted production to low-wage countries to increase short-term profits. In some cases this process has involved shutdowns of facilities that were viable but not bringing in enough profit. In such situations, it may be possible for the employees to buy out their company and run it themselves.

Among the successful large buyouts have been Weirton Steel in Weirton, West Virginia, and Algoma Steel in Sault Ste Marie, Canada. Both buyouts saved thousands of jobs in companies that would otherwise have closed, devastating their local communities. In the original buyouts of both companies, employees owned a majority of the company stock. Their ownership was subsequently diluted by the need to raise additional investment capital through stock offerings. By 1999 employees owned only a quarter of the stock in each company.

When I visited Algoma Steel in spring 1999, the company was facing some difficulties because of lower-than-anticipated sales. Integrated steel companies such as Weirton and Algoma face constant competition from minimills that utilize scrap, from imports of Asian low-cost steel, and from substitution of plastics and other materials for steel. The company had been earning profits since the buyout, but in January 2000, union and management agreed to cut 400 jobs over the next two years, which represents a little less than 10 percent of the jobs.[7] These cuts are to be accomplished as much as possible by early retirement and attrition. Despite recent losses in 1998 and 1999, the price of steel is edging upward, providing hope for the continuation of this enterprise.

Algoma hoped to expand sales with a brand new integrated strip mill that became fully operational in 1999. The company will also need to produce more steel with fewer workers to remain competitive. So far, the reductions in the number of steelworkers have been accomplished through attrition, mainly retirements. If steel sales remain sluggish, however, Algoma may be forced to lay off some of its workforce.

Despite their many advantages, worker cooperatives also face some problems attributable to their structure. And struggles between managers and ordinary workers persist, though probably to a lesser extent than in capitalist companies.

PROBLEMS AND PITFALLS

Participatory democracy requires time for members to take part in meetings and arrive at consensus decisions. The participatory process is important. Even if decision making takes more time, it helps guarantee greater commitment to the outcome. Not all members want to spend the extra time and effort to participate in meetings. Some would be just as happy to collect their paychecks and leave responsibilities and worries to activists and managers. To cope with this attitude, co-ops try to educate members about the importance of participation. Like other organizations, worker co-ops also delegate various issues to small committees and pay members for time spent in meetings.

A difficult issue for cooperatives is the hiring of nonmembers. Many cooperatives find it necessary to hire nonmembers to meet extra seasonal or project demand, but are reluctant to grant them full membership. Regular members share the profits and have equal rights to vote on general matters and on elections to the governing board; new workers become full voting members at the end of their probationary period or are let go. Unless there is a limit on the number of nonmembers, however, co-ops may degenerate into workers' capitalist organizations whose worker–owners exploit hired labor at lower wages. This re-creates the gap in power between owners and hired labor. At two of the O&O supermarkets in Philadelphia, for example, the original members were reluctant to accept new employees as owners because it would have diminished their own share of actual or potential profits. This lack of solidarity weakened the supermarkets (Lindenfeld, 1992).

A further problem for cooperatives is conflict between ordinary workers and managerial and professional staff over control of the workplace and shares of the profits. In theory, workers and managers cooperate for the good of the company. In practice, so long as an organization includes salaried professionals, managers, and hourly workers, there is a potential for conflict. A company can address this issue by reducing income inequalities and having professional staff train understudies from the workforce. However, even in the most egalitarian co-ops, those who do higher-skilled and technical work may push for a

wage differential, as well as for a greater say over issues they claim fall within their area of expertise.

At Algoma Steel the professional and middle management employees formed their own union local after the worker buyout, and joined the USWA. There are now two union locals at Algoma, a larger one representing the hourly workers and a smaller one representing the salaried professionals and other staff. When I interviewed union officials at Algoma, the tension between the two union locals was apparent. The biggest issue is how to handle reductions in the workforce to reduce costs. If it comes to a showdown, top management may well side with the hourly worker local's claim that there are still too many supervisors and other salaried employees.

WHY AREN'T THERE MORE WORKER CO-OPS?

If worker cooperatives are such a good idea, why are there not more of them in this country? Part of the answer lies in the pervasiveness of the capitalist ideology. A major problem facing the cooperative movement in the United States is the dominance of the capitalist culture. The mass media and even educational institutions help to propagate the myth that with the demise of Communism in central and eastern Europe, there is no alternative to corporate capitalism. Rising stock market prices have enticed people to invest their savings in mutual funds in the hopes of reaping large returns. Right-wing politicians have promoted the idea of transferring Social Security funds into stock market investments. Television programs, newspapers, and magazines tout the virtues of transnational corporations and globalization. Such procapitalist propaganda makes it more difficult for people to seriously consider the potential benefits of worker cooperatives.

A further problem is lack of capital and access to credit. Many banks distrust worker cooperatives and have been reluctant to extend them adequate credit. Almost by definition, capitalists have equity capital to invest. A group of ordinary workers, even with pooled assets, may not be able to come up with enough equity capital to provide their co-op with a cushion against minor business setbacks. For example, if the O&O markets had begun with $50,000 from each member instead of $5,000, more of the markets might have been able to survive in the cut-throat retail food industry, dominated by giant corporate chains with deep pockets.

In the United States there is not enough of the kind of a financial, educational, and organizational infrastructure that could help worker cooperatives succeed. If the cooperative movement is to grow, it needs to develop such an infrastructure, which might include regional cooperative development groups able to provide funding as well as technical assistance to new cooperatives.

At the university level, we need to change business education courses to turn out more managers who understand worker cooperatives and are willing to work in them. We should set up MBA programs with a specific emphasis on cooperative organization.

At the community level, we need to make available the capital needed by cooperative firms. In Canada labor-sponsored investment funds provide venture capital for community businesses, including cooperatives. Tax credits have encouraged thousands of Canadians to contribute to these funds. Such a system could be copied by this country. We also need ways to encourage the use of the enormous assets of public and union pension funds to help finance worker-owned, democratically organized firms. Loan

funds and other community development financial institutions are another potential source of credit for cooperatives.

CONCLUSION

As more and more people become disenchanted with corporate capitalism, the lack of family-wage jobs, and the inevitable downturns of the global financial system, the development of regional networks of cooperatives may appear increasingly attractive. Building worker co-ops and cooperative networks will not be easy. These democratic alternatives may expect opposition, especially once co-ops grow large enough to present a credible challenge to corporate capitalism. As cooperatives proliferate, they will be fair game for economic and political warfare against them by major corporations and by governments beholden to corporate interests.

As potential agents of social transformation, cooperatives embody the kind of participatory democratic structures that would predominate in the good society. As networks of cooperatives and democratically managed organizations proliferate, they may reach enough of a critical mass to transform the entire society into a cooperative commonwealth.

NOTES

1. For an overview of the worker cooperative movement, see Krimerman and Lindenfeld, 1992.

2. At the same time the union persuaded A&P to reopen most of the other markets under the Super Fresh label in return for wage concessions.

3. Rothschild and Whitt (1986) see collective organizations as an antithesis to bureaucratic ones. Collectives operate by group consensus, deemphasize rules, rely on normative appeals for social control, and emphasize wholistic, affective relationships within the workplace. Collectivist organizations tend to be egalitarian, have a minimum division of labor, and rely on normative and solidary work incentives instead of material ones.

4. The Mondragon co-ops were influenced greatly in their development by a local parish priest, Jose Maria Arrizmendi-Arrieta. Don Jose served as unofficial godfather to the local cooperative movement. Through his efforts a local technical school was established, five of whose graduates

founded the first of the Mondragon co-ops, ULGOR. Don Jose was also influential in the development of the cooperative bank, the Caja Laboral Popular.

5. See, for example, the 1999 issues of the *Grassroots Economic Organizing (GEO) Newsletter.*

6. An extensive literature on worker participation suggests that workplace participation is linked with higher productivity and profits. Summarizing some 43 economic studies, Levine and Tyson (1990) maintain that worker participation usually increases productivity, especially when combined with profit sharing, guaranteed long-term job security, a relatively small wage spread, and guaranteed worker rights.

7. Algoma's top management provides strong leadership to the company. However, the situation at Algoma is fairly unique in that the current contract provides for virtual co-management of the company by the steelworkers' union, USWA. Union representatives sit on the company board of

directors; the company's books are open to union inspection; and major decisions such as investing funds outside of Sault Ste Marie must be approved by vote of the union members. A joint union–management council revises and reviews the company's strategic plan, and joint union–management committees are responsible for day-to-day implementation within the various departments.

REFERENCES

Curl, John, 1980. *History of Work Cooperation in America: Cooperatives, Cooperative Movements, Collectivity and Communalism from Early America to the Present* (Berkeley: Homeward Press).

Ellerman, David, 1990. *The Democratic Worker-Owned Firm: A New Model for the East and the West* (Winchester, MA: Unwin Hyman).

Frolander-Ulf, Monica, and Frank Lindenfeld, 1985. *A New Earth: The Jamaican Sugar Workers' Cooperatives, 1975–1981* (Lanham, MD: University Press of America).

Korten, David, 1999. *The Post-Corporate World: Life after Capitalism* (San Francisco: Berrett-Koehler).

Krimerman, Len, and Frank Lindenfeld (eds.), 1992. *When Workers Decide: Workplace Democracy Takes Root in North America* (Philadelphia: New Society Publishers).

Levine, David, and Laura D'Andrea Tyson, 1990. "Participation, Productivity and the Firm's Environment," in Alan Blinder (ed.), *Paying for Productivity: A Look at the Evidence* (Washington, DC: The Brookings Institute).

Lindenfeld, Frank, 1992. "The O&O Supermarkets: Achievements and Lessons," in Krimerman and Lindenfeld, *When Workers Decide*.

Lindenfeld, Frank, 1997. "The Cooperative Commonwealth: An Alternative to Corporate Capitalism and State Socialism," *Humanity & Society*, 21, 1.

MacLeod, Greg, 1997. *From Mondragon to America: Experiments in Community Economic Development* (Sydney, NS: University of Cape Breton Press).

Rothschild, Joyce, and J. Allen Whitt, 1986. *The Cooperative Workplace* (Cambridge; UK: Cambridge University Press).

Shuman, Michael, 1998. *Going Local* (New York: The Free Press).

Whyte, William F., and Kathleen K. Whyte, 1988. *Making Mondragon: The Growth and Dynamics of the Worker Cooperative Complex* (Ithaca, NY: ILR Press).

10

Applied Sociology
and Organized Labor
On Going Better Together

ART SHOSTAK

Editors' Note: Art Shostak tells of lessons learned in his 40 years working with organized labor. In his adventure he has found various sociological roles useful, including those of advocate, consultant, board member, meeting convener, researcher, and teacher.

Looking back now over nearly 40 very satisfying years as a labor-focused applied sociologist, I recognize five related roles I have learned much from taking. I hope I have made a contribution to both the discipline I am proud to be employed in, and the labor movement I am proud to assist.

After first explaining how I came to my focus on organized labor, I plan to comment briefly on each of five roles—in alphabetical order, as each is valuable in its own way. I do so to encourage you to take up some of these roles yourself, and I fully expect you to do a helluva better job that I did.

Coursing through all of this will be my conviction that organized labor—here and abroad—needs all the help it can get, especially the kind of help possible from sociologists like ourselves. I take this position conscious of the disparity between it and the profession's preference for value-neutral posturing. I believe that an open declaration of bias is far more honest, and preferable to the myth of value neutrality.

BACKGROUND: TRYING TRADE UNIONISM

In 1958, immediately after my college graduation, I held the last of my summer student jobs. It was prob-

ably the most consequential of them all, as it helped free me of one lingering career alternative I had to dismiss before I could seriously consider the option of a career in applied sociology.

I worked this time for a wild and woolly labor union that was located in mid-Manhattan but was eager to organize workers anywhere in the Greater New York region. Indifferent to jurisdictional lines drawn to inhibit interunion warfare, my summer employer was willing to fight almost any other union for new members (drawing the line only at Mafia-linked locals known to maim and murder—without hesitation—to protect their worthless union contracts).

A no-nonsense, hard-boiled outfit, my union, District 50 of the Mine Workers, helped eliminate naive illusions I had held about organized labor. Every day I accompanied a business agent in search of shops to organize, by whatever means necessary—including signing a contract with a boss eager to freeze out other more powerful unions, a contract we would later assure bewildered workers was the best we could get for them.

Once we actually "kidnapped" the employees of a shop as they showed up for work, driving them to a storefront we had rented for the day. We then offered to release them if their desperate employer would immediately sign with us. Careful never to blatantly break the law, we bent it and manipulated it to advantage, believing the other side was doing as much in turn.

Opting Out

By the summer's end I had decided not to pursue a career as a union staffer. I understood the harsh pressures with which my union staff friends wrestled, including the need to defend their lives against Mafia mis-leaders of mobbed-up locals; the need to outmaneuver union-busting lawyers and antiunion consultants; and the need to constantly add new members to replace the small undercapitalized shops that were always suddenly going out of business.

I appreciated the argument that our members were better off for having our (top-down) contract and representation than if left entirely at the mercy of the boss. But something still nagged at and bothered me.

I realized I lacked the ability to give unquestioning loyalty to incumbent officeholders, favoring as I did something called "union democracy," a soft-headed matter that evoked wry smiles and laughter when I brought it up. I lacked the ability to hold myself above the rank and file, favoring as I did respect for and trust in the membership, another disparaged soft-headed matter. And I lacked the ability to wheel and deal in an agile and amoral way, favoring as I did the idealism I associated with (soft-headed) textbook notions of a labor "movement."

Over the years, I have often had second thoughts about this career resolution, especially as I have had the privilege of getting to know (and teach) hundreds of union staffers who live and act in the idealistic spirit of my imagined labor movement (Geoghegan, 1991). But back in 1958, it seemed wisest to move along to something more in keeping with my values and my eagerness to work with, rather than on top of, union members.

Questioning Sociology

Professors at the New York State School of Industrial and Labor Relations, from which I had just gradu-

ated, urged me to consider sociology—a discipline whose influence I had noticed coursing throughout my undergraduate years. I had never taken a course in the subject, but I had read a considerable amount of sociology written by classical theorists (Marx, Michels, Veblen, Weber, etc.) and by a smaller number of modern theorists (Bell, Lynd, Merton, Mills, Reissman, etc.). Various courses in industrial and labor relations had also made good use of books by then prominent industrial sociologists (Dalton, Gouldner, Hughes, Kornhauser, Sayles, Strauss, Purcell, Whyte, Wilensky, etc.).

Much of this material, however, was avowedly descriptive or analytical. Very little of it reported on an author's deliberate interventions based in sociological reasoning. I found this quite vexing, as I believed then (and do now) that "sociological practice" should include deliberate intervention. I did not consider library and hardcopy research "applied," regardless of how novel, difficult, or esoteric the endeavor, unless and until it resulted in an actual intervention. I wondered if sociology had room for my activist orientation, and resolved to try and prove that it did.

FIVE ROLES AS AN APPLIED SOCIOLOGIST AND UNION SUPPORTER

Now, reflecting back over several decades of mischief and possibly some accomplishment, I can "package" it all in terms of five major roles, as follows.

Advocate

Unlike some applied sociologists who shy from taking a position, believing it the prerogative only of the client, in my consulting work I champion a lot of reform options, and I urge them where appropriate on my union clients.

Some of these reforms are far less controversial than others. Typical is my urging the client to survey the ideas of the membership whenever possible, and to explain much of the rationale for a decisions once taken unilaterally by union power holders. I operate here from a foundation of basic respect for the rank and file, and I find most (though not all) union leaders willing to go along.

Other positions I advocate are far more contentious, such as favoring the (far too rare) unionization of the field staff of a union. The opposition inside labor argues this will tie the hands of the leader and force the retention of poor performers—two arguments, I remind them, we hear commonly from rabidly antiunion employers. I also recommend benign quotas to speed the advancement as staffers of talented women and people of color. And I champion more mediation and less militancy whenever a company seems trustworthy (a far too rare occurrence).

Most recently, I am busy advocating a fresh approach to informatics, the heart of the computerization process, which I regard as the single greatest opportunity for union renewal to come along in decades: the powerful mixture of telecommunications advances (fiber optics, fax, satellite waves, etc.) and computer information technology possibilities (hardware, software, the Internet, the World Wide Web, etc.). Informatics illustrates the concept of synergy, in that the result is greater than the addition of the parts would first suggest. I believe that at present informatics is the single greatest lever of change, one that is thoroughly transforming everything we know of reality—and ourselves, to boot. Informatics is making possible the "most extensive communications system on earth" (Ogden, 1995, p. 17). Organized labor thus confronts a new economy—one "all about . . . the ability to transform [organizations] into new entities that yesterday couldn't be imagined, and that the day after tomorrow may be obsolete" (Tapscott, 1996, p. 43).

As an applied sociologist I have studied labor's computerization process in considerable detail, both here and overseas (Canada, England, Israel, Norway, and Sweden). I have interviewed scores of pioneer users, observed many applications, assessed results, and especially sought out visionaries (in and outside of labor) with "blue sky" ideas about possibilities.

I now write papers, speak at union functions, and in 101 other ways struggle to get labor to appreciate how it might use computers far more creatively to reinvigorate itself. My 1999 book *CyberUnion: Empowering Labor through Computer Technology* offers fresh thinking about novel applications and aims to help labor get beyond limiting conventional ideas about this unlimiting phenomenon (Shostak, 1999).

For example, I urge unions to create interactive, rather than static, Web sites, inviting prospective members to e-mail tough questions that the union can answer in public for all to read. I urge unions to create on their Web sites a section of typical contract clauses, the better to advertise concretely what organizing can help workers secure. I urge unions to highlight very recent success stories showing just how unionizing has actually helped an employer improve its bottom line, thereby bolstering the chances the workers will continue to have a payroll. And I urge unions to study one another's Web sites so as to adopt the very best of the 21st-century innovations that pathbreaking unions continuously offer in cyberspace. I call all of this a CyberUnion model, one that can help labor organizations match the employer's formidable progress with computer applications, show the membership that the union proudly "computes," and bolster chances of making a desirable difference in American life early in the "information age" century.

As an applied sociologist with rare entry behind the scenes, I have taken to urging an ambitious alternative to the labor–computer status quo. This alternative model dares to incorporate futuristics, innovations, services, and labor traditions (F-I-S-T)—all of which go better when they build on the mind-boggling gains that have been made in computerization. Labor urgently needs the rewards possible from reliable forecasting. And the rewards that 21st-century innovations, such as computer data mining, uniquely offer. And the rewards that computer-based services, such as volume discounts on PCs, can provide. And the rewards possible from the computer-aided modernization of traditions (as in the production of interactive software rich with labor history material).

Why this unusual combination? Because in my own role as a professional futurist, I think labor has much to gain from this ancient and yet also avant-garde art form. Similarly, in my role as a labor educator, I believe labor needs the public to associate it with cutting-edge innovations. And like most labor educators, I champion both extending union-offered services (as in offering cheaper PCs for members) and celebrating labor traditions (as in offering "edutainment" prolabor videos). Overall, my CyberUnion model goes farther than anything now on the scene, and has already earned much valuable attention from a growing number of intrigued union reformers.

Consultant

Thanks to the mystique that accompanies the label "applied sociologist," I have been invited over the years to serve as a (moonlighting) consultant on a wide range of challenges. (I do not use the term "problem," as it invites mind-dulling defensiveness and unduly hasty and conservative responses.)

Typical of the many consulting jobs I have had with unions is the survey research and advising role I occupied from 1980 through 1982 with PATCO, the now infamous and no longer existent union of air traffic controllers. I prepared four national surveys of the union's 13,000 members at 4-month intervals, interpreted the data, and traveled widely to explain my findings to high-level PATCO gatherings. My major forecast—that more than 85 percent of members would honor a strike call—was vindicated by ensuing events, though nothing could have prepared PATCO for the Reagan-initiated firestorm. When the smoke lifted, the union had been decertified and 12,400 of the 12,900 PATCO strikers had been fired by the president—two events without precedent in federal employment history.

Far more positive in results was the consulting I did more recently for the American Federation of Government Employees (AFGE). This unique and progressive union asked me to survey its membership about the pluses and minuses of their computer use. I discovered far more use being made by far more AFGE members than we expected. I also found that many members were eager to get more help raising their skill level than the union could immediately provide. Further research is now seeking inexpensive and effective ways to provide such educational aid. Above all, the findings underlined high-order acceptance of computerization and even eagerness to computerize union realities. As well, AFGE asked for advice based on my findings—just the sort of request

I welcomed, as I was then spending three years writing *CyberUnion*.

Another type of consulting has had me serve labor union clients as a long-range forecaster (a very special role inside applied sociology). The Transportation and Communications Workers Union (TCW), for example, hired me to address their constitutional convention about the changes union members should expect in their industries, especially in the railroad sector, over the next 10 or so years. I have done similarly commissioned "crystal ball" talks for unions in the communications field (CWA), the electrical field (IBEW), and steel (USW), among others.

"Green Power" Board Member

For the past six years (1994 to date) I have served as a nonpaid member of a multimillion-dollar mutual fund pioneering in bringing "green power" (financial resources) to bear in labor–management relations. The fund was created after a longshore union officer, Bob Eason, read in my 1991 book *Robust Unionism* about how millions in jointly managed (union/company) pension funds might be leveraged on behalf of improving labor–management relations. Eason persuaded a finance company in Boston (MFS Investment Management Company) to back a one-of-a-kind mutual fund, Union Standard Equity, which invests 80 percent of its assets in unionized firms with a good record in industrial relations.

I serve on the USE fund's Labor Advisory Board and help vet the names of companies that are being considered eligible for investment (the fund manages more than $200 million and regularly trades in nearly 70 companies). As an applied sociologist, I offer advice about demographics that bear on company prospects, consumer market trends, company reputations, and other such social science material (Shostak, 1996b).

I also go to union functions and urge switching of pension money into USE. I believe the fund's ability to vote its proxies for good causes in tandem with other "white hat" organizations, its support for best-practices management, and its boost to labor solidarity (as from pride newly taken in "green power") make USE a very admirable social invention.

Meeting Advocate

Given how little sociologists seem to know about organized labor and the less-than-obvious aspects of this social invention, I have tried for years to help close the information gap. As a regular presenter at annual meetings of the several sociological societies in which I maintain membership, I focus each paper on some aspect of unionism I am currently studying here or abroad.

As well, and especially for the receptive annual meeting of the Society for the Study of Social Problems, I have often arranged for a panel of area union activists to share ideas with my sociology peers. These high-energy events commonly win accolades from both sides of the podium.

Similarly, wearing my hat as an applied sociologist and futurist, I regularly put together a panel of union representatives (carefully mixed by gender, race, and type of union) for the annual meeting of the World Future Society. As highbrow (and/or New Age) attendees are generally skeptical, if not downright suspicious, of labor's place in a 21st-century postindustrial world, these events are often a well-applauded and long-remembered aspect of the meeting.

Researcher and Writer

Most of the 19 books I have written, edited, or co-edited have dealt with some aspect or other of working-class life and/or labor unionism (Shostak, 1962, 1964, 1968, 1980, 1986, 1991, 1992, 1996b, 1999). Believing themselves ceaselessly under siege by the enemies of labor, most union leaders shy away from academics, talk to them only guardedly, and expect the worst from the subsequent writings of the "eggheads." As an applied sociologist I have worked very hard to earn union leaders' trust, and it has always helped to be able to note that I carry a union card myself—with Local 189, the Workers Education Local of the CWA union (Shostak, 1995).

Pervading all of my research and writing are four thoughts about the role here of the applied sociologist. First, I think it helpful to remember the First Rule of Consulting: "The client's definition of the problem is part of the problem." Accordingly, I try

never to take what my union friends (or their management counterparts) say as the gospel. This philosophy helps them—and me—struggle toward still finer insights and more honesty about the matter.

Second, I remember the First Rule of Forecasting: "A trend is not a law." Accordingly, I try never to take the 30-year decline in labor's percentage of the workforce (now down to barely 14 percent) as irreversible. I thereby remain alert to possibilities that organized labor may yet turn this around—for example, through creative computerization projects.

Third, I remember the First Rule of Sociology: "Things are seldom what they seem to be" (Berger, 1963). Accordingly, I try never to take for granted what appears obvious, what calls out for casual acceptance. I thereby force myself to search deeper, longer, and far more creatively for masked, evasive, and consequential truths.

Finally, I remember the First Rule of Communications: "Before uttering or writing a word, ask if it is truthful, kind, and necessary." Accordingly, I try never to say or word-process anything that I am not firm about, that cuts or wounds someone, or that fails to make a contribution.

Unionists seem to appreciate my use of these private guidelines, and they reward me with fascinating anecdotes and insider material that endlessly remind me of how much more there is always to learn—and how much an outsider like myself will never really entirely grasp. In turn, I respect their confidences and tell and write far less than possible—this arguably the First Rule of the Applied Sociologist; at least, if he or she wants further business from clients distinguished by very private realities and unsparing anxieties.

Teacher

In traditional university classes, I always invite in union friends as classroom speakers. Their presence helps demystify unionism, puts a human face on the movement, and provides a chance for some tough questions and worldly answers to expand everyone's grasp of labor realities. I also urge students to see various related feature films (*Norma Rae, Silkwood, Working Girl, Hoffa, On the Waterfront, Killing Floor,*

Pushing Tin, Blue Collar, etc.); and I try to process ideas spurred by such films afterwards in classroom dialogue. I recommend interviews with family members who are unionists, and I call attention to various unions on campus, the members of which might cooperate with cordial interviews. I highlight any union function occurring during the term (rallies, strike lines, etc.) and maintain that a focused and searching visit could prove worth a thousand pages of text.

Believing as I do that applied sociology requires some actual resulting change, and not simply research into or teaching about the matter, I hesitate to include this role—but think I can show some justification. Since 1961 I have taught college courses in industrial sociology and in social change and social movements. Since 1975 I have taught these two courses, and also introduced the first-ever "Futuristics-for-Unionists" course, at the AFL–CIO George Meany Center for Labor Studies, the only such resident campus in the United States.

What qualifies any of this as applied sociology is my development of a one-of-a-kind listserv (e-mail discussion group) for those who complete my course. Many continue their learning and aid the lifelong learning of all of us (especially me!) by exchanging a few times a month fresh insights, better questions, and even an answer or two via the cyberspace e-mail system we share. In this way, I like to believe my teaching may truly impact the off-campus world—a litmus test for me of what is meant by "applied sociology."

SUMMARY

The labor movement is on a roll, and more significant changes are tumbling after one another now, at the beginning of the 21st century, than ever before in labor history. If you are interested in trying out a role here as an applied sociologist, you will need to add a union bug to your business card, join Local 189 of the CWA (Workers Education), subscribe to the *Labor Studies Journal,* and accept an apprentice role and welcome the mentoring of battle-scarred veterans.

In short, if you would help here, please get in touch with me (shostaka@drexel.edu) and tighten your seatbelt! The rewards—spiritual and mental, in particular—cannot be matched. The camaraderie (known in the movement as solidarity) is priceless. And the accomplishments are the sort that the founders of our discipline envisioned at their best.

REFERENCES AND BIBLIOGRAPHY

Aronowitz, Stanley. 1973. *False Promises.* New York: McGraw-Hill, p. 22.

Bell, Daniel. 1953. "Hard Times for the Intellectuals." *New Republic,* 129, 8–10.

Berger, Peter L. 1963. *Invitation to Sociology: A Humanistic Perspective.* Garden City, NY: Doubleday, p. 21.

Dalton, Melville. 1950. "Unofficial Union Management Relations." *American Sociological Review,* 15, 5, 612–616.

Geoghegan, Thomas. 1991. *Which Side Are You On?* New York: Plume.

Gerth, Hans H., and C. Wright Mills, eds. 1946. *From Max Weber: Essays in Sociology.* New York: Oxford University Press.

Gouldner, Alvin W., ed. 1950. *Studies in Leadership.* New York: Harper and Brothers.

Halle, David. 1984. *America's Working Man.* Chicago, Ill.: University of Chicago Press.

Hamper, Ben. 1991. *Rivethead: Tales from the Assembly Line.* New York: Warner Books.

Hughes, Everett C. 1937. "Institutional Office and the Person." *American Journal of Sociology,* 42, 404–413.

Kornblum, William. 1974. *Blue-Collar Community.* Chicago, Ill.: University of Chicago Press.

Kornhauser, William F. 1952. "The Negro Union Official: A Study of Sponsorship and Control." *American Journal of Sociology,* 57, 443–452.

Lester, Richard. 1958. *As Unions Mature.* Princeton, N.J.: Princeton University Press.

Lipset, Seymour Martin, et al. 1956. *Union Democracy.* New York: Free Press.

Lynd, Robert S., ed. 1948. *Knowledge for What: The Place of Social Science in American Culture.* Princeton, N.J.: Princeton University Press.

Merton, Robert K. 1949. *Social Theory and Social Structure.* Glencoe, Ill: Free Press.

Michels, Robert. 1949. *Political Parties.* Glencoe, Ill: Free Press.

Mills, C. Wright. 1948. *The New Men of Power.* New York: Harcourt, Brace.

Mills, C. Wright. 1951. *White Collar.* New York: Oxford University Press.

Moore, Wilbert E. 1962. *The Conduct of the Corporation.* New York: Random House.

Ogden, Frank. 1995. *Navigating in Cyberspace: A Guide to the Next Millennium.* Toronto: Macfarlane Walter & Ross.

Pfeffer, Richard M. 1984. *Working for Capitalism.* New York: Columbia University Press.

Purcell, Theodore V., S.J. 1953. *The Worker Speaks His Mind.* Cambridge, Mass.: Harvard University Press.

Purcell, Theodore V., S.J. 1960. *Blue Collar Man.* Cambridge, Mass.: Harvard University Press.

Reissman, David. 1950. *The Lonely Crowd.* New Haven, Conn.: Yale University Press.

Sayles, Leonard. 1958. *Behavior of Industrial Work Groups.* New York: Wiley.

Sayles, Leonard R., and George Strauss. 1953. *The Local Unions.* New York: Harper and Brothers.

Seider, Maynard. 1984. *A Year in the Life of a Factory.* San Pedro, Calif.: Singlejack Books.

Seidman, Joel, et al. 1958. *The Worker Views His Union.* Chicago: University of Chicago Press.

Shostak, Arthur B. 1962. *America's Forgotten Labor Organization: The Role of the Single-Firm Independent Union in American Industry.* Princeton, N.J.: Industrial Relations Section.

———. 1964. *Blue-Collar World: Studies of the American Worker.* Co-edited with W. Gomberg. Englewood Cliffs, N.J.: Prentice-Hall.

———. 1965. *New Perspectives on Poverty.* Co-edited with W. Gomberg. Englewood Cliffs, N.J.: Prentice-Hall.

———, ed. 1966. *Sociology in Action: Case Studies in Social Problems and Directed Social Change.* Homewood, Ill.: Dorsey Press.

———. 1968. *Blue-Collar Life.* New York: Random House.

———, ed. 1972. *Sociology and Student Life.* New York: David McKay.

———, ed. 1974. *Putting Sociology to Work: Case Studies in the Application of Sociology to Modern Social Problems.* New York: David McKay.

———. 1974. *Privilege in America: An End to Inequality.* Coprepared with Jon and Sally Bould Von Til. Englewood Cliffs, N.J.: Prentice-Hall.

———. 1974. *Modern Social Reforms: New Answers for America's Social Problems.* New York: Macmillan.

———, ed. 1977. *Our Sociological Eye: Personal Essays on Society and Culture.* Sherman Oaks, Calif.: Alfred Publishing.

———. 1980. *Blue-Collar Stress.* Reading, Mass.: Addison-Wesley.

———. 1984. *Men and Abortion.* Coauthored with Gary McLouth and Lynn Seng. New York: Praeger.

———. 1986. *The Air Controllers' Controversy.* Coauthored with Dave Skocik. New York: Human Sciences Press.

———. 1991. *Robust Unionism: Innovations in the Labor Movement.* Ithaca, N.Y.: ILR Press.

———, ed. 1992. *Guidelines from Gomberg: No-Nonsense Advice for Labor–Management Relations.* Philadelphia: Chapel.

———, ed. 1995. *For Labor's Sake: Gains and Pains as Told by 28 Creative Inside Reformers.* Lanham, Md.: University Press of America.

———, ed. 1996a. *Private Sociology: Unsparing Reflections, Uncommon Gains.* Dix Hills, N.Y.: General Hall.

———, ed. 1996b. *Impacts of Changing Employment: If the Good Jobs Go Away.* Thousand Oaks, Calif.: Sage.

———. 1999. *CyberUnion: Empowering Labor through Computer Technology (Issues in Work and Human Resources).* Armonk, N.Y.: M. E. Sharpe.

Straus, Roger A., ed. 1994. *Using Sociology.* Dix Hill, N.Y.: General Hall.

Tapscott, Don. *The Digital Economy: Promise and Peril in the Age of Networked Intelligence.* New York: McGraw-Hill, 1996.

Veblen, Thorstein. 1921. *The Engineers and the Price System.* New York: Viking.

Whyte, William F., ed. 1946. *Industry and Society.* New York: McGraw-Hill.

Wilensky, Harold L. 1956. *Intellectuals in Labor Unions.* Glencoe, Ill: Free Press.

Wolff, Kurt H. 1950. *The Sociology of Georg Simmel.* Glencoe, Ill: Free Press.

PART TWO

Applications to Specific Settings

11

Politics on Campus
The Janitors and the Sociologist

COREY DOLGON

Editors' Note: Corey Dolgon illustrates putting sociology to use in this account of how custodians and sociologists became unlikely allies in a campus janitors' strike. When research is shared, it can change the nature of research. Both the sociologist and the janitors learned, and the outcome of a political struggle was shaped. Corey details how the sociological imagination helped forge a coalition past racial identities.

On February 14, 1997, the custodial workers at Southampton College of Long Island University were essentially sold to Laro Management Company, an outside firm that specialized in maintenance services. Custodians suddenly found themselves forced to fill out new job applications for positions some had held for almost 30 years. Laro supervisors told custodians that no one's job would be guaranteed and that changes in workforce, schedules, and procedures would soon follow. As one custodian told the local press a few weeks later, "we felt like dogs kicked onto the sidewalk."

At a faculty meeting a few days later, the college's provost announced that the management company had been hired to oversee custodial work. He explained that faculty, staff, and students had long complained about the appearance of the campus and that since the new contract with Laro involved only a 1 percent budget increase, it was essentially a "budget-neutral" decision. One faculty member protested the move, asking whether the custodians had been involved in the decision. He also wondered aloud what would be the ramifications of inviting "sleazy" outside companies onto campus to exploit workers who had been part of the college's community for so long. The provost visibly reddened and scolded the professor for commenting on the character of the college's new "partner" without any background knowledge. While custodians were not part of the decision, he continued, the conditions of their employment "would remain much the same." No other faculty spoke up on the issue.

By the next week, the provost's comments proved curious at best. Background research by the custodians showed that Laro had a history of National Labor Relations Board violations and had tried to bust union locals throughout the New York metropolitan area. Meanwhile, the work conditions and compensation for custodians changed significantly: They lost eligibility for TIAA–CREF retirement benefits; they lost tuition remission benefits; they lost access to emergency loans and other perks offered to college employees; and they experienced immediate changes in work, pay, and vacation schedules. Laro threatened and intimidated custodians, asserting that they "knew" some of them were "lazy workers and thieves." Laro also warned custodians that "fraternizing" with students, faculty, and staff would not be permitted. It became clear that the custodians' conditions of employment had not only changed; they had been radically transformed.[1]

On a small scale, this event is an example of a continuing crisis of the modern academy. Universities are under attack for losing a coherent identity, mission, and purpose. Meanwhile, continuing financial crises have inspired institutions to infuse their educational mission with a bottom-line mentality. Some suggest universities model themselves after corporations, privatize "nonessential" tasks, and terminate "nonproductive" people.[2]

Many universities seek new markets. Professional scholars find the need to demonstrate their relevancy by retaining government grants and administrative favor. There is talk at least that we need to link academic work to what Michael Berube calls "public access," connecting the "real world" with a more practical approach to research and teaching.

In response, many universities have sought to create or expand programs in which academics are linked to so-called "community" interests. These efforts span a wide range of activities that include private sector research projects, student internships, government agency collaborations, distance learning programs, and experiential education centers. For administrators, professors, and students, these programs solve a double dilemma—they expand funding possibilities, and they make participants feel they are an important part of the world outside the ivory tower. However, as sociologist Sam Marullo has written, efforts such as service learning are "widely perceived as 'charity work' or 'volunteerism' and hardly pose a threat" to the institutional status quo.[3]

We need to apply our research in ways that challenge both the corporatization of the university as well as the elite nature of scholarly knowledge.[4] An important aspect of applied sociology must be a commitment that allows non-elite groups to shape both the questions and the applications of research. The Southampton College custodians' situation marked a historic convergence of institutional *and* individual crises. It brought together the interests of the sociologist and the janitors.

A BRIEF POLITICAL ECONOMY OF LONG ISLAND'S EAST END

To understand the campus labor struggle, we need to understand the social and political history of the area. Southampton and East Hampton ("The Hamptons") have been a famous summer resort for much of New York City's elite since the late 1800s, when the completion of the Long Island Railroad allowed urbanites access to the area's pristine beaches and sprawling countryside. During the stock market boom of the 1920s, expensive summer retreats were built along the south shore's Atlantic coast. Since the 1920s, between Memorial Day and Labor Day, the Hamptons have hosted important artists, entertainers, publishers, bankers, CEOs, and politicians, whose million-dollar mansions along the sandy shores create a kind of beachfront skyline that resonates as New York City's companion "antiurban" landscape.

Over the past two decades, changes in the transportation and telecommunications industries have increased access to the area for people no longer interested only in a summer retreat. Even the city's wealthiest population cannot ignore the rise in urban blight. In reaction, fortress-style architecture now characterizes an economically separated city landscape. As Teresa Caldiera has written, "In cities fragmented by fortified enclaves, it is difficult to maintain the principles of openness and free circulation which have been among the most significant organizing values of modern cities."[5] These constrictions weigh heaviest on the poor, who have little economic access to private space or control over public space; but even the wealthy have felt the negative impact of having to live in a fortress with constant surveillance.

This social dynamic has converged with the eastward movement of developers. Little open space remains on Long Island, except at the East End. Even the region's famous Pine Barrens forest and preserve (over 50,000 acres of pine forest and wildlife) had to be "saved" recently by allowing some residential development on 10 percent of the area's perimeters. Meanwhile, houses and condominiums, megastores and outlet centers are sprouting throughout the Hamptons. The town of Southampton is rapidly becoming not so much a suburb from where people commute but more a distant borough of New York, where executives, attorneys, and entertainers send faxes, use electronic mail, and participate in teleconferences.[6]

These changes have also been accompanied by new labor relations and migrations. Meeting the increasing demand for low-paid, nonindustrial workers, the population of "new Hispanic" immigrants (Latin Americans who are not Mexican, Puerto Rican, or Cuban) has grown significantly since the beginning of the 1980s throughout the New York metropolitan area.[7] Latino/a workers from Central America make up the fastest-growing segment of the minimum-wage service sector. Most interesting is the changing pattern of immigration that brings Latinos directly to Long Island instead of through New York City first. Although Catholic Charities has documented a segment of Latino migratory workers in the area since the 1950s, the last decade has marked a rapid rise in the number of full-time, year-round Latino families who have settled in the area. Public school statistics show an increase of almost 200 percent in the enrollment of Latino students in both Southampton and East Hampton. Meanwhile, labor statistics show that although most of these immigrants are still employed in agricultural-based occupations (farm workers, vineyards, nurseries, and landscaping), many now hold a much greater diversity of low-wage, service sector jobs.[8]

For many years Southampton remained complacent in its race relations. African Americans (who lived in small and segregated neighborhood pockets throughout the East End) and American Indians (who lived predominantly on the Shinnecock Reservation across the road from Southampton College) formed the core of a low-wage and often seasonal workforce. Those lucky enough to have service or maintenance jobs in the public schools, at the college, or at the local hospital made up the bulk of the African American and American Indian middle class. Rapidly changing economics and demographics, however, created simultaneously an overabundance of lower-paying service jobs in retail and domestic work. A growing number of immigrant workers and even unemployed workers from "up Island" began commuting to seek those jobs.[9] It was within this context that the college custodians (predominantly African Americans and American Indians) were "sold" to a management company that would use the growing local labor surplus to reduce wages and bust the union. Within this context, the custodians organized a community-wide effort to challenge the contract and build community support.

THE SOUTHAMPTON COLLEGE COALITION FOR JUSTICE

A few days after their contracts had been outsourced, custodians began passing around a petition among students. It called on the college's administration to cancel the new contract and rehire them directly. Although the petition did not circulate for long, it did succeed in gathering student support; and it demonstrated that workers were unhappy with the new situation and would work to change it.

During the next week, I sat down with Michelle Wattleton, a junior at Southampton College with whom I had worked as part of a welfare rights organization in the previous year. Michelle was a "nontraditional" student in all aspects of the description. She was 29 years old, part American Indian and part African American; she was a single mother of three children; and she had received welfare assistance since she had left an abusive husband a few years earlier.[10] She worked part time at the school's switchboard and part time at the campus Center for Racial and Cultural Diversity, making barely enough to support her family and pay tuition. She was also an "A" student who had become increasingly active in local and national politics by speaking out on issues such as welfare reform, running for the New York State Assembly, and being elected as the president of the regional NOW (National Organization of Women) chapter. The custodial situation also affected Michelle in a direct way, as she was engaged to the custodians' shop steward, Malcolm Day.

Michelle and I decided that a group comprised of students, faculty, staff, and interested community members might be able to help the custodians pressure the college. By supporting the fledgling petition drive or by creating other means to publicize the situation, perhaps we could encourage the administration to change its decision. We called a meeting for Monday, February 18, and placed announcements in the campus and local press.

On the 18th, the professor who had spoken out at the faculty meeting, a couple of students, a campus secretary, and about eight of the custodians showed up. Immediately, the Southampton College Coalition for Justice and its work took shape. The custodians talked about their situation and experiences. Michelle and I tried to use those experiences to lay out a variety of strategic and political options for the group's work. From the first meeting it was clear the custodians were angry about the way they had been treated. They wanted to act in some way, and appreciated the support from others on campus and in the community.

That first meeting also demonstrated that the situation was a complicated one. The custodians themselves had many different analyses of what had happened and why. I offered research evidence that outsourcing had become a prevalent institutional strategy for universities, but the custodians explained how the decision had racial overtones, as they were the only campus unit comprised predominantly of people of color. The custodians had been pressuring the administration to promote more minority members. In 30 years only two custodians had ever been promoted to the next highest level—mechanic—and neither of them had been a person of color. Custodians were sure that it was the increased pressure that had inspired the administration to find a private management company.

Although the custodians had already dropped the petition, the new group decided to meet again the next Monday and embark on a letter-writing campaign to the local press. Everyone agreed that the more pressure the college received from local people and groups, the more likely they would be to terminate the contract. We also began collecting more information about Laro and about other colleges and universities that had experienced similar labor problems. In essence, part of our strategy was to educate the community about the issue. Another part was to educate ourselves by conducting research so as to better analyze our own situation.

Over the following weeks the coalition brought together students, faculty, staff, and concerned members of the community to work with custodians. The group leafleted the campus, coordinated a letter-writing campaign, held the first political rally at the campus since the 1960s, and took the issue to the local Anti-Bias Task Force and County Human Rights Commission. Our most powerful tactic was to intervene in the college's attempt to get $5 million in funding from the town of Southampton for a swimming pool. The college proposed to make the pool available for public use (with a $500 annual family membership fee), but it would be located at and operated by the college. The coalition informed the college that we would publicly oppose the pool project because the college had shown poor citizenship by negatively impacting the employment conditions of residents. We argued that the college's policies could influence a downward spiral for employment conditions throughout the region if the wages and benefits fell for unionized workers in maintenance and service positions.

In response, the college offered numerous concessions to the custodians: (1) restoring tuition remission; (2) revisiting the promotional issue; and (3) incorporating the coalition in the college's evaluation of Laro's performance. After much debate the coalition accepted these concessions and decided not to publicly oppose the pool project. This was a difficult decision, as some members of the group believed that the pool represented a very strategic opportunity to expose the college's duplicity in claiming to be "good citizens" and part of a "caring community" while (in the words of one of the custodians) "treating its employees like slaves at the auction block." In the end, it was the custodians themselves that swayed the coalition to accept the concessions and back off on the pool project. The workers believed that students and faculty wanted the pool and that public opposition would damage the Coalition's support on campus.

These concessions took place in May 1997. The coalition continued to meet throughout the 1997–1998 academic year, maintaining varying levels of pressure on the administration through rallies, letters, meetings with civic groups, and a sit-in in the provost's office. In the summer of 1998, the custodians affiliated with the Teamsters Union. Meanwhile, the coalition held meetings to plan for fall demonstrations and publicity. Intimidated by the prospect of another September barrage of bad press, the college agreed to terminate the Laro contract and rehired the entire custodial unit under the same terms they had before the outsourcing. The college also promoted an African American custodian to mechanic, breaking the campus color line. The provost told custodians not to think of the contract termination as a "victory"; but, as custodians later told a coalition meeting, "It felt like a victory to us."

APPLYING SOCIOLOGY: UNDERSTANDING THE STRUGGLE

As a frequent convener and facilitator of coalition meetings, I had opportunities to employ my skills as an activist and sociologist. I helped frame local issues in a larger context and participated in a democratic process developing a strategy for action. From these experiences I also learned much that influenced my own understandings of social theory and practice. The coalition applied our constantly evolving knowledge to the political conditions at hand.

I began to understand how the custodians' cultural heritage and everyday experience shaped their strategy and protest. For centuries the American Indian and African American residents of Long Island's East End had resisted the expansion of white domination. Sometimes resistance was explicit and overt, as in early raids on encroaching colonial settlements or in recent demonstrations against police brutality. Mostly, though, the resistance has been much more subtle. Historically the Algonquian Indian culture maintained powwows and other customs despite European settlers' attempts to restrict them.[11] Similarly, African Americans had a long history of covert resistance dating back to their first days in the region as slaves.[12]

In the first few months of my work with the Southampton custodial workers, I began to understand the importance of this multidimensional tradition of resistance. Even before the outsourcing, custodians had a long history of discrimination and degradation at the hands of the college and the community.

It would be too simple to understand the workers' previous lack of organized protests and overt collective resistance as simple accommodation and complacency. Accommodation is never simple. As Eugene Genovese has said of slaves' accommodation:

> *Accommodation itself breathed a critical spirit and disguised subversive actions. . . . In fact, accommodation might best be understood as a way of accepting what could not be helped without falling prey to the pressures for dehumanization, emasculation, and self-hatred.*[13]

In fact, historian Robin D. G. Kelley argues that, for any oppressed people, resistance "manifests itself daily in conversations, folklore, jokes, songs, and other cultural practices . . . [as well as in] theft, foot-dragging, the destruction of property. . . ."[14] In Southampton acceptance often masked a history of complaint, informal protest, and sabotage as a minority workforce asserted power in strategic ways.

For the custodians, even with union protection and representation, open and organized resistance to job discrimination or racial indignities was rare. As one custodian put it, "We were used to being ignored by white employers or even talked down to and mostly just let things roll off our backs. We had some of the best jobs around and there wasn't any need to make a big deal about it." Still, not all custodians of color reacted in the same way. Ella Hamer, an African American woman who had worked at the college since its inception, had a reputation for "speaking her mind," and admitted to more than once telling a student, colleague, or even supervisor how she felt about being disrespected.

Senior custodians possessed a great deal of control over their work schedules, which allowed informal and covert methods of resistance. This power also resulted in a reluctance to "make waves" about larger issues such as racial discrimination, the lack of promotional prospects, and the overall hierarchy of status and power. Most custodians felt lucky to have good-paying jobs in which they had some control over their own workdays and weren't under the kinds of surveillance and insecurity most low-paid, working-class people of color in the region experienced.[15] Many were willing to put up with both institutional discrimination and periodic personal indignities because they were afraid to lose the power they had achieved.

According to one custodian, when the unit did complain about inefficient or discriminatory management policies, they received threats and intimidation from university personnel. As Malcolm Day explained, "I tried to talk with [the provost] numerous times and finally wrote a letter about the management of the custodians. In return, I received a threatening letter from the college attorney that I should apologize for negative comments made about the college or I would be sued." The college's refusal to address concerns and its attempts to quiet "troublemakers" exposed certain divisions and produced new schisms within the custodial unit. Some workers were willing to settle for the previous "peace" and imbalance of power and would not support Day's confrontational efforts; others, especially those who had convinced Day to become shop steward, wanted to continue to press for better treatment and more power.[16]

The complexity of issues such as worker resistance, accommodation, and power, as well as race and class consciousness, became crucial elements as we tried to piece together a coalition of students and community supporters who looked to the custodians for leadership. I also had to learn, however, to respect the varying levels of resistance that workers had always participated in. We as a coalition were openly and purposefully heightening levels of conflict, but the custodians' response to this militancy differed from worker to worker. On more than one occasion, we discussed the fact that, as Dr. King had explained about the Civil Rights Movement, we were not creating conflict and tension but merely exposing conflicts and tensions that already existed. The college's decision to outsource workers created a lens through which we saw a historical process of oppression and protest. Thus, the variety and ranges of custodial responses could not be easily reduced to categories of complacency, fear, complicity, or bitter betrayal. They had to be understood within the entire histori-

cal, political, and cultural complexity of the workers' daily lives at the college.

Racial divisions represented a complex area of stress among the custodians. African Americans and American Indians in the region had a history of both conflict and solidarity. Although many families could trace some lineage back to both groups, cultural and status tensions periodically caused friction between the Shinnecock residing on the reservation and African Americans living in the "Hill" section of Southampton. Some of these animosities could be seen at the college, where custodians would sometimes take sides along racial lines on a variety of issues. The most significant racial division was between white workers and custodians of color. Even before the custodians' contract was switched to the Laro Management Company, "people tended to stick to their own camps." This hindered any serious collective action. And, although white workers did not receive significant privileges, they were often referred to by administrators as "the good workers" who didn't "make trouble." In return, white workers received disproportionate unofficial perks such as overtime and use of college vehicles.

An interesting example in which these racial divisions could be observed was Manny, who with his mother was one of two Yugoslavian immigrants working as custodians. Manny, who spoke English well but with a distinguishable accent, was one of the newer and younger custodians. Although he was very angry about being outsourced and wanted to protest, he was reluctant to accept the idea that race had played a part in the college's decision. In fact, Manny had been told by supervisors on numerous occasions that he was not like the "lazy ones" who did not pull their weight. He believed that he might have a future at the college, especially because he was taking courses there. While not exactly the beneficiary of a white identity, Manny made it clear that he thought of himself as white. Others had encouraged him to identify with the management's conception of a "good" (read white) worker. As one custodian explained, Manny was in the process of becoming white and receiving the privileges that accompany such an identity.[17]

From the beginning of the coalition's meetings, the racial divisions were obvious. Custodians of color argued vigorously that race played a crucial role in their treatment; white workers felt that the college had betrayed them primarily in order to save money and break the union. Some workers (both white and minority) thought that workers of color who were becoming more militant—such as Malcolm Day—were actually to blame for the decision. Thus, although they acknowledged race as an important issue, they did not blame the administration for discrimination. Instead, they wanted the increasingly vocal workers to stop "making waves."

When the unit was contracted out, many workers had mixed emotions. The most militant immediately protested and accused the administration of betrayal. Those less militant supported protest, but still blamed the activists for the situation. The most antimilitant refused to get involved in any action and hoped they could still do well if they supported management and the administration. For the most part, custodians of color fell into the first two categories and white workers belonged to the second and third groups.

Race was important not only in explaining what had happened but also in creating solidarity. The Coalition decided that we had to include open and honest discussions of race. Much of the analysis I have given of the racial and political divisions among custodians is based on the sometimes volatile conversations that occurred during our weekly meetings.

Two discussions, in particular, show that the custodians themselves possessed a sophisticated understanding of class and racial identities. Although they had not been able to employ this analysis in unified action, it informed much of their daily experiences and actions.

In our second meeting as a coalition, we discussed strategies about how to present the issue to the public. We had decided to embark on a letter-writing campaign and talked about the possibility of going to the Town's Anti-Bias Task Force. Some of the white workers were apprehensive about making race a significant issue. In part, some didn't think race was that important in the decision while others didn't want to "press any buttons" on highly sensitive race issues. It seemed in part that the prevailing white desire to avoid discussing race openly stemmed from white workers' concerns about how the predominantly white community would respond to claims of racism. Manny explained that he agreed with both premises. He knew some workers were racially discriminated against, but he was concerned about jeopardizing his own status as a "good worker" by protesting on this issue.

Leonard (a Shinnecock) had been described to Manny as one of the "bad workers," and the two were not on speaking terms. Management had successfully played them against each other, convincing Manny that his best interests lay in identifying with their interests while convincing Leonard that Manny simply accepted management's line. At the meeting Leonard argued that race had separated the workers for too long; custodians of color "always got the short end of the stick," but white workers had not benefited all that much either. In fact, only two white custodians had ever been promoted. As the group discussed who was known as "good workers" and "bad workers," Manny came to realize that the identity of "good worker" was a racialized one: It had more to do with his skin color than with his performance.

When Manny said that he was still discriminated against because of his noticeable accent, Fred, an African American custodian, explained that Manny, as an immigrant, was still only part white and that until he could blend in better and move out of a custodial job, he would not be completely white. Another custodian, Jesse, compared the situation to an outburst by our provost directed at me, a faculty member. The provost scolded me for writing a letter critical of his decision without talking to him first, and said, "I thought we were colleagues." Jesse said, "What he really meant was that he thought you were one of them, not us."

Weeks later, Manny and Ella got into verbal sparring over an incident on the job. Although the actual event was never fully described, it was clear that both had used harsh words and racial slurs in fighting with one another, words that they repeated at the meeting. Many of the custodians intervened and tried to determine what had happened. Jesse looked across the circle at Manny and said, "Manny, you know I've never said anything bad about you and I've always been with you, but you can't say things like that. We have to be able to disagree and argue without using that kind of language." Ella was still hurt and told Jesse to just "forget about it." But Jesse continued, "We have to fight like we're a family, you know? We can't let arguments break us up; we can argue but we have to stay together like a family."

The group struggled with the ways in which race and class affected our social identities and class positions. Our greatest success was that we continued to embrace these discussions, not as asides, but as part of the organizing itself. As I facilitated our meetings, I realized that the struggle itself had become a site where limiting racial and class identities were being challenged. I believe it may be exactly the kind of "opening up" for radical democratic politics that Howard Winant writes about in "Racial Dualism at Century's End." Winant argues that we need

> to understand the malleability and flexibility of all identities, especially racial ones. One of the recognitions hard-won by the movements of the 1960s . . . was that identity is a political construct. Not carved in stone, . . . our concepts of ourselves can be dramatically altered by new movements, new articulations of the possible.[18]

The custodians were successful in large part because they were able to forge an identity beyond racial boundaries. This solidarity was made possible only by their being able to have an informed and open discussion of the sociological dynamics of race and power. The coalition created a new place that nurtured the convergence of personal honesty and collective commitment. It also tested and challenged racial boundaries. As Stuart Hall asserts, political struggles "constitute the terrain for producing identity."[19]

Our hope is that we can use the fluidity of these identities to recognize the larger implications of our struggles. For me, when Jesse pointed out that I had transgressed class boundaries by incurring the provost's wrath when I spoke in support of the custodians, he also challenged me to recognize the significance of class differences within our group. I was able to inform discussions of organizing strategy and

racial discrimination with historical and sociological perspectives on the labor movement and racial identities.[20] I could not have explained, though, how those very forces had shaped the experiences and strategies of local workers. Therefore, the best strategy and most accurate theories of social action had to be researched and created collectively.

I have also been able to link these local efforts with other similar protests occurring at institutions such as Tufts, the University of Rhode Island, the University of Pennsylvania, and elsewhere. The administrations of these universities have all caught the downsizing bug and either contracted out their maintenance units or, in the case of Penn, their entire plant facility.[21]

AFTERWARD

Despite the coalition's victory in September 1999, the group continued to meet. We organized a conference that brought in a wide range of local community groups to discuss how a changing political economy was impacting particular issues. More important, the conference got participants to discuss how a variety of local problems were interrelated and how networks of support could be created to address them. The coalition has begun reaching out to support other groups and share our strategies and experiences; we have also tapped into a budding labor movement on college and university campuses across the nation. We appeared at University as Workplace conferences sponsored by Massachusetts Jobs With Justice in Boston and at labor teach-ins at Brown and Yale Universities sponsored by a new group called Scholars, Artists, Writers for Social Justice.

The other "sociological" arena for the coalition is to further explore the implications of such a struggle for the local and regional political economy. Corporate ability to downsize workers, break unions, and create a downward spiral of wages and benefits is pretty much taken for granted these days. But the political solidarities and communities of struggle that are being nurtured by the coalition could challenge the dominance of corporate morality. As we reach out to others in the community, especially the area's few unionized workers in the public schools and sympathetic professionals and politicians, we plan to raise other, more broad-scale issues such as "livable wage" legislation, the need for safe and affordable housing, and so on. In other words, part of our social knowledge will be created as we expand our struggle from the particular to the collective, from the campus to the community.

As a sociologist, I am struck with how this political struggle has changed my notion of applied science and applied research. Within the context of an institutional crisis and of my own professional crisis concerning the social responsibility and relevancy of intellectual pursuits, my work with the Southampton College Coalition for Justice focused these dilemmas. Research and theory that comes from a particular struggle forces a practicality that frames questions and applications in a powerful way. This approach takes authority out of the hands of the professional researcher. It not only democratizes the search for knowledge but demands applications that must be continuously tested and validated in action. As applied sociologists, we take on the crucial challenge to all scholars to move beyond ivory tower speculation. As Marx noted, "Philosophers have only interpreted the world in various ways. The point is to change it."[22]

NOTES

1. For a full account of this administrative decision to outsource custodians and the formation of the Southampton College Coalition for Justice, see Corey Dolgon, "Cleaning Up the Hamptons," *Z Magazine* (June 1997), pp. 16–17.

2. Richard Mahoney, "Object Lessons from Big Business," *The Chronicle of Higher Education* (October 17, 1977).

3. Sam Marullo, "The Service Learning Movement in Higher Education: An Academic Response to Troubled Times," *The Sociological Imagination* (Fall 1997).

4. Abigail Fuller, "Producing Radical Scholarship: The Radical Sociology Movement, 1967–1975," in *The Sociological Imagination* (Fall 1997). For more on this subject, see Dick Flacks, "Making History and Making Theory: Notes on How Intellectuals Seek Relevance" in *Intellectuals and Politics: Social Theory in a Changing World*, edited by Charles Lemert (Newbury Park, CA: Sage Publications, 1991), pp. 3–19.

5. Teresa P. R. Caldiera, "Fortified Enclaves: The New Urban Segregation" *Public Culture* (Winter 1996), p. 303.

6. In the late 1980s, Robert Fishman coined the term "technoburb" in his book *Bourgeois Utopias* (New York: Basic Books, 1987) to describe some of these dynamics. Yet the kind of suburban industry relocation that Fishman describes is more common in Long Island's Nassau County and Western Suffolk County. In contrast, the East End remains economically and culturally linked directly to New York City's urban core.

7. Saskia Sassen, *The Mobility of Labor and Capital: A Study in International Investment and Labor Flow* (Cambridge, UK: Cambridge University Press, 1988).

8. Southampton Planning Commission, *Tomorrow, Volume 2: Plan and Implementation Strategy. Town of Southampton Comprehensive Plan* (Southampton, 1997).

9. While those commuting from up Island are also disproportionately from the "new Hispanic" group of immigrants, the largest segment come from more established migrant groups and African Americans.

10. I use Melissa's real name here, as her story has been told often in the local and regional press. The rest of the names in this article have been changed.

11. T. H. Breen, *Imagining the Past: East Hampton Histories* (Reading, MA: Addison-Wesley, 1989).

12. For important discussions of this multidimensional nature of resistance see Eugene Genovese, *Roll, Jordan, Roll: The World the Slaves Made* (New York: Vintage Books, 1976), pp. 597–598, and Ronald Takaki, *A Different Mirror: A History of Multicultural America* (Boston: Back Bay Books, 1993), pp. 110–131.

13. Genovese, pp. 597–598.

14. Robin D. G. Kelley, *Race Rebels: Culture, Politics, and the Black Working Class* (New York: New York University Press, 1994).

15. Interviews with Ella Hamer, Malcolm Day, and Fred Washington.

16. Interviews with Jesse Jordan and Day.

17. Interview with Manny Kukoc. Minutes from coalition meeting, 17 March 1997. For discussions of the historical and cultural construction of whiteness and its social significance for workers struggles see David Roediger, *The Wages of Whiteness* (New York: Verso Press, 1991).

18. Howard Winant, "Racial Dualism at Century's End," in *The House That Race Built: Black Americans, US Terrain*, ed. by Wahneema Lubiano (New York: Pantheon Books, 1997).

19. Stuart Hall, "Subjects in History: Making Diasporic Identities," in *The House That Race Built*, ed. Lubiano.

Others have discussed these issues of identities and political struggle in depth—see, for instance, Bernice Johnson Reagon, "Coalition Politics: Turning the Century" in *Race, Class and Gender,* ed. Margaret Anderson and Patricia Hill Collins (Boston: Wadsworth Publishing Company, 1995).

20. These are the kind of educational dynamics of multiculturalism that scholars and teachers have discussed over the last few years. See Leslie Roman, "White Is a Color! White Defensiveness, Postmodernism, and Anti-Racist Pedagogy," and Roxana Ng, "Racism, Sexism, and Nation Building in Canada," in *Identity and Representation in Education,* ed. Cameron McCarthy and Warren Crichlow (New York: Routledge, 1993).

21. "Workers Fight U. of Pennsylvania Plan," *Chronicle of Higher Education* (October 24, 1997).

22. Karl Marx, "Theses on Feuerbach," in *Writings of the Young Marx on Philosophy and Society,* ed. and trans. Loyd Easton and Kurt Guddat (New York: Anchor Books, 1997), p. 411.

12

Safety from Personal Violence
Empathy and Listening

HAL PEPINSKY

Edited by *WILLIAM DU BOIS*

Editors' Note: Hal Pepinsky, cofounder of Criminology as Peacemaking, shows how his experience working with child abuse and victims has taught him that true safety from personal violence depends upon listening and empathy. He shares his knowledge and experience listening and working with victims, offenders, and professionals.

It has been just over a decade since I turned explicitly to studying how to make peace instead of making war on crime and violence. Criminology and criminal justice are essentially negative enterprises, focusing on what not to do. In studying peacemaking I sought to understand how we can get the kind of human relations we *do* want.

From a war-making perspective, safety from crime and personal violence lies in making individuals obedient to commands from the proper authorities. From a peacemaking perspective, safety from personal violence lies essentially in building empathy rather than in commanding obedience. Signs of obedience such as remorse are inherently unreliable indicators that people are safe company. When it comes to safety from personal violence, empathy works; obedience doesn't.

This article was created by Bill Du Bois weaving together "Safety from Personal Violence," *Humanity and Society* (1998), and "Empathy Works, Obedience Doesn't," *The Criminal Justice Policy Review* 9, 2 (1998). Hal Pepinsky is most grateful for this adaptation. Bill also contributed to the original "Safety" article.

I began my explicit inquiry into peacemaking by stating a theory that peace supplants violence whenever interaction becomes "responsive" (Pepinsky, 1988; expanded in Pepinsky, 1991). Violence and the fear and pain it engenders come from people pursuing their own independent agendas and objectives regardless of how others are affected. Responsiveness is interaction in which actors' personal agendas shift constantly to accommodate others' feelings and needs.

INFORMATION SHARING AS SAFETY

Taking child sexual abuse as a case in point, I believe that making peace with and working with victims promotes safety and healing from personal violence, whereas making war on offenders further jeopardizes the victims. Safety from personal violence rests essentially on the art of listening and empathy.

For potential victims, information sharing is the best protection. Recent experience with the burdens of proving child abuse has made me share a concern for safety from personal violence. A child, my child or yours, could be seriously sexually assaulted by virtually anyone. I have come to the point at which I can well imagine that unbeknownst to me, some of my best friends are child molesters. The child abuser I know about may be less threatening than the one I do not, but knowing a child abuser on my street protects no one against the high probability that others on virtually every block have abused and will abuse. If I were to tell my daughter to watch out for the known abuser, I would be doing her the disservice of having her lower her guard for others.

If she is threatened or assaulted, I want her to be able to tell me or others promptly and to find refuge among those whose presence, concern, and company will protect her against further assault. Neither she nor I can predict who will assault us next, but friendship can offer a virtual guarantee that personal violence will stop.

The more any of us conveys being open, with friendship readily at hand, the less likely we are to be targeted for personal violence. It is universally acknowledged that those who seek out victims for personal assault look for vulnerability: for the kind of person who craves attention of any kind too much to object to assault, or who is so quiet that she or he will never tell anyone about an attack. Victims often fail to tell others what has happened to them because they feel like offenders—ashamed, embarrassed, worried about what others will think of them if they find out.

When I think of safety for victims of personal assault, I think of the apocryphal story about George Washington telling his father that he had chopped down his dad's cherry tree, and the father rewarding George for telling the truth. I want to create that kind of climate for all children. For that matter, we adults also need to find someone empathetic and reliable to tell about being victimized when it happens. That is the safest world I can imagine for us all.

Survivors I know call this form of safety "light." They want others to know and care about harm and danger that they have encountered, and to have anyone who would consider hurting them again know that they will be missed or that if something is wrong with them, someone outside an assailant's domination will know and react. Experience has taught many

survivors that "light" is the only safety that they can depend on. Sharing information is a form of safety.

RESPONSIVENESS

When we are truly living *with* one another, each of us repeatedly shifts course based on what we learn from those with whom we interact. Interaction becomes social death or violence when any of us does not let what we are after be affected by information from those we affect. Violence begins when we fail to take time out to listen and respond to one another's information.

Violence means persisting in trying to reach a single objective (including remaining detached from others). I call the opposite kind of interaction "responsiveness" or "democracy" (see Pepinsky, 1991). Responsiveness means that those whose actions affect other people keep shifting their own agendas as they hear and see how they are affecting others. Violence including crime is persisting in trying to get someone's personal valuables or to conquer someone's body, but also includes any set agenda or objective.

Making peace in place of war is a matter of choosing responsiveness over violence at any moment. Listening and changing course is how we humans can make ourselves safer rather than more at risk with one another. Let children be able to tell and be heard when violence hurts or threatens. That is my safety wish.

PEACEMAKING

Responsiveness is nicely portrayed by diverse accounts of indigenous practices, notably in Navajo accounts of how to go about restoring balance to human relations disrupted by violence (as by Yazzie, 1998). The Navajo tribal community in the southwestern United States has reinstituted a tradition, which they call "the peacemaker court," as an alternative to common-law prosecution of crimes. The "court" is an extended process of talking and listening among parties even in cases of serious violence like rape. Eventually the "court" convenes in a circle. There, parties to disputes and those who live with them gather with someone recognized as handling disputes wisely, and take turns speaking freely.

As the Navajo see it, violence means that human relations are out of balance. I think of "out of balance" as meaning some people are getting over on others. The remedy for violence is to restore balance, which is predicated on having everyone in the circle have her or his say. The theory is that when everyone has a chance to express freely and fully, all can adjust their own courses in their own directions and emerge from the circle in harmony with one another. The Navajo and outside observers report considerable success in uncovering and ending personal violence in this manner.

To the Navajo as to me, it is a contradiction in terms to make someone responsible. A peacemaking process liberates one's heart to be in tune with others and to continue taking turns in interaction. Participating in a balanced conversation stimulates one's assumption of responsibility. Safety lies in networks that are committed to reaching out to hear and amplify the voices of those least heard among us, and to let the knowledge we gain from listening manifest itself in what we do.

DISSOCIATION

Alice Miller (1990 [1983]) calls commanding obedience the "poisonous pedagogy." Your pedagogy is your style of teaching children. As children we learn that to please the parents and avoid pain and rejection, we must smile when we are supposed to and say the right thing, no matter how tempted we may be to protest or to show fear or pain. We learn, in other words, to lie. The poison in this pedagogy is that as children we are taught to dissociate from our own feelings and inclinations, to reject our own true selves.

Nothing is more fundamental to safe social relations than honesty. Insofar as we manage to bury our true feelings and to respond—mechanically—as instructed, we are essentially what psychiatrists in my culture these days call sociopathic. We are essentially expedient. We are in the dissociated frame of mind.

Rapists who talk about it characteristically express surprise that those they have raped are complaining; they think "they asked for it" or "they deserved it." While those being raped fear that their attacker is so out of control that "he could kill me," those who are raping are oblivious to the pain and fear they cause. As a friend, Cynthia Ford, infers of her father's state of mind when he ritually tortured her during her childhood:

> *My sense is that abusers dissociate first, and that the part that arises when harming another isn't oblivious to the pain and terror inside themselves. They project their own helpless inner kid onto the victim, and then destroy the pain and terror inside themselves by harming another. Or that is one reason. My father, for instance,* needed *my pain and terror in order to feel better. The sexual release was only a sort of artifact or perhaps a symbolic finishing or denouement.*

Violence begins in a state of dissociation or detachment from the feelings, needs, and wishes of the person victimized. That dissociation permits violence to begin and to repeat itself.

We put a premium on obedience. We do so at our peril, I believe. Both ends of the spectrum of obedience are dangerous, from those who subordinate others wantonly, to the yes-person who conforms to our norms. Personal violence does not happen unless the assailant dissociates. At one end of the spectrum, you don't know whether you can count on those who learn to turn their true feelings off and tell you what they think you want to hear. This is what the effect of poisonous pedagogy—doing and feeling as you're told—produces. When the conformist who promises "I'll be there for you" feels the demand to shift allegiance to some other power figure at your expense, you lose. The promise is oriented toward an external set of rewards and punishments, which may shift with political winds, away from your needs. One common promise made for obedience's sake is to apologize for one's violence and promise never to do it again. The promise is an act of obedience, not of empathy.

REMORSE AND EMPATHY

It is remarkable that we so admire remorse. Remorse is in thorough disrepute among those who work with those victimized by domestic violence. In the run-of-the-mill cycle of repeated assaults, each assault is followed by a "honeymoon period" in which the assailant expresses remorse, says he's sorry, tries to do anything to make it up. People who work with those who most regularly are battered, including those who are routinely raped, regard remorse as worthless. Experience tells them so. I find it quite remarkable that we can find remorse, whether in criminal defendants or in children, so reassuring.

Conversely, empathy may supplant violence with no remorse expressed. Since I began supposing empathy might be a reliable ground upon which to build trust and become safe in others' company, I have noticed how hard it is for those who are at risk of continuing emotional or physical assaults to fake empathy. Remorseful violators can go on and on about how terrible *they* feel over how they hurt you; but until they become honest with themselves and you about getting what they want, they suffer what I might call "emotional attention deficit disorder." If they are forced to talk about how they think *you* feel and what they think you want, it just won't sound like you to you.

I have learned to depend on empathy to decide whether I can afford to let down my guard with others. Empathy may come and go, of course, mine included. It is not that the world can be separated into empathic and sociopathic people. Rather, empathy, while it is being shown, indicates that any of us can be depended upon to be responsive rather than untrustworthy. Empathy amounts to letting others' true selves into our conversations. When we do so, we are literally there *with* others, in a frame of mind to notice others' fear and pain and offer validation and reassurance.

In recent years I have gotten to know a number of children and parents caught in struggles over evidence that the children have been seriously assaulted by a parent; and to know large numbers of those who describe having been raised in horrendous violence, commonly known as ritual abuse; and to know people who have treated these victims for the trauma such violence leaves behind. I have gotten to know these people in the context of offering a seminar on children's rights and safety and another class in which I introduce peacemaking. I invite these people to meet with these classes. I seldom have money even to cover their expenses in coming, but I do offer my

home to those who stay overnight. Among these guests is a woman who I believe indeed was born in a prominent cult bloodline and, long after she thought that she had renounced, still got "triggered" into an "alter" state to impose "discipline" on member groups in a multistate region. I asked my students how they felt about my inviting this woman and several survivors of like violence into my home. Some were outraged and dismayed that I could do so. I sent their comments to my friend, who wrote back a long letter.

The letter, which I have shared with my students and others, is not long on remorse. My friend says that she herself did hands-on "sacrificing" of people only until she rose high enough to let others do it instead. She says that she did it without feeling, knowing that she would be killed if she did not. She explicitly distinguishes herself from despicable serial killers such as Ted Bundy.

She also describes going through books of pictures of missing children, looking to see whether she recognizes any of her victims. She offers assistance to law enforcement, including telling them about her past (which is unprosecutable because bodies would not be found). She takes in others who are trying to escape. She is in touch enough with what she now regards as an alien part of herself—the part that could be triggered and called out to cult activity—that she takes care to ensure that she is always in safe company so that she has no chance to "lose time," as happens when people switch among multiple personalities. In so doing she is in touch with her real self, just as she pays attention to others. On her own initiative, she started visiting a prisoner with whom I have been corresponding for some years. She not only shows sensitivity and empathy for those in whose company I see her; ultimately she shows empathy for me. She is, for instance, scrupulous about honoring my requests that her visits fit my family schedule. She and her guests notice and express appreciation even for little demonstrations of hospitality. Noticing their empathy, I am confident that they will in no way hurt me or my family. Their displays of empathy are exercises in taking personal responsibility—in becoming different from the way they were when they tortured and killed others. To become responsible and empathetic, you have to have confidence in the value and legitimacy of your own feelings and needs. So my friend may show some remorse implicitly; for example, by having tried to identify her victims—but in my judgment my safety with her now rests on her knowledge that it was a part of her that she now considers alien. She is better and more trustworthy than the part of her that formerly hurt others. You have to like and accept a part of yourself and not dissociate if you are to be honest with others about what you do feel and want. It appears to me in this and other cases that one's *empathy sets in only as one feels one can be oneself without being rejected for it*. Trying to induce remorse and shame is therefore counterproductive. Being shamed makes one loathe, reject, and demean oneself. Martyrdom and servitude are inherently instrumental. Empathy is not. Empathy is an openness to new experience, a relaxing of preconceptions as to what is expected; in English metaphor, an opening of the heart. In Buddhist terms it is pure life(-giving) energy, compassion in action. As Quinney (1991) tells us, we end suffering by noticing it and responding openly. Empathy is captured in this saying attributed to the Navajo, which I have posted outside my office in bold letters:

> SHOW UP
> PAY ATTENTION
> TELL THE TRUTH
> DON'T BE ATTACHED TO OUTCOME

Being "attached to outcome" means that you know, before you hear from others, what needs to be done. If you already know what needs to be done, you have nothing to learn from listening to others before you make your next move. Your priorities are not up for discussion.

The energy in compassion or empathy lies in learning something new to do by listening to those who will most be affected by what you do next. Empathy is a suspension of one's agenda to "pay attention" to what they say, and to let their feelings soak into one's own conscious nervous energy. Empathy begins with unencumbered listening (Pepinsky, 1998a). Of course, in order to pay attention you have

to "show up"—or, as I hear people in my daughter's generation say, "be there." Paying attention means showing interest in and drawing out the voices that are least heard in whatever setting or reference group you find yourself, in order to introduce balance into the conversation—the structural manifestation that peace is being made.

I have been close to people who I believe to be repeatedly assaulting or harassing others. I have heard plenty of remorse. I have seen how hard it is for those at risk of repeating their violence to empathize. They are too hung up on their own problems, and desperate to do whatever they feel they must to cling to others. I find that empathy, unlike a polygraph, is hard to fake. And when people like the houseguests I have described show empathy to one another and to me, I find that I can afford to let down my guard and enjoy safety in their company. I also notice that I receive ample warning as empathy shuts down before someone bursts into violence, which helps me relax and empathize myself, rather than having to be continually on guard for renewed attack.

BALANCING PARTICIPATION

"Someone raped me last night." If someone told you that, what would you want to know next? When I ask students, the answers fall into two categories. (1) A few people want to know how the person is feeling, and just let her (or him) talk—to be there and wait to see whether the person asks for any other help. (2) Most people want to ask the person what happened—so as to judge whether a crime was in fact committed—or they want to know who did it.

This second reaction is a form of tuning out—a "professional" response that rape survivors describe as making them feel raped again. It makes them feel that they are being treated like vehicles of someone else's agenda rather than someone whose feelings matter to others. In making war on crime we are efficient at dispatching "justice": at labeling people and treating them according to these labels. We are not so good at healing lives.

When children are being sexually assaulted by one parent, one of the greatest frustrations for the children, and for those close to them who are trying to rearrange custody and visitation, is delay in hearing of the children's trauma. It is common for protective parents to spend tens of thousands of dollars and wait years without ever quite getting around to hearing what the children are feeling and saying. I have often heard a mother who has concluded that her child has been sexually assaulted by the child's father berate herself, "She was trying to tell me! I told myself there was nothing wrong, that my child was just being emotional. I couldn't imagine anything bad was happening. I feel so guilty that I didn't take it seriously when she screamed before or after his visits." On the other side is the common child's plea: "I tried to tell you, but you wouldn't listen." Or, "I didn't want to bother anyone. . . . You were so busy; I didn't want to disturb you. . . ."

Personal violence, especially violence committed by someone the victim knows, is generally accompanied by threats not to tell what has happened. The victim also typically feels shame that he or she has let this happen, or even has somehow invited it. There may also be ambivalence—loyalty and love toward the assailant as well as rage and fear over the assault. When victims begin to disclose what has happened and to ask for protection from further assaults, they do so hesitantly, timidly, by allusion. Therapists are accustomed to having clients' disclosures that they have been personally violated take a long time to begin, and to emerge in bits and pieces, as clients gain confidence in their own memories and come to trust therapists not to take the memories over and make them into something the clients cannot control (see Whitfield, 1995, for further discussion).

It is also hard for a married parent to hear and accept a child's report that the other parent is molesting the child. Validation of the child's disclosure may require the parent to consider moving, changing economic circumstances, changing an array of arrangements that depend on the status of being married. We have a tremendous investment in not hearing.

There is no magic we can perform that will suddenly make us open up and reveal all of our own sense of personal threat and injury, let alone make others open up to us. But we all know of people who are known as "good listeners." Those who convey that they listen relatively well notice people often open up and share pain and fear with them that they share nowhere else. Listening pays. Listening is a quality worth nurturing. Being heard at all can and often does make the difference between remaining a victim and becoming a survivor.

A survivor is someone who knows she or he did not deserve the pain and fear—and that it is not crazy to feel hurt and afraid. This conviction requires validation by others. Validation, in turn, lends the victim ego strength to carry resistance beyond just this one disclosure. The more readily and more widely that the story of victimization can be shared, the greater the chances the survivor will find safe refuge from further victimization. The assailant will become so conscious that others might learn what is happening that he or she will no longer feel "safe" enough to carry on the attacks.

HONESTY AND DIALOGUE

"Telling the truth" refers to honesty. If you want someone honestly to talk about his or her reaction to having committed a crime, you don't set up plea bargaining or ceremonies of remorse in order to draw out how the offender honestly feels and believes. The condition for honesty is essentially acceptance of this principle: When I ask you for truth, I grant you the responsibility for deciding how what you tell me gets used next. We may experience frustration when a complainant declines to report a crime to police or the prosecutor. But the rule of confidentiality and abiding by complainant wishes is ironclad.

This is precisely the rule followed by therapists and rape or domestic violence crisis counselors. The one who has been victimized suffers a loss of control. Restoration of a sense of personal safety rests on the one who has been victimized resuming control of life. Since the victim is the one who has most been stripped of a voice by what happened, the victim's voice is the one that most urgently needs to be drawn into the ensuing conversation. If that voice matters, it will guide and be supported. Let the one who has most been traumatized by victimization be the primary guide to what comes next.

At the individual level one's capacity for empathy with others remains in balance with what I consider empathy for oneself; that is, "telling the truth" to oneself and others about what one feels. We need to feel validated and connected to others merely for being ourself, not for denying our own needs and feelings in martyrdom or self-sacrifice. In enjoying the safety of empathy, one takes heart from watching those who have been victimized gain voice and assume responsibility for their lives; one's satisfaction rests in being there to validate and honor the occasion. In martyrdom or self-sacrifice one becomes codependent, burying one's own feelings and needs while assuming responsibility for others' needs rather than enhancing others' assumption of responsibility for meeting their own needs.

When enjoying empathic relations, one loses "attachment to outcome"; one develops faith that balanced participation in itself increases the chances that one's own most crying needs will be met. This supplants the belief that *someone else* has to do something as a predicate to safety. Trying to make anyone else empathic or responsible commits the fallacy of making empathy an act of obedience. The logic on which empathy rests means that we can invite empathy and responsibility only by showing empathy and responsibility. This means listening down—drawing out the voices most excluded from our conversations and being guided by them—rather than subordinating others, which literally is a refusal to grant empathy. It means listening down to others in balance with listening down into one's own self. It is by allowing one's sharing of one's own feelings and self with others to emerge that one can feel at all, truly feel, and hence feel what others are expressing in the event.

When one turns off one's own feelings and denies one's own sensibilities, one turns instead to connecting with others in the manner of one of Milgram's (1973) obedient subjects. This includes feeling too ashamed and inadequate to deserve having one's feelings and sensibilities count, or enter the conversation. Ultimately, shame deprives us of the capacity to have empathy with others or with oneself. It is, as Ernest Becker (1968, pp. 327–346) concludes, our self-esteem rather than our shame that allows us to connect safely and honestly with others. That is no less true of one's worst enemy than it is of oneself. We must value ourselves and others. One cannot dictate whether anyone gives empathy, but safety lies only where feelings of the moment are noticed and recognized, and acted

upon. Empathy rests on embracing a part of one's own inner self before rejecting what has been wrong with oneself.

THE DYNAMICS OF JUSTICE

From the peacemaker point of view, I am safer the more readily those who are obedient find relations in which they pay attention to one another's will and needs. If I extend the boundaries with those I share empathy and trust, I become safer. If I raise the number of those whose fates I separate from mine via subordination, then I become endangered, not only by those authoritatively subordinated—"you offender, you"—but also by all those who empathize and share destinies with them. Thus, justice is something that happens to me and my fellow creatures together, one way or the other. The gods who render the justice I see don't much care who started violence. It is simply that the more firmly separated enemy fates become, the more endangered we are. Justice happens. In the peacemaking frame I describe, justice is what Hindus call karma. In terms of how likely some friend will feed, shelter, and hold me in need, insofar as we enjoy empathy, we enjoy safety. Insofar as we resort to violence, we fear and hurt from violence. That is not a prophecy. That is simply how justice works.

Wagner-Pacifici (1993) has analyzed transcripts of negotiations between the MOVE group and the city of Philadelphia, confirming the hypothesis that violence escalated and eventually erupted as MOVE members' voices and concerns were taken out of officials' conversations in the negotiation process. As Fisher, Ury, and Patton (1992) depict peacemaking in international diplomacy, "getting to yes" entails "moving from position to interest." Parties are able to move to inventing ways to accommodate one another's concerns once they take for granted that everyone's interests equally deserve airing and hearing. Democratization is the path to peace. Responsiveness is how people act in participatory democracy.

Balancing conversations in response to personal violence also makes us safer and more secure in everyday life. Within the microlimits of our individual lives, just having friends with whom we can safely, honestly share fear and pain is the essence of being safe from personal violence. Personal investment in empathy pays off in personal security and self-esteem.

When we seek safety, we look for those who are prepared to pause to listen. We look for those who might be oriented toward sharing feelings here and now for its own sake. Even while walking streets in strange urban neighborhoods late at night, it is safer to carry a friend than to carry a gun. Someone who will notice and react if you are hurt or threatened makes you safer.

REVEALING ABUSE

I operationalize child abuse as doing something with a child that you would not wish the child to describe to others as the child chooses. It is the essence of abuse for someone to require someone else to keep a secret about how they themselves relate. When secrets entail not telling what is happening to oneself for someone else's sake, that becomes oppressive.

Good therapists buck the trend toward quick fixes. They play with child clients and let the children talk any way they would like about how things are going. With adult clients, they recognize that opening up to talk about private trauma takes more trust than their clients have otherwise managed since early childhood, and that clients have to set their own pace at exploring what they can handle talking about.

People will be drawn to you if you are known for having listened and empathized with tales of childhood trauma. Therapists and survivors have an experience I share in the classroom when I talk about cases I know. People come up to tell you that they too have been hurt, as in being raped at home. Survivors affirm that all you need to do then is to thank the person for trusting you with the story and say, "I'm sorry." In fact they admonish against leaping in and trying to do more straightaway. A *big* part of what makes a listener trustworthy, I gather, is that the listener will not freak out at the horror of it all, or start to offer all kinds of advice or ask all sorts of questions.

Psychologist Sidney Jourard (1971) has written extensively about disclosure. In reference to a romantic relationship, he writes:

I love her. What does this mean? . . . As she discloses her being to me or before my gaze, my existence is enriched. I am more alive. I experience myself in dimensions that she evokes, such that life is more meaningful and livable. My beloved is a mystery that I want to make transparent. But the paradox is that I cannot make my beloved do anything. I can only invite and earn the disclosure that makes her transparent. I want to know my beloved. But for me to know, she must show. And for her to show her mysteries to me, she must be assured I will respect them, take delight in them. (p. 52)

A similar dynamic takes place in disclosures of abuse. Certain people invite disclosure, while others have styles that make it unlikely. "For me to know, she must show." And the only way she will show is if she is sure that I will respect her truths. A person must be sure that the listener will not use the revelations for other purposes; that is, that the person will be valued in and for himself or herself. Listening is learning about another person's life; it not just collecting evidence to make a case. In peacemaking, people are treated as ends rather than means.

If you are perceived to be empathetic and open, you have already heard stories of victimization yourself. Looking back, survivors see themselves searching for someone safe to disclose to first, a friend as often as a professional. One thing this means is that even if your child is not being victimized, s/he may well have friends telling her or him that they are being victimized. Your child might be some other child's best therapist. Many readers of this text will be the first line of defense or safety for childhood victims of personal violence by adult caretakers, even without going around talking about child abuse. Students in my seminar on children's rights and safety sometimes tell me how a roommate or a special friend has confided a terrible secret of victimization. When students start talking with friends outside class about what seminar guests have been saying, the disclosures multiply.

LEARNING HOW TO LISTEN

Social worker/ritual abuse survivor/activist Jeanette Westbrook advises that if you are going to open up to victims and survivors and stick with it, "You have to take care of your own stuff." Like others in this position, I found that I needed to ask for help from a therapist whose empathy and capacity for understanding I trusted. Empathy I had given others eventually led me to ask for some of the same back, to share ways in which I had grown up scared silent. One thing I noticed is that I could be as disturbed, invaded, and traumatized by legally innocuous behavior as others had been by felonious acts like serial parental rape. As I learned not to trivialize my own private terrors, so I found myself more responsive to others' depth of feeling than to my assessment of how serious a thing had been done to them. It was easier to notice and respond to others' pain and fear when I *stopped* worrying about how badly I *ought to* feel about it.

I have come far enough in my own healing process to notice how it feels to receive empathy for suffering one has borne alone. I expected to feel waves of happiness, and indeed I do notice and acknowledge my own emotional highs and lows more readily. To my astonishment, though, the healing I notice is more an absence of anxieties, stillness in my head.

In my own case, one of my compulsions was to daydream and elaborately rehearse what I would say and what others would say in forthcoming interactions. When I noticed what I was doing, I also noticed that the interactions invariably went differently from my elaborately laid plans. Ironically, I felt as though conversations were unreal insofar as they departed from my fantasies of what they would be. Interaction was hard work! The fact that I had empathetic listeners, including my therapist, let me notice and marvel at what I was doing—and enabled me to recognize that although once it served to get me attention I craved, it was superfluous to the attention I receive now. I began to catch myself starting to rehearse, and sometimes even cut it off by laughing out loud to myself. I noticed I could begin to assure myself that I could afford to lighten up, the way I had sought to assure others. Eventually, I began to catch myself *not* rehearsing. In these moments I also noticed that I was paying more attention to what was happening around me then and there. I didn't feel puffed up with self-assurance, but I did seem to be

conversing with others more effortlessly, and to be interested without feeling that listening obliged me to make new plans. My therapist assures me that this is how healing feels. A result is that I'm less distracted and more relaxed when I'm with people. My hearing improves.

This transformation allows me to listen to voices that otherwise might not have seemed important enough to matter. I am less impatient to end conversations and get on with business. This experience has brought home to me that giving empathy eventually requires gaining empathy; otherwise it burns out. It is as crucial to explore avenues for being heard as it is to hear. The trick, as Navajos recognize in their "peacemaker courts" (Yazzie, 1998), is to allow balance in one's conversations.

WHAT HAPPENS WHEN WE LISTEN?

One of the hardest things about making peace with personal violence is letting oneself listen without trying to jump in and fix it. Violence cannot be "solved" like a math problem. Seeing someone's problem as neatly solvable allows us to deny the scope of the problem and move right on. That may be part of our fascination with television murder mysteries. When the murder is solved, the threat is over. We can roll over and go to sleep. So too with sex abuse and other crimes: By concentrating on solving the crime, castigating the offender, and imposing a sentence, we have done something and can leave the victim's pain behind. "Justice has been served." There is a conclusion. We can return to our lives and avoid letting the nightmare disturb our sleep.

Jumping in to fix things may make us feel better, but it may make things worse for the person involved. It may be quite a while, if ever, before a victim is prepared to have anyone go and confront an offender. Therapists such as Whitfield (1995) warn clients contemplating confrontation with childhood assailants to hold off until they feel they will gain from telling the assailants how they feel regardless of how the assailants respond. In matters of secret violence, the first response to an accusation is bound to be denial. The accuser who counts on receiving remorse may only be traumatized by another attack.

Happily, confrontation—daring to face one's attacker without fear of retaliation—may be broken down into small next steps that may take any form with which the victim feels comfortable. For example, one common step people take in therapy as they begin responding to having been raped by someone they know is to write the offender a letter and read it out loud to a friend. Exchanges may take many forms, such as exchanges of letters or videotapes, besides sitting in the same room. As in diplomacy—the art of negotiating with group leaders—things like where people meet and how they sit at face-to-face meetings may mean a lot. Peacemaking presupposes that no one is qualified to decide which step should come next until decision makers learn how people feel after the first.

Will the unconfronted attacker prey on others? Perhaps, and so perhaps will most anyone who has not been identified as an attacker. Victims can gain safety far more readily than attackers can be caught, labeled, and subdued. The urge to do something to offenders does not warrant forcing victims to jeopardize themselves further.

PERILS IN LAW

Performing one's role without letting others' feelings interrupt and change one's course is robotic. Remaining on one's preset course without regard for the other is violence itself. Sometimes this violence manifests itself in what we call crime, such as by "taking" someone sexually without noticing her or his feelings, or taking someone's wallet over their objections. Violence happens when you play roles you will not interrupt for others' pain or fear. In going by the book, players in our criminal justice system join others doing violence to victims.

Our preoccupation with quick and simple solutions drowns out our system's ability to listen for helplessness—to offer a guarantee that if we are in trouble, we will have someone to tell who will believe us, who will give us a place to stay, and who will grant us the right to dissociate from them as well as to associate with them.

Goodness knows how many people I know who cannot get justice—for whom the bastard is still out

there—and yet who have a real chance to survive and thrive among people who let themselves be interrupted by another's fear and pain. In worlds like that of child sexual abuse, it seems to me that most of the safety I see people gaining comes from private support, whereas legal status leaves everyone unsettled at best.

We should bear in mind that if it seems cruel and unfair to force victims of personal violence to face their assailants in mediation, victims face even worse abuse in court. In court, they face people whose job it is to discredit them and their stories. There they risk having an outsider authoritatively decide that they are fabricating their complaints. Accused persons often get threatened enough in such cases to countersue complainants and their supporters. Those who seek vindication are instead overwhelmed with legal retaliation. Victims commonly report feeling "raped again" by the system. Along the way, they are admonished to stop acting "emotional" and are told they have "credibility issues" by prosecutors, who are often under pressure to relieve heavy caseloads by dropping or reducing charges in less winnable cases, or even by their own lawyers' concerns for their professional appearance. Here and there, often seemingly everywhere, professionals and officials have a personal stake in discrediting victims.

The judicial system is a power game. It decides whose voices get to be heard. It defines who the offenders and victims are. Growing up in the game of obedience, it doesn't take long to learn that those who monopolize power over others get to decide that "what I say goes." The realities of subordination manifest themselves repeatedly. Nowhere have these realities more clearly manifested themselves to me than in contests between children who say that a custodian is sexually assaulting them and the caretakers accused. It often appears as if the more corroborative evidence there is, such as a child's having a sexually transmitted disease or a torn anus or vaginal opening, and the more serious the assault would be if the fact of it were recognized, the greater the odds that officials will refuse to believe the accusation and will rule that evidence of the caretaker's assaults is inadequate to find fault and that hence the child should be taken from the presence of any parent or therapist to whom the child complains (Pepinsky, 1998b; Rosen and Etlin, 1996). In the face of the fact that those who hold more power are more likely to win power games, we who continue to seek safety via subordination of miscreants find ourselves in ever more jeopardy, caught in a world where inequalities and injustice harden and grow.

Some parents I have met have decided to drop legal action in order to keep their children from having to be alone with the other parent who sexually assaults them. These "protective parents" have learned what happens to other parents who press the matter once officials fail to "substantiate the abuse" (well described by Rosen and Etlin, 1996). Parents who persist in trying to get protection from the courts are virtually bound to have adverse rulings compound one another. Eventually protective parents can lose custody and go to jail for defying court orders requiring them to stop acting as though the abuse is happening. Sometimes children and parents in these cases disappear.

The question arises whether victims and survivors do not have a duty to do all they can to help put perpetrators away so that the perpetrators will not go on hurting innocent people. One case comes to mind: A pair of primary schoolers have apparently had the continuing threat of unsafe visitation with their noncustodial biological father lifted after four years of court struggle. I am persuaded by the evidence that sexual assault persisted well into this period with the collusion, if not participation, of some supervisors, and the children have hinted at much worse things having to do with blood, killing, and torture. For now the children do not seem to want to have to talk about their father when they are not with him. The mother told me not long ago that it would mean nothing if the father now admitted the assaults and apologized (which he sort of did to the children about a year ago). She and I have talked about what happens to the father and what he might be doing. Visitation is now well supervised, so he is not continuing to assault his own children. If he is hurting other children, odds are that he does so in groups that would carry on even if he died.

Experiences like these humble me. The subtleties and complications of responding to personal violence hold me back from presuming what, if anything, ought to be done to offenders. I put a premium instead on helping victims survive and become safe, on helping them gain control of their own safety. I can do that only by letting them take their time taking each next step. The happy part is that in cases all around me, victims are breaking silence about their victimization. Children are managing to stop having to be alone with assailants, where once there would have been no way out but suicide, collapse, or disappearance. Adults are resuming emotional contact—this time with trustworthy people—which they severed in self-defense in childhood when their trust was betrayed. We can proceed far along the way of freeing people from risk of further personal violence by empathizing with victims and letting them take the initiative in responding. We can concentrate on this effort when we let go of the imperative to take care of offenders first.

MAKING PEACE

Our ultimate cultural barrier to substituting empathy for obedience is our presumption that adults know more than children. In a sense, of course, that is true. But as children we have some vital gifts of our own to add to conversations. Chief among these is our blatantly honest desire to please and be accepted by adults. We bring honesty to conversations, unless adults shut us down. We may be the first to cry when we are all scared.

Adult–child relations are the master template on which we design social control. Empathy and respect for wisdom and knowledge we possess in childhood translates into empathy and respect for all those whose interests are formally subordinated to others. It translates into recognition that whatever human problems you face, you need to listen first for the weaker, smaller voices before gaining a balanced idea of what to do next. In criminal justice classes where I introduce peacemaking, conversations sometimes run like this:

STUDENT: What would you do after you talked with the victim?

ME: I don't know until I have listened to the victim.

STUDENT: But what would you do then?

ME: I would use what the victim tells me to help decide. . . .

STUDENT: You're not answering my question. What would you do then?

ME: I'm sorry, but that's my whole point. I think the right thing is to let the victim take the lead in orienting what comes next. If I'm a police officer and she or he doesn't want to give a statement or be examined, then I'd see respecting her or his wishes as the right next move in my job of making peace.

Literally and metaphorically, we have predicated social control on the master model in which parents know better than children what is good for them. Every bid we make to have others take care of our problems for us is an extension of this model. Police, judges, and prison wardens are supposed to make us safer than we know how to make ourselves. Balancing voices in our conversations requires that we individually feel secure enough to dampen our narcissism. This means letting go of getting our own points across and relaxing our determination to reach some objective we have set for ourselves or for others in advance.

I figure that beginning in childhood, the most reliable guide to anyone's personal safety is oneself. I figure that power over others puts parents at a greater risk of doing violence to children than the other way around. I figure that at any age, those of us who suffer the violence know what is happening and what safety requires better than I or any other social planner does. I had better listen.

BIBLIOGRAPHY AND REFERENCES

Becker, E. (1968). *The structure of evil: An essay on the unification of the science of man.* New York: George Braziller.

Bianchi, H. (1994). *Justice as sanctuary: Toward a new system of crime control.* Bloomington, Ind.: Indiana University Press.

Carpenter, M. (reporter), & Dietrich, A. (photographer). (1997). Children of the underground. *Pittsburgh Post-Gazette* (Dec. 14–18; five-part series).

Christie, N. (1977). Conflicts as property. *British Journal of Criminology,* 17, 1–19.

Cohen, S. (1979). The punitive city: Notes on the dispersal of justice. *Contemporary Crises,* 3, 339–363.

Consedine, J. (1995). *Restorative justice: Healing the effects of crime.* Lyttleton, N.Z.: Ploughshares Publications.

DeMause, L. (1982). *Foundations of psychohistory.* New York: Creative Roots.

Finckenauer, J. O. (1982). *Scared straight: And the panacea phenomenon.* Englewood Cliffs, N.J.: Prentice-Hall.

Fisher, R., Ury, W., & Patton, B. (1992). *Getting to yes.* New York: Houghton Mifflin.

Gross, E. K. (1996). *A preliminary evaluation of the Navajo peacemaker court.* Paper presented at the annual meeting of the American Society of Criminology, Chicago.

Harris, M. K. (1991). Moving into the new millennium: Toward a feminist vision of justice. In H. E. Pepinsky & R. Quinney (Eds.), *Criminology as peacemaking* (pp. 83–97). Bloomington, Ind.: Indiana University Press.

Knopp, F. H. (1991). Community solutions to sexual violence: Feminist/abolitionist perspectives. In H. E. Pepinsky & R. Quinney (Eds.), *Criminology as peacemaking* (pp. 181–193). Bloomington, Ind.: Indiana University Press.

Knopp, F. H., et al. (1976). *Instead of prisons: A handbook for abolitionists.* Orwell, Vt.: Safer Society Press.

Marx, K. (1963 [1843]). Bruno Bauer: Die Judenfrage. In T. B. Bottomore (Ed. and Trans.), *Karl Marx: early writings* (pp. 3–31). New York: McGraw-Hill.

Milgram, S. (1973). *Obedience to authority: An experimental view.* New York: Harper and Row.

Miller, A. (1990 [1983]). *For your own good: Hidden cruelty in child-rearing and the roots of violence.* New York: Noonday Press.

Pepinsky, H. (1995). Peacemaking primer. *Peace and Conflict Studies,* 2 (Dec.), 32–53.

Pepinsky, H. (1997). Geometric forms of violence. In D. Milovanovic (Ed.), *Chaos, crime, and social justice* (pp. 97–109). Westport, Conn.: Greenwood Publishing.

Pepinsky, H. (1998). Transcending literatyrrany. *Contemporary Justice Review,* 1, 189–212.

Pepinsky, H. E. (1973). *Toward diversion from the criminal justice system: With a written reply by Robert Maynard Hutchins.* Paper presented at a conference on diversion from the criminal justice system, Center for the Study of Democratic Institutions, Santa Barbara.

Pepinsky, H. E. (1980). On handling contradictions between dynastic tradition and Marxist humanism: The new criminal law in Communist China as an effort to legitimize the post-Mao state. In Tsai, W. (Ed.), *Struggling for change in Mainland China: Challenges and implications* (pp. 180–198). Taipei, Taiwan: Institute of International Relations.

Pepinsky, H. E. (1988). Violence as unresponsiveness: Toward a new conception of crime. *Justice Quarterly,* 5, 539–563.

Pepinsky, H. E. (1991). *The geometry of violence and democracy.* Bloomington, Ind.: Indiana University Press.

Pepinsky, H. E., & Jesilow, P. D. (1992). *Myths that cause crime,* 3rd edition. Santa Ana, Calif.: Seven Locks Press.

Pepinsky, H. E., & Quinney, R. (1991). *Criminology as peacemaking.* Bloomington, Ind.: Indiana University Press.

Quinney, R. (1991). The way of peace: On crime, suffering and service. In H. E. Pepinsky and R. Quinney (Eds.), *Criminology as peacemaking* (pp. 3–13). Bloomington, Ind.: Indiana University Press.

Reiman, J. (1997). *The rich get richer and the poor get prison: Ideology, class, and criminal justice,* 5th edition. Needham Hts., Mass.: Allyn and Bacon.

Rosen, L., & Etlin, M. (1996). *The hostage child: Sex abuse allegations in custody disputes.* Bloomington, Ind.: Indiana University Press.

Schaef, A. W. (1992). *Co-dependence: Misunderstood, mistreated.* San Francisco: Harper Publishing.

Sullivan, D. (Ed.). (1998). The phenomenon of restorative justice. Special Issue of *Contemporary Justice Review,* 1, 1–174.

Wagner-Pacifici, R. (1993). *Discourse and destruction: The City of Philadelphia versus MOVE.* Chicago: University of Chicago Press.

Weber, M. M. (1999 [1904/5]). *The Protestant ethic and the spirit of capitalism* (Talcott Parsons, trans.). New York: Routledge, Chapman and Hill.

Yazzie, R. (1998). Navajo peacemaking: Implications for adjudication-based systems of justice. *Contemporary Justice Review,* 1, 123–131.

Zehr, H. (1990). *Changing lenses: A new focus on crime and justice.* Scottsdale, Pa.: Herald Press.

Zion, J. W. (1985). The Navajo peacemaker: Deference to the old and accommodation to the new. *American Indian Law Review,* 11, 89–109.

Coming Full Circle

A County–Community
Restorative Justice Partnership

DARROL BUSSLER AND MARK E. CAREY WITH WILLIAM DU BOIS

Editors' Note: Darrol Bussler and Mark Carey instituted the first Peacemaking Circle in a non–Native American setting in the United States. Circles are a wonderful example of a social invention. These authors offer insights into how and why circles are used, and they discuss the process of making circles. Restorative justice provides a new way to solve community and social problems.

DARROL'S STORY

Late one April evening in 1994, two juveniles checked a rear door of a home in their neighborhood. The lock had given way, and they quietly entered. There was no one home. Later, when the owner arrived home, he discovered what looked like a war zone: broken glass and furniture, damaged appliances and walls, destroyed family keepsakes and art. In the middle of the kitchen floor, there was a mound of food: flour, eggs, chocolate, and mayonnaise. The contents of the cupboards and refrigerator had been emptied into a heap. All light fixtures in the house were broken. Dishes were smashed, table tops scratched. The boys had a tool that they used to break into cars—hold this tool up and it would shatter glass. That meant that every picture and every mirror in the house were in pieces on the floor. The offenders would later say they'd needed a rush. The insurance company would set the damages at $16,000. The emotional toll was even higher. I ought to know. I was that homeowner.

When something like this happens, your security, your self, and your whole world are invaded. As I struggled through a sleepless night, two questions kept running through my mind: Who? and Why? I needed to make some sense of it. Family heirlooms lay broken at my feet. My parents had died. What little I had left was now in pieces. It had to mean something. So much was irreplaceable. When I was a high school teacher, 100 kids had collected money to buy me a stereo system. The speakers and the receiver were now destroyed. I just couldn't sweep up the pieces and go back to living as usual. I couldn't just let it go. Something good had to come out of all this.

I work with kids; I teach for a living; I believe in kids. I am not ready to throw these kids away. This vandalism was a symptom of something gone wrong in my neighborhood, our community, and our society. By the time the police called the next morning, informing me that they had identified the offenders, I had already made a decision: "I will work with whoever did this."

After the investigation, charges were filed against two neighborhood juveniles. I received the usual forms requesting the name of my insurance company and my deductible. Upon signing the form, I asked myself, "Is this all there is?" I decided it wasn't and attached a letter to the form explaining my ideas for working with the boys. A couple of months passed. I received no response. I decided to check the status of my case and was told, "The court is not interested in creativity. The court is interested in consistency." I quietly hung up the phone, disappointed and hurt. My disappointment soon turned to anger. However, I continued to believe that I had a good idea. Working with these two juveniles seemed like the right thing to do. But how could I? Where would I go? Who would listen?

Several days later, the phone rang. The voice said, "We just received a copy of your letter. We think it's creative, and we'd like to talk to you." The caller from the local Citizen Council explained something about "restorative justice." I had never heard of it, but what she said seemed to make sense. In fact, it sounded exactly like what I had proposed in my letter: meeting with the two neighborhood juveniles face-to-face and making decisions about how they and I, together, could resolve what had happened. My anger turned to hope.

A couple months later, I participated in a victim–offender mediation with the two juveniles, their mothers, and two mediators. Seated around my dining room table, we discussed restitution and accountability. I told my story about what their vandalism had done to my life. We also discussed what we could do to restore trust in our neighborhood. The two juveniles had been the primary reason for the high crime rate in the area. I had them identify five people they had harmed in the neighborhood, make an appointment with them, and then deliver a written apology in person. This is just the kind of face-to-face contact that our present justice system doesn't often afford. Another aspect of our restitution plan was to give the entire neighborhood a dinner party in my home with the two juveniles helping me, purchasing and preparing the food, inviting neighborhood residents face-to-face, greeting and serving the neighbors, and cleaning up. To apologize to their neighbors face-to-face was quite a step. It was a first step toward direct accountability and healing.

Practice in Partnerships

South St. Paul is a first-ring suburb of the Minneapolis–St. Paul metropolitan area. At one time, it was home to two large meat-packing plants and the world's largest stockyards. They disappeared in the 1970s, and our community was declared a depressed area by the federal government. We experienced high unemployment rates, an aging citizenry, a declining tax base, and a 55 percent loss of students in our public schools. It was not only an economic depression but a psychological one as well.

In the early 1980s, I served as the South St. Paul Public School's community education director. My job was to facilitate Community Partnerships, a process designed to bring the community together. It was based on an educational reconstruction philosophy which sees education as the primary means for change in society: it changes the community and facilitates the democratic process. Once a month, citizens and leaders from the public schools, the city, the chamber of commerce, the Housing and Redevelopment Authority, churches, and service organizations met at 7 A.M. Combining their individual and organizational resources, these groups began to identify and address community issues. In 1990, our community was recognized at a White House ceremony: We were named an All-American City for our grassroots efforts in community redevelopment through democratic practice.

As I sat staring that night into a broken piece of mirror that had been part of my parents' dresser, I realized I hadn't talked to my neighbors in years. I had gotten busy. We had all become strangers to each other. We had lost our connection. I felt a need to reconnect, to restore authentic relationships in my neighborhood.

One of the boys once asked me, "Why are you doing this?" He didn't understand. Someone caring was foreign to his world. But he finally got it. This boy would turn his life around. It is still too early to tell about the other boy. He spent six months in a juvenile facility for his part in the incident, and later was in custody again. His family eventually moved away, and I honestly don't know what happened to him.

I grew up on a family farm and attended a one-room school; community was the basis of our life. As a teacher, I maintain that relationships are necessary for effective teaching. Strangely, this vandalism was the beginning of restoring right relationships in our neighborhood.

Rather than fixating on punishment, restorative justice focuses on making things right. I didn't know it at the time, but victim–offender mediation has some history. In New Zealand, Maori tribal rituals for dealing with juvenile crime became the law of the land in 1989 and led to an 80 percent reduction in juvenile cases referred to traditional courts. This process, which is called *family conferencing*, involves the victim, the offender, and their families sitting down with the arresting police officer. Australia widely copied these programs, which are designed to reconcile the offender and the victim through conferencing in face-to-face meetings. In the United States, Mennonite minister Howard Zehr (1990) was influential in creating victim–offender reconciliation programs (VORP). VORP believes crime is a violation of people and relationships. These programs provide a mechanism for face-to-face meetings between victims and offenders. This facilitates victim restitution, allows an opportunity for victims to express their feelings, and provides ways for the offender to "make right" the wrongs committed. The language of restorative justice emphasizes restoring relationships. It's my belief that if right relationships are restored, everything else takes care of itself.

MARK'S STORY: THE CONVEYER BELT OF JUSTICE

As probation and parole officers at Dakota County Department of Corrections, we see countless faces every day. They line up outside the courtrooms. They wait in our lobbies. As on an assembly line, they travel the conveyer belt of justice. On any given day we have about 8,000 offenders under supervision. By

year's end we have monitored more than 14,000 offenders. Over time the faces become a blur. For many the caseloads are so high that remembering a name to go with a face is an accomplishment. Usually, being memorable is not a favorable attribute. It means that you stuck out, you were noticed. It probably means that you are uncooperative or at high risk of reoffending. The probation officers that have high-risk adult caseloads average 140 apiece. Officers with high-risk juvenile caseloads average 50. These workloads are approximately double what we'd recommend as a maximum caseload. On one occasion we conducted a time study and discovered that the highest-risk adult offenders received 35 minutes of a probation officer's time per month. It was the "squeaky wheel" that got our attention. Staff estimated that 20 percent of their clients consumed 80 percent of their time and resources. These conditions caused one high-ranking official to call probation in Minnesota "a fraud" on the public's trust.

And then there is the justice machinery, which includes the courts, prosecutors, defense attorneys, guardians and so forth. Each player has a distinct role to fulfill. Each depends on the others to do their jobs well and in a timely manner. That is how the assembly line can process the myriad of cases without backlogging and dragging the entire system down.

Despite the demands and the working conditions, staff members are hardworking and highly dedicated to their profession. They remember the days of the past, when working with offenders was more meaningful, and when they worked closely with the community on each case. The offenders were not faceless but were seen as neighbors, spouses, employees, and someone's best friend. Today, each offender is still someone's brother or teammate. Yet somehow, something bigger and more demanding has taken precedence in the justice system. Somehow, in our scurrying to keep up, we have lost our way. There is still the occasional breakthrough and success story, but it seems as if staff tell those stories less often.

When the concept of restorative justice was introduced, I was skeptical but intrigued. The department had various restorative programs. I soon discovered that every correctional agency has some restorative responses but that most fall far short of full systemic change. It is not a matter of whether you are restorative, but to what degree. There was a significant gap between the talk and the walk.

So although the concept made sense to me, I was not about to jump on a bandwagon full of rhetoric and little substance. As the director of the department, I knew I needed to do something that would serve as a compass and lead us out of the maze called case processing. Eventually, I agreed to be a pilot site for the federal Office of Juvenile Justice and Delinquency Prevention. I committed to exploring the principles of restorative justice; and, if those principle and values resonated well with the department, I agreed to align policy and practice with them. Little did I know the extent of the changes that were just beginning to unfold for us.

Changing the System: A New Vision

The first step was to acquaint ourselves with the concept through training and development. We provided four different speakers over a period of nine months. Each speaker spoke on one aspect of what was called the "balanced approach." Restorative justice identifies three objectives: competency development, public safety, and accountability. It suggests that the justice system has not one but three customers—the victim, the offender, and the community.

The Victim: When an individual commits an offense, the individual then has an obligation to the victims as well as the community. *Accountability* means making things right with the victim. This process includes providing time for the victims to tell their story—how they felt and how the crime affected their lives. It usually also includes some form of restitution. Too often in the traditional system, the victim is only a bystander in the process.

The Offender: Offenders should leave the criminal justice system more capable than when they entered it. Making the offender more competent must be one of the outcomes of the system.

The Community: The criminal justice system has a responsibility to protect the community and to ensure public safety.

The initial staff reaction to the training was sharp and varied. Most expressed strong support for the concept, noting that many of these principles used to be emphasized and that the field had strayed away from them in support of monitoring and surveillance duties. Paperwork, formal structures, and legal liabilities were taking up more and more of their workday, taking away from their job satisfaction. Staffers pointed out that they entered this field to help people but that over time they found less and less opportunity to spend meaningful time helping people reconstruct their lives. That is what they were passionate about, what fed their drive to show up for work.

Another group of staffers were reluctant to eagerly embrace the philosophy. They needed more information. They needed concrete examples of how this would be any different from what they were doing now. Many were veterans who had seen new waves of philosophy come and go. They were not going to jump on board for just any new idea that came along. They didn't dismiss it, but they didn't commit themselves.

The last group, a small minority, was clearly not convinced that this philosophy made any sense. They raised many questions. What was broken? What was wrong with what they were doing now? How could they possibly add two more customers to their workload (victims and community) when they couldn't get the job done now with offenders? Why should they believe that they could get communities involved? Who had any spare time to do the difficult work of creating the cultural change necessary for personal and collective responsibility? How could we respond simultaneously to the voices of victims and offenders when they had conflicting goals and perspectives? They wanted to stick to what they knew best and let others worry about meeting victim and community needs.

After hearing the speakers and the staff responses, I was convinced the philosophy of restorative justice resonated with my personal values and where I wanted to take the agency. Furthermore, it gave us a language and symbols to use as a rallying point, and a locus where we could align our energies and resources. It had the capacity to redesign who we were as an agency and what direction we could take. In short, it gave us a vision.

Mission: A New Life

The majority of staff agreed that the principles of restorative justice should be embraced and that we needed to start from the beginning. Our first step was to review and alter our mission statement. It was an older document, and it was long. Staff could not remember what it said, let alone recite it. I created a staff committee who debated long and hard what our new statement should say. They surveyed their peers and other jurisdictions. In the end, it took us an entire year to finish the mission statement. Why? We knew it was extremely important, because we were going to breathe life into it. It was going to be our touchstone for everything that followed.

One word tripped us up. The word *victim*. Internal staff debate was intense over whether that word belonged in a correctional agency mission. Many argued that we should refer victims to other agencies rather than accept them as one of our primary customers. Others, who understood that we had a lot to offer victims, especially information and access to influence, believed it was imperative that we include them. In the end, victims were named as a primary customer in the new mission statement.

Implementing restorative justice required nothing less than changing the organizational culture. Culture might be described as a "set of basic assumptions which members of a group invent to solve the basic problems" (Schein, 1981). This implementation meant significant change at the agency and staff level, including new values, new skills, new roles, and new expectations. We needed to focus on repairing the harm done; we needed to learn victim–offender mediation and community organizing; and we needed to learn how to provide ongoing victim input and communication. This required training the staff and developing new sources of social support and new resources.

DARROL'S JOURNEY: ESTABLISHING COMMUNITY PARTNERSHIPS

I wasn't always sure that my work with the boys was worth the effort. It had been extremely successful, but it had required a tremendous investment of my time. A friend remarked that I should consider the al-

ternative: While many victims still had wounds, I had healed. I think conflict resolution means exactly that. It affords the opportunity for issues to be resolved so that you can move on with your life unencumbered. A year to the date of the break-in, I had a nightmare and woke up in utter terror that it was happening again. By the second year, I had healed enough that I wasn't even aware of the day of the anniversary.

We were successful in restoring trust in our neighborhood. This success led to new questions and ideas. What about other neighborhoods? What about the entire community? My initial idea for a communitywide process in South St. Paul occurred when the National Council of Churches aired their yearly documentary on NBC in July 1996. The one-hour documentary on restorative justice concluded with my story. As I watched, I noted that the opening and closing of the program made references to faith communities. I thought, "Where are churches in this whole process? Instead of just talking about forgiveness, we really should be living our values." This rekindled the anger I had felt when some fundamentalist Christians on my block had challenged me 2 years earlier: "How can you let those boys back in your house?" In my mind, I asked, "How can you, as Christians, be asking me that question?" The television program posed another question: What is the role of faith communities in addressing community crime? With that question I began a six-month reflection on how the neighborhood experience could be expanded into the entire community. The result of the reflection was a decision to use my experience as the former community education director. I conducted one-on-one meetings with positional leaders in the community such as the police chief, the superintendent of schools, and the director of a private community organization connected to area faith communities. Each agreed to the need, and each agreed to participate in an initial community meeting to explore a communitywide approach to addressing crime. In addition to positional leaders, youth from the schools and citizens of the community were invited. Two volunteers from faith communities came who had seen the television documentary and thought, "Our churches should be doing that."

In early 1997 I facilitated our first meeting of community volunteers and representatives from the schools, the city, county corrections, county courts, faith communities, and eight school youth. The invitation to the first meeting was sent by the superintendent of schools on school stationery, inviting participants to meet at the community center, a facility managed by the schools. This process built on the schools having successfully launched other community initiatives, which were later owned and managed by the community. This beginning process was based on the belief that the public school has a responsibility to serve as a center for the community and can serve as the facilitator of a democratic process for community development.

Beliefs, Mission, and Vision: In the second meeting the superintendent of schools led a conversation on beliefs. Some of the key ideas were the importance of connections, especially between youth and adults, and the community's role in connecting with youth; the importance of systems' working with community; the importance of care; the need to be proactive.

A volunteer from a faith community led a conversation on vision: If everything were in place, what would be happening? The vision dialogue included ideas such as neighbors working together, parents relating to their children, adults interacting with youth in their neighborhoods, timely help given to those in need, faith communities taking leadership roles, youth and adults trusting each other, expanding clubs, saying hello.

These early discussions developed a foundation for action and the South St. Paul Restorative Justice Council was born. Within the next year, we agreed to develop belief, mission, and vision statements that would serve as guidelines for behavior. In our council meetings and circles today, it is not uncommon for discussions to be guided by ideas from these statements: "Does that action reflect what we believe?" "But is that our mission?" "Is that really the direction we want to go?"

Our beliefs guide our desired actions. We believe in a democratic ethic: Every citizen has the right to influence any decision affecting that citizen's life. All have the right to an equal voice and the right to be heard. We practice decision making by consensus. Our mission is to develop and sustain restorative processes in our community to promote healing, increase accountability, and provide support. The mission helps us stay focused on our tasks. Our vision is a community living in justice, safety, health, and respect. The vision provides an image of being our best in actions, social relationships, thinking, feelings, and our spiritual connections. The beliefs, mission, and vision are printed on newsprint-sized paper and are posted during our meetings as reminders of who we are and what we do. We decided addressing crime should include relationship building (love) within accepted community norms (law), and the community should develop an ability to solve problems (learning). Love, Law, and Learning became our slogan.

We included faith traditions such as the Old Testament law of the Ten Commandments and the New Testament law of love. I wanted to emphasize the importance of principles rather than rules. I chose a statement from Oren Lyons, Faithkeeper of the Turtle Clan of Iroquois:

> *What happens, say, if there is an act of violence by one Indian against another?*
>
> *All I can tell you is that every situation is seen as entirely different. We really don't have the kind of specific rules or laws that you have. Nothing is ever written down . . . If you write the rules down, then you have to deal with the rule rather than figuring out what's fair. We're interested in principle. The principle is to be fair. We know everybody, we know their families, what they like, what they don't like, what's troubling them, what the kids may be going through. We have all the problems any community has. When one member intrudes on another, we have a situation. We meet and just keep talking until there's nothing left but the obvious truth.*[1]

The impact of Lyons's statement, I contend, has been a major factor in our work as a council and, ultimately, in choosing circles as a primary means for restorative justice. We are principle-based rather than rule-based. And within the practice of circles, we are learning to speak and listen, rather than speak and write.

Moving to Circles

Dakota County Community Corrections, under the leadership of Mark Carey, provided the context for the development of the South St. Paul Restorative Justice Council: a partnership of the public schools, city law enforcement, county corrections, county courts, and community volunteers through faith communities and other community organizations. When presented with our first case, we proceeded with two conveners originally trained in family group conferencing: a probation officer from Dakota County and a volunteer from a church.

In Minnesota, we were lucky. We have both victim–offender mediation and family group conferencing available to us. We were encouraged to also look at a third process—circles. Circles seemed natural as they emphasized our belief in community development based on democratic principles. However, our awareness of circles was limited to some reading and a few conversations. On the wave of the increasing awareness of restorative justice, the Minnesota Department of Corrections hired Kay Pranis of the Citizens' Council as a restorative justice planner, the first such position in the world. She brought in Judge Barry Stuart (1997) to talk to local judges about sentencing circles, which he uses widely in the Canadian Yukon. He lent credibility to the idea of trying a circle in South St. Paul.

Circles are similar to the Navaho Peacemaker Courts that Hal Pepinsky outlines in his article "Safety from Personal Violence," which appears in this book. The circle invites all voices to be heard: offenders, victims, and community. The circle provides all participants the opportunity to see, hear, and speak to each other face-to-face. All are seated without use of tables. The "circle keeper" begins the process with a welcome and sets a comfortable tone with an opening ritual—a reading, poem, song, or presentation of a visual object. Introductions and guidelines are established; everyone is invited to "speak from the heart" and "in a good way." The "talking piece" is introduced—an object such as a stone, feather, or other meaningful object. Only the participant holding the talking piece has the right to speak. The talking piece moves to the left of the keeper. When finished speaking, the participant passes the talking piece to the next participant in the circle. Everyone has the responsibility to respect the time of others and also has the right to remain silent by passing the talking piece.

The keeper's role includes clarifying, summarizing, making sure participants respect the guidelines, and moving the process to meet the circle's purpose. Purposes vary and may include learning, providing support and healing, decision making by consensus, problem solving, conflict resolution, and sentencing.

The keeper closes the circle with a closing ritual such as brief reflection, a reading, shaking hands, or connecting as a group. Some form of breaking bread together afterwards is a helpful part of the process. It invites informal reflection and provides opportunity for closure.

The council implemented the first circle sentences in South St. Paul. These are probably the first non–Native American circles in the country. Our first case involved two teens who slashed tires on the cars of 50 victims. The two boys and their families met in a circle with the restorative justice council and approximately 30 of the victims. Each victim shared his or her own pain. Most of them didn't want money as restitution. A victim who knew one of the boys suggested that he clean his grandma's house 10 times. In another early case there was a 35-year-old woman with a drug charge. Rather than having a felony on her record, she is becoming an articulate, reflective, responsible, contributing member to our community; we are confident she will not reoffend.

The primary work of the council has been offering education on the circle process and implementing circles. We have also worked with local public schools and managed to get full-time restorative justice planners in the three elementary school buildings. The school circles are used for behavior issues and for learning. In one case, half a dozen sixth-grade students were caught using inhalants. The principal could simply have automatically applied the suspension rule; instead, the students were given a choice of going through the restorative process. Students chose the latter, which included in-school suspension but also included reintegration into the community.

Circles in schools have also gone beyond student issues and have included issues related to teachers and staff. For example, one building used the circle process to determine what positions should be cut in the building for the next school year. Another planner served as the circle keeper for employees working on solving conflict within a department of the school. And the circle process has been carried into other community groups such as faith communities.

I view the circle keeper as a "keeper of a democratic process." The circle process is voluntary and has no predetermined script, no concrete step-by-step agenda, and no predetermined outcomes. The keeper needs to be in tune with the thoughts, feelings, and dispositions that people with varied perspectives bring to the process. The circle process is viewed as a spiritual experience by many of us. Three qualities characterize this spiritual experience: (1) connecting with ourselves and with others, (2) recognizing that we are part of something bigger, and (3) experiencing beyond the cognitive through "speaking from the heart."

One of our cases involved 12 teenage boys and girls who vandalized a house that was up for sale. The 80-year-old man who owned the house gave the circle the history of the house. It had been his family's home. He told them that they had vandalized the bedroom in which his mother had died. The man would succumb to cancer before the house was fully renovated, but he died knowing that the 12 juveniles and their families were restoring the house.

The spiritual component can also be illustrated by a story a friend of mine told me of a process that took place in Des Moines, Iowa. Someone had broken into a synagogue and painted swastikas on the walls. Members were horrified beyond belief. When the offenders were paraded in front of the congregation, there a gasp: It was a young man and woman in their late teens; two frail skin heads who had done it partially to impress their friends. Synagogue members were able to tell them how they felt seeing the swastikas painted on their walls. Part of the restitution agreement involved the youth taking classes in Jewish history from seven Holocaust survivors. They also repaired the physical damage. And oddly through all the pain, a bond developed between the two offenders and the congregation. When they got married and had a child, they brought the baby to their own church to be baptized and then also to the synagogue. One must understand the depth that is often experienced in the restorative process. Feelings can be expressed, wounds can be healed, and

there is room for the spirit to move in the midst of our lives.

Lessons Learned

Restorative justice is voluntary. Initial meetings are conducted one-on-one to insure personal and organizational commitment. When we convene as a group, we sit in a circle. This makes a silent statement about equal accessibility and voice. Council members learn the circle process by doing it. There are no observers; all participate, including the media if they are present. We come to the circle as citizens with names, but no titles. Judges, probation officers, and such are welcome in the circle, although they have no special privileges. However they may have special information they can contribute.

Council beliefs and principles guide the circle process. Guidelines for the circle keeper have been developed. It is important to note that these are not rules, criteria, or checklists, but guidelines that encourage freedom for the keeper and participants to determine the process. Guidelines allow the keeper to bring his or her unique ideas, skills, and dispositions to the process. Cokeeping is preferred, and each is encouraged to keep the circle at least twice in order to practice what is learned. For continuing circle processes, the circle keeper role may be shared. That allows the circle to experience new keepers on a continuing basis. Thus, routine is avoided and the components of the circle (opening, purpose, and closing) are addressed in different ways by different keepers.

Participants learn to "trust the circle" and allow the "magic of the circle" to work. All participants sit where they choose. A focal piece such as a meaningful object, a candle, or flowers may be placed in the circle's center. This may be helpful for times when participants have difficulty in having direct eye contact with others. The talking piece may be selected by the keeper and may have individual or group meaning. The meaning may be shared in the opening of the circle. The keeper may decide when to use the talking piece and when to set the talking piece aside for open dialogue. Any participant may request either the use of the talking piece or open dialogue at an appropriate time.

The circle process is useful beyond problems and behavior issues. The circle is also used for classroom group learning, family communication, and organizational meetings. The use of the talking piece helps create a safe environment. It can also be helpful during discussions when tempo and interruptions increase. The use of the talking piece can restore a sense of calmness and order, allowing all to contribute. It helps stop knee-jerk reactions and ensures more individual listening than speaking.

When the council conducted an informational circle with positional leaders in the community, a council member said, "I have always been a person who dots the I's and crosses the T's. I have learned to work beyond just the details." A holistic view is helpful in the circle process—seeing both details and the big picture. We should know the law but also include love (relationship) and learning. We need to include cognitive, affective, and intuitive ways of knowing. Restorative justice requires both sense and common sense. The original meaning of the latter focused on a sixth sense, the common, a process in which information from the five senses was brought together and combined in the sixth.

Originally, a jury of your peers meant people who knew you and could use their personal knowledge to judge your actions. Judges were also there to judge—to trust their intuitions and use human abilities to make decisions about how to fit abstract principles of justice to the situation at hand. It is only more recently that we have moved to a detached, objective theory of justice. Today, judges are there more to act as a referee between competing sides rather than to offer their wisdom for inventive solutions. Historically, the jury and judge were not supposed to be just objective observers of the facts, but were there to lend a human component to the wheels of justice. Restorative justice brings us full circle back to the earlier wisdom of the jury and the town hall meeting.

In a high profile case, we were referred a man who could have been sentenced to 10 years in prison for assaulting a police officer and for possession of an illegal substance. We had three circles and still could not come to consensus, mainly because the police officers really wanted to put him away. The judge

finally took the case back and sentenced him to 2 years prison and 10 years on probation with us. The Appellate Court ruled the sentence illegal and remanded him back to the judge. Meanwhile, the circle had supported him while he was in prison. Dozens of people had visited him in prison talking about what was going on, how he was doing, and how we were going to ultimately try to reintegrate him back into the community.

The night before the judge was to resentence him, she called a circle—she wanted to hear from the community about their perceptions of what had happened in court. This was not a sentencing circle. But during the process of the circle, the judge came to her decision and announced what she was going to do. The next day she released him from prison. She set up a co-probation between the probation officer and the restorative justice council. This is brand new, and to our knowledge has never been done before. The arrangement is to last ten years.

After release from prison, he was ordered to chemical dependency treatment and from there to a halfway house. As the council representative, Darrol sees him weekly and the support council sees him monthly, as does his probation officer. While he was in prison, we actually got him enrolled in a restorative justice class that Darrol teaches at Minnesota State University, Mankato. This is a bringing together of two systems: the prison system and the university system. Since he was in prison, he could not attend class so Darrol would see him on a weekly basis. Every student in the class has a buddy so his buddy became part of that process visiting both with Darrol and alone. Darrol's prediction is that eventually we will have an ex-con with a degree in sociology and psychology who will work in the prison system.

Students in Darrol's classes at Mankato are encouraged to use circles. Students often show how they have integrated restorative justice into their lives. One student's sister had made the decision behind everyone's back to commit the grandmother to a nursing home. In response to this, a circle was actually convened in the hospital room with the student, the sister, grandmother, parents, and minister. The decision was made that the grandmother would return back to her own home. The discussion centered around who is going to make sure she is all right. A family commitment was made that everyone would take responsibility. The sister had made the original decision to commit her to a nursing home because she feared she'd have that responsibility alone. In this instance, the talking piece utilized was a family picture. Three generations made the decision together and a commitment to make sure it worked.

In another instance, a student's parents owned a home that was rented out to college football players. A neighbor threatened to call police and have them evicted because of their loud parties. As a result, the student called a circle of the parents (owners), the football players, and the neighbor. The result was an agreement that if the football players were planning a party, they would call the neighbor. If he was to be at work early, they would call the party off or make sure all the windows were closed so the noise would not disturb him. Interestingly, the football players had a hard time waiting for the talking piece because they always wanted to interrupt. The talking piece in this case made listening possible.

It is common to have the circle process reveal information about other issues that need attention. Once, during a circle training going on in a church basement, we looked out the window and three kids were smoking pot. A police officer and some of the circle members gave the kids a choice: go with police officer or the restorative process. The kids choose the circle. During the circle, the three shared their previous talks about committing suicide. As the circle participants dealt with the substance abuse, they also saw the need to address the issue of suicide. Rather than just reacting to a criminal act, the circle often leads to prevention.

Developing Structures to Support Action

Systems are powerful forces in how we think, what we say, and what we do. Restorative justice is going to become a system whether we like it or not. The question is: What kind of system? How do we refrain from becoming too efficient, too organized, and too routine? Our experience in systems has taught us to dot I's and cross T's, but in circles we often question not only *when* we should, but *if* we should. What or-

ganizational structures are helpful and which ones interfere with practicing our beliefs and carrying out our mission? We have developed five organizational components: the council, an executive council, a coordinator, key case contacts and school restorative justice planners, and the community itself.

The monthly restorative justice council meetings, conducted by two circle keepers, are a continuing process to clarify and to practice our understanding of restorative justice, to become informed about our work, and to make decisions.

After the opening, meetings often begin with the use of metaphor. A keeper may present an object that sometimes becomes the talking piece. In circle each participant shares his or her interpretation of how the object symbolizes restorative justice; this becomes a way for new participants to learn and for others to clarify and strengthen their understanding of restorative justice. This process reflects our continuing emphasis on learning.

The council makes decisions by consensus, as does the Executive Council, which meets prior to council meetings to explore issues needing attention and to prepare the agenda. The coordinator supports both and is the primary contact for information and for keeping financial records and other records.

As the council has accepted additional cases, a decision was made to identify a key contact for each case. The key contact coordinates information, activities, and circles for victims, offenders, and the community involved with the case. Related to key contacts are the restorative justice planners in the public schools. Each of the three public school buildings is served by a full-time planner who implements restorative justice processes supported with grant funding.

The fifth component of our organizational structure is the community; or, perhaps more realistically, a sense of community. We believe wisdom can be gained through community and that community is the ultimate reason for our work.

Our beginning structure was housed in a public school, which also served as the fiscal agent for grants and related matters. This will change, as the St. Paul Restorative Justice Council becomes an independent nonprofit organization. The school has a history of facilitating community initiatives that later become independent of the school.

We continually ask ourselves: Are we becoming too organized? We are aware that the existence of structures such as the Executive Council can create a class structure. We have experimented with calling it other names. However, having a separate decision making entity could create an elite no matter what you call it. To help prevent this and encourage democracy and openness, we make a point of inviting participants from the community to Executive Council meetings.

We have become more conscious of our language, the language of systems. We seek to use language that invites dialogue: principles, guidelines, and agreements rather than rules, criteria/checklists, and contracts. We believe that our continuing focus on our mission and beliefs, especially on principles related to democratic process, will provide the greatest support in keeping us from becoming like traditional systems. Our goal is to keep our language and behavior from becoming so routine that we forget to be conscious of what we are doing.

One time circle members were discussing what should be done to juveniles who were not carrying out their restorative agreement following vandalism. We caught ourselves speaking in traditional systems language: "rules," "punishment," and doing something "to" them. We reminded ourselves of our guiding mission to promote "healing, increase accountability, and provide support."

The Role of the Professional

From the beginning, we have had the support of Dakota County. The involvement of their professional staff has been crucial to our success. However, we view professionals and the community as partners. Consequently, we leave titles at the door; we bring our knowledge and skills to the circle.

With the increasing involvement of the community, some have expressed concerns about job security for professionals. We believe that no one will lose his or her job. However, roles will shift from doing "to" and "for" to doing "with." It is a shift *from* the professional doing the community's work *to* helping the community to do its own work in community

development. Rather than having the police officer, the attorney, the probation officer, and the judge decide what will be done, professionals can help offenders, victims, and the community develop healing, accountability, and support. The system cannot achieve this alone, nor can the community do it without the aid of the professionals.

There should be an interdependence between professionals and the community. We remember a case in which the judge stepped down from his bench and participated in a circle. The parents and the child met authentically with the support of the judge and the community. Hurt and disappointment were openly expressed in this family for perhaps the first time. During the tire slashing case, an angry victim began by saying that she had checked into the matter, and "we can sue the parents to get our money." The judge reported that yes, she could do that, but went on to explain why this case had been referred to the Restorative Justice Council. As the process continued, it became evident that there was no "we" in the room. Later, this same victim became the first participant to suggest a community program that could provide these 14-year-old boys with job opportunities to earn their $4,000 for individual restitution. Through this simple exchange, both the professional and the victim played important parts in the process.

Results: Organizational Change

Mark is no longer with Dakota County Corrections. He is now deputy commissioner of the Community and Juvenile Justice Division of the Minnesota Department of Corrections. In other words, he is head of juvenile and adult probation for the state. Restorative justice continues to be an important part of his vision.

In Minnesota, an 8-point-plan of research validated practices has been developed: (1) A risk-tool and level of services inventory have been created; (2) Those needing cognitive behavioral intervention need to be helped; (3) Probation officers need to develop a case plan emphasizing both risk reduction and restorative elements; (4) Minimal standards of restorative justice should be established in every county. At the least, there needs to be community conferencing, victim offender mediation, and a community involvement board; (5) Attention should be given to aggressive restitution collection; (6) There needs to be aftercare and a transition plan for anyone entering a residential adult or juvenile program; (7) Primary services are important. There are things that you would think are everywhere but are not. The list includes presentence investigations, domestic abuse assessment, urine testing for drugs and alcohol; (8) Workload standards need to be enforced. There are caseload sizes above which you just cannot be.

Minnesota has the highest ratio of probationers to people in prison in the United States. There are roughly 22 times as many people on probation as in prison. The states that rank second through fifth all have a ratio of roughly 5 probationers to every one person in prison. Minnesota may be over using probation—other means need to be explored. Restorative justice offers an exciting opportunity. This is particularly true if we are going to reduce case loads.

This is an exciting time. The experience in South St. Paul is a work in progress. People have been energized and done great work. At the same time, they have been frustrated with the system (parts of it have been eager and parts have held back).

Mark thinks the keys to organizational change are going to be what he calls the four P's.

1. *Passion:* There is a huge difference between having a passion for a mission as opposed to just doing a job.
2. *Persistence:* To break barriers, we are going to need persistence.
3. *Patience:* We need a sense of urgency—we are not going to tolerate the status quo—and at the same time we need to not get burned out because it is not easier.
4. *Perspective:* We need a set of values that line up with our idea about humanity: a sense of humility about who we are; a shared understanding that says "there but for fortune go I."

Finally, we must not underestimate the importance of joy in organizational change. We all perform better, and are more likely to adapt to changes, when we have a sense of purpose at work; are appreciated for our contribution; and have fun doing it. A revolution for change in society must be a joyful revolution—no whipping and grim looks. It must be a party so others will want to join in (Carey, 1998).

OUR STORY: DARROL AND MARK'S CONCLUSIONS

In the first 3 years after getting trained, we have implemented crime repair crews, family group conferencing, circle sentencing, cognitive probation, a repeat drunk driving program, a continuum of juvenile nonresidential programs aimed at restoration, and expanded victim–offender mediations, among others. Currently, risk assessments and restorative case plans are being put in place. We have held both victim and community forums to learn how the justice system could improve its sensitivity and also meet the public's needs. Mentoring programs are beginning, and community justice councils have begun in three cities. As restorative justice got more attention, the print, radio, and television media have begun running special-interest stories. Legislators grew interested and attended short informational sessions. School personnel invited us to speak to their staff to consider conflict resolution techniques and alternative discipline procedures. Soon we discovered that the concepts of restorative justice were beginning to take hold in other settings. We were no longer the initiators. As we listened to the police, community groups, schools, businesses, and faith communities, we learned that the concepts of consensus decision making, personal responsibility, peer conflict resolution, and communitarianism were becoming commonplace in many different settings. The ideals of restorative justice fit nicely in these other movements.

Perhaps most rewarding was watching what was flourishing in our three communities of Hastings, Burnsville, and especially South St. Paul. Community members became involved in problem solving over crime issues. These issues soon spilled over to other areas such as racism, quality of life, illicit use of alcohol and drugs, and so on. School personnel in the South St. Paul public schools began using the circle process to deal with all sorts of school issues, including resolution of conflict among elementary kids, a program that was initiated by the kids themselves. While anecdotal testimonials abound, the statistical data on violent acts per day confirms the success in our schools. The first elementary school using circles for learning and for behavior issues reported a drop in violent acts per day by as much as 50 percent per month. Recently high school kids brought up the idea of getting students trained as circle keepers.

Within three years, over 300 community citizens have been directly involved in South St. Paul Restorative Justice processes along with hundreds of students in the schools. Our culture was beginning to change. What had begun as our dream, soon started to take on a life of its own. Our struggle to influence soon gave way to trying to keep up with all of the change generated naturally by citizens. A struggle to get our citizens involved transformed itself into trying to figure out how the justice system could find the time and resources to participate in the exciting, life-changing process being held in our church basements and community centers.

This is not to say that all is well. Challenges remain for us. Government can be a reluctant partner, especially if some players perceive a loss of control or power. We have concerns about vigilantism and about community members' expecting too much from the justice system. Still, if you were a government official, with which would you rather be burdened? A complacent, apathetic community that criticizes decisions made by you and your peers? Or eager and engaged citizens who may stretch their participation beyond your comfort zone and even make some mistakes? We don't think that this choice is even a close call. We are just learning what it means to be partners. It means that each of us has a role to play, but that we are all pulling in the same direction. We once got the feeling that a government official could not be a citizen at the same time. There was a "we–they" feel. Now we no longer feel disconnected. The lines are blurring as we experience what it means to govern by the will of the people, and what it means for citizens to take responsibility for peace and harmony. We are democracy at work. Our slogan, Love, Law and Learning, is a constant reminder that we view ourselves as partners in learning organizations.

Coming Full Circle: Moving to Community

Darrol began his journey when two neighborhood juveniles vandalized his home. Among the things they left, was a piece of broken mirror from his parents' dresser. Staring into that mirror, he wrote this poem:

Take a look at this piece.
What do you see?
A broken mirror?
That's easy to see.

Take a look at this piece.
What do you see?
Your community? My community?
You? Me?

Take a look at this piece.
What will we do?
Will our actions reflect
What we need to renew?

NOTE

1. Quoted in Jerry Mander, "The Gift of Democracy," in *Absence of the Sacred* (San Francisco: Sierra Club Books, 1991).

REFERENCES

Carey, Mark. 1998. "Infancy, Adolescence and Restorative Justice: The Timing of Strategies in Promoting Organizational Change toward Restoration," Washington, D.C.: United States Department of Justice at http://www.ojp.usdoj.gov/nij/rest-just/ch3/infancy.htm.

Schein, Edgar S. 1981. "Does Japanese Management Style Have a Message For American Managers?" *Sloan Management Review,* Vol. 23, No. 1.

Stuart, Barry. 1997. *Building Community Justice Partnerships: Community Peacemaking Circles.* Ontario, Canada: Department of Justice.

Zehr, Howard. 1990. *Changing Lenses, A New Focus for Crime and Justice.* Scottsdale, PA: Herald Press.

14

There Are No Secrets Here
Secrets and Privacy in Juvenile Group Homes

WILLIAM DU BOIS

Author's Note: This paper originated out of an action situation. I was consulting with a juvenile group home for delinquent boys. I was doing staff training every other week on how to work with delinquency, and once a week I was holding a 3-hour session with the youth teaching them power skills. One evening I really got the kids to open up. They discussed the problems they were having with the cook. Most initially voiced the opinion that they thought she was "just a bitch" and nothing could be done. (This was a characterization both youth and staff had shared with me privately many times.) But in the discussion, people actually came to some appreciation of the cook's situation and who she might be. We invented ways they might successfully deal with her. In confronting a real-life problem, it was possible to teach the kids prosocial conflict resolution skills, assertiveness, and how to get what they wanted without negating another's self-esteem.

The next morning all the kids were grounded and lost their allowance for having referred to the cook as a "bitch" in my session. One youth had mentioned it to a counselor, who had informed the administrator. I was outraged. I felt that I had unwittingly tricked the kids into opening up and that they were now paying the consequences. How could one effectively help the kids if they couldn't open up and be themselves? When I was unable to change this, I resigned, but I told the administrator that in my consulting, either party could withdraw at any time; however, I got one more session to explain what was going on. I spoke in frustration. In reality I had invented this condition on the spot. I marvel to this day that the administrator agreed to allow me to present one more workshop to him and the staff.

What follows is the presentation that I gave him and the staff in a 3-hour session. After it was over, several of the staff told me privately that I had voiced what they had been wanting to say for years. Unfortunately, my talk did not change the situation. However, a later administrator of this same group home would make this paper required reading for staff.

The paper itself has an interesting history. Students tend to like it, finding it reasonable. Many group home staff say it honestly articulates the dilemma they find themselves in all the time. Administrators and group home supervisors often hate it, saying it is impractical and dangerous.

One clichéd argument is that once someone has broken the law, he or she has forfeited the right to privacy. But we must wonder at the effectiveness of such a stance. Is that practical?

The impeachment of President Clinton and the death of Princess Diana have made us more aware of the nature of front stage and backstage. Is privacy something people who lead a public life must surrender? Does committing a crime mean you are no longer entitled to a backstage? Or is backstage a crucial need for healthy people?

I would argue that by outlawing secrets, juvenile group homes create an atmosphere where youth are always on stage and all acts are available for public inspection. Counseling depends upon the bond of trust and intimacy fostered by secrets. Without such private spaces, effective counseling cannot take place. The realistic administrator recognizes this and balances kids' needs for privacy with organizational needs for information. Privacy is not some privilege to be forfeited for "bad behavior"; nor is it a luxury people must forgo when they enter the public arena of politics. Having a backstage region of privacy is crucial to good mental health.

We must be doing something wrong. Research shows that of offenders not caught and processed by the system, only 6 percent go on to a life of crime. Studies reveal most youth commit crimes and then simply age out. However, of those we treat in group homes and other institutions, many get stuck and can be expected to go on to repeated criminality. The cure seems worse than the disease.

Yet group homes are staffed by dedicated, underpaid counselors who give of themselves and labor with their hearts and souls because they care about helping youth. Whatever we are doing wrong must be fairly subtle.

SECRETS AND INTIMACY

One thing we are doing wrong is the way we deal with secrecy and privacy in the group home. Normally, counselors are required to share privileged information with other counselors and staff. Records are often logged with information that was intended by the youth resident for the counselor's ears only, now available to the entire staff and court officers. This is normally justified in terms of security and better knowledge to enhance treatment. However, something subtle is awry here.

Early sociologist Georg Simmel (1950) tells us that "the secret" is the foundation of intimacy. We know who our friends are precisely by their willingness to keep secrets. Indeed, a friend is someone we can trust not to reveal our secrets. It is with friends that we can lower our guard and be ourselves. Without secrets, this intimacy and trust are destroyed. According to Simmel, the secret is so crucial that without it, friendship and close bonding are impossible.

Now, we might question whether counselors can or should be "friends" with clients. However, something akin to the bonding process found in friendship is necessary in the therapeutic process. Psychologist Sigmund Freud echoes the same sentiments as Simmel. With his normal propensity for big terms, Freud calls it "transference" and "countertransference." Transference is the bonding of the patient to the therapist. Countertransference is the similar bonding of the counselor to the patient. And Freud (1950) says that without this transference/countertransference, *healing and the therapeutic process are impossible.* This pseudo-friendship process of trust and rapport is essential. Freud even suggests that the counselor must wait for transference to occur before productive counseling can begin.

Contemporary psychologist Scott Peck (1978) recasts Freud's transference language in more human terms. He says he regularly "falls in love" with his patients—although, of course, he does not act on this sexually. Without this involvement of caring for the person counseled, nothing can happen. I personally know many psychologists who accept as patients only people they like or are interested in. At first this may seem like the luxury of the successful therapist. However, these psychologists conclude from experience that without a bonding between counselor and client—liking, caring, trust, something approximating friendship in a therapeutic setting, or at least some genuine interest—counseling never works.

The seemingly subtle ritual of confidentially shared information being passed between staff and logged as open records takes on new meaning. Juveniles themselves see nothing subtle in the process. They feel betrayed. And rightly so. Many counselors will even tell a youth not to share certain information because they will be compelled to report it. However, such a barrier makes the counselor more remote from a child's life. The youth are unable to discuss certain subjects—to relax and lower their guard. The counselor can't counsel on problems youth are forbidden to share. Nor can an atmosphere be created in which youth can relax without always having to be on their best behavior. Despite pretenses of camaraderie, juvenile residents perceive the counselor as a cop monitoring their behavior. The seasoned juvenile resident will report that "you can't trust anyone here." And unfortunately, that is an accurate portrayal.

Of course, the group home originated the policy to prevent problems. The administrator obviously wants to know if one of the juveniles has a large quantity of heroin stashed away or is planning a major crime spree. In such cases, of course any responsible counselor would report this to all authorities. However, most secrets are not nearly so sinister. They may pertain to possession of a bottle of beer or a condom, or a 5-minute curfew violation. They may not even involve minor rule violations: In this consultation it was logged into the official record that a youth thought the cook was a "bitch." This was a common perception among residents. However, sharing the information certainly didn't improve the youth's rapport with the cook.

Every secret is an occasion for dialogue, problem sharing, trust, and support. Some information needs to be shared with staff, but each occasion may require a separate decision and a weighing of the factors involved, as would be true in any other social or professional setting. Should I violate a confidence in this instance, and if so how much should I tell?

As human beings, counselors will also naturally treat some youth differently than they treat others. To pretend that you are equally involved with each youth is simply a lie. Justice must be fair, but liking and bonding follow individual preferences. We all remember the one or two teachers who took a liking to

us. This special interest had lasting effects. A similar process of finding a "pseudo-friend"—someone you can rely on—is at work in the counseling process.

INSTITUTIONAL SCHIZOPHRENIA

Dramaturgists are sociologists who examine the social rituals of life. Many dramaturgists contend that schizophrenia, the mental illness, is nothing more than the "inability to get offstage" (Messenger, 1974). Most of us know the difference between "front stage" and "backstage." We select what kind of information to share in public and what kind to leave at home in the closet behind closed doors. Schizophrenics blur this distinction. If you ask them, "How are you?" they are as likely as not to respond, "My hemorrhoids are killing me—would you like to see the pictures?"

The schizophrenic doesn't recognize the need to present some information publicly to the world and keep other information private. If any of us were to share our failures, fears, awkward moments, and sins in the wrong setting—a job interview or judicial disposition review, for instance—we could come off looking bad indeed. (How many juveniles would like to have entered on their official record the comment "Masturbates frequently"? And yet I've seen a frequently locked bathroom door get it logged.) On front stage, the successful high school student learns to present a social image. We know from self-reported studies that half of all high school students have done drugs and 95 percent have consumed alcoholic beverages (Bartollas, 1990), yet the "normal student" learns to hide such behavior backstage rather than having it presented publicly on front stage.

The juvenile group home has created *institutional schizophrenia* by forbidding secrets between staff and youth, and by destroying privacy. Youth residents find it impossible to get offstage. They are always available for public inspection. There is no way to retreat backstage and regroup.

We must look, here, into the nature of *home*. Home is normally where we can get offstage and let our guard down. It is where we can be ourselves without worrying about consequences. But in many group homes, the rooms of residents do not even have doors. The normal privacy in which to recover from the outside world has been destroyed. (Now, we may say that you forfeit this privilege by violating the law. But this is not a privilege but the normal way people construct a healthy self.) *Anyone* living in an environment where you can't get offstage—an environment of institutional schizophrenia—would suffer problems (Rosenan, 1973). For a youth already experiencing problems, such an environment will make recovery much more unlikely.

We must ask if we are really creating a juvenile group "home" or only the illusion of a homelike environment. The issue of secrets is far from subtle—it is actually crucial.

Family is also one of the most crucial variables in delinquency. Family members are normally people we can count on to be "on our side." They are people we can be ourselves around. For the group home atmosphere to approximate a family setting, then, bonding and trust must be encouraged as well as concern and respect. We can expound on the value of the warmth of hearth, home, and family. But if we are to teach youth to build healthy relationships, we must begin with the interactions between staff and residents. We must practice what we preach.

MANAGING A GROUP HOME

Managing a juvenile group home is a tough business. From the organization's standpoint, the goal is to stay open. Success is measured in terms of occupancy rate. The reputation of the facility and its rapport with local officials, such as judges and school principals, and the general community are crucial. Without respect and referrals from the judicial system, a group home is doomed. Most homes must maintain at least an 80 percent occupancy rate just to cover expenses, salaries, mortgage payments, and insurance premiums. A group home's reputation in the community is worth its weight in gold. But to be effective, an administrator must do a balancing act between the organizational reality and the youth's reality (Figure 14.1).

When there is a conflict between the organizational reality and the youth's reality, the organization has a tendency to win. The board of directors live in fear of a front-page news story. Community leaders fear the worst from a group home in their neighborhood. A lawsuit, a runaway kid raping and killing, a drug racket inside the home—these are all a board of directors' worst nightmare. There are also court officials and social workers *who would ideally like to know everything.* When decisions on rules and policies are made, they are usually made in fear of a worst-case scenario. But rules should be made for normal everyday. If worst cases arise, they should be dealt with as exceptions. In my classes on the sociology of work, I teach that if we make policies by worst-case scenarios, then we make bad rules and policies. In juvenile group homes, living in fear of worst-case scenarios will prevent normal "home" and "family" functioning.

There are few advocates for the youth's reality on a daily basis, but the organizational reality meets the administrator's ears constantly. So the balance normally tips heavily in the organizational reality's favor. From the youth's standpoint, success is measured in terms of recidivism rate. Is the group home rehabilitating youth? The question gets lost in the shuffle. Youth are *without the power* to lobby effectively for their interests—after all, they are delinquents. Counselors may voice their concerns, but they also lack power when confronting their superior. Too often the youth's reality is left up in the air

FIGURE 14.1   Ideal Balance of Organization's Needs and Youth's Needs

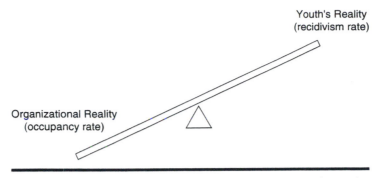

FIGURE 14.2   Typical Balance of Organizational versus Youth Needs

(Figure 14.2). The administrator is the only one with a foot in both worlds. He or she knows the needs of the youth and the home from daily experience; he or she also is the one who must deal with the judicial system, the board of directors, the school board, community concern, and local as well as state government. *It is the administrator's job to balance both realities.*

Secrets and privacy are critical issues. If we respect the youth's perspective, they are essential for normal functioning. From the counselor's perspective, they are necessary for effective remediation. From the organization's standpoint, they occasionally create problems that could prove explosive. But if we are to be effective, we must not outlaw *living* in group homes.

CONCLUSION

Being able to get offstage is essential to good mental health. We abolish backstage regions at our own peril. In adult prisons, I have had many inmates tell me they purposely got themselves thrown into the hole for a minor infraction to gain a few days of solitude. All people need a backstage.

Too often, we objectify and distance ourselves from youth. We seem to have developed two theories of behavior. One theory explains "our behavior." The other theory explains "their behavior." It was classic sociologist Charles Cooley (1962) who recommended

"sympathetic introspection" as the method for sociology. We must be very suspicious of theories of "their" behavior that aren't grounded in reality enough to also provide some insight into "our" behavior. That is, if something is not good for normal people, then it probably is not good for delinquents. Secrecy is fundamental to forming close, caring relationships. Elements of privacy are essential to each person's feelings of self-worth. If we are to be effective in rehabilitating juveniles, each group home should rethink the issues of privacy.

Students and the general public find these recommendations to be obvious, but many practitioners have been very threatened by these ideas, saying they are impractical. An approach involving even some trust undermines both these practitioners' worldview and their therapeutic approach, which demands control and total knowledge. I am reminded of the insight by psychologist Gerald Jampolsky (1983) that we really have only one choice in life. The choice is between two different paradigms: love and fear.

We must be streetwise. But we must not abolish our humanism. We must not build a world strictly on suspicion and distrust. We know what we get if we do that. Fear then becomes a self-fulfilling prophecy with all its evil consequences: Our group homes do not rehabilitate, our counselors do not humanize, and our juvenile institutions produce increased crime instead of reform.

I've often heard prison guards say doing a favor for an inmate opens you up to being blackmailed. If you look the other way at a rule infraction, the inmate may come to expect it. The inmate now has the power to betray you by turning you in. Secrets end up making both parties vulnerable to each other. Seasoned veterans say that you must always treat everyone exactly the same.

But one can be blackmailed only if the administration is responsive to it. If favors and secrets are forbidden, then guards, counselors, and staff are vulnerable for any thoughtfulness they show prisoners or juveniles. However, if the administration realizes the necessity for secrets and friendships, then such blackmailing becomes impossible. Indeed, the inmate or youth may try it, but it won't work. This takes the fear away for staff. However, this approach requires a certain amount of maturity on the part of staff, administrators, and the general public. And it requires that we trust the judgment of our staff.

If we keep a person's secret, we are treating them as special. Many have criticized special treatment because it is unfair to others. But we need to recall the haunting statement with which Erich Fromm ended the section on "The Practice of Love" in *The Art of Loving* (1956): "The practice of love begins with realizing the difference between love and fairness."

Fairness is not mistreating anyone. But if we reduce all interaction to the common denominator of fairness and treat everyone the same, then there is no room for love. Love and fairness are entirely different paradigms.

Love *is* special treatment. We don't emotionally click with everyone. No one person can give everyone special attention. Love needs to be more than just universal love for everyone. In order to grow we need to be loved *in particular.* It is just such special treatment that has made a difference in our lives: the teacher or coach or aunt or uncle who took the extra time. If we believe such an insight, then our strategy must become finding ways to match people so that everyone will find someone who will give them special attention.

Secrets involve a risk. They make us vulnerable. They are a leap of faith. When we bare our souls to others, we can only hope that our truths will be respected. Without people who'll keep our secrets, we live in a place where we are perpetually strangers.

REFERENCES

Bartollas, Clemens. *Juvenile Delinquency.* New York: Macmillan, 1990.

Cooley, Charles. *Social Organization.* New York: Schocken Books, 1962.

Jampolsky, Gerald G. *Teach Only Love: The Seven Principles of Attitudinal Healing.* New York: Bantam Books, 1983.

Messenger, E. A. "Life as Theater" in Denis Brissett and Chris Edgley, *Life as Theater: A Dramaturgical Sourcebook.* Chicago: Aldine, 1974.

Fromm, Erich. *The Art of Loving.* New York: Harper and Row, 1956.

Freud, Sigmund. *Collected Papers of Sigmund Freud* (trans. J. Riviere). London: Hogarth Press, 1950.

Peck, Scott. *The Road Less Traveled.* New York: Simon & Schuster, 1978.

Rosenan, Daniel. "On Being Sane in Insane Places," in *Science* (1973): 250–258.

Simmel, Georg. "The Secret," in *The Sociology of Georg Simmel* (ed. Kurt Wolf). Glencoe, Ill: Free Press, 1950.

15

Marriage Is for Life

SIDNEY M. JOURARD

Editors' Note: In a classic paper, Sidney M. Jourard offers a model of marriage as dialogue. It may seem strange to include a piece by a psychologist in a book on sociology; but Jourard shows how cultural myths influence our behavior. We shouldn't talk about role models; we should talk about relationship models. Our model of a relationship influences our roles and how we act. He suggests a more healthy cultural model for relationships.

I feel rather honored to have been invited here, and I am rather dismayed, and delighted in a way, to see how many people there are fighting the good fight. And it is indeed a good fight. I'll throw in my 10 cents' worth or whatever denomination you might want to put after it.

The title of my talk has nothing to do with chronological time. When I chose the title "Marriage Is for Life" I meant that marriage is to enhance life, and it is not so much an answer as it is a search. I want to direct my remarks to that search, the search for life itself.

IDEAL (AND FALSE) IMAGES OF MARRIAGE

The image of the good marriage is perhaps one of its most destructive features. The ideal marriage is a snare, a trap, an image the worship of which destroys life. The ideal marriage is like the ideal body or any other ideal, useful only if it engenders the divine discontent which leads to questing and authenticity.

Taken from tape recording of the plenary address at the annual meeting of the American Association of Marriage and Family Counselors and the National Council on Family Relations, St. Louis, Missouri, October 26, 1974. Reprinted by permission of Antoinette Jourard.

Whose image of a way to live together will guide a relationship? This is a question relevant for a president and his electorate, a doctor and his patient, a parent and child, a researcher and his subject, or a husband and wife. Shall it be an exercise in the concealment and display of power or a commitment to dialogue? Failure of dialogue is the crisis of our time, whether it be between nation and nation, us and them, or you and I.

I had thought of putting together a book of my several writings on marriage, education, psychology, politics, and business and entitling it "Disaster Areas," for that indeed is what they are. The state of marriage and family life in this country can easily be called a disaster. I think it stems in part from unrealistic expectations and in larger part because of a culturally induced arrest of growth in adults. Perfectly good marriages are ended because something has gone wrong. Actually, I would say they are ended right at the point where they could begin.

There are two fallacies perpetuated which keep the disasters happening. One is the myth of the right partner. The other is the myth of the right way to act so as to ensure peace, joy, and happiness. People believe, or are led to believe, that if they just find the right partner, the right answer to the riddle of their existence will be found. Once having found the right person and the way of relating that is satisfying at this time, the partners try to do everything to prevent change. That's tantamount to trying to stop the tide. Change, indeed, happens, but it happens underground, is concealed, and then it's introduced and experienced as a catastrophe. Instead of welcoming it, the partners find it devastating. Each may then seek to find someone who will not change, so that they never need face the need to change themselves.

MARRIAGE AS DIALOGUE

Marriage at its best, according to the image that is making more sense to me, is a relationship within which change is generated by the very way of relating—dialogue—so that growth as well as identity and a sense of rootedness are engendered. Change is not so much a threat as it is the fruit of a good marriage, according to this image. Marriage is for growth, for life. It's a place to call home, but like all homes one must leave it in its present form and then return, and then leave it, and then return, like Odysseus, leaving Ithaca and returning.

Kierkegaard refused to marry and thereby defied the nineteenth century. I have refused to divorce, and I defy the twentieth. When 1 marriage in 3 is dissolved, or maybe it's 2.6, to remain wedded to the same spouse is virtually to live an alternate lifestyle. If so few marriages endure, then something is nonviable about that way of being married. I have tried in the 26 years of my marriage to be married in the ways designated by tradition, by the mass media, by my friends, by textbooks on marriage, by my wife's image of a good marriage—but none of these ways were for life. None were life-giving, but were rather images, or better, idols. To worship idols is idolatry, a sin. To worship means to live for, to sacrifice what is of ultimate value. To worship an image of marriage is, like any other idolatry, the expenditure of one's own life, time, and vitality to enhance the image. That such marriage is disastrous is self-evident. When it endures it becomes a major cause of psychological distress and physical illness in our land.

Conventional medicine, psychiatry, and psychotherapy, and, for that matter, marriage counseling and family counseling, frequently function very much like combat surgery. The illness and suffering which reach the healers stem from the stress and "dispiritation" engendered from inauthentic family relationships. Laing and Esterson (1965) documented the way a family image can be preserved at the cost of one member being scapegoated as a schizophrenic. The wards for cancer, heart disease, gunshot and knife injuries, suicide attempts, and other stress ailments provide evidence that nondialogic family life engenders unrelenting and destructive stress. To be married is not an unmixed blessing. If marriage is hell and family life is a major cause of disease, which indeed it is, why stay in it, or get in it?

Is the family dead, as David Cooper (1971) observed? If it's dying, should we then kill it, put it out of its misery?

What do people do who have tried marriage and then gotten out of it? The overwhelming majority remarry, and try to live the second, third, or seventh marriage in a way that is more life-giving for the self and others than the first. Frequently these marriages "fail" as did the first. And I put "fail" in quotes, because I don't think marriages fail; I think people fail marriages.

Wherever I go in this country I get uncomfortable. I think it's more so in California than elsewhere, and it's not with smog or even the inhabitants of Orange County, but with the people one encounters everywhere. I am a trained and rather experienced psychotherapist, tuned in to the nonverbal expressions of despair, loneliness, anguish, and need. So many of the adults I encounter casually or in depth are suffering a rupture of their last lawful or common-law marriage, and are desperately looking for a new one or despairingly avoiding all but superficial relationships in order to avoid risk. The silent shrieks of pain deafen me. To be married is for many boredom or hell. To be unmarried, legally or unlegally, as many experience it, is hell and despair. Is there an alternative?

Everything depends on the model or metaphor which defines the marriage one will live, seek, grow in, or die from. There are lethal images of marriage and family life, and there are life-giving models. I take it that enduring, growing relationships are essential for truly human life and for personal fulfillment and growth. I take it that happiness, pleasure, or growth, if sought as ends in and of themselves, will not happen. They are by-products of a fully lived life. A life lived in continuing dialogue with some few others will encourage, even force growth.

I take it as true that there is no way to go through life without some pain, suffering, loneliness, and fear. We can help one another minimize the shadow side of life; none can avoid it completely. To seek to avoid pain at all costs is to make an idol out of pleasure or painlessness. To avoid solitude at all costs is to make an idol out of chronic companionship. To avoid anxiety and depression at all costs is to make an idol out of safety and elation. To have to achieve orgasm with somebody in particular is to make an idol of that person or of the genital experience. To sacrifice everything for the breathless experience of being in love is to make an idol of breathlessness.

Many people live in such idolatrous fashion. They marry for those ends and divorce when the other side of reality creeps or bursts into the magic circle, only to seek another playmate or protector in relation to whom the idol may once again be worshiped and the sacrifice of life continue afresh.

Marriage as dialogue through life is for me a viable image, one that engenders life and growth as the conversation unfolds. Dialogue for me, as for Martin Buber (1937), is the appropriate way for human beings to be or to strive to be with each other: not imposition, power plays, and manipulation. Family life is an appropriate place for dialogue to be learned and practiced. And through dialogue it's a place to grow in competence, self-sufficiency, and self-esteem.

To me the great failure in marriage, as in American education, is that neither institution as lived and practiced fosters enlargement of self-respect, respect for others, or growing competence in the skills that make life livable. Deception, manipulation, bribery, and threats are as American as apple pie and mother. These skills are learned in relation with Mum, Dad, the teacher, or the teaching machine.

There is, as near as I now know, no assured way to practice marriage as dialogue except by living it. As soon as a relationship becomes habitual, dialogue has ended. Predictable, habitual ways for people to act with one another are simply nonverbal ways to say the same things to one another day after day, year after year. Habit is the great anesthetic, the annihilator of consciousness.

Nondialogic ways of being married are either exercises in a chronic struggle for power and control or they are harbors to escape those aspects of life that would engender growth. Some people stay married so they will have someone to control. Some people stay married so they will have an ear to talk into. Some people stay married so they can suffer or make their partner suffer. Most curiously, some get divorced when their partner will no longer be controlled, will no longer listen, or will no longer consent to suffer. The other's changes may be, indeed, a sign of the other person's personal growth. The one who gets a divorce may find yet another partner with whom control can be practiced or who will listen to undisciplined chatter with apparent interest or who will accept pain.

All this is by way of saying that I think in America and in the countries that follow the example set by the American way of life, we expect more out of marriage than it could ever deliver, and we expect the wrong things. God, in Her infinite wisdom, so designed us that we are of two kinds and we find one another irresistible at various stages in our lives, so much so that we decide to live together. So far, so good. It's joyous to find another person attractive who finds you attractive, then to make love, even to have children.

Then the honeymoon ends and the marriage begins. It is at this point that I think most divorce happens. We are hung up on honeymoons. My honeymoon was a disaster. I knew next to nothing about tenderness and solicitude, sex, women's sexuality, my bride's sexuality. I was incapable of dialogue. I wanted to be seen in a certain way. I needed my wife to be a certain way, and, obliging girl that she was, she obliged. She seemed to be the kind of person she thought I thought she was, the kind of person she felt I would like. We carried out this double masquerade for about 3 years. It took me that long to cheat. By 7 years I was an accomplished dissembler in the realm of my sex life—not my love life, where I was a truth-teller in all realms except that.

With our first separation I had a modest collection of female scalps, so to speak, to my credit; and my wife, to her credit, after the shock of disclosure wore off, discovered the dubious joys of semiguilty infidelity. Through some fluke, though, within a month of a decree of divorce, we decided to resume our by now somewhat scarred relationship, rather wiser and more honest with one another about who we were. This openness, for those not practiced in it, was pure hell. It was painful, I assure you. It was painful for me to learn that my wife had a mind, a perspective, and feelings of her own different from mine. She was not the girl I married; in fact, she never was. I married my fantasy, and so did she. She had some coping to do, discovering that I was not the saint I had once seemed. She learned I was, and still am to some extent, a scarcely bridled privateer, a pirate, an adventurer, barely domesticated to her or American conceptions of married males.

How do two or more eccentric and energetic people live together? With humor or not at all. I did not become selectively gelded upon marriage. The more I reflect upon it, the more I like myself, having had the courage to pursue those ways of keeping vital and alive as nondestructively as I did. I could have done worse. I could have sought a divorce or have been divorced by my wife. If the first 3 years were the honeymoon—actually, only about 1 year was honeymoon—boredom and pretense at joy in our sameness is a better description of our next 2 years. My cheating was the beginning of a marriage with some authentic companionship, some lying and getting on with the career, and the experience of living with several very young children. This marriage or this way of being married lasted until 7 years, when I experienced the death of my father, the completion of my first book, and the dreaded disclosure of my rather complicated affairs with several other women. Here was a real opportunity to be taught a lesson or to learn a lesson. I didn't divorce, however, nor did my wife divorce me, because we retained some recollection of affection between us, we had some children to care for, and a vast amount of anger and mutual reacquaintance to go through. It is, I assure you again, a painful experience extended through time to make yourself known to the person with whom you live and to learn aspects of her experience,

attitudes, hopes, fears, and so on which shatter your image of her.

But my marriage and family life were not all my life. I had friends, other interests, and I pursued these, as did she. My life did not begin when I met her nor end when we were out of contact with one another.

My third marriage to her began with hope and resolve, as we struggled to find some enjoyment in living and to care for our children. I suspect we were growing in experience, self-sufficiency, and self-esteem. I hesitate to use certain words, but I'll say them. The point I was going to make is that marriage and family life is a wonderful place to learn shit, fecal detritus, because if you don't know shit, you have not lived. But if that's all you know, you have not lived.

I don't know how many marriages I have had by now, but I am married at the present time to a different woman of the same name in ways that are suited to our present stage of growth as human beings. I am not breathlessly in love with my wife, nor is she with me. Now, she read this and there are some asterisks in her handwriting. It says, "Maybe not breathlessly, but I do love you now with more intensity and depth and true caring than I ever have in my life."

When we spend a great deal of time in one another's proximity, we can both know irritations, even rages of astonishing intensity. It is difficult for two strong and passionate and willful people to share space and time without humor and respect for the other—even though she is wrong, as from my point of view she is. It would be so much easier for me to divorce her and to live with, even marry, some younger woman who has firmer breasts, a smaller waist, who is as sexy as a civet, who worships me and wants to have an intense and meaningful relationship with me, who would attend to my every word and think I was the Messiah or at least worthy of the Nobel Prize. Many of my colleagues have done that. I could never see—except when I was most exasperated with my wife and fed up with being a father—why these friends of mine, otherwise sensible, wished to play the same record over again. I find someone whose perspective is smaller than mine, or who wants me to be their father, or who is but an echo of my own perspective, rather boring. Flattering, but boring. And I don't want to father anybody, because I've been a father. I find a grown person of the opposite sex incites me much less to rape or riot than a young girl but is more interesting, by and large, at least to listen to.

It takes a long time to give up manipulative and mystifying ways of relating to others in order to trust oneself in dialogue. My training and experience as a psychotherapist has influenced my conception and experience of marriage, or perhaps it's the other way around. My colleagues in the American Academy of Psychotherapists are indeed a rather eccentric lot with many backgrounds and theoretical orientations. All were trained in some way of acting with a patient which was believed to influence, heal, or otherwise impose magical power upon the sufferer. All learned through experience that whatever else they did, they helped people grow by entering into dialogue with them, by being fully present, struggling through impasses, and growing through those struggles. Impasses were not to be avoided, they were to be sought out and celebrated, as painful as they were. They helped their patients grow by staying in relationship with them. The growth that is crucial in this conception of therapy is increased awareness of one's own worth as a person and a realization that one is vastly stronger than anyone had ever imagined. This sense of worth and of strength protects one from entering into and staying in a way of relating to another that is devitalizing and sickening.

A book on marriage which I have read—and I have read many, including the O'Neills' (O'Neill and O'Neill, 1972)—and which addresses this mystery of growth with some of the respect that it deserves is a small volume written by Israel Charny called *Marital Love and Hate* (1972). Compared to Charny's vision, many of the other books fail to acknowledge, I think, the depths of misery and destructiveness which are the other side of personal growth. Charny sees the family not strictly as haven or a place for fun and games, although it can be that, or as a place for sexual delights, but as a place where that most savage of all creatures, man, can learn to share time and space nonviolently and nondestructively. Armed by his vi-

sion, as well as by my own, I can see that many so-called successful marriages and happy families are that way because someone is repressing his perspective or is colluding with others in the destruction of his own perspective.

According to this view, marriage is not for happiness, I have concluded after 26½ years. It's a many-splendored thing, a place to learn how to live with human beings who differ from oneself in age, sex, values, and perspectives. It's a place to learn how to hate and to control hate. It's a place to learn laughter and love and dialogue. I'm not entirely persuaded that marriage and family counseling is a profession with any particular contribution to make to the quality of life. There is, so far as I now know, no way for people to live alone or with others that God endorsed as the way that She intended. *[Laughter.]* Why is that funny? Certainly She intended that we cohabit to conceive and then to rear children, but the exact way we should live with one another was never specified. We have to grope and search, according to this view. As near as I can see, such groping for viable, nondestructive ways proceeds best within a context of dialogue.

Dialogue takes courage and commitment to honesty. When people find they can no longer live with their partner, it is not divorce or separation that is indicated. This is in some ways like suicide. The person who tries to kill himself is being unduly literal. By his act he is saying that he no longer wishes to live in the way he has been, and he is also saying that he can imagine no other way to live. He doesn't necessarily wish to stop living, just to stop living in that way. His failure is a failure of imagination as much as it is a failure of nerve.

Divorce too frequently means that one partner or the other refuses to continue living married in that way. The divorcee then finds someone with whom some other dimension of himself can be expressed. This looks like change or growth. I have wondered whether hitherto unexpressed dimensions of self could not have emerged in relation to the spouse, because with the new partner an impasse will arrive and there will be the necessity to struggle with it.

If there is growth in serial marriage—and there is—one wonders why there could not be growth in the first. I know of many marriages in which one partner or the other refused to acknowledge or value the change in the other. The unchanged one ordered the changed one to revert to the way he or she was earlier, on pain of divorce.

The failure of marriage is the failure of our culture to provide models and reasonable expectations about human relationships. Because we lie so much about our relationships, especially to our children, and because the breadth and depth of authentic experience is not presented in movies, comics, books, or TV, nobody knows what is expectable or what is healthy or life-giving or potentially life-giving in marriage. People think that if they get angry or bore one another or fail to respond sexually that the marriage is finished, that they are out of love. Perhaps the overestimation of romantic love is one of the more pernicious patterns in our society.

When spouses deceive one another for the first time, that is the time the potentially life- and growth-promoting aspects of marriage can begin. When the couple find themselves in rage, that is the time not for divorce but for celebration. Whimsically, I thought that the first betrayal of marriage should come on the honeymoon, so that it can be gotten over and the dialogue resumed.

Marriage is not an answer but a search, a process, a search for life, just as dialogue is a search for truth. Yesterday's marriage or way of being married is today's trap. The way out of the trap is to resume the dialogue, not to end it, unless someone is pledged not to grow and change. One of my colleagues is being divorced after 22 or 23 years of marriage. He is a Southern fellow; his wife, an extremely pious member of the Methodist church, is a "lousy lay," he assures everyone; and he explored another young woman. And the way he put it, "You know, when I went to bed with her she liked it." He carried on, "It was great, and I discovered there was another way, but then my wife found out about it and she made me confess to our children and then made me give her up" and so on. And, sadly, he is divorcing her, or she is divorcing him; they are divorcing each other, because she wants to remain exactly as she was when she was 14 or 15. He's growing and searching. Yesterday's way of being married is today's trap. The

way out of the trap is to resume the dialogue, not to end it.

If marriage counseling is not training and experience in dialogue, then it falls short in my opinion of its help-giving potential. How does one function as a marriage and family counselor? In the same way two porcupines mate—with difficulty and great care. I know of no techniques for counseling individuals, or couples, or entire family units. There is something about the experience of having struggled to retain one's self-respect and *joie de vivre* in the face of marital disaster, one's own marital disaster, that helps one to listen with empathy and humor to others' difficulties. I think that inventiveness and a profound faith in every individual's capacity to overcome all disasters and to find their own strength is helpful. I am always astonished at how couples convince themselves that they cannot live more than 5 minutes if their partner changes in one way or if they are incommunicado from their partner for 5 minutes. That is astonishing when you think about it: Two reasonably adequate human beings live together, and then if one of them changes in one jot or tittle, the other person is either to commit murder, suicide, or divorce. Or if they split for a day or a week or a month to recenter themselves, the one who did not choose to be apart for a while will very frequently do everything in their power to punish the one who is seeking to recenter herself or himself.

In various earlier papers I have explored the importance of modeling—of being an exemplar of viable ways to live, or of the possibility of overcoming difficulties in living. Theory and technique are valuable in counseling, as they are in any other enterprise; but they can be the refuge of scoundrels and fools, like patriotism. If he or she is not a spokesman for and an exemplar of dialogue, integrity, and a relentless commitment to a search for viable ways to live and grow, then he or she will be found out. There is no way to impersonate integrity for very long. As in all realms where human beings deal with one another, there is no place in family counseling for dissembling and technical manipulation by the professional person. Marriage and family counseling to enhance or to terminate marriages proceeds best, perhaps only, through dialogue.

DIALOGUE WITH AUDIENCE

QUESTION: Explain what you mean by dialogue.

RESPONSE: The image of dialogue that I speak from is dialogue as expounded by the philosopher Martin Buber in rather poetic terms. As a conversation between I and Thou, is the way he put it. But to put it in prose, dialogue is to speak your truth in response to the other person's truth, with no effort in a concealed way to lie or to con or to manipulate the other person to be in some way what he is not. It's speaking your truth and then waiting to hear the other person's truth, which you can never predict or control. As soon as you try to predict or control it, dialogue is ended. Out of it, incidentally, comes growth. Without it there may be change, but it's not necessarily the change you would call growth.

QUESTION: Is this view of marriage as dialogue an appropriate view of human relationships outside the marriage—relationships within the community and so on?

RESPONSE: I would say, absolutely, that it is the failure of the desire for and the trust in dialogue that engenders the way of life of power manipulation, the desire to influence friends and to control people. Business and politics are the refuge of liars and cheats. *[Comment from audience].* Absolutely right. The comment was, "Dialogue works only if both are committed to it and understand something of its rules." And this raises the question—and it's more than a question, it's a challenge—where do you learn dialogue? When you've never experienced it or encountered it within your own family, where let's say your mother and your father for cosmetic reasons lie to you about themselves or about their own relationship, where your teachers in school lied to you in one way or another by withholding personal perspectives in order to be functionaries and spokesmen for those who wrote the curriculum—where do you learn dialogue? I'm still learning, but I've thought of changing my professional title from Professor of Psychology to Professor of Dialogue to express a commitment to learn dialogue and to teach dialogue. But the way that you teach it is by living it. It's one of those ironies where you can't talk about it, you live it. And the only way to learn it is by example, by invitation. And I think that the real challenge for the so-called helping professions is not to become more sophisticated in the design of research to prove that they are more or less effective than somebody else. And the real challenge is not to develop even more sophisticated theories of influence and technique and theory. The real challenge is to learn oneself how to achieve greater competence and capacity for dialogue with a wider range of humanity, people who differ from you. Growth in dialogue is growth in two ways: growth in the capacity to enter into and sustain a relationship of dialogue with someone radically different from you, increasingly different from you; and/or the ability to commence a dialogic conversation with another person and follow it where it will lead without resorting to lying or evasion. That kind of growth is extremely rare.

QUESTION: *[Inaudible.]*

RESPONSE: First part of the question: Such integration is done with difficulty. That's glib. I think it's absurd to separate the two. Not to be concerned with your own growth and integrity is to be out of touch with something very important. To be concerned only with your own growth and integrity is to be shortsighted. They are coterminous, for want of a better word.

QUESTION: Do you believe in justifiable divorce?

RESPONSE: Absolutely. Please, do not construe what I have said as being the path for everybody, because that's not my intention nor my belief. Human beings being human beings, we have many ways to find our own way of life. We have our own styles and places for growth, and I have no reason to doubt that for those individuals who have chosen to further their quest for life and meaning and growth by moving out of one relationship into another that there are nondestructive and lifegiving and growth-promoting ways of doing this. There are some good books that have been written by people who, loaded with their scars, can actually say, as a friend of mine said on being divorced, that it really is not as bad a state of being as my enemies could wish—or as blissful as my unhappily married friends would hope. Dialogue is not just words. You see, actions are words, and a friendship, a marriage, a parent-child relationship is a dialogue; words and a dialogue in actions; my turn to bow, your turn to curtsy. We're saying something about ourselves by our actions and what we are saying. What I do is in some way an expression or a continuation of my dialogue with the persons I am involved with. Dialogue is in words and it is in those actions that are words too. Actions speak louder than words lots of times.

QUESTION: Is dialogue to be limited and its contribution to growth limited only to one's personal relationships, intimate personal relationships? Can one not engage in dialogue and grow through one's work, through one's reading, one's contacts with nature?

RESPONSE: I have to say yes. What we're talking about, really, both in dialogue and in being in nature is—again I'll quote Buber. Buber made some such comment as this, that the essence of human life involves distance and relation. To put something at a distance is to let it be itself, and in letting the other be itself/himself/herself, one is being oneself and letting that which is reveal itself, so that you're not imposing your preconceptions on the tree, the car, the book, the other person. The response is on the other side, and for me my relationships with people involve distance and relation. One cannot stay chronically in relation. If you can't back off, it's devastating, but if you can't enter into relation, it's devastating. It's never either/or, it's both.

QUESTION: *[Inaudible.]*

RESPONSE: The comment is that this conception of dialogue seems utopian. To some extent I agree, because I think it takes growth, courage, and commitment to enter into and stay into dialogue, and it's difficult and I think it's a manifestation of growth. You start out unable or unwilling to enter the rigors of dialogue or to stay in them very long, and depending on the degree of enlightenment, really enlarged awareness, that you

will achieve will depend whether or not you grow in the capacity to enter into and stay in dialogue or whether you will choose to live a life of seeming semblance and power manipulation games. It's a matter, I think, of experience, the practicality of it.

QUESTION: *[Inaudible.]*

RESPONSE: To have been reared in a culture that predefined roles, where everyone was told how men are, how women are—and, for that matter, in a white-dominated society, how blacks are.... Because he was never equipped by training, experience, or example, let's say to deal with a woman who wasn't just an itty-bitty thing. If you're a "good ole boy," women are "li'l ole things." And for the "li'l ole thing" to prove to have a mind of her own is mind-blowing and very threatening. How to address this problem? Again, I know of no solutions. With humor, I think. I don't mean to laugh it out of existence; I mean, it's part of the human comedy. We've got to learn how to change our views and our expectations about what other people can be like and what their capacities are, and it very frequently means giving up some prerogatives and privileges, which is done painfully and reluctantly. And, I think, increased awareness is very helpful, but I don't know any way of easing the pain unless it's to stay drunk all the time. It's desirable to ease the pain. The question is, are there some rules and guidelines? Well, yes is a better answer. One rule is to try truly to listen to what the other person is saying with their words and their nonwords: truly to listen, because truly to listen is to explore your concepts of what the other person is like. So, to learn through practice, to suspend preconceptions, and truly to listen to what another person is saying with their words and gestures. And the other rule is to struggle painfully to find the courage and the words to speak the truth of your reaction. There's no recipe there, man!

QUESTION: *[Inaudible.]*

RESPONSE: Let's see if I can grasp the sense of the question. I'll restate it and see if I have a part of what you're saying: "Is there a place in relationship, is there a time and place to be nondialogic, but instead to be manipulative or commanding?"

QUESTION: Can dialogue be destructive?

RESPONSE: Yes, the whole function of dialogue is to destroy false images of one another. The very nature of dialogue is to destroy illusion. Now that's frequently painful, and there's a time and a place, I suppose, that comes with wisdom and experience to choose one's time to destroy illusions. Because sometimes you can destroy someone's illusions and maybe they can't cope with that right now. They might be able to cope with it the day after tomorrow, however. No, dialogue is destructive of illusion and that's what it's for.

QUESTION: *[Inaudible.]*

RESPONSE: Fundamentally, when I'm working as a psychotherapist in trying to develop a relationship of dialogue with the other person and within the framework of that relationship I don't have in advance any preset agenda—that I'm going to make sure that we get some Gestalt exercises in and some bioenergetic exercises. For me the ongoing conversation is the process; and if in that context it's meaningful as my next response to put my arm around a person, I have no reason not to, unless common sense tells me that's not appropriate. That doesn't elaborate much, but that's as much as I can tell you.

REFERENCES

Buber, M. *I and Thou*. Edinburgh: T. & T. Clark, 1937.

Charny, I. *Marital love and hate*. New York: Macmillan, 1972.

Cooper, D. *Death of the family*. New York: Random House, 1971.

Laing, R. D., and Esterson, A. *Sanity, madness, and the family*. London: Tavistock Publications, 1965.

O'Neill, N., and O'Neill, G. *Open marriage: A new lifestyle for couples*. New York: J. B. Lippincott, 1972.

16

Parenting without Controlling
Caring for the Relationship

WILLIAM WAGNER

Editors' Note: In a thought-provoking and perhaps controversial article, Bill Wagner offers a realistic model for parenting. Today we are accustomed to hearing about "postmodernism." Bill Wagner offers practical, easy-to-understand applications. In the modern scientific world, we expected that we could find the truth and that the truth would then tell us how to live. In the postmodern world, we learn that there are many truths and many different interpretations of it. You have yours and I have mine. How do we get along and share the world? Perhaps this question is never more critical than when we live with children.

Parenting is hidden among the habits of everyday life. Most of the time we don't even think about what our parenting patterns really are. If we take specific situations and look into them for some clue as to what we are doing, we can gain some insight into what we are and into how we parent. It is important to be able to see what we are doing in order to do a better job. The problem is that most of the time we can't see the meaning of our behavior and we don't take the time to carefully consider it. We act automatically without thinking about our behavior. It is the automatic parenting that gets us into trouble. When we take the time to think about our behavior we must admit that we look pretty stupid; and if we think that this stupidity gets by our children, we are in serious need of a reality check. Actions of our children are reactions to our behavior, and unless we can see that, we can get nowhere. Thinking about parenting situations and how they developed can be instructive.

Years ago, when I was just out of graduate school, my uncle called me on the phone and asked if I would come over. It was an emergency. When I got

there, my uncle announced that his daughter, 16 years old, had run away. He and my aunt wanted to know what to do.

"We called you because you have studied about this kind of thing and we don't know what to do next."

"Well, yes, I have." I felt uncomfortable. The theories are clear; I can teach them in my sleep; but what *do* I tell my aunt and uncle about this specific act of delinquency, about my cousin?

"We need some help. We have to get our daughter back!"

I had never felt so useless. A Ph.D. in sociology with juvenile delinquency as a special area of study and I didn't have anything to say that any other caring person would not have to say. "My" sociology told me to stay objective, merely to explain how these kinds of things happen in this culture. In my head I was saying, "Well, what we have to do is to start over. You've done a lot of things wrong. You created a juvenile delinquent, and as a scientist it is not my place to tell you what to do. What do I look like, a social worker?" My science made it impossible for me to do much at all that I could not have done as any other member of the family.

Today I would know how to help. Today I could help them to understand what was happening, and why running away "made sense" to my cousin, and, most importantly, how they could begin to construct a relationship in which running away would not "make sense."

For the last 7 years, I have been teaching a course on parenting called Parenting without Controlling: Caring for the Relationship. Most of the students are graduate students who are teachers or who are working in the areas of child care and development, juvenile justice, or adolescent treatment programs. These students have done much to challenge and refine my thinking on parenting.

I can no longer think about parenting as I once did. So much of what made sense about parenting 10 years ago is unthinkable for me today. Fifteen years ago I spanked my eldest son because I thought it made sense. Today I can't imagine any justification for spanking a child. Ten years ago I used threats and fear of punishment as a way to gain compliance. Today I see such techniques as totally unacceptable. The process of transforming my parenting has indeed included a different way of thinking about parenting and the role of children and parents.

The greatest confirmation I have ever received came one night as my daughter and I bummed around Minneapolis–St. Paul waiting for my wife to get out of an evening class. We had had a fun evening, visiting a children's book store, doing sixth-grade homework at a Dairy Queen over french fries, and then just generally clowning around. In the midst of it all Brittin said, "You know, Dad, I think we have the best father–daughter relationship in the world." I think the emphasis upon building a good relationship with children has had positive results in our particular situation, and I think it can have a positive impact on any parent–child relationship.

THE POLITICS OF CONTROL

The notion that punishment will "teach a lesson" still dominates a lot of parenting. It does teach a lesson, but not the one we think. Most parents who use this approach do so because their parents used it—and because there are still many individuals offering advice about parenting who have never been able to think their way out of one variation or another of the gun-to-the-head logic that says the reason for following parents' rules is to keep from getting punished. If the gun to the head is the reason I dance, what happens when I get the gun? What happens when children grow up or when parents forget to be vigilant or when parents get too tired or "soft-hearted" to punish? Punishment has been the cornerstone of parenting. It is a constant threat to happiness for children and a dreaded task for adults.

Our culture still conceptualizes good parenting as behavior that ensures that the parent will be obeyed, that the child will do as the parent wants. It is a model in which there is only one valid point of view, only one way to look at things, and that is the way the parents see it. The model is still the monarch and the loyal subjects. Parenting today does not work very well this way. To be truthful, the old monarchies didn't either. History is clear on the fact that the monarch dictated and the people deviated until they could throw the royal bums out.

We live in a postmodern world, a world in which there is a great deal of conflict over just exactly what is right, what is good. In the minds of our children, and, indeed, in our own minds, the notion of respect for authority and blind obedience has been clouded with cautions concerning whom children can really trust and who deserves respect, and a notion that local and national leaders may very well not lead us to virtue. When I was a kid, adults, parents, teachers, priests and ministers, local and national politicians—gosh, even lawyers had an air of respectability. We live in a different world. At 9 years of age my daughter commented on a political commercial, "They're lying to us, aren't they, Dad?"

THE MODEL

Michael, 12, refuses to eat his corn. "I don't want it, I'm full."

I go into "automatic parent." "You have to eat your corn before you watch that show."

The world will not come to an end if Michael does not eat his corn, but I'm on a mission. This corn thing is important. Michael repeats, "I don't want it, I'm full." If my wife left her corn, this would be a reasonable response. If any adult left the corn, this would be a reasonable response. As a matter of fact, I would not think of suggesting to any adult that their corn needed to be finished up! But for a 12-year-old boy, this is not a reasonable response.

I may decide to "make him" eat his corn. If the issue gets defined as an act of "disobedience," we may both dig into our positions, and Michael may get sent to bed. He is not willing to give in and contribute to a pleasant evening for just two bites of corn.

Or other scenarios may ensue:

"Come on, Michael, it's just a little bit."

"I'm too full, I'll eat it later."

"OK," I say, "but you have to eat it before you eat anything else."

Not a great piece of parenting. Some give and take, but a clear message that I still make the rules. You may choose not to eat the corn now, but you will eat it later or starve.

So now it's later that evening, Saturday, and Saturday night is our "game" night. The game of Clue is under way and out come the cookies. Everyone reaches for one. Michael does not get a cookie unless he eats his corn first. Of course, he is not willing to do that. He pouts, plays without enthusiasm, and ruins the game for everyone.

"Come on, Michael, play right."

"I will for a cookie."

"OK, but you are still going to have to eat that corn." I'm thinking it is no big deal, and we all know what Michael is capable of. This will save the night. The game continues. Michael knows he has won this battle. His sibling wonders how Michael always gets his way. My wife is unsatisfied with the outcome, and we will have a discussion about it after the kids go to bed. Everyone "knows" I took the "easy" way out.

Both scenarios leave us acting in a silly kind of way in dealing with the corn problem and, in a more general sense, whenever we deal with struggles with our children. So what is the option? The process of "parenting" (really, relating to and assisting your children) demands careful analysis of the dynamics of human social behavior. Taking the conventional parenting advice is just the same old "control" game with the new twist of new techniques that promise to get them to "behave." Such techniques can make us look rather foolish to our children—but even if looking foolish does not bother a parent, we should see that none of these techniques construct the kind of day-to-day relationships that we cherish.

In order to know what to do in the corn situation, we have to take a detour into some assumptions about how things work. Watch out now, here come the big words for which sociologists are famous.

Principle Number One

Understand that any interpretation of social truths rests on values and perspectives and will eventually give way to new truths.

The cold hard truth about social issues keeps changing from time to time. Humans have a history of believing a single interpretation as the truth. It makes sense to hold a belief (interpretation or "truth") because it can be defended as part of a reasonable value system. It also makes sense to assume that others may very well hold truths (interpretations) different from our own. The struggle over the reasonableness of competing truths (interpretations) has to do with how well one can defend an interpretation and where that interpretation will take you.

I am getting to the corn and Michael. Hang with me.

It is easy to see how truths change and give way to new truths. I was taught that working on Sundays was completely wrong unless it was an emergency. This was truth. Today people generally laugh at such an interpretation. There was a time, not long ago, when smoking cigarettes was not only inoffensive but debonair. This was truth. Today it is considered somewhat deviant and generally very offensive. Not long ago it was acceptable for a husband to hit his wife if she "got out of hand." This was truth. Today we define this as totally unacceptable.

These examples demonstrate the point that we keep changing our interpretation of what is true in the social world. Human beings create the nature of the social world and then proclaim these creations reality. But there are a lot of people and groups defending their own interpretation as the one and only truth. This is exactly the issue in the postmodern social world. The idea that truth is clear and the same for everyone gets us in trouble when someone cannot see the truth as we can. Actually, we make stuff up (through a complex process for sure) and then declare it as the truth with the authority of a father, a supreme being, a scientist, a philosopher, Oprah, or whatever we can get people to buy into.

The problem here is what sociologists refer to as *reification:* the process of taking an interpretation of something and acting as if that is the only, or true, interpretation. Think of the interpretation, or reification, of the concept *girl* when girls were defined as being incapable of performing athletically as they do today. The old truth about girls is no longer the truth. Think of the interpretation, or reification, of the concept *father* when fathers were defined as not being able to be "nurturing" to their children. It was not in men's nature to do these things. The old truth about fathers is no longer the truth. We can think of all kinds of truths that we have changed. Women have forever changed our social world with their reinterpretation of what is appropriate for women and men.

Reification is a concept that is useful in a discussion on how and why we should behave in society. It also gives us reason to reject the idea that there is only one way to look at the world, which is to face "reality." Realism suggests that we observe the social world from the "outside" and discover "the nature of things." But realists have problems when they have to explain why women today are not the same thing they were 100 years ago. It was a realist who spoke of the objective fact that the sun rotated around the earth. It was a realist who spoke of the crossbow as the ultimate weapon. It was a realist who claimed women did not have the necessary biological makeup to vote intelligently. Things that seem true, or are held as true, get us to act in a way that is consistent with the interpretation we take as true. Complex!

The social world has an arbitrary nature. The power of reification is in passing off our values or wishes about something as the truth. When we acknowledge this, we can bend minds. To reify things and not acknowledge it is detrimental to building relationships with our children.

Human beings create the social world through a very complex process. This social construction of reality is for the most part hidden from us and becomes understandable only with significant work. Most of us are not prepared to do this, but if we consider the construction of the meaning of the contemporary conceptualization of *wife,* we can begin to see how we "give things meanings."

When my wife and I got married the first time (we have married each other about six times now), we eloped to Mexico and were married by a guy named Walter who asked my wife if she would promise to love, honor and *obey.* She did promise, although she now claims that marriage and its promises are valid only in Mexico. Even that would be too much for most women and men in our society today. "Wifeness" does not imply obedience as it did in the past. The point is that we have now given *wife* a new meaning that rejects the notion of obedience. This new creation of the meaning of *wife* has been accomplished through the actions of many individuals and through many struggles on a micro and a macro level. The meaning of social concepts, such as *wife,* emerges out of a process of power and struggle.

So, back to the corn problem. When we accept the model, we accept that it is good to "eat the corn when I say so"—because it has been set up that way, not because it is better than any other option. Given the arbitrary nature of the social customs and meanings, we assume that there is nothing wrong with rejecting the interpretation someone else, even "society," gives to "eating corn." Would anyone like to defend the notion that it was wrong for women to reject the obedient role of wives?

When we give up the idea of one single all-powerful and correct interpretation on anything, we make room for negotiation and for the reasonableness of working to defend our position. It makes it necessary for us to explain why our position on a given issue is a reasonable one. We should expect to struggle over these explanations and be ready to set out our argument. Eating corn is like every other situation in this regard.

Principle Number Two

As human beings, we try to construct situations that make sense to us—that fit our interpretation of the situation.

I believe we should accept an understanding of human beings that allows for the hope for change, human dignity, creativity, and critical thinking. In our postmodern world, different populations have diverse perceptions of what "makes sense." We attempt to create social worlds that are consistent with what "makes sense." This is a positive application of power; it is not rebellion, it is not just wanting attention, it is not bad choices, it is not lack of control. It is the struggle to construct social situations that make sense. Does "eating the corn" make sense? To me it does. To Michael it does not. Well, that is perfectly reasonable. We both interpret the corn deal differently, we both act to try to get our interpretation to work for us, and we both try to get the other to go along with our interpretation.

Principle Number Three

Human beings struggle over how things should go. Consensus and conformity on issues should not be expected.

Have you ever known a married couple who totally agreed about what makes sense? It does not happen; and if it did, I don't know that it would be much fun. "Good" marriages incorporate an acceptance and an understanding of differences—the spouses expect struggle and learn how to struggle at higher levels. The notion of conformity incorporates an unrealistic expectation. To conform is to be passive, and to be passive is to be powerless, and powerlessness leads to decay or violence.

The model suggests that struggle is at the center of human experience. If we pay attention we can create and implement methods of struggle that will not devalue human beings, lead people to develop resentment, or contribute to powerlessness.

Principle Number Four

The behavior of any single actor in a situation is a reflection of everything going on in the situation.

It makes no sense to attempt to explain behavior as if it were related solely to the characteristics of a single individual. We cannot understand the behavior of a single individual without considering the entire social context out of which the behavior emerges.

Michael's behavior is reflecting my behavior, and my behavior reflects his. To assume that there is something "wrong" with Michael is to miss the interactive nature of behavior. To think that any behavior does not play off the behavior of others is to be unaware of the dynamics of human behavior.

These four principles set forth a model of behavior that is the core of this entire approach to parenting: Struggle is at the center of the understanding of human behavior.

The struggles emerge out of contact between human beings who have various perspectives, values, interests, and understandings. As an example, I can readily see that my daughter, Brittin, has very different perspectives concerning the issue of horses than I do. Teachers and students often have very different interpretations about what is important. Children generally have perspectives, values, interests, and understandings that parents cannot come to share with them. We should understand this and expect it. The result of these differences is struggle. The nature of these struggles will shape relationships and, indeed, the social world we share. If we struggle by beating our children with a belt, we cannot hope for social relationships characteristic of more empathetic struggling. Parents and children can create a social world with enough diversity to allow satisfaction and growth for both children and parents, but you have to work toward that end. Trying to beat the truth into children will result in a social world painted by violence, deceit, power plays, and "war."

If we understand how the model can be used to raise the plane on which we struggle, and if we understand how using these principles can make us able to treat each other with respect and dignity, respect and dignity have a chance. So how does it work in the corn issue? Here is a third secenario.

"Wait a minute, let's get out a model and take a look."

I get a piece of paper and roughly draw a diagram (Figure 16.1).

"Here's you and here's me. As the arrows show, we are involved in a struggle."

"Duh," Michael responds.

I start out, "We are struggling over eating corn, and neither of us seems to want to give in. Remember, with this model all we have to work with is a difference in what we want. Not a difference in who is right and who is wrong, just a conflict over eating corn or not eating corn. So we have to talk about why we want the corn thing to turn out in the way we want it. This is the way I see it. I think you should eat the corn because it is good for you and it is good that you develop a habit of eating vegetables."

Michael comes back quickly, "Yeah, but I almost always eat the vegetables Mom serves and I like corn. I just did not want to eat it tonight and I don't feel like eating it now."

"Well that sounds reasonable," I say, "but what about the tactics you are using to keep from eating the corn. You said you would eat it later, and then when I remind you you go into your I'm-not-going-to-have-any-fun deal, and you know that drives me crazy."

Michael knows I have identified his plan. When you identify behavior as a tactic, it loses its power. Michael picks up on this and "names" one of my tactics. "Well, you are using the 'I'm the dad and I know the best about what you should eat and vegetables are good for you' thing."

"OK," I say, "I know that is a tactic, but I do think I know more about nutrition than you."

"Yeah, about nutrition maybe," Michael admits, "but I know that vegetables are good for me to eat, and I eat them, and corn is my favorite anyway. So

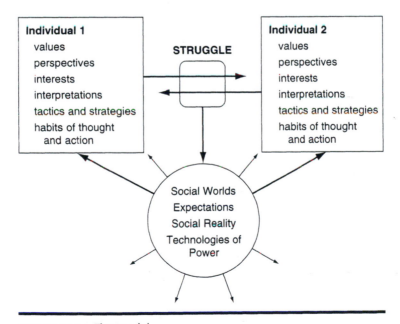

FIGURE 16.1   The Model

this is just about you telling me what to do because you are the dad."

The discussion goes on for about 30 minutes. The discussion includes exchanges about our values, how we interpret things, and our habits. Both of us clearly state that one of our values is the relationship we have. We talk about how this little deal over corn will help to shape, maybe in just a small way, what we will expect about what is fair in our relationship in the future. The conversation is characterized by differences between Michael and me and by mutual respect for those differences. We learn much about how the other feels about a lot of issues, but we do not let the thing get ugly. Time and time again we assent to the fact that we do not agree and that that was to be expected.

We struggle, but on a higher level, and on a level in which we both grow in understanding ourselves and the other. We also say a lot of things that will become the foundation for future struggles. The "corn thing" becomes an opportunity to learn more about how to struggle in a manner that does not rest on beating the other person down or asserting your perspective as "right" and his as "wrong."

The key is to focus the discussion on the aspects of the model: on values, perspectives, interests, interpretations, tactics, strategies, habits of thought and action. And, most important, make sure that you both do about the same amount of talking and listening. The discussion that emerges helps respect to grow between individuals. It moves the focus of action to understandings that can contribute to stronger relations between parents and kids. Talking about how you parent forces you to make sense. When you have to defend the things you do, you usually do more defensible things.

Oh, people ask how the corn thing turned out. Did Michael eat the corn? You know, I don't remember. It became so unimportant compared with the real stuff that was happening, or compared with the building of a stronger relationship, that I will just have to ask Michael, and I bet he doesn't remember any better than I do.

APPLYING THE MODEL

Parenting must involve teaching children to think through issues with an understanding of what is in-

volved, and then trusting them to choose a path that is reasonable to them. This kind of teaching depends on the maintenance of trusting relationships between parents and children. The teen years, in particular, will be blessed by these relationships. Trusting relationships will allow us to assist our children as they confront the difficult issues that emerge for teenagers.

Teenagers, Sex, and Parenting

Parents, teenagers, and sex! Now here is a real challenge. Our own understanding of this wonderful aspect of our lives will have profound effects on our children's lives. Can we trust our kids? You bet we can, if we do our job well. Will there be mistakes and problems? You bet there will, regardless of what we do. Will our children have better-integrated sex lives? You bet they will. Will we be in a position to assist them? You bet we will.

To think of sex as if it is only about those acts that directly relate to physical intimacy is to make it impossible to deal with sexuality in any kind of reasonable manner. To think about sex as if the choices for our children are abstinence or intercourse is a sure way to kill their chances of developing a wholesome sexuality. Sexuality is not a simple take-it-or-leave-it proposition. Our sexuality is woven into the fabric of our lives to the point that it both reflects and shapes who we are. The thought that we can deal with it as if it were a separate topic to be learned at a specific time in our lives is kind of a crazy idea. Yet this is exactly the approach we often take in this culture.

So much of what we do in the name of sex education is not about sexuality in the broad sense I am trying to get to, but about the war that goes on in our attempts to control teenagers. You can see the battle being waged over the hearts, minds, and bodies of teens. How do they learn to delight in sexuality when we focus our teaching on opposing pregnancy, venereal diseases, and even sex itself?

Human beings are sexual beings, and they will get involved in sexual intimacy. Teenagers are also human beings and, like the weather, will not be controlled. Despite our culture's "just say no to sex" strategy, in the United States today, fully 80 percent of men and 75 percent of women have intercourse before age 20, and survey after survey puts the percentage of high school seniors who have had intercourse at close to 50 percent. The Centers for Disease Control report that 1 in 3 girls and 1 in 7 boys will be molested at least once before age 18. The secrecy fosters abuse.

Breaking the silence with teens should help them be comfortable talking about all aspects of a healthy sexuality, and they will be helped immensely when parents are comfortable. Given the nature of our culture's take on discussing sex, comfort is sometimes hard to develop. Honesty about our lack of comfort is the next best thing. There is embarrassment over some sexual issues. Humor always helps! A quick look at the teen chat lines on the Internet and teen magazines such as *Seventeen* will give you a current idea about the kinds of issues teens want to discuss. Here are some random issues teens bring up: Does it hurt? Are two condoms better than one? Why don't I have hair "down there"? How important is it to be a virgin? How do I know if my girlfriend has an STD? Can friends have sex and stay just friends? How do I tell her no? Fruitful discussions can take place with the help of some of these articles or issues. I know of one family that set up a chat line on their computer for questions "too embarrassing" to ask face-to-face. It worked well, and grew from specific sex questions to more broadly based issues. Some way or another teens have to get various types of information.

Teens need to know about the biology of reproduction and pleasure. They need to know why different approaches suggest that abstinence is the best, the only, or the most unrealistic approach to dealing with sexuality. They need to know how sexuality is associated with every aspect of their lives. They need to know that how a young man or young woman treats others in school says a lot about his or her sexuality, and that respect for others translates directly into more enriching sexual relationships. The farther away we can stay from making sex a "big deal," the more likely it is to be integrated into the lives of teens in a reasonable manner. Again the theme should be some understanding that sexuality can be a natural and wonderful part of life.

Fear-based approaches attempt to exert overt control or to mythologize sex. The sexual bogeyman uses all the ugly faces of sexuality as a means of keeping teens away and fails to balance this image

with all the beauty that is possible. Such approaches rely on only part of the story. A good sex education program will provide teens with the necessary information to avoid unwanted pregnancies and sexually transmitted diseases. These programs should also be able to speak to the notions of friendships, cultural messages related to sexuality, responsible decision making, lifelong sexual development, sexual identity, male and female roles, building and maintaining supportive relationships, and the preparation for parenting.

Brittin, Shari, and I sat down to watch a video of the movie *Dirty Dancing*. My wife taught ballet for years, loves to dance, and loves the movie. I had seen the movie before but had forgotten almost everything except that there was some cool dancing. This time the movie hit me like a ton of bricks as the perfect movie to open up a meaningful discussion about sexuality and relationships. Brittin and I had a wonderful discussion about the positive and negative sexual relationships we saw in the movie. As we drove around doing errands, we shared perspectives on the characters, the relationships, and the story. We did not talk about the actual sexual acts that were suggested in the movie, but I got a chance to tell her that I hoped that she would be able to understand the kind of sexual exploitation that was modeled in the movie and be able to avoid it. We also spoke of the more positive relationship between the two main characters. I told her I hoped she could experience such a relationship.

It was a serious talk, and I deliberately directed it toward giving her a clear idea of the kinds of things I wished for her in terms of her own sexuality. As we pulled into the garage, I said, "Brittin. I hope you will be able to experience a relationship like that." "Yeah, Dad," she said, "but the girl was not 13." "That's right, and very astute of you to see the importance of that little issue." I responded with a little prayer of thanks.

Sex, like fast food, has been mythologized and packaged so that sound decisions are difficult to make. Sex, on average, is probably not as threatening to the planet as McDonald's; but outside of responsible situations, it does carry the potential of real harm. Teens need to be able to make decisions concerning sexuality that will allow them to develop as whole persons. They need to learn what is healthy for them and what is not. They need to develop tastes that fit them. It is hard to develop a positive sexuality when the messages one hears are always negative, just as it is hard to understand nutrition with only messages about what not to eat. Our teens should learn to make decisions about sex that will allow them to avoid exploiting others, avoid diseases, and avoid unwanted pregnancy. But we also have to help them avoid understandings of sexuality that disregard the many beautiful aspects.

There are some values that are fairly general and can provide a starting point for sex education discussion at home or at school. Most of us agree that every person deserves to be respected and cared for. We also generally agree that exploiting someone else is not appropriate and that unambiguous consent is essential to any healthy sexual contact. Further, we share the notion that not all feelings should necessarily be acted upon. More basically, we share the belief that 15 is probably too young for teens to become parents. With some agreed-upon values, parents and teens can facilitate the development of a sexuality that incorporates sharing, joy, pleasure, excitement, anticipation, contentment, love, responsibility, empathy, and eventually the ability to procreate under favorable circumstances. It is like learning to properly nourish our bodies. When we follow a healthy diet we just feel better, have more possibilities, and enjoy a fuller life. When we develop a healthy sexuality we just feel better, have more possibilities, and enjoy a fuller life.

Teenagers, Drugs, and Parenting: "It's Not about the Drugs"

How do we assist our kids in making reasonable decisions about drugs? Two short stories:

At 15, James has gained a reputation as an experienced shoplifter, school truant, and all-around troublemaker. He is a likable kid with a ton of problems. He doesn't much speak to his parents, because "they wouldn't understand anyway." His reading stands at about a third-grade level, but his knowledge of cars is extensive. James pretty much hates school and the teachers that come with it. He enjoys hanging

with his friends and working on cars. James is no stranger to alcohol or illegal drugs, and he makes sure he always has a stash of pot. He has been on legal drugs also, but they didn't work out for him. Over the last 5 years, James was put on Ritalin (methylphenidate), Dexedrine (dextroamphetamine), and Cylert (pemoline). He had all the common side effects: lack of appetite, trouble falling asleep, headaches, stomachaches, irritability, crankiness, crying, emotional sensitivity, staring into space, and loss of interest in friends. He only suffered from one of the "serious" side effects, muscle tics or twitches and jerking movements; but when it finally hit him that these embarrassing problems were related to his meds, he refused to take them any more. The illegal stuff is much more friendly for him. About twice a week James finds himself walking to school with two of his friends and sharing some dope to get into the "proper" mood for school. The friends laugh and kid around as they walk. The friendship and the dope make the prospect of school seem much less foreboding.

Allison is just turning 15 and she wants to do something exciting for her birthday. Allison is a very good student who plans to study medicine when she goes to college. She has a fairly good relationship with her parents. They trust her, and she gives them good reason to do so. Allison has been curious about what marijuana is like, and she has even read up on it. She bought into the DARE (Drug Abuse Resistance Education) classes she attended in the sixth grade, but has since discounted most of the message as a scare tactic. Allison has two close friends, Tracy and Emilie, who have tried smoking dope. Tracy, who lives on a farm, offers to join Emilie in hosting a private little birthday party for Allison. Tracy's parents will be gone all day Saturday and the three girls will have the whole farm to themselves. At the "party" Tracy brings out a joint and invites the others to get high with her. The three girls share the marijuana and end up having a great time, laughing, clowning around, and devouring snack food.

If we can consider just these two specific situations of drug use, most would agree that we have two very different things going on. The difference emerges not out of the actual smoking of marijuana, but out of the very different contexts in which the act takes place. I know we want to talk about where this will lead, and what happens next for Allison and her friends, but it is pretty clear that Allison and James are heading in vastly different directions. Drug use for them is clearly not the same thing. For James and Allison the use of marijuana is put into the context of who they are and what they hope to accomplish.

The life that surrounds the use of marijuana defines the drug use more than the drug use defines the life. This can be put into perspective when one considers that it is estimated by the National Institute on Drug Abuse that 70 million Americans over the age of 12, about 32 percent of the American population, and nearly 50 percent of high school seniors, have used marijuana at least once, with about 26.2 percent using during the past month. In a piece of research I conducted, about 62 percent of a sample of first-year college students admitted to using marijuana within the last 12 months. It is obvious that the vast number of Americans who use marijuana do not fit the stereotype of "drug users." Allison is one of those "users."

Allison thinks about using marijuana in a much different way than does James, and their behaviors reflect this perception. Marijuana fits into Allison's life in a very different way than it fits into James's, and she makes different decisions about how and when to use marijuana.

This is where parenting comes in strongly. Parents have a lot to do with the relationships they have with their children, with their children's relationships to school, and with their children's sense of who they are and who they are going to be. Both Allison's and James's parents have a lot to do with their relationship to the use of drugs. James's priorities, his relationship with his parents, his sense of who he is and where he is going, put drugs into the category of a substance that assists him in developing the "proper" mood for school. One way or the other, by omission or by commission, parents play an important role in the lives of their children. This is not to blame James's parents, but to recognize that they did contribute significantly, but not alone, to the process of creating the person James is becoming.

Allison knows that it makes no sense to smoke pot on the way to school, but she reasons that it will be fine for her, and her friends, to experiment with pot at the farm. She sees it as kind of exciting and she expects it will be fun. Allison knows enough about herself, her friends, and marijuana to make a reasonable decision about when and where to smoke. She can make judgments about drugs that will lead to her being one of those who "have used" marijuana but who, like the majority of teens, will not become regular users. Many simply leave pot behind as they grow older; others continue to use drugs recreationally with no negative side effects. I assume that good parenting helped her to come to the decisions which will guide her life.

To James, smoking pot on the way to school makes a lot of sense. It is his way of connecting with something or somebody. It is his decision to use drugs to alleviate the anxiety, the uncomfortable feeling, associated with school. Some who become locked in heavy drug use report that the decision to use drugs when they were young was, for them, a decision to save themselves from a reality they couldn't face sober. For them, drugs were their salvation. It is hard for us to think of drugs in this manner because of the reigning myths about what drugs are and what they can do to us. In reality, they can act like a rope when we create cliffs too difficult for some to climb. James is in such a place. And, it is here that we find the distinction between drug use and drug abuse. The concept *drug abuse* is so misleading. It is a matter of focus. *Abuse emerges not out of the use of too many drugs, but out of a life that calls for too many drugs.*

What we call drug abuse can be solved only if we can find a way to change children's reality when that reality gets too difficult to face without drugs. I don't know how much longer it will take us to hear the message of drug addicts who have kicked their habits. Time and time again they tell us, "It was not about drugs." It was about the struggle with failure or success, with loneliness, with insecurity, with pain, with lack of understanding. Instead of mindlessly allowing the local cop to provide Drug Abuse Resistance Education, we have to create situations in which drug abuse does not fit.

Parenting without controlling suggests a way to think about parenting that allows development and assistance to foster responsible decision making and to build a basis for trust in the decisions our teenagers will make.

When Brittin was about 9 years old, we went into a bar and grill for lunch. On the table was a stand-up advertisement for some kind of beer. Brittin was horrified, "We can't eat here. They sell drugs here." "Well," I said, "beer is not really 'drugs' like other drugs. It is legal for them to serve it here." Brittin argued, "In school they told us that beer is a drug."

What could I say? All kinds of things ran through my head.

"Yes, Brittin, I am a user."

"Look. Alcohol is not really a drug like all that illegal stuff."

"It's no problem for me to have just a couple."

"Alcohol is OK for adults, and for kids if their parents allow them to have some. Here, have a taste."

I simply said, "Don't worry about it. We will talk." And I ordered a beer. Later, when Brittin excused herself to visit the rest room, I looked at my wife and asked, "What in the hell are they teaching them in school?" Shari shook her head. "She is right, you know. Alcohol is a drug." "Yea, but it's just not that simple. I feel like we brought her into an opium den or something." My overly intelligent wife responds, "So does she."

My mind was reeling. What must have been going on inside Brittin's head? "My dad is a drug user." "Alcohol must not be really that dangerous." "Drugs can't be as bad as Officer Tennety (DARE presenter) said they are." "This situation scares me." "Hey, maybe I should try some, too." She was confused, and to tell the truth, I felt a little funny myself. There was major explaining to do.

Our children need to be able to think about drugs reasonably before they can make reasonable decisions about drugs. They need to be able to discern the difference between myths and reality. Teens don't learn to take themselves seriously and make responsible decisions when they just take our word for something. They gain strength from knowing the realities of drugs and struggling over their own decision making. They should be able to explain the difference between Allison's experiment with drugs and James's. They should be able to articulate what drug use means for Allison and James, and what it may mean for their families, their community, the quality of their lives, and their future. Teens would be much better off being involved in the discussion of the relative merits, purposes, and appropriateness of using any kind of drugs, rather than listening to sermons about the evils of illegal drugs.

Unfortunately, the simplest answer to the question of why some drugs are illegal is that some people got together and decided to pass bills that made them illegal. History indicates that the majority of these decisions were shaped by perceptions influenced by reigning myths rather than by careful debate about the facts. People simply had something against the use of a given drug and enough clout to get a law passed. Some of these people had individual stories about how drugs devastated their lives, and these stories contributed to false generalization to all drug use. We don't often consider the history of our laws and the knowledge that was available at the time they were passed. Laws come and go as our knowledge changes. What seemed reasonable and workable at one time becomes rather silly in the light of new knowledge. It is worth the effort to research and discuss the formation of drug laws with your children.

We have to remember that because we make some drugs illegal, it is much more difficult to engage teens in the discussion of how to handle them. The label "illegal" already defines them in a way that limits thought. I would like to begin with the assumption that there is a responsible and an irresponsible way to use any drug. From this premise we can move to a discussion of the kinds of situations in which using a specific drug might be some combination of dangerous, harmful, painful, harmless, fun, exciting, or pleasant. Such discussions rest on the assumption that human beings are capable of thought and careful consideration. Such discussions would challenge us and our teenagers. Can you imagine considering drug use with the aid of thought and integrity rather than myth and distortions? Now this would be an enterprise that could put drug use into its proper place and also contribute to thinking teenagers. I can hear the negative reactions. "Kids can't think that carefully." "They are not capable of such thought and maturity." Kids, like all human beings, will do what makes sense to them. We use the techniques that are effective for us in building a life or a situation. Once kids get the feel for thinking through issues and see the power in the process, they apply it to decisions.

Making a distinction between behavior that emerges out of the youth culture and behavior that is the result of serious personal struggles is important. It is here that we can find the meaning of use and abuse. Try as we may, I don't think we as parents are going to beat the odds on drug *use*. However, *abuse* emerges out of serious problems that good parenting can do something about. The reasons teens go from "safe" drug use to more dangerous use are tied to the reasons they are involved with drugs; drugs themselves don't capture people unilaterally. There is a reason why I use no illegal drugs, and it has to do with the nature of my life. The same is true of my daughter, Brittin. I know that I cannot control her or her environment closely enough to keep her from ever coming into contact with and using drugs; but I can support her, teach her, provide a model for her,

and try as much as possible to support a life for her that will not call for drug abuse. This is my role. I am not a police officer, I am a parent.

"It is not about the drugs." If we want to avoid the serious problems associated with drug abuse, we have to understand how important we are in all those "nondrug" aspects of our teenagers' lives. What happens to teens when they use drugs has a lot to do with us. As can be easily seen, some drug use is not serious, but other drug use may contribute in a negative way to preexisting problems. If we can teach our children how to build lives that speak to higher purposes, and learn to support those efforts, teenagers will make good decisions about drugs. They will be able to see that some types of drug use can get in the way of what one hopes to accomplish and others will not. They will be able to see that some types of drug use are indeed dangerous, whereas others may not be. If we do it well, our teens will be capable of thinking about drugs in a reasonable way and will be able to control their own drug involvement responsibly.

17

Sport Is Too Important
to Be Just a Game!

MARTIN G. MILLER

Editors' Note: Bringing sociology to life, Marty Miller offers an example of positive youth development. Famed UCLA Coach John Wooden, known as "the great motivator," was once asked what is the key to motivation. He thought about it for a moment and then said, "Well, I think it would have to be love." He went on to say, "You have to treat people fairly. That doesn't mean you treat everyone alike. People aren't the same, so that wouldn't be fair." The old cliché is that sports builds character. Marty Miller shows us how sports can build the type of character and values we want. You may want to post his "Sportparent's Creed" on your wall.

Sport is too important to be just a game. It is one of the few times when we get to spend quality time with our kids when we have their full attention. You have to be inventive. A lot of the ideas here are new to coaching. With children we need to be especially creative.

The numbers are awesome. There are 26 million youngsters between the ages of 6 and 18 participating in nonschool athletics in the United States. Millions more participate in interscholastic sports. Three million adults are also involved in youth sports. It's the minority that run the show. Adults select the teams, teach the kids skills, organize the kids' recreational programs, control the kids, officiate at their games, select their uniforms, build them stadium-type ballparks, drive them to practices and games, and so on.

Youth-driven recreation has given way to adult-driven youth activities. I tell my grandchildren about my sandlot days of baseball. When I was their age my school chums got together every day after school and played baseball in any open space we could find in the neighborhood—schoolyards, streets, alleys, backyards, and vacant lots. We didn't have much equipment. The kid with the ball and bat was in. We chose up sides. We set the rules. First base was the tree, second was the bush, and the sewer cover was third. We used "take it over" often, and a ball batted through the Murphy's window was an out and an out-of-there as fast as our little legs could take us. We didn't practice; we wouldn't have tolerated throwing drills, hitting drills, infield drills, outfield drills. We played the game, and we got better at it the longer we played. What fun and excitement!

Adults are now in charge of the younger generation's games, and we won't return to those nostalgic days of yesteryear. Therefore, we elders have a serious responsibility to the younger generation: the responsibility to preserve the best of the past while contributing to the healthy socialization of youth. This means making sports fun, exciting, and competitive for kids while allowing opportunities for kids to cooperate, achieve, make decisions, handle success, handle failure, and deal with stress. Because the older generation insist on running the kids' show, and because they feel it's for the kids' own good, they must provide the younger generation with healthy competitive environments.

Now, I'm one of the paternalistic elders. I've coached youth softball and volleyball for 18 years. Though I've coached my own children, I've mostly coached others' offspring. I've officiated youth and high school sports for just as long. I've been an administrator of a junior sport club for the past 10 years. But by trade, I'm an academic sociologist. My sociological self has given me perspectives that guide my approach to youth sport and my interaction with the young people in my charge.

Each new season for all these years, I have endured the "activity trap" of tryouts, practices, schedules, lineups, and so forth by considering why I'm doing all this ... and for no financial compensation. I visit my coaching philosophy and get in touch with my goals. Each year I study how to resolve circumstances I experienced the previous year that affected the healthy sport environment I attempt to construct for my young athletes. This article presents the issues and the outcomes of my contemplations. My purpose in sharing these ideas is to assist the older generation in establishing healthy, successful, and developmental sport environments for the younger generation.

COACH—GET IN TOUCH WITH YOUR GOALS!

The season is upon you. You're feverishly preparing your team for the league or tournaments. You continue your activities day after day with precious little time for thought or awareness of your reasons and goals for doing all this. You are caught in the *activity trap*.

When I ask coaches why they're working so hard, a common response is, "For a winning season." Is this what we ultimately want for our youngsters and ourselves? Wasn't our original intention in getting into coaching closer to wanting to achieve success for our athletes and teams, whether or not our team has more or less points than the other team at the end of the contest? Are our coaching goals *ends-oriented* or *means-oriented?* If our goals are *ends-oriented,* then our athletes are happy only when winning. If *means-oriented,* then they feel happy with the play and satisfied with personal success. *Means-oriented* goals value play as a spontaneous, expressive experience.

In the mid-1980s I came across a pamphlet published by the Institute of Sports at Michigan State University for those who coach youth sports (Gould, 1980). Over several years, MSU researchers asked sports-involved adolescents the simple question, "Why do you participate in sports?" The three top choices were consistent: (1) to have fun; (2) to be with friends and/or to make new friends; and (3) to improve sport skills and learn new skills. "To win" was in 12th place. The study also found that about 33 percent of all youths drop out of sport participation each year. The three top reasons were: (1) no fun, (2) too much pressure, and (3) too much emphasis on winning.

The results of that study revolutionized my coaching style. The youngsters' answers made sense to me. I asked myself, Why was I playing racquetball and being a member of my department's volleyball team? The three main reasons were: (1) to have fun; (2) to enjoy a recreational relationship with my university colleagues and students outside the context of our formal academic pursuits; and (3) to be a better racquetball and volleyball player. If those are my reasons, then it makes sense that the young girls I coach in softball and volleyball should feel the same way. Successful coaches are those who instill an enjoyment of the sport they teach and who encourage a desire in their young charges to pursue lifelong activities in sports and wellness.

The intensity of a coach's environment is a product of our culture. Sport is not only a major form of leisure activity; it is a means through which children achieve physical health, leadership skills, and team loyalty. Sport also provides a training ground for competitiveness and give-and-take relationships. However, visible emphasis on sports in our communities is grounded in *winning achievement.* Parents stress the importance of self-development and fair play in their preadolescent children; but as their offspring mature into adolescents, the "good plays" and "scoring points" become burning issues. Parents' behavior as spectators reflects this shift. Notice how parents overlook unseen fouls or referees' questionable calls when such occurrences favor their child's team, and note the hostile verbal references when the call goes against their youngster's team. Many critics of youth sport have pointed out the professionalization of children's recreation; that is, the substitution of skill and victory for fun, enjoyment, fairness, and equity as the paramount factors in play activity. The older the children get, the more they act like their parents—they want to win at any cost and have temper tantrums if they lose. This is a process that sociology refers to as *anticipatory socialization* or rehearsal for adulthood.

Coaches' behavior reflects pressure for winning achievement from athletes and parents as well as from the general community. Such an intensive environment masks sensitivity to the difference between *winning* and *success*. Coaches agree that both are important and indeed realize how important both are to their young athletes. Constantly emphasizing winning distracts from the goal of success.

In fact, winning and success are not synonymous. Neither success nor failure depends on the ball game's outcome or the won-and-lost record. Success is effort, good feeling, camaraderie, making a contribution, gaining skills, and having fun—all things we have some control over. Coach John Wooden, the renowned retired coach of UCLA, won national basketball championships 10 out of 12 years. However, his version of success wasn't winning; it was "peace of mind, which is a direct result of self-satisfaction in knowing you did your best to become the best that you are capable of becoming" (Wooden and Jamison, 1997, p. 170). Individuals have control over the amount of effort they put forth in a game, but they may have limited control over the final points on the scoreboard. Success is what youngsters strive for, but winning is what adults value, and the kids know it.

Coach, take time out from the daily activities of tryouts, practices, schedules, lineups, and so on, and consider your coaching philosophy. Assess your perceptions of success and failure and winning and losing. What do these dichotomies mean to your young athletes and to you? Get in touch with your true goals. By doing so, you will avoid the activity trap.

DEMOCRATIC COACHING: SHARING THE COACHING RESPONSIBILITIES WITH YOUTH

One of the highlights in my busy and predictable life is coaching girls' softball and volleyball. The coaching seed was planted years ago when my daughter

Sharon began playing softball in our community girls' softball league. She was 11 years old at the time. As I watched her team's practices and games, I became impressed with these youngsters' abilities, enthusiasm, and enjoyment. I expressed these feelings to my daughter's coach—and also the thought that coaching is an ideal way for youth and adults to be involved in positive interactions and quality time.

In a small town it doesn't take long for a parent who expresses interest in a youth program to become involved. When my youngest daughter, Amy, signed up for softball, the commissioner, having heard of my interest, called me to say that Amy would be a member of a team of 12 enthusiastic fifth- and sixth-grade girls. Since no volunteers had come forward to coach the team—no coach, no team, no play!

With that phone call I became the coach of the Clothesline Consignment Store Girls' Softball Team. With some ambivalence. What did I know about softball? I did pitch for my high school baseball team, but that was a long time ago. What did I know about coaching? It was clear that I was a rookie coach and had to sink or swim.

As it turned out, my rookie season was great. We had fun, we acquired some softball (and coaching) skills, and we even won two games. Not only was there improved performance on the ball field between the first and last games; I learned a lot too.

In one of our first practices I was trying to instruct the girls on how to throw the ball overhand with a wrist snap for distance and speed instead of shot-putting the ball. Try as I might, I could not get the girls to throw the way I showed them, and my frustration was apparent. My older daughter, whose softball career had skyrocketed, was watching. "Dad," she said, "get them down on their knees and have them throw." She demonstrated, the girls followed, and they began to throw correctly overhand. Aha!

On another occasion, I was trying to get my pitchers to throw the ball so that it traveled over home plate, a not-too-easy task for 11-year-olds. Again Sharon came to my rescue. At her suggestion she and four members of my team went to another part of the field. In a half hour they returned and proceeded to throw strikes. What a look of accomplishment Sharon and the pitchers had. Aha!

The object lesson was: I needed a partner coach, one who could relate to the players: a youth coach.

I didn't want the season to end. Coaching had been such a rewarding experience, and I had become so attached to the kids. I knew that coaching was in my blood and that I would be a volunteer coach in the years ahead. I also knew, sadly, that I'd never coach this particular team of girls again. The girls move on, and teams are reformulated each season. A coach's first team is special.

Suggestions for Democratic Coaching

In my evaluation letter at the season's end, I thanked the league commissioner for the opportunity to develop coaching skills and to make new young friends. I also submitted the following recommendations:

1. Each team should have an adult and a youth coach. Youths should not be designated "assistant" coaches. Adult and youth should have equal status.
2. Youths should be actively sought and trained as umpires. Youths and adults should have equal status, working side by side in officiating games.
3. Youths should be actively sought and trained as managers and scorekeepers. Youths and adults should have equal status in these roles.
4. Youths should be actively sought to be on the executive board of directors and league commissioners. Again, youths and adults should have equal status.

I would like to see these recommendations implemented in all community youth sports. Youngsters from the older leagues, junior high school athletes, and senior high school athletes should be actively recruited as coaches and officials for the younger teams.

Developmental Time-Outs

All sports have time-outs. I've always been curious about what goes on between the coach and players during these breaks. Time-outs are necessary for the team to regroup and receive instructions. But they are entirely *coach centered*. The players surround the coach and quietly listen as the coach pontificates, and then it's back to the game. What a waste of a developmental opportunity.

A few years ago, I turned the time-outs for my volleyball teams around. I made them *player centered*. The captains of my teams are more than figureheads; they have analytical, strategic, decision-making, and communication responsibilities. When a time-out is called, the team huddles around the captain and she's the first responder. This makes sense to me, for it's the players that are experiencing the action, not the coach. The captain reflects on what's happening on the court and suggests adjustments; the team listens and responds. Then I get my chance, which is usually to agree with the captain's analysis, though I may elaborate on her suggestions. The captains come up with just about what I would have instructed the players to do. The youngsters learn to express themselves precisely, for in junior volleyball time-outs are only 30 seconds. The girls are given the opportunity to analyze and problem-solve. And most importantly, they are given a meaningful role on the team. The coach is still the coach, but a little control is exchanged for a lot of learning.

Empowerment of Young Sport Participants

Missing in the history of youth sports is youth and adult colleagueship, with adults learning from youth as well as vice versa. Those athletic youngsters can teach a lot of skills to coaches. As coaches and athletes learn from each other and share responsibilities, there will be a change in adults' attitudes on the abilities and roles of kids.

The point is that meaningful roles, other than that of athlete, should be readily available to youngsters. It is interesting that we develop the role "athlete" at an early age, but seldom develop the roles of coach, manager, referee, or commissioner. These are reserved for those possessing "adult" status. In reality, they are satisfying participatory roles that are not age specific.

Empowerment is the cornerstone of a democratic society. Our sport programs can provide opportunities for youngsters to participate in the process and governance of community programs. Our youth are a valuable resource. Elders need to help them develop as responsible community members. This can be accomplished through democratic participatory youth sport and recreational programs.

Coaching through Mistakes

At my first practices I have worn a most special jade and white T-shirt. The statement written on the front was authored by the renowned adolescent social psychologist H. Stephen Glenn. My approach to coaching is grounded in Dr. Glenn's "building capable people" approach to the socialization of youth.

The motto on the shirt reads, MISTEAKS R WUNDERFULL OPPERTUNITEEZ 2 LERN! This is my favorite shirt, for it captures so well a major premise of my coaching approach—the *mistake center* concept. The only way I know to teach skills to kids and at the same time establish a fun environment is to encourage them to take risks in trying new things. We all learn by attempting, observing our mistakes, considering the correction, and being congratulated for the effort. So I emphatically communicate to my athletes and their parents that the practice field or gym and the ball game field or court are "centers of mistakes," where we don't worry about goofing up.

If you want a child not to be fearful of and therefore inhibited by making mistakes, you must show that you can be relaxed about those mistakes and can still laugh when nothing much is going right. One way to do this is for the coach to learn to talk in a voice that's supportive, projecting the spirit that "making corrections is useful and fun." By proceeding with patience and a positive approach, you will establish a learning climate in which the child understands that you have a genuine desire to help. Your corrections will be welcomed, because kids will recognize that your intention is not to hurt in any way but to offer solutions that may make it possible to serve or pass better and thus have more fun. This is so important, for fear spoils the fun kids should have with sports and makes them hide their mistakes, instead of recognizing them and going to work on solutions. Fear causes youngsters to drop out of sports and therefore lose the opportunity to engage in lifelong wellness and enjoyable recreational activities.

ACCENTUATE THE POSITIVE (AND ELIMINATE THE NEGATIVE)

I don't believe in recording individual statistics on my athletes. Such figures are meaningless to those under 13. I do want to record and communicate to players the positive things they do that show teamwork, sportsmanship, and self-awareness.

The Team Applause Sheet

In my early years of coaching, I felt a need to record things the players did during their games as a reminder of good plays and also of things we needed to work on in practice. I composed a simple sheet with all the players' names down the left-hand side about an inch apart. At the first game of the softball season, I put a clipboard with this sheet and a pen on the bench. I was going to record my observations while the game was in progress. I got so wrapped up in the game that I never gave it another thought. At the end of the game I was kicking myself for being so absentminded. Where was my clipboard anyway? There it was, still on the bench. To my surprise it was completely filled out with statements and drawings. While players were waiting to enter the game, they wrote about each other's accomplishments. This clipboard, with a pen and a sheet that now includes the coaches' names, has been placed on the bench of every game I have coached for many a year. I have never written on it, and I have never instructed the players regarding it. I have always found it on the bench at the end of the game, filled with praises and drawings. A negative has never appeared.

At the end of the season, instead of giving the kids a bunch of numbers indicating what a good or bad batter, pitcher, or fielder they are, I hand them a compilation of their teammates' acclamations. They beam. What use are batting averages, RBIs, ERAs, and fielding percentages to 10- to 12-year-olds? It's more meaningful for them to know that their teammates care about them.

A Positive Sandwich Is Nutrition for Success

Mistakes are part of athletics. I coach girls' volleyball. Volleyball is a game of mistakes. We shank balls, we serve them into the net, we hit them out-of-bounds; balls roll up our arms, and so forth. Volleyball athletes even celebrate each other's mistakes with a high five and a *"good try!"* How coaches and parents react to mistakes is critically important. If adults handle them wrong, there is a risk of creating a fear of failure in our young athletes that can harm not only their performance but also their outlook on themselves, the sport, their parents, their teammates, and their coach.

Notice how your player hides her face in her hands when she shanks a pass; she's embarrassed. The most useful thing you can do is to give her immediate encouragement. This is when she needs it most. At the same time, mistakes should be golden opportunities to provide *corrective instruction.* She wishes she had done it correctly, and the instruction may be particularly meaningful at this time. A general principle to follow is: If you are sure the athlete knows how to correct the mistake, then encouragement alone is sufficient. To tell an athlete what she or he already knows is more irritating than helpful.

Athletic motivation takes several forms. Many athletes try to achieve because of a positive drive to succeed. Others are motivated mostly by fear of failure. The success-motivated athlete welcomes and peaks under pressure, whereas the fear-of-failure youngster dreads critical situations and the possibilities of failure and disapproval. Fear of failure is an athlete's worst enemy. It harms performance and detracts from the enjoyment of competing.

The positive approach to coaching creates the motivation to try again and strive to improve, rather than the fear of failing. If coaches deal honestly and openly with their own mistakes, their players will be better able to accept their mistakes and learn from them. We can do no more than our best. This is one of the most valuable lessons to be learned. Coaches make mistakes, players make mistakes, parents make mistakes, officials make mistakes, club program directors make mistakes. A sense of tolerance is needed to save us all a lot of emotional wear and tear.

There are times when we have to give corrective instruction to assist an athlete striving to improve. To be effective, it must be encouraging and positive. Don't focus on the bad thing that just happened but on the good things that will happen if the athlete follows your instructions. Your instruction should have three elements:

- Start with a *compliment.* ("Way to hustle. You really got to that ball.")
- Give the *future-oriented instruction.* ("If you stay low, I know you'll get the ball to Jessie next time.")
- End with another *positive statement.* ("Hang in there! Work hard! I know you'll get better!")

This "positive sandwich" (two positive communications wrapped around the instruction) is designed to make the youngster positively self-motivated to perform correctly rather than negatively motivated to avoid failure and disapproval. Try it; I think you'll like it.

THE BENCH IS NO PLACE FOR A KID

Every youth sport program has grappled with the "benching" problem. It's serious. If you want a damaged relationship between parents, their kids, and the coach, then bench a child, even for one game. You'll hear from these folks—pronto!

When I debate this issue, this is what many people argue: Youngsters should earn the right to play on the field or court. Life is tough, and kids need to learn early on that they will not get far without working for it. Those who strive to make the starting lineup will be better for their effort than those who are just given their position. This is a common view of youth sport management and is summarized by what is referred to as the revenue sports model; see Jack Hutslar's book *Beyond X's and O's: What Generic Parents, Volunteer Coaches, and Teachers Can Learn about Generic Kids and All of the Sports They Play* (1985), a book all program administrators, coaches, and sportparents should read. In the revenue sports model, the reason you are here is to make money: We need high attendance, sponsor support, a successful program. We need to win to make a profit. A major philosophy of professional sports and increasingly of amateur sports is to view it as a business. I am not downgrading professional sports, but that's just a different approach to life and recreation.

Here is my perspective on this issue of playing time.

Although millions of youngsters enthusiastically participate in organized youth sports each year, as many as one-third voluntarily drop out. Eighty percent of kids drop out of youth sports programs by age 13, the age when junior high school sports kicks in. The cause, as reported by young people: disappointment about not getting to play and being scolded for mistakes by coaches and/or parents (Wolff, 1998, p. 30).

Adult wisdom states that children should play in programs in which they sit on the bench and "earn" their way onto the starting lineup. I refer to this as a "myth of adult wisdom."

Adults do not tolerate bench sitting in their own sporting activities. They want to play. When denied this, they move on to other activities in which they do get to play. Kids are no different. When they do not get to play in one sport, they move on to another sport or, unfortunately, just leave sport altogether. If we agree that sports are good for kids, should we not want to get them involved and keep them involved so they can profit from what is to be learned?

When we rely on the bench to motivate youngsters to improve, only certain ones will respond to that challenge. When "everyone plays," on the other hand, youngsters learn what it takes to get better under the guidance and motivation of the leaders, teachers, and coaches. Let's not perpetuate the view that sports programs for youngsters should follow a one-size-fits-all approach. Age and ability are inconsequential.

If we restrict youngsters to the revenue sports model, it is like saying to students in school, "You students who are not doing well, sit there, watch, and learn from the better students. Go study on your own and improve. If you catch up with the others, we'll give you books and let you participate with the better students." We would not tolerate this approach to education. Yet this is exactly what occurs in the revenue sports model. Are we mainly interested in what we can gain from kids' achievements—whether it is more money or more wins? We must consider other models of sports programs and coaching for children. Youngsters who leave or are driven out of sports because of the revenue sports model will have been denied all of the good that might have occurred if they were involved.

Should we run our programs so that only a few benefit? I'd like to see as many kids play as possible. It is unfair to serve only those who are the best at that moment in time. The important thing is for youngsters to get involved and learn. Why should we subject them to the "survival of the fittest" model? If we adopt for our program's mission statement the motto of the USA Coaching Accreditation Program, *Athletes First—Winning Second,* we will be on the track of healthy sport environments for all kids. Let them play, not sit!

CONFLICT RESOLUTION AND SPORT

Conflict is endemic to sports. Tryouts! Cuts! Team selection! Playing time! Winning! Losing! Coaching! Officiating! Benching! Personalities! Playing politics! Is it any wonder?

Anger Needs to Be Dealt With

Coaches receive training on how to teach sports skills—but how do you handle the out-of-control angry parent who is in your face because his daughter is crying in the car because "You didn't play her at all in the championship match!" No coaching clinic addresses this situation. Let's make some sense out of dealing with flaring tempers.

To deal with another's anger, realize you have to control your own feelings—a hard thing to do when your defense mechanism is telling you to yell back. These suggestions should help:

• *Acknowledge* the other person's anger quickly. Listen closely; never ignore or try to laugh off the anger.

• *Remove the audience and keep the ball in your court.* Often angry players, parents, coaches, officials, and so on appear out of nowhere and pin you to the wall. You don't want your team, parents, and everyone else to witness what might be an ugly confrontation. Say to the angry parent, coach, or official, "Let's step out into the hall (or office), and I'll be happy to discuss this with you." Or tell the angry player, "I'll be happy to talk about this with you after practice, but I can't discuss it with you now." This catches them off guard and makes you appear to be much more in control. It also puts you in a one-to-one situation, which is better for both of you. Remove the audience and the situation has a better chance of becoming calm and stabilized.

• *In your mind, separate the angry person's emotion from his or her point.* The fact that this person is angry and hysterical doesn't mean the person doesn't have a point.

• *Communicate* that you are concerned. Say something such as, "I don't blame you for being upset—this is an important matter." Active listening always works better than demanding messages.

• *Don't hurry* the person. Never try to shut the person up. Frequently all the person needs is the opportunity to talk through their anger. Listening helps.

• *Asking the antagonist to calm down rarely works.* It makes people madder, because angry people interpret this to mean you don't care, or feel that you don't see the same urgency of their point. It's best to let people know that "they do seem to have a good point" and then let them talk themselves to closure.

• *Keep calm.* Many people express anger in an emotional way and say things they don't really mean. If you must react to those statements, do so after the immediate outburst is over.

• *Encourage* the angry person to talk about solving the problem that caused the anger. If you've been calm, courteous, and concerned, the anger should subside. Talk reasonably with the person, propose a specific solution to the problem, and agree on a schedule to implement the solution. If the person is still too angry to talk about solutions, find an excuse to postpone action.

If there is, in fact, a problem that you can or should solve, then do so. It doesn't matter whether you were right or not. You won't want to admit that the angry person was right, but if solving the problem leads to a smoother-running program, team, or tournament, haven't you ended up gaining the most?

The Conflict Resolution Process

Youth sports are notoriously totalitarian. Coaches kick kids off of teams. Parents kick coaches out of programs. Neither kids nor coaches have the right of due process or the avenue of problem resolution. Most conflicts between a youth and coach are non-negotiable—coach wins, kid loses. The same can be said about parent–coach conflicts—the powerful parent wins, coach loses. Ironically, both the youngster and the coach are victims of the old cliché, "might makes right." But it makes more sense to resolve than to remove. If those in conflict work out a solution, it is healthy, successful, and developmental. Being ousted is destructive to both the individual and team.

The *conflict resolution process* should be prominent in a sport program's governance document. The athletes, coaches, parents, administrators, volunteers, and officials need to be aware of this process and assured that it will be activated when needed. It is important that young athletes realize there can be fairness and justice in sports. Their sport organization should have a process that listens to them, lets them express themselves, and respects them.

Box 17.1 shows the conflict problem-solving process that has been placed in the bylaws of the youth volleyball program that I administer. The use of trained mediators, as called for in our bylaws, may be problematic if program administrators are unaware of such professionals in their community. However, conflict resolution has blossomed throughout the country. Conflict resolution is in schools, and family conflict resolution and divorce resolution programs are increasingly popular. Restorative justice and mediation processes are emerging in court systems everywhere. Mediators are nearby; you have only to seek them out. If such expertise cannot be found in the community, then it is well worth sending a staff member, parent, or volunteer to conflict resolution training. This knowledge is crucial to the success of your program. This trained mediator also can become the program's ombudsman.

THE MEANING OF FUN

At my first practice I ask each athlete to write the reasons why she wants to play on the team. The ranking has always been the same: *fun* first, *friends* second, and *skills* third. As their coach, do I respect

Box 17.1

The Conflict Resolution Process

An athletic team is a quasi-community and therefore is subject to such occurrences as conflicts, stresses, anger, hard feelings, jealousies, and misunderstandings. Healthy and well-functioning communities establish for their members a fair and trusted process of conflict resolution.

The Iowa Heart Juniors Volleyball program's policy is to encourage the least drastic alternative in person-to-person and team-as-a-whole conflict resolution, which is: Those in conflict will attempt to work out the problem and agree on a solution. However, if this method of problem solving fails, then *Conflict Mediation* will be activated. It should be noted that the majority of the conflicts and problems could be resolved in a way satisfactory to all those involved through person-to-person or team problem solving. Mediation will occur when necessary, but it will be a rare occurrence.

Conflict Mediation is based on the premise that conflict in a community (team) is not the major harm to the group. Rather, it is the method of coming to solutions that hinders group functioning and achievement. If members of the conflict do not feel they have ownership in the solution of the problem, they will feel hurt, frustrated, angry, and resentful. The purpose of mediation is not to win arguments (a win–lose situation), but to solve the problem (a win–win situation). Mediation is a healthy method of problem solving and it is an indicator of a healthy community.

The Conflict Mediation process will be initiated by the Program Director through a written request for mediation by a player, a coach, or a staff member. The request must include:

1. A complete presentation of the problem.
2. What activities have been completed in an attempt to solve the problem.
3. The reasons felt that mediation is necessary.
4. Any additional information or comments.

The Program Director will evaluate the problem circumstances and verify the efforts attempted to resolve the problem. If it is apparent that the conflict has reached the mediation stage, the Program Director will activate the conflict mediation process.

The following are some circumstances that would qualify for mediation:

- Unresolved team conflict.
- Unresolved feelings of unfairness.
- Unresolved tension.
- Unresolved conflict between two or more players.
- Unresolved conflict between a player and a coach, players and coaches, a coach and a coach, a player and an administrator, or a coach and an administrator.
- Lack of improvement in a player's attitude and/or effort after coaching assistance has been given.
- Any serious unresolved concerns affecting players, coaches, the team, or the program.

Conflict Mediation involves a private meeting attended by those involved in the conflict, arranged by the Program Director. A trained mediator will conduct the meeting. The mediator will be a person not affiliated with the club, who will be impartial. The mediator, selected from a list of trained conflict resolvers, will be briefed on the conflict circumstances by the Program Director. The day, time, and meeting place will be indicated by mail to those to be involved in the meeting.

Others may be asked for their input and assistance. At the gathering the mediator will facilitate the expression of concerns and views and guide the problem-solving process. No more than two mediation sessions will be scheduled to resolve the conflict.

In a healthy, well-functioning community (team), community members abide by the group-resolved solutions. The Iowa Heart Juniors Volleyball Club expects compliance to the mediated solutions by all those involved in the mediation process. Noncompliance is most damaging to the welfare of the team as well as the entire program. Noncompliant persons will not be allowed continued participation in the program.

It should be noted that a club member has the right to resign from the club at any time without ridicule or embarrassment from team members, coaches, or the club administrators.

their meaning and facilitate their desire for valuable recreational participation? Just as important: Do I have fun coaching kids, and do the parents have fun, pride, and satisfaction in watching their children play the games? These are the most important questions we can ever ask about youth sports.

We all agree on the importance of fun in sport, but we seldom take the time to reflect on its meaning. If we know what fun means, then we have a better chance of establishing it in our programs and teams. We will be better able to meet the needs of our athletes. So here is my shot at the meaning of *fun*.

Having fun is participating in meaningful activities, being with people who don't yell and who offer encouragement. Fun is using a ball, bat, glove, stick, or racquet as often as possible. It is serving an ace, hitting a softball, shooting hoops, pitching balls, kicking goals, splashing water, playing games, being with friends, eating pizza.

Fun is not being yelled at. It is not being on a team that fights and argues. Fun is not enduring long boring practices, coaches who talk too much and don't listen, or sitting on the bench too long. Fun is play, venturing out, trying new things.

Fun is being understood; having a coach who cares about the team and who knows the game and how to execute skills; having shared team experiences; learning new sports skills. Fun is not having a coach who does not understand what it is like to be a child, or not having a team that has no spirit or unity, or missing out on learning the technical aspects of the game. Fun is having a coach who knows the game and teaches it in a way that makes you feel free to try and learn new things.

Creating a climate of fun means that the youngsters will practice and play harder and take a personal interest in their team, in each other, and in their own learning. It can make a big difference in how young athletes play—as a team or simply as a group of individuals—if all the players truly enjoy the sports experience created for them.

If fun isn't evident with your team, then it's time to rethink and change coaching styles and program goals. A guiding coaching principle should be: *No matter what, keep it fun!*

THE REAL MEANING OF WINNING

Coach, have you had a serious discussion with your team about what *winning* and *losing* mean in the scheme of things? If you haven't, do it soon! Both are going to happen, so be prepared. Understanding such important phenomena in one's life is more important to the human development of young athletes than all the laboring on learning to pass, serve, transition, defend, and so on.

Young athletes can learn from both winning and losing. But for this to occur, winning must be put in a healthy perspective. This means:

• *Winning isn't everything, nor is it the only thing.* Young athletes can't possibly learn from winning and losing if they think the only objective is to beat their opponents. If at the end of the season your players feel they have enjoyed relating to you and to their teammates, feel better about themselves, have improved their skills and are looking forward to playing next year, you have accomplished something far more important than a winning record or a championship. And, Coach, you will be a successful coach!

• *Failure is not the same thing as losing.* It is important that athletes do not view losing as a sign of failure or a threat to their personal value. Young athletes should be taught that losing a game is not a reflection of their own self-worth. And Coach, it certainly is *not* a reflection of your self-worth!

• *Success is not equivalent to winning.* Winning and losing apply to the outcome of a game and match, whereas success and failure do not. How, then, can we define success in sports?

• *Athletes should be taught that success is found in striving for victory.* The important point is: *Success is related to commitment and effort!* Athletes have complete control over the amount of effort they give, but they have only limited control over the outcome that is achieved. If you can impress on your athletes that they are never "losers" if they commit themselves to doing their best and giving maximum effort, you are giving them a priceless gift that will assist them in many of life's tasks.

We have won tournaments with our approach. We have also had losing streaks. On three occasions we have won the state tournament; and we have taken three teams to the Junior Olympics, the most prestigious national tournament. In all these events, everyone played and everyone contributed to decision making on the court and off the court. We have also learned to celebrate smaller victories: She threw the ball in the right direction! She actually swung the bat this time rather than standing paralyzed! She served the ball over the net for the first time!

Competition Teaches "Winning"

What is winning? Consider what "winning" means to each of the following people. Do you agree?

1. When Jessica returns home from a soccer game, her father says, "Did you win?" (Winning means scoring more points than the opponent.)
2. A football coach tells his players they will have to work extra hard in practice tomorrow, because their defensive skills were poor even though they won today. (Winning means playing the best you can.)
3. A softball coach says to her worst batter, "I'm really proud of you. Today you dared to try those tips I've been giving you about batting. Yes, you struck out, but your form and swing are so much better. Soon you will be hitting that ball!" (Winning means never giving up.)
4. Jessica's mother asks, "How did you enjoy your game today? What did you learn?" (Winning is having fun in learning new skills.)

If winning depends on outscoring the opponents, then half the participants will win. If winning depends on bettering personal performance and striving for excellence, then everyone has the opportunity to win. Beating another team is exciting, but performing better than you ever have before is winning.

Competition Teaches Losing

The following statements were made after a loss. What do they teach about losing?

1. "You bunch of sissies! How could you have lost to a group that plays like that?" (Losing means being put down by the coach.)

2. "I know it was a tough game for you and that you feel miserable, because we know we can play much better. We'll work extra hard in practice tomorrow. You are still my number one team." (Losing a game is OK. There is always a tomorrow when I can try again.)
3. "All right, so we lost the game by 20 points and the other team outplayed us. We are still a good basketball team." (Let's hold up our heads and be proud of the way we played.)
4. "Since you lost we're not stopping for ice cream on the way home!" (Losing means we have to be punished.)

Losing a game is never as joyful as winning it. However, a true loser is one who yells, cheats, hollers, and sulks. A true loser is one who refuses to think, "How can I play better tomorrow?" or "I played my best; therefore, the other team must have played better today than I did." How you handle a loss determines whether or not you are a true loser.

What is *losing?* Losing means:

- cheating to win a game
- using abusive language
- describing opponents in a negative manner
- not doing the best you can

What is *winning?* Winning means:

- running farther than you ever have before
- practicing those free throws to increase your free-throw percentage
- playing as hard as you can
- going out for pizza with your opponents after the game
- mastering a new move
- enjoying the game regardless of the outcome

In my team discussions on winning and losing I present this quote from John Wooden, the former basketball coach of UCLA, renowned as a successful and winning coach: "The real contest is striving to reach your *personal* best, and that is totally under your control. When you achieve that, you have achieved success. Period! You are a winner and only you fully know if you won" (Wooden and Jamison, 1997, p. 171).

Coach: Celebrate your wins, strive for victory, accept and learn from your losses, respect your athletes, and you will find peace of mind.

THE SPORTPARENT'S CREED

There are three major participants in youth sports: the athletes, the coaches, and the parents. The least prepared members of this triangle are the parents. As I observe sportparents I am impressed with how much anguish and aggravation they experience while supporting their children in sports. If you take a moment to pan the bleachers, it's quite revealing: moms burying their heads in their hands, dads pacing the sidelines, parents wringing their hands, looks of distress. Are they having fun yet? It doesn't look like it to me.

All parents feel frustration when their child is performing. Parents have no control over their child's actions during a game; they have no control over the coach's behavior; and they have no control over how the game will turn out. Lack of control is the basis for frustration and anxiety. The problems and the pressures parents feel are often brought to the courts and playing fields.

It isn't easy being a sport mom or dad. Parenting is the most difficult, sensitive, and stressing role that adults can have. We want the best for our kids. Most of all, we want them to be happy. It isn't easy for us to watch the pains our children go through in striving for their achievements and identity. Being a sportparent should take as much effort as it takes to become an excellent athlete or coach. An interesting concept that has occurred to me: In order for parents to be allowed to come to their children's games, they should be required to complete a set amount of training and be certified as a sportparent. They would have to pass a written examination and be rated while at their children's games by an upper-level certified sportparent. We already have certified coaches, officials, and scorekeepers; is being a parent less important? Of course, this won't happen—but you get my point.

In March 2000, Dave Epperson, George Selleck, and I established *Positive Sports Parenting* (Epperson and Selleck, 2000). We train sportparents to train other sportparents how to relax and how to cherish their children's endeavors in sports. Parents convey a lot in their language. How they talk at home and what they do when they come to the games are important. Sports can reinforce values and life skills; sports can teach parents how to realistically assess the child's abilities, to respect themselves and others, to communicate effectively with the coach, to cope with frustration, and to deal with difficult problems such as controlling their anger. Parents and children shouldn't have to go through the anxiety and the frustration. We need to make everyone a winner and to accentuate the positive. This program offers the hope that both kids and parents can enjoy themselves and have fun.

I've been a sportparent, it seems, forever. My four kids were involved in a variety of athletics. I enjoyed those years immensely, but it took effort on my part. I educated myself by reading literature on human behavior, the socialization process, achievement motivation, active parenting, parent and teacher effectiveness, and the psychology of preadolescent and adolescent behavior. Much of my training came from years of experience as a participant–observer at games and tournaments. This education is lifelong. Though my biological children have left the nest, my surrogate parenting continues in my role as a coach. As I did when I was my young children's sportparent, I continue to revisit my goals as a sportparent coach. Box 17.2 outlines my understandings of my role as a sportparent. Of course, the Sportparent's Creed is not gender specific. Because I coach females, my copy reads "she" and "her." A coach of males would use "he" and "him."

The Sportparent's Creed has been a handout at my preseason parent meetings. I display this Sportparent's Creed prominently at my home and in my office. I've read it so often through the years that I can recite it. It has helped me relax and be reassured that I remain healthy in my perspective on children and on myself. I'm a happy sportgrandparent and coach.

CONCLUSION

Because adults now organize, manage, and control the recreation of youth, they are obliged to preserve the fun of the sandlot days. But those elders who

Box 17.2

Sportparent's Creed

I understand my child is unique. She has her own gifts and develops at her own pace.

I understand that my child has her own goals in sports as in other aspects of life. I will support those goals and keep them separate from my own.

I understand that I am a mirror to my child's feelings about herself. If I value her and show her respect and compassion, she will know I love her for who she is—not what she does.

I understand that my behavior off the playing court or field is as important as my child's behavior on the court or field. My actions and my words have an impact on my child's behavior.

I understand my child has her own inner voice. My job as parent is to help her recognize it, listen to it, and act on it.

I understand that the coach needs to hear my feelings, feel my support, and understand that our common interest is the well-being of my child—not the scoreboard.

I understand that attaching blame to outside factors—luck, fate, officials, teammates—teaches a lack of responsibility for one's actions.

I understand that youth sports should enhance and not dominate my child's life. Overemphasis on sport reduces the balance in her life and creates undue pressure to perform and excel.

I understand that the other children on the playing court or field are equally important and as special as my child. They deserve my love, support, encouragement, respect, and blessings too.

I understand that I can change any negative patterns that have developed between myself and my child.

As a sportparent, I pledge to continue to see my child as a whole person. I want to understand her *emotionally, socially, mentally, physically, and spiritually.*

---

affect the lives of young people through sport need to do more. We need adult coaches who are the architects of empowered and contributing citizens. What better places for this to take place than on the ball fields and in the gyms? Sport is too important to be just a game.

BIBLIOGRAPHY

Epperson, David Canning, and George Selleck. *Beyond the Bleachers: The Art of Parenting Today's Athletes.* Sugar Land, TX: Alliance Publication, 2000.

Epperson, David Canning, and George Selleck. *From the Bleachers with Love: Advice to Parents with Kids in Sports.* Sugar Land, TX: Alliance Publication, 2000.

Gould, Daniel. *Motivating Young Athletes.* East Lansing, Mich.: Institute for the Study of Youth Sports, 1980, pages 6–9.

Hutslar, Jack. *Beyond X's and O's: What Generic Parents, Volunteer Coaches, and Teachers can Learn about Generic Kids and All of the Sports They Play.* Kernsville, N.C.: North American Youth Sport Institute, 1985.

Miller, Martin. "Developmental Coaching: An Approach to Positive Youth Development in Sports." *New Designs for Youth Development,* Vol. 9, No. 2, 1989, pages 31–35.

Miller, Martin. "The Spectrum of Coaches' Attitudes and Behaviors toward Young Athletes." *New Designs for Youth Development,* Vol. 10, No. 3, 1993, pages 7–13.

Miller, Martin. "What Young People Learn through Competitive Sports." *New Designs for Youth Development,* Vol. 12, No. 1, 1996, pages 44–47.

Wolff, Rick. *Sports Parenting: Encouraging Your Kids on and off the Court.* New York: Pocket Books, 1998, page 30.

Wooden, Coach John, with Steve Jamison. *Wooden: A Lifetime of Observations and Reflections on and off the Court.* Chicago: Contemporary Books, 1997.

18

Creating Grassroots Change through Service Learning

BARBARA A. CARSON

Editors' Note: We don't see our environments, because they surround us. As John Culkin says, "We don't know who discovered water but it certainly wasn't a fish." An outsider may see things that the insider takes for granted. Bringing problems to the blackboard can allow us to step back and see new solutions. Barbara Carson discusses using the university as a platform for community change.

We in universities believe we are fairly smart people. After all, we have degrees to prove it, and others pay us to read, think, and teach. However, we have a long history of not being able to leave the ivory tower and do anything practical. This is particularly so when it comes to solving social problems or applying our knowledge in everyday settings. Sometimes we rationalize that we are helping our community through writing and teaching others, who can take our insights and reduce the world's problems. However, as Herb Blumer (1970) wrote, the process of implementing social policy is a unique sociological process in and of itself. We in academia should go beyond the traditional classroom settings and take some responsibility for how our knowledge is utilized. A method of teaching called service learning is one means for academics to promote local grassroots social change.

SERVICE LEARNING

Service learning is a form of experiential education in which students perform service within the community and then spend classroom time reflecting on and analyzing their experiences. In sociology courses, this often means focusing on some social concern or working with agencies or community groups addressing social problems. As a teaching approach, service learning helps students understand concepts, theories, and applications of sociological knowledge (Corwin, 1996; Everett, 1998; Marullo, 1996, 1998; Rundblad, 1998; Stoecker, 1996). It also can be beneficial in linking faculty and other community members together to respond to social problems.

Service learning programs are organized in various ways. Students may work independently on special projects; a class may provide service to one specific agency or community site; or students in a class may be dispersed to multiple agencies. Regardless of the approach, weekly class time is spent having the students share and reflect on their experiences with their classmates and their instructor. This is a marvelous means for stimulating class discussion. Each student has the specific information and personal experiences to bring to discussions. This keeps things interesting, as the faculty member has no idea what the specific daily content may be!

Field supervisors are considered co-teachers, even though they usually are not involved in the classroom discussions. Practitioners benefit from the service learning program—not only from free labor, but because they get to show the future generation of professionals what the real world is like. Faculty members usually maintain direct contact with the field supervisors throughout the course to monitor the students' work. It is this relationship that is the springboard through which a sociology professor can become involved in grassroots social change.

The faculty member and community-based field supervisor also have indirect contact. Service learning students describe their field experiences in the classroom and, similarly, describe classroom activities to field supervisors. From a faculty member's viewpoint, it may seem that students are spying on the community agencies. The extent of "espionage" varies with the number of hours and weeks students are involved in service learning activities; but the result is that students spend considerable class time describing and analyzing agencies' activities, policies, and personnel. In the course of a given term, a faculty member may learn much about an agency's inner activities. If this agency is used several semesters, the dossier of information known by the faculty member is extensive. Likewise, agencies learn much about the classroom instructor.

If students are performing well, there may be rather limited direct dialogue between the university instructor and the field supervisor. When the opposite happens, however, there are extensive discussions and a sharing of information and ideas on how to address the student's difficulties. One person or the other may agree to take responsibility for speaking with the student about the difficulties and devising plans for change. There also may be times when seriously inappropriate behavior requires drastic intervention, such as removing the student from the service learning site or reporting illegal behavior. For example, recently we had to remove an intern from a prison because she was alleged to be flirting with the inmates. Dialogue between the instructor and the field supervisor in situations such as this may be lengthy, particularly if the two disagree on what the issues are or on how to resolve them. All of these activities lead to considerable dialogue on how to teach the college student in a real-life setting.

A structural factor that influences the dynamics of the relationship between community practitioners and faculty is that service learning partnerships may exist for a long time. The contacts described above are not necessarily episodic. They can become routinized across many semesters and even, perhaps, many years.

TRUST

For the partnership between the community supervisor and the classroom instructor to exist beyond the offering of one class, there must be trust. I suspect such partnerships probably do not last more than two semesters if trust does not develop quickly. Trust is important when an instructor is making the initial service learning arrangements for placing college students. It can also facilitate academic sociologists' working on community social problems and promoting social change.

Trust is the mutually acknowledged evaluation of a relationship in which the participants' behaviors can be predicted to be caring and supportive, and where there exists no fear of being harmed. Trust takes time to develop. It involves a reciprocal process of gradually sharing private information. Trust strengthens as it becomes apparent that partners will keep each other's secrets; that information will not be used to hurt an individual.

As partners affirm their respect for each other, trust may evolve into mutual support. When one person has considerable background information about another, it is easier to sympathize, empathize, or even provide useful advice to assist the other in his or her struggles. Trust implies that the close and supportive characteristics of the relationship will continue to exist in the future. Trust is always sought between close friends and intimates, but it can also be useful for building professional relationships among people who share a desire to eradicate social problems.

Implications of Trust in Service Learning Relationships

Service learning is an extremely useful way to initiate and develop relationships of trust between faculty members and community members. Often students are placed in service learning sites that are tied to their majors or to an area that interests their instructor. Interests and concerns of the field supervisors and classroom instructor are probably very similar—a good foundation for building trusting relationships.

Developing trust facilitates easy transitions for students and undoubtedly makes the learning experience more fruitful. Trust helps create a continued relationship for the field supervisor and the classroom teacher as they share information and express concern about social problems within the community. The faculty member, from listening to students' classroom descriptions, learns more about issues in the community and about how existing agencies or social groups are trying to respond to social ills. The faculty member also learns more about the struggles of these agencies, be they personnel problems, financial troubles, or political issues.

A shared concern for the dilemmas faced by community organizations develops. Agency people may express relief and appreciation that a relative outsider understands. In trusting relationships, classroom instructors undoubtedly will make the agency people aware of the results of students' "espionage." There also may be a sharing of vulnerabilities. Between the two instructors, there may be a sharing of the critical issues surrounding attempts at social change.

This may lead to an exchange of resources. Academic sociologists, based on our particular skills and training, may actually be able to make a contribution to the community in supporting positive social change. This can take place in several ways. The faculty may be able to guide the service learning students to initiate change. The instructor may be able to provide ideas and information useful to the practitioner. Finally, the instructor can take advantage of being an outsider possessing insider's information and work with community leaders to facilitate the change advocated by the field supervisors.

AN EXAMPLE OF A
SERVICE LEARNING PROGRAM

I have taught a service learning course every term for the past 6 years. The objective of this class is to expose students to individuals who have been convicted of a crime. Students are required to provide 6 to 10 hours of service per week in some local organization throughout the entire semester as well as to participate in the weekly classroom reflection activities.

Approximately two-fifths of each week of course time is spent reflecting on service learning experiences. Each student describes his or her own experiences for the week, and then the entire class assists in analyzing the events. During the remainder of classroom time other topics are addressed, but service learning experiences are used frequently as examples to help students understand class material.

My university's service learning program, and my particular course, were jointly created by students, local agency staff, and faculty. The way the program was created is important, because it demonstrates that from the beginning the service learning program was designed to be mutually beneficial to all parties. I have worked with agencies such as our local YMCA, a shelter for abused women and children, a crisis hotline, our local jail programs coordinator, youth mentoring programs, and several local public schools. Many of the following examples come from my partnerships with local schools.

In any given term, 8 to 15 of my students are placed in numerous junior and senior high schools in nearby communities to work with children who have been permanently or temporarily removed from traditional classrooms because of behavior problems. Many of these children are on probation for activities such as truancy, shoplifting, drug use, and assault. The college students assist the younger students by tutoring, teaching study and organization skills, and becoming informal mentors for the younger students.

An additional advantage of linking college students with these public school students is that many of the younger people have never met someone who is going to college. The younger students typically are shocked that college students would voluntarily attend school beyond the legally required age. These young students hate school, and they have difficulty imagining why anyone would actually pay money to go to school.

Similarly, many of the participating college students have never met individuals from lower socioeconomic classes. Typically, they express shock when they confront realities such as the fact that six siblings may share a single bedroom or that there are households in our community with no telephone or alarm clock. With the proper guidance by all instructors, the personal change resulting from this introduction to members of different social classes may, by itself, effect social change in the long run.

Over the course of 6 years, the instructors (as well as some principals) at several schools and I have worked on building trust. This has not been an overt issue—it just happened, and it was necessary to keep our service learning arrangements functioning. As a result, I have learned much about the inner operations of the schools. I have heard about the behavior of excellent teachers and also learned about the problem teachers. I have learned much about the constraints and lack of funding. I have also learned about racist policies in these schools.

I realize that many of the reports I have received are from naive reporters. Most of the college students I teach have had very little contact with members of lower social classes or with younger people with tremendously troubled lives. The college students are also profoundly unaware of how political issues affect the operations of schools. By teaching a service learning course, I have learned many secrets about my community and our schools.

HOW SERVICE LEARNING CAN LEAD TO GRASSROOTS SOCIAL CHANGE

There are at least three ways in which service learning can lead to social change. Students may initiate change; faculty may provide ideas and information directly to practitioners; and instructors may act as "outsiders with insiders' information." What follows is a more thorough description illustrated with stories based on my personal experiences.

Students Initiating Social Change

Over the course of several semesters, college students in my service learning classes who were tutoring junior high students with behavior problems became quite concerned that students were often given the answers during tests by their teachers. It appeared that the teachers felt students were incapable of learning and so would give them answers instead of making them learn the material. Some teachers also let these younger students use calculators to solve simple math problems, assuming that they were incapable of learning math. The college students disagreed. The college students felt these practices not only deprived the younger students of the chance to learn necessary skills but also communicated a stigmatizing message to the younger students—that teachers thought they were stupid. As a result, in the classroom component of the service learning class, we reflected on labeling theory. Labeling theory illustrates the consequences of stigma. A label such as "bad" or "dumb" has a tendency to become a self-fulfilling prophecy. Teachers act on the basis of such definitions, and students may internalize such expectations. The college students questioned the junior high teachers about the legitimacy of these practices. This questioning occurred every semester for 2 years. Over the course of time, I saw a significant decrease in these teaching practices. This may not seem like massive social change, but the overall effect of changing the stereotypes held by some teachers improves the likelihood that troubled youth will stay in school long enough to graduate.

Another example of college students' promoting change occurred when it was reported during the reflection component of our class that public school students who received subsidized lunches were publicly stigmatized. When kids went to lunch, everyone in the school had to type into a computer a personal identification number that subtracted the current lunch from the funds sent in by parents. Students receiving subsidized lunches typed in their identification number too, but the recorded balance, visible to every other student in the lunch line, was always zero. When students in my class were discussing how embarrassing this was, I would simply ask, "So what are you going to do about this?" The students contacted local school board members, and the practice was quietly altered. Again, this was not a tremendous social ill, but it was a wrongdoing that got stopped. Perhaps this act also helped educate school board members about the need to avoid labeling students.

Examples such as these provide excellent illustrations for classroom discussions of *The Sociologi-*

cal Imagination: C. Wright Mills's (1959) work contending that personal problems reflect social issues. When college students are exposed to the depth of injustice experienced by the disadvantaged in our society, they respond passionately. We often see this in typical classroom settings, but in service learning courses students meet and learn the names of real people who are socially exploited. Many students have only recently emerged from the relatively powerless status of childhood and are eager to respond to injustices. However, particularly with traditional-age college students, they may not know what they can do. Instructors as well as more experienced students can offer suggestions. These suggestions may involve anything from organizing letter-writing campaigns, conducting public hearings, writing newspaper editorials, meeting with community leaders, and lobbying congresspersons to holding demonstrations. These are all activities that will draw attention to community problems and bring together other concerned citizens to work on the problems.

If students stay organized beyond the term of a specific semester, their range of activities can expand further. Regardless of the length of their involvements, impassioned college students can be very effective in making bureaucratic organizations stop and ponder the social ills in their community.

Faculty Assistance to Community Agencies

College faculty can be involved in social change by being a resource for community agencies and/or activists. As sociologists, we understand power relations: We know where to look for sources of power, and we understand when power is being abused. We are skilled at teaching others how to apply the sociological imagination to understand how social forces create individual problems. With these skills, we may be able to assist local activists in promoting change.

In addition, most of us know how to research topics, and we understand the use (and abuse!) of statistics. When agency people are attempting to justify change, they need information that we know how to find. Some of us are also very good at writing grant proposals. This can be a useful service to many organizations.

As a result of my involvement in this service learning class I have been invited by community members and agencies to help them work on sensitive, difficult issues. For example, one of my students urged a younger student to have her parents get in touch with me about incidents of racial harassment in the schools. This was a family new to the area who were at a loss as to whom to contact. I became an advocate for this family.

I have consulted privately with teachers on how to handle difficult situations, such as issues that arose when one school had a sudden large influx of international refugee children. I was able to give the school resources, such as published research findings on working with children who have grown up in war zones, and I was able to find contacts in other communities who had successfully responded to similar issues.

I was invited by a high school principal to meet with faculty to discuss possible responses to a rash of racially motivated fights among students. The political environment surrounding the school was such that the faculty did not want their problems publicized, but they also realized that they needed outside help. Faculty at this school had helped me in a previous situation when my college students acted inappropriately in their service learning site and had helped me decide how best to approach my students on difficult issues. I was eager to assist them.

Let me add that not all agencies like my responses when I have been invited to assist with internal problems. I suspect there are often times when they wish they had not asked me, such as when my assessment in a particular school was that the teachers were very poorly trained to handle racial conflicts in the classroom and that the curriculum needed to be more multicultural. In this case, and in others, my "brilliant," "insightful" sociological wisdom did not always create the change I thought necessary. However, as one of many professionals making similar assessments over time, I have seen change occurring in this school.

At other times and other places, I have chastised school administrators for not having students well informed on how to report incidents of harassment. I have criticized school board members for placing the responsibility for responding to racism in the school on students instead of taking responsibility themselves. I have said things that I felt needed to be said, and privately I have received support from many teachers. Because of my relative power status in the community and because I am an outsider (remember, they can't fire me), I can say things that many others know about but feel unable to say openly.

As a sociologist, I am not surprised that all of these situations occurred. However, as a traditional academic teacher, I probably would not have learned about these specific incidents in my community and would have had little opportunity to respond to them. Because I have been involved in service learning classes, not only have I learned of these social ills, but, like my students, I know the names of people in my community who are exploited or who are suffering. This is a powerful motivator to get involved.

An Outsider with Insider's Information

Another process   mulating social change that emerges from s   ning requires academic so-ciologists to be   ve. Through service learn-ing, classroom   learn the "dirty secrets" of the community   may be actual abuses of power, or they   lemmas the community ei-ther does not kn   to address or has chosen to ignore. These can   stacles stopping change in the community or within the particular agencies. Responding to this knowledge requires academic sociologists to act as an outsider with insider information.

The range of possible resulting activities is varied. It may involve "whistle-blowing" either on community activities or on issues within a specific organization. It may involve becoming an advocate within the community. It may involve working within an organization where a trusting relationship already exists and helping that organization overcome obstacles.

The beauty of the outsider's role is that the university faculty member cannot be fired by the agency for exposing difficulties. Nor can the faculty member be accused of supporting the personal agenda of some group, because he or she is not a member of the group. The status of university faculty may be used to lend credibility and balance the power of the relatively powerless.

To be most effective, actions must be directed toward addressing problems without destroying the relationships and trust among those involved. If there is something wrong within a community agency (such as a personnel issue) or if an agency is misdirected (such as focusing on the wrong aspect of a problem), critiques must be offered with the understanding that there is support and a commitment to a future relationship. As such, the sociologist not only takes responsibility for pointing out the problems; he or she must also take responsibility for helping the group find means for resolving the problems.

At times, I have felt morally compelled to do something with the knowledge I learn from my students. Once an African American student was harassed by a white bailiff in our local courthouse as she was accompanying a younger student who was picking up some legal papers. The bailiff wrongfully assumed that the college student, undoubtedly because of her race, was an offender awaiting a court hearing. In this case, I called the probation officer who was the field supervisor for students in that site, and he shared my complaint with the judge, who then attempted to educate the bailiff on the dangers of stereotyping.

I have had a student working with residents at our local shelter for battered women experience a landlord's saying an apartment was already rented when an African American woman applied, but that it was still available when a white woman later inquired. I have had students witness a white police officer attempting to choke an African American junior high school student. I have had students witness teachers hitting students—an illegal act in our state.

In all of these cases, I became involved. I have reported incidents, I have demanded investigations, and I have contacted community leaders in an attempt to raise their awareness of these activities. I suspect such abuses of power would not have taken place in front of me, a white university professor. I also suspect that my students' simply reporting the incidents would not cause much to happen. And I am not so naive as to assume that all such abuses ended because of my responses—as in the case when service learning students reported on the white police officer's choking an African American junior high school girl.

When this happened, my students called me immediately, asking what they should do. I contacted their field supervisor to make sure that the incident had been reported. It had, and an investigation ensued. I made it clear that I had college students who could testify as witnesses; in fact, they wanted to testify. But they were never contacted. I later learned that the mother of the student came to the police department the next day and demanded to know how to file a complaint against the police officer. Despite what appeared to me fairly strong evidence (including bruises on the girl's neck), no charges were ever filed. Perhaps this failure had something to do with the fact that the mother was arrested for robbery several days later and was charged with participating in a gang-related crime. Whether or not the mother committed the crime, and regardless of whether or not she was a gang member, based on my students' reports, a student had been assaulted by a police officer and nothing happened.

It is frustrating when abuses of human rights are not resolved. In this particular case, the same police officer was investigated several years later for similar offenses. I made telephone calls again, stating that I had students who could testify about an earlier incident. Although they were never contacted, the officer was eventually fired. However, no charges were ever pursued. Minimally, while coping with frustrations over events such as this, I can make sure that my community does not forget that such abuses occur.

Sometimes it is not a crisis that motivates me; I simply get tired of hearing about the same problem semester after semester, and eventually I feel compelled to act. After hearing my students complain about a certain alternative school, I finally asked to meet with its board to discuss their admission policies, the need to update textbooks, and concerns about gender inequality in programming. In this situation, I was advocating the very issues the school's teachers had been trying to vocalize to the board. I came as an outside community member, acting on behalf of the teachers, *and*—I did not have to worry about being chastised or fired. At worst, I risked having the school decide not to accept my service learning students; but they needed the labor!

Let me add that I also learn much about the excellent practices that occur in these schools. As an outsider with insider information, I am able to brag and publicize outstanding policies, programs, and teachers. For example, I have spoken at state gatherings about one school's use of community circles for responding to racially motivated conflicts between students. I have invited alternative high school students into my classes to demonstrate peer mediation programs. I have also written letters of recommendation for wonderful junior high and senior high school teachers seeking tenure. The only reason I have information on these subjects, and thus can take some responsibility for helping excellent practices survive, is because of my service learning courses.

CONSTRAINTS OF TRUSTING RELATIONSHIPS

Using service learning as a means to promote social change can be extremely successful, but it also has several potential problems. Local agencies or service learning field supervisors may limit the effectiveness of the sociology faculty member in two ways. The first kind of constraint is rejection of the advice or services of the faculty member. The second is the specific request that public exposure of an agency's problems be suppressed. The strength of these constraints becomes greater when it is remembered that these are relationships of trust built on the assumption of continued working relationships.

As I mentioned earlier, my advice to one school for creating social change was ignored. Let me add that this has happened many times, with different agencies; probably it should be an expected outcome. University-based sociologists may have to be patient, waiting to see if their advice is ever accepted. And the reality is that at times it will not be. The intermingling of social activism and the classroom may present difficulties. At times, either the field supervisor or the classroom teacher may have such different views on how to create social change that it makes it impossible to continue the social learning relationship.

The second way that service learning relationships may constrain sociologists from promoting social change is that agencies or individuals may ask the outsider to *suppress* insider information. Sometimes this request may be evaluated as reasonable. At times, it may not. The ethical issue for the classroom sociologist is that the only reason he or she knows private information is that trusting relationships have been created. Constraints on behavior are being requested as a component of that trust. Clearly, decisions must be made dependent upon the severity of issues and the context of the dilemma.

Both requests to suppress information invoked on the basis of trust and rejection of the professional advice of the classroom sociologist have the potential for terminating service learning partnerships and thus ending the sociologist's access to activism through these channels. Although I have not experienced this, I have taken measures to prevent it from happening and to avoid the inevitable bitterness. The potential for this kind of breakdown needs to be analyzed while we are in the process of developing the relationship. As trust is developing, a history of ways to handle ethical dilemmas should also be developing. Combined with this should be an evolving pattern of communication between the classroom sociologist and the field supervisor—a pattern of listening to each other yet recognizing that each is from a different work environment. Differences should be expected, but learning about each other can still take place. When constraints are placed upon the classroom sociologist, there are times when they should be ignored and when the trust relationship will therefore be terminated. However, perhaps because of respect for these trusting relationships, extended efforts are usually made by all participants to find mutually agreeable solutions to the differences in opinions.

SUMMARY

Service learning can promote both student and faculty involvement in creating grassroots social change. It is an excellent means for academics to make links and develop relationships of trust with existing activists in the community. Trust implies that no harm will come from these relationships and that the partnerships will continue in the future. At times ethical dilemmas may arise because of constraints placed by those in trusting relationships. However, service learning programs can foster the development of trust that can then continue to create strong partnerships for resolving grassroots social problems.

I believe that it is critical that we function as *sociologists* when getting involved in community social problems. We must remember that most of our society analyzes problems at a psychological level, looking just at the individual. It is possible to be seduced by that level of analysis. Although there are benefits to that approach, our most valuable contribution as sociologists is our specialized insight and knowledge. We have professional training for understanding social behavior, power relations, and social movements. We know what it takes to generate interest in a social problem, and we can research what strategies have worked in other communities. Service learning is the vehicle for making ties with the community through which we can share our knowledge.

REFERENCES

Blumer, Herbert. 1970. "Social Construction of Social Problems." *Social Problems* 18: 298–306.

Corwin, Patricia. 1996. "Using the Community as a Classroom for Large Introductory Sociology Classes." *Teaching Sociology* 24 (3): 310–315.

Everett, Kevin D. 1998. "Understanding Social Inequality through Service Learning." *Teaching Sociology* 26 (4): 299–309.

Marullo, Sam. 1996. "The Service-Learning Movement in Higher Education: An Academic Response to Troubled Times." *Sociological Imagination* 33 (2): 117–137.

Marullo, Sam. 1998. "Bringing Home Diversity: A Service-Learning Approach to Teaching Race and Ethnic Studies." *Teaching Sociology* 26 (4): 259–275.

Mills, C. Wright. 1959. *The Sociological Imagination.* New York: Oxford University Press.

Rundblad, Georganne. 1998. "Addressing Social Problems, Focusing on Solutions: The Community Exploration Project." *Teaching Sociology* 26 (4): 331–340.

Stoecker, Randy. 1996. "Introduction to Special Issue: Sociology and Social Action, Part II." *Sociological Imagination* 33 (2): 91–93.

19

Tramp Training
Constructing a Service Learning
Program in Homeless Intervention

R. DEAN WRIGHT

Editors' Note: Dean takes students to the street to learn from the homeless so they can design more effective programs. It may seem like a strange thing to get college credit for sitting under a bridge at 4 o'clock in the morning talking to a homeless person. However, it is here that theories get punctuated and needs animated.

This is a story about how students became a part of an outreach program that had been invented to address the needs of homeless persons. As I look back, it is hard to identify an exact starting point. The coming together of students and the program was a natural expansion of the classroom into the streets for the validation of academic ideas and then back into the classroom for discussion and critique. Staff and board members of the local Salvation Army operation had decided they needed to construct a program to address the yet unknown needs of a new foundering group that had been identified in our community: homeless children. Those of us who became members of the newly created Salvation Army outreach team had only limited knowledge of what we were doing—there was no blueprint, no set of cheat notes, no textbook from which we could gain an understanding of what we were supposed to try, let alone accomplish. All we knew was that we wanted to find out what it was like to be homeless and that at the same time we had the ameliorative goal of "helping" those who were forced to live on the street. In some ways, we were a bunch of do-gooders in search of a group in need.

When we started this program, there was never the intention to do something that would become a must for social service students; but it, like Topsy, just grew. For those of us who charted a path to deal with "feeding breakfast to the homeless," the journey took us to a point where we suddenly realized that what we were doing was taking on meaning far beyond the immediacy of our personal lives. That is what C. Wright Mills had taught us in his writings. He wrote about personal biography and how it is shaped by and at the same time shapes the social worlds in which we live. That made sense. It is through personal biography that we suddenly come to realize that the worlds in which we live are very different from what we thought. In addition, we came to realize that the lives others live are far different from what we had assumed. Sharing the worlds of people from profoundly different life circumstances forces us to come to a better understanding of our personal lives.

At the same time, these realizations may provide us with an opportunity to question the traditional view of individualism that so often undermines how we look at others. Homelessness is a nation wide social

201

problem. As sociologist Emile Durkheim said in the late 1800s, "If someone gives an individualistic interpretation of a social problem, you can be sure that it is false." The social causes of homelessness include a decreasing supply of affordable housing; an unemployment rate that, although low, still does not provide adequate jobs for many who are simply unemployable; and the cadre of social reasons that lead people to seek escape in drugs and alcohol. To save money (among other reasons), society has deinstitutionalized many who were formerly cared for in mental institutions and veterans' hospitals and who now have difficulty fending for themselves. After a short detour in temporary assisted living, most of these people went straight to the streets. The ever increasing youth population on the streets is a product of alienation and a lack of anywhere viable to turn. Homeless youth are increasingly on the margins of society, and with our "get tough on kids" mentality we are making certain they stay there. Individualistic explanations remain popular, but in reality the factors underlying homelessness repeat in a familiar pattern across many different personal lives.

THE ACADEMIC CHALLENGE

For decades those of us who teach undergraduate students have tried to explain what we do as sociologists: how the worlds in which we live are shaped by ideas, and ultimately how students, when they leave ivy-covered halls, can do something that has the potential of making a difference. With pride, we often point to the masters from the heritage of our discipline who taught us that if we are to have meaning as sociologists, we must have that ameliorative focus for our lives and our professions. A perpetual struggle exists between the theories, often abstract, of the folk heroes of sociology and the needs of teachers, often practical, to make their words meaningful in the worlds in which students live and work. How often have I heard former students tell me, a year or two after they graduate and face the real world of the paycheck, that what they were taught often had little parallel with reality? There is a struggle, a conflict between the high ideas and ideals that we as academicians talk about and the real world of everyday

problems shared by people who live the lives about which we talk.

In the late 1970s and early 1980s, I came to the personal realization that the voice calling for social action was not being realized through any personal action with my students—or, for that matter, in my life. Over the next few years, I became a member of many boards and committees in my local community. One of the boards that I joined was that of the Salvation Army of Greater Des Moines. Sally, as most of us called the organization, was ready for change. About the same time, do-gooders of the city had discovered the plight of the homeless. especially the new group of women and children that then constituted the most rapidly growing category of homeless in Iowa (and in the rest of the United States). The Army and the need went through a brief courtship, with marriage occurring soon thereafter.

THE PROGRAM

Some of us believed that Sally needed to develop a program that might both benefit people who lived on the street and at the same time provide a learning experience for students. Our answer was a breakfast program that would go on the street to provide food to the homeless. It was a natural for us, and fit very well into the goals of the Salvation Army of Greater Des Moines. We were confident that this program could help address a need that had recently been discovered and was now a popular cause. Ever since the time when William Booth founded the Salvation Army, it has enjoyed a reputation of helping the most needy of the needy. Having been chair of the board of the local Salvation Army for some time, I had been searching for something to rejuvenate a basically paralyzed organization that no longer seemed to have anything to offer the local community. For several months we had searched for a realistic and vital program, discarding most suggestions as being unrealistic or overly ambitious. Finally, we came up with the idea of taking breakfast to the streets each Tuesday morning and providing a warm meal for the homeless, especially the children, who we had come to realize resided in several abandoned and substandard houses and under some of the more protected bridges of the city.

The local Salvation Army owned an aging and seldom used $100,000 emergency vehicle fully equipped for assisting people during disasters. It had a stove, a refrigerator, coffee makers, and a generator that could supply power to microwaves. It was ideal for an outreach program. We visualized taking that oversized vehicle onto the streets of the city to offer food to those who lacked even this minimum need. Through these efforts we had the opportunity to provide a beneficial service and at the same time to help the local Salvation Army better achieve its mission and, we hoped, become more viable in the community.

It took a while to translate our intentions into reality. Some people cautioned us about legal issues, others about financial stability. Many questioned where we would find sufficient volunteers. Other issues emerged: Where would we find adequate supplies of food? Were there really enough homeless to justify our actions? Were we actually "enabling" people? Were we doing this to make ourselves feel good rather than to help others? And what about the danger? Answering these questions increased the length of time before we started the outreach. Some of us were concerned that we might be delayed until the winter months, and in Iowa, winter can be a brutal time of the year. Finally, on a warm June morning some 11 years ago, we took to the streets with the goal of providing a "warm and nourishing" breakfast to those who live in various dilemmas of homelessness. Factually, we had little understanding of what we were doing—but we all agreed that it was time to stop talking and "just do it."

The first day of the program, we went onto the downtown streets of the city at about 5 A.M. We tried to distinguish the homeless from early arriving construction workers. Often we approached a person we thought might be homeless, only to discover that she was simply going to work or just walking. That first morning we were able to give food to 12 people. (Last week some 350 persons were served by the same outreach program.)

Within a few weeks, the program was better established and the numbers that we served started to climb. Our ability to identify potential clients and to interact with them improved. Those who were active in the program were so satisfied with the operation that a "satellite" vehicle was added. This van allowed volunteers to go into the more remote arteries of the community where the homeless lived a more private life. The main emergency vehicle quickly developed a standard itinerary. With time, residents of homeless shelters and street people who lived together came to anticipate the emergency vehicle to be at a certain corner on or about a given time. For instance, at 6:30 A.M. it was expected to be at the YWCA in downtown Des Moines. Over 3 or 4 years the YWCA had changed its local mission and had become a shelter for adult women and their children. It was a natural. Emergency housing was scarce in the city, and 70 or 80 rooms had been opened up for homeless women and their children. Meals were not available at the YWCA, so the Salvation Army van provided a welcome meal that supplemented the needs of these families. Several minutes before the arrival of the vehicle, residents started to form lines, and by the time the van stopped, 20 or 30 people were waiting for breakfast. The satellite van added more flexibility and could go off the established route and seek out those homeless who move from bridge to bridge, from abandoned house to abandoned house, from tent location to tent location. By almost any standard, the program had become a success.

STUDENTS BECOME A PART

Students soon heard about the Tuesday morning homeless run. I was teaching classes with titles such as "Homeless in America," "Throwaway Kids," and "Poverty in Rural America." Several students in these classes came to know that a group of us were going to the streets during the early morning hours. Many students wanted to share the experience so they could meet the homeless under bridges and wherever they routinely lived. It seemed logical that students be invited to participate with us; but should the experience be as a volunteer, or should there be some academic networking? The students and I pondered and discussed how to make the experience worthy of academic credit. That was not an easy job because many of the faculty within the college and university with which I am associated have a traditionally snobby point of view when it comes to experiential learning, internships, and other nontraditional educational experiences.

How does one tell students (and others) about those dark nights and mornings when my friends and I crawled into the recesses of abandoned buildings in hopes of finding a person who was escaping the world? One of the real fears was that we might actually find someone in the caverns of an abandoned building and then not have any idea of our next step. How does one respect the dignity of a person living on the streets and weigh it against the need to let a student witness, as a part of the learning experience, the plight of the homeless? Drawing that line is difficult. You are never sure when you have stepped over the boundary into something that is so personal that it should remain a part of the private life of the street person.

At first, I invited students to participate through providing a secondary level of service that Sally needed to have done. Meanwhile, we were learning from the satellite van through trial and error. We had no script that could hint what we might expect. We did have the experience of another outreach van that had worked the streets on Saturday night. I had gone with the organizer of that outreach several times, talked with street people, entered and crawled through abandoned houses, entered my first crack house, gone under most of the major bridges in the city, and walked the wooded areas in and near parks and on the riverbanks where the Des Moines and Raccoon Rivers meet just below downtown.

PLAYING IT BY EAR UNTIL IT WORKED

Folk wisdom and trial and error, along with impressionistic evidence of how to interact with the homeless, guided us during the first few weeks we were on the street. Because of local television accounts of the Des Moines homeless, most of us expected that we would be regular victims of panhandling and conning and would always be looking over our shoulder for fear someone would mug us and take our valuables. With time we came to realize that the opposite was closer to true. The homeless we first met in hidden corners of the community were friendly, inviting,

talkative, sharing, open. But at the same time it was obvious that many of them, especially street people, were not about to let their guard down. Over the years they had become accustomed to people like us invading their space and using them to gain warm fuzzy feelings. Legions of volunteers had the option of later returning to the safety of their warm and comfortable suburban homes. In time, we realized that homeless men and women came to resent this intrusion, yet they knew there was nothing they could do about it. Such futility, almost a sense of alienation, marks the ongoing routine of the street people we met.

In the classroom, students came to know Erving Goffman, whose writings had introduced us to concepts like the back face—that part of our selves and identities that we preserve for our quieter moments. If and when we decide to share our back face, we do so with a very limited number of people. Yet, we outsiders would crawl through a window or come down a river bank and invade the space that the homeless had come to occupy and perhaps call home. Each article that a student read invited more and more discussion and critique. Students challenged the reality of the words that scholars had written on the pages of journals and books. Often there was considerable disagreement, sometimes based on methodology, at other times on theory, but more often based on values and norms that impacted and often challenged what students saw and how they interpreted their experiences.

With the passing of time and the changing of semesters, more students were invited to come with us and participate as we interacted with the homeless. Most students seemed to have positive encounters. They would come back to class and talk about their experiences, commenting that they had seen this or that and it either supported or refuted what they had read in books, articles, or the newspaper, seen on television, or discussed in class. The experiences served to give credibility to or further challenge their opinions, and they could now offer their own informed perspective on what they had seen. I came to realize that the experiences with the homeless had become something that was going to last a lot longer than any one class. The students were going to remember going under a bridge or into an abandoned house during darkness and relate that story over and over all of their lives. The stories that they brought back into the classroom often took the form of "I can top that story" or "You should have been there: Then you would understand."

THE ACADEMIC DILEMMA

Now, with these positive encounters happening, how was I going to incorporate the student's experiences as a part of service learning, give academic credit for the activity, or in some other way legitimize the accomplishment within a college that did not have a history of seeing such experiences as related to intellectual pursuits or academic potential? The answer was simple. Using the old philosophy of "It is far better to ask for forgiveness than for permission," I continued as if I knew what I was doing. I started to treat the community experience as part of the academic experience. Some students tested different methodologies, qualitative and quantitative. We were able to critique the positive and negative experiences in light of the results they produced. Other students started to do life histories of homeless persons, spending hours recording the experiences that the homeless were able to share and then molding them into an academic narrative. Some students, for personal or ideological reasons, wanted nothing to do with the street experience, and these wishes were honored. There were plenty of alternative research projects available, and the skills of students could be called upon for critique and questions about the social worth of what other students were experiencing.

The breakfast program became fairly well known, having been highlighted in the local newspapers and on television and radio. After all, the Salvation Army shield, bridges, and abandoned houses make good photo opportunities. After a few months some of the local high schools and middle schools asked if their students could accompany us on Tuesday mornings. The answer was yes, of course, but within certain rules. No more than six people other than regulars should go out on any morning. There was a number, a critical mass, above which we would become overly intrusive. At the top of our agenda, each and every time we went into the field, was an examination of our intrusiveness. We knew we were intrusive, but we

worked to keep our invasion at a minimum. We never surveyed the students or their sponsors; no quantitative numbers exist, other than raw numbers of things such as people fed and people volunteering. We can offer no elaborate data or subsequent mathematical modeling. Nothing can be offered other than the words people said; what we saw people do; the expressions on their faces; the simple ways in which common, everyday people met those who lived on the streets.

Some students never allowed themselves to consider anything other than individualism as the cause of—and way to address solutions to—homelessness. Attributing responsibility for homelessness always provided heated discussion in any classroom. It was not unusual for students to murmur that we were "enabling" those on the street to develop a lifestyle of homelessness: an argument that resembled what advocates of welfare reform were voicing at the same time. Some students, like many political officials, argued that all a homeless person needed to do was assume personal responsibility, get a job, rent an apartment, and take the straight and narrow path—and thus be "cured." These ideas have historically guided how the general public thinks about and deals with persons occupying negative social categories, including homelessness.

One teacher from a local suburban high school became concerned about her students. They were, after all, traveling into what had become perceived as the high-crime part of the city. For a while it seemed that every evening the TV news showed photographs of buildings in the part of town where the outreach program started. In the 9-second clips the news anchors highlighted drug dealings, drive-by shootings, prostitution, muggings, and all sorts of community problems. Even though not one person on any Salvation Army homeless outreach program was ever harmed or in any way threatened, this concerned teacher was afraid. This fear built as the weather turned toward winter and we went onto the streets long before sunrise. After one local TV station aired an intensive series of drug stories focusing on the "inner city," the concerned teacher abruptly called to inform us that she would not be sending her students because of the potential danger. In retrospect, I cannot blame her for her fears or for her desire to protect her students.

There were times when we did see bad things in the early morning, but these were often the residuals of the previous night: spent needles, empty Night Train or Mad Dog 20/20 bottles, and the traces of a lifestyle that differed from that of more affluent parts of the city. Sure, particleboard over the windows and doors of abandoned houses was often pushed aside so a street person could catch a few hours of sleep out of the cruel elements of an Iowa January night. What we saw more often was the residual poverty, the violence of the powerful as they constrained the less powerful: houses that had not been repaired, an infrastructure belonging to the city that was decaying under benign neglect, uncut weeds in city parks, abandoned cars—things that one never observes in the "better" parts of Des Moines where officials opt to live.

THE POLITICS OF SERVICE LEARNING

We almost never had violence directed toward us. Now and then we would be told to "get the hell out of here, this is my place"—and we would, for they were justified in their comments; we were the outsiders. In all of that time, we never saw one gun or one knife; nor did we hear a voice raised in anger, except from some officials from the city of Des Moines, who told us on more than one occasion that we were enabling rather than helping homeless people. Several officials told us to "leave them on their own and force them to make a responsible decision and find work." There was much emotion, from all sides, directed at homelessness.

The city of Des Moines passed rule after rule after rule in an attempt to keep the homeless from the front door of the city. The city manager commented in a public forum that if the community were to increase the number of shelter beds, Des Moines would become a mecca for the homeless, drawing them from near and far. The city passed a rule, still in effect, limiting shelters and group home facilities (not only for the homeless but for all needy) to no more than one "every half mile." Any variation would have to be approved by a zoning board, an event about as likely as a hijacker's commanding a pilot to "take me

to Des Moines." As officials representing the city of Des Moines became more hostile to the homeless, they started inspecting shelters, finding numerous rule violations, and demanding that they be repaired quickly. Failure to agree would result in closure. The war lines were drawn between the city and advocates for the homeless. And this battle rages to this day. In return for financial support, the city demands that shelters "police" their clients and protect the innocent citizen from their potential danger.

A new committee was recently formed by downtown business interests and charged with devising a plan for keeping the homeless out of sight so as not to "frighten" customers and staff. One of the first efforts by the committee was to investigate "crime" committed by the homeless against innocent citizens and businesses near a major homeless shelter. The committee pretended to be objective; they wanted to see their thesis supported and thought data were just sitting out there to prove it. When it became apparent that data did not exist to support or refute the "rampant crime" theory, the committee ceased meeting. More recently, the group commissioned the writing of a manual on techniques, which have been effective in other cities, for moving the homeless out of the downtown. What would benefit us even more would be a manual on how business and community leaders can better understand and deal with the homeless.

INCREASED STUDENT INTEREST

Requests from students to accompany or volunteer for the homeless program multiplied. Instead of having to find volunteers among students, we had to limit the number who could accompany the shelter van. Waiting lists were started and bureaucracies emerged. One parochial middle school asked, and was granted permission, to have their students volunteer as a part of their confirmation procedure. A high school asked that their "peer mentors" participate as a part of their training. A local community college asked that students in upper-division human services courses be permitted to participate. And the requests continued. About 2 years into the program a second morning, Friday, was selected as a time to send another group into the community and serve a new near-homeless population whose need had not been addressed by the original plan. The near-homeless population was defined as persons who without entitlements would be homeless within a month. Although it may not be very "scientific," anyone who deals with poverty populations understands exactly what is meant by that definition.

A few of my students wanted to participate more actively in the program, to do something other than provide a meal and a friendly ear once a week for a few hours. For these students, a more formalized internship was devised, one that would require the students to work approximately 11 hours per week for 3 hours of academic credit. These students would work directly with organizers to help develop goals and objectives, draft procedural documents, coordinate volunteers, solicit food and items to be dispensed to the homeless, and contact referral agencies (drug, alcohol, shelter, etc.) to which those on the street or "quasi-homeless" (living in abandoned houses, cars, tents, etc.) could be taken for services or a change of lifestyle. The students were to keep a journal (not a *Dragnet*-style journal—"just the facts, Ma'am, just the facts" but a flowing journal in which interpretation, barriers, assets, etc. were outlined and discussed), prepare an annotated bibliography associated with the activity, meet regularly with the social service supervisor or contact persons and the faculty member, and come together with other interns in similar placements to share their experiences and tie them back to classroom learning. Providing the academic context is especially time-consuming for the faculty member, but if there is to be academic credit such commitment is a necessity.

In a few instances the student either was not able or did not care to complete a formal internship. In those cases the student was often provided the opportunity to integrate the experience into general requirements for a course. For instance, during the summer I teach one-hour courses that last for one week, three hours per day for five days. They are topical: I treat them as courses that provide me the opportunity to learn and the students the opportunity to expand their understanding of focused topics. These summer courses average about 20 students each. The students may have a specific set of readings, and I will have a specific set of objectives to accomplish in

that short period of time. As a part of these mini-courses, students may have the option to go on the Salvation Army breakfast program; participate in the satellite program; meet and talk with homeless men, women, and children; and write a quick, impressionistic paper about those experiences. In addition, they will be called upon to report their observations back to the class, where they will be critiqued by other students, many of whom have experienced similar activities during the past. Some of the students themselves have been homeless at one time or another; many of them will be welfare recipients and progressing through programs that are designed to provide them with self-sufficiency.

BARRIERS TO SERVICE LEARNING

There are several barriers that act to prevent service learning of the type I have described from being a regular part of the academic experience for students and faculty. Within the academy, especially in private colleges and universities, one finds a cadre of faculty who oppose almost any form of service learning, labeling this type of educational process as being appropriate only for technical schools, community colleges, and land-grant institutions of higher learning. They argue that the only legitimate educational experience is one related to the classroom, and any teaching must be through traditional methods legitimized over the centuries by pure scholars. Term or research papers, reading and critiquing original texts, and other orthodox academic exercises are seen as the only legitimate means of ensuring academic integrity. These faculty members think that "soft" fields of study that incorporate experiential learning do so because they lack academic rigor, lack appreciation of the academic enterprise, or simply have a faculty or student body that is too weak to succeed at more demanding academic experiences. How does one win over people with this viewpoint? It is not easy; it takes considerable logic and argumentation within the confines of the academic community and in other arenas where faculty governance of the curriculum takes place. All of this requires time and energy, but the outcome is a more relevant academic experience.

Evaluation can be difficult for the instructor concluding a semester of academic credit that hinges on service learning. Universities require that academic credit carry with it some sort of evaluative notation, most commonly a grade. To differentiate between an A and B, a B and a C, is difficult at best. I have always envied but at the same time suspected faculty members who "knew" that a student whose work involved service learning had earned a grade of A, B, or whatever. After a few semesters of attempts to grade each student, it became apparent that the concept of using traditional grading for experiential learning was flawed. Thus, as a department we opted to grant credit or no credit rather than a grade. One could consider pass, high pass, or something similar; but unless there is a compelling reason for making such a distinction, it seems better to focus on the experience rather than on the grade.

A BAG OF STORIES TO TELL

One of the most valuable things about being on the street with students and among the homeless for 5 years is that you develop a bag full of stories to tell, stories about people who live in conditions of homelessness and whom you get to know on their own turf. The title of this piece, "Tramp Training," came from an encounter my students and I had one warm July morning. Most of the men's basketball team had remained on campus to take summer courses, and several of the players were in my minicourses. When we stopped under the University Avenue bridge that crosses the Des Moines River, we looked up to a flat concrete landing just below the bridge structure where many homeless sleep at night. Coming down the steep grade toward the river was a young man, perhaps 25 years of age. His hair was unkempt and his clothes were in need of a washing, but he was bouncy and cheerful. I met this man each week, often at different locations, and had come to know him as Rick. Rick looked at me and my students and in a voice echoing with happiness said, "What do we have here?" As he looked upward from his just over 5 feet in height at these men who probably averaged 6 foot 8, I replied that my students were out to understand more about living under bridges and being

homeless. He said that he would teach them. "I'm a tramp and I will teach you how to be a tramp if you will give me your time," Rick shouted. "Yes, I will be your trainer—I will do tramp training." And with that my students, mostly from the inner cities of larger metropolitan areas, walked up and sat in his imaginary home on the slabs of concrete, drinking coffee, eating stale doughnuts, and talking about being a tramp. I don't know for sure how much academic credibility the experience carried, but I do know that this was an encounter that will last in the memories of all involved, including Rick, as long as they live. They will never forget each other.

On the Streets during Iowa Winters

Another story focuses on the fact that Iowa winters are dangerous to the health of anyone who lives outdoors. One of the most difficult parts of meeting homeless people over a prolonged period of time is that you come to know them as the human beings they are. Their lives are full of the same high points and same difficulties as anyone else's. It was the first day of the year. On our way to the major bridge in the southeastern part of the city, we had difficulty driving through the 2 feet of recently fallen snow; the plows had not fully cleared the roadway. We looked from our vehicle down a pathway to an area where homeless people typically live, hoping to see nothing and move on to what would eventually be a warm breakfast. Instead there were distinct imprints in the pathway, footprints, now a few hours old. We followed the prints to the "camping" area, some 100 yards to the north. There we found a small, heavyset man the locals called Shorty. Shorty had been a backup cook at Sally until mid-November, the date of the fourth anniversary of the death of his son and wife. He always said that they had been killed by a drunken driver. With time, you eventually came to realize that Shorty had been that driver. The guilt ate him alive, and on that anniversary he abandoned Sally and took to the street.

When we found Shorty he was sitting on a wooden crate with another box in front of him, on which were three bottles of MD 20/20. Two were full and one was about half empty. He wore gloves, but his fingers were exposed through well-worn holes. He had planned, he told us, to drink until he could sleep and hopefully sleep into eternity. Fortunately, we were able to immediately contact an outreach program at the local public hospital, and they quickly sent their van and emergency crew to the bridge, where they were able to talk Shorty off of the street and into treatment. Shorty had suffered frostbite on his hands, face, and toes. Eventually, he lost two joints on his right hand and two toes, one on each foot. Students, upon critiquing our experiences, commented more than once on how guilt, personal troubles, and problems with substances greatly impact the daily lives of homeless people. C. Wright Mills's written words about social issues and personal troubles had now taken on a practical meaning that in the past had been only an abstract set of ideas.

Living with Mental Illness

Michael had been diagnosed as a schizophrenic, having endured catatonic states during several earlier periods of his life. He resided in an old house that lacked utilities. Every room of the house was stacked with throw-away materials that Michael had picked up over the years during his roaming and Dumpster diving. Michael was a man in his early 40s who had worked at various jobs but was no longer able to hold permanent employment. The house in which he lived had belonged to his parents, and when they died, it became his property. He, however, lacked the skills to maintain it, and the place had slowly deteriorated to a state of disrepair. (Eventually it would be condemned and demolished by the city.) I considered it important for students to spend as much time as possible with Michael and to do so inside his residence. Besides the visual mess that students saw, there was decaying food throughout the house, and it was not uncommon for students to see large rats dart from one place of hiding, grab some food, and return to another pile of "stuff."

An outreach worker and I became concerned when we discovered that Michael had found an old open-fronted gas heater and was burning wood as well as paper in its hollowed-out inside. There was some venting that he had constructed, but we were fearful that the trash piled around the burner might ignite and cause a major fire. In addition, Michael was now self-medicating. He had been taking lithium for some time but had decided to sell it on the street and self-medicate with alcohol. Drinking often led him to lose control of his behavior. The outreach worker and I went to his house daily as the late November days became short and bitterly cold.

Students spent considerable time with Michael talking about his past, his daily activities, the things that he held to be important and unimportant in his life. This provided a good opportunity for students to practice life-history research, biographic accounts, and other techniques of qualitative data finding whereby they could act as validators of what others had heard and recorded. The experiences with Michael, and with many others, helped students understand better the difficulties of gathering valid and reliable data in field situations.

Hobos Living in the Jungle

Timothy was the first true hobo that the students and I came to know. They had learned the distinctions among *tramp, bum,* and *hobo,* and were acutely aware that for some time the traditional hobo had been disappearing from the scene of the American homeless. There is a place along the Raccoon River, just down the hillside from Terrace Hill (the home of Iowa's governors), that became known as the "jungle": a wooded area where homeless men came from around the country and settled. It is located near the large bridge that spans the river and under which numerous railroad tracks enter and leave Des Moines from and to the west. Over the years, students had gone with me to meet and talk with several of the men who took up residence, usually in tents, along the river. One morning we found this new man, Timothy, living in a blue pop-open tent. After making initial contact we asked him if he would like to join us for a cup of coffee, some breakfast, and a little talk. He agreed, and this became the start of a relationship that was to last over a period of 4 years.

Timothy, he told us, had been on the road for some 14 years. He had abandoned his wife and three children and left them in West Virginia after he came back from his tour as an infantry soldier during the Vietnam War. He had gone back to his home but was unable to find steady employment. This, coupled with his war memories, had led him to abandon his family and spend the next 14 years riding the rails, staying here and there, and now finding his way from Austin, Texas, to Des Moines, Iowa. As students read narratives from the past that involved hobos and their experiences, as well as the works of those few academicians who have researched the topic, Timothy provided real-world parallels and enriched their readings with tales from his own life. He told of being socialized into hobohood by "No Thumbs Joe," a picture that every student delighted in imagining. He described being beaten; being thrown off trains by railroad officials; spending winters in Key West, where he fished and lived on the sands; and generally living the life of adventure.

Timothy survived on a military pension that followed him around the country. He collected cans and scavenged a variety of items that he could either sell or use. His tent grew into a very elaborate living area that had tables, chairs, couches, and even hanging plants to brighten the landscape. He told of traveling to all corners of the United States, living in camps similar to this one on the riverbank, and always being careful that he did not antagonize people who could bring harm his way. Timothy liked living outside, even though heavy rains ruined most of his possessions. He simply regrouped and started his habitat again. When the winters approached he packed his most needed "stuff" into a backpack and took off for somewhere in the South. This cycle led him to return to Des Moines for three out of four summers. During the second year he did not appear in Des Moines, although we routinely went back to the location where he had set up camp. There were, however, plenty of people coming and going as well as some regulars—enough to keep students occupied as they engaged a diverse homeless population.

On the third summer we went down to the Raccoon River on our regular Tuesday morning run and noticed a new tent. The students and I approached the tent in our regular fashion, and to my surprise out came Timothy. Our greeting took on the aura of meeting an old friend. The hobo described his past

two winters and the previous summer. He had been from Florida to California, Oregon to Maine. He told of finding a "safe harbor" in Maine and deciding to spend the summer there. As the year progressed, however, some of the locals decided that he and other transitory homeless residents might be having an impact on the dwindling tourist business and in a forceful manner suggested that he move to another part of the county.

Timothy explained that this reaction characterizes many parts of the country: parts of Arizona, California, Florida. More and more there seemed to be a sense of rejection of the stranger by established communities. Students, through their interaction with the reality of the homeless, come to better understand the multitude of personal and social experiences that define the worlds in which we all live.

USING SERVICE LEARNING TO INVENT SOCIAL PROGRAMS

With the passage of time several of the students who had become actively involved in service learning went on to work in programs in the private and public sector. Many of the social phenomena that these students had observed on the street impacted their decisions as they worked for and eventually managed social services and agencies. The void of child care, for instance, was obvious, and several students later worked with major organizations in creating ways to deliver child care to homeless families. The greater the familiarity that students have with the real world, the more possibility there is for them to invent or modify programming in ways that actually make a difference in the lives of homeless men and women. Child care was only one of the many areas in which students had an impact; many went on to make their career pathway in service agencies, while others found new avenues of volunteerism for themselves, their friends, and others.

One of the skills that students offer social service agencies is the ability to do good evaluative research and to assist in constructing realistic outcomes. Through good research and the collection of respected data that focused on homelessness, many agencies were able to demonstrate needs that could be translated into private and public grants. As more and more information was amassed, groups came to depend on many of these students to provide credible information that could be used to support their activities. As these students matured, they became major assets for the community.

The Salvation Army homeless program had sprung from ideas that were germinated by a Saturday evening outreach program that was a part of Bethel Mission. As the Sally board looked for a program, they reinvented what was being done on Saturday night. Similarly, several other programs were in part or totally the consequence of the Sally program. Unlike Athena, however, they were not born full-blown but came to fruition slowly as needs with the community were discovered.

For example, volunteers participating in outreach often carried ideas back to their groups. Several community volunteers saw the need for a "last resort" shelter. Eventually, several of these people formed Churches United Shelter, a facility that today serves more than 100 residents each night. This independent shelter is the only free shelter in the city of Des Moines and serves those who are "falling through the cracks."

Another spin-off that was a social invention and was closely associated with the Sally homeless program was the Port of Entry, a housing program for substance-abusing homeless men. As the name implies, the facility serves as a place where homeless men who are both substance abusers and living on the street can try over and over to come from the street into the halfway house until such time as they are comfortable with entering treatment. It was noted by people on the Sally van that many substance-abusing men who live on the street cannot enter treatment directly—it is much too intimidating. They try, often fail, try again, fail several more times, but eventually are able to make a decision to leave the street. Had we not learned this through the Salvation Army team, programming would never have been made flexible. The conventional wisdom of many providers is that street people who are abusers have to make a decision to leave the street completely. Our findings led us to the decision that an alternative approach was much more realistic. Social inventions, such as Port

of Entry mesh the understanding of sociological ideas with application being made in the real world.

The outreach program developed by William Penn College, in which student tutors come from Oskaloosa, Iowa, to Des Moines twice each week to offer help to children and mothers in shelters, was another direct spin-off. In this program, students from the college's School of Education help to improve reading skills, first of children and later of mothers as they came to see the importance of reading well. Another program was a day shelter for children of homeless parents. Homeless people need somewhere to leave their kids during the day so they can take care of business—perhaps look for work, food, and shelter for the next night—or possibly just take some time off from the responsibility of constant child care while on the street. This shelter provided a place where homeless parents could feel comfortable that their children were safe. Other examples could be provided, but the point is consistent: One invention leads to another and even to another. Once started, these social inventions have a tendency toward self-perpetuation. The condition for everyone is what some people term "win–win": Every part of the community comes out ahead.

BRINGING IT BACK INTO FOCUS

There are many reasons why a person spends time under a bridge or in an abandoned house. The stories that people tell give an insight into their reasons and give depth to their personal biography. Some are there to escape a society that has been overly harsh. A few are running from something that to them is bad—violence, the police, a spouse, life. Still others have no other place to go. Some are young, as was one 16-year-old who had run away from a violent home and had no place to turn where he might be safe. Some are looking for closeness, as was a woman in her mid-40s who stayed under a bridge because her "meat" was spending time there and she would do anything to be with him. Still others are running from a family that does not understand their personal lifestyle or shuns them because of religious belief; when one young man told his family that he was gay, they immediately ordered him out of their house and their life forever. Other young people are escaping families that cannot accept or tolerate their friends, their taste in music, or their beliefs—as was a young man who was running from his authoritarian father, a professional in the U.S. Army. A few are there because they have problems that result in their minds' being clouded and their not really realizing where they are or what they are doing; a college graduate from St. Paul, Minnesota, who held a B.A. in journalism, believed that there were rays coming from outer space that would eventually kill him and all other living things. Some are there because of demons in their mind or because of guilt over things they had done, as was Shorty. There are a multitude of other stories, each constructed to provide those on the street with reasons for being where they are.

So what does all of this mean? Like so many things that happen, the homeless outreach program started involving students and then took on the legitimacy of a learning experience more by accident than by design. Many students wanted to experience what it was like to live on the street, but to do so from a safe and secure distance and with the knowledge that they could return to their residence hall, shower, and have a good meal in the dining hall. Other students wanted to experience the reality of the homeless in their natural habitat, having selected a social service career for their lifetime of work. Would what they found lead them to look for a change in majors? Or would it strengthen their resolve to commit more

firmly to the applied areas of sociology and the other social sciences as their profession?

For the average student, the experiences of being on the street afforded the opportunity to encounter, one-on-one, the lives of people who otherwise would never become speaking acquaintances to the average student. What can they learn from such an encounter? The nature of the outsider, the person who lives beyond the margins of everyday life, that character that Simmel termed "the stranger." By taking ideas from the classroom, interacting with personalities in the real world, and ultimately merging those experiences with classroom work and academic writings, the students were provided with a unique opportunity to test social theory and methodology. These everyday experiences guided students in their quest for something different, something that took the traditional academic field of sociology and gave it a real-world flavor.

At the start there was never a defined objective of taking students outside of the classroom as a part of their learning experience. Yet that was something that happened as challenges and questions from the classroom could best find potential answers when all of us became as much a part of the real world as time and opportunity would allow. Even though no student has become a tramp and the training of Rick could be challenged, interaction with Rick and his colleagues from the street undoubtedly made my students much more aware of what being a tramp means to those who will live in the new century.

20

Caring about Each Other
Churches, Public Health, and Community

GARY GUNDERSON

Editors' Note: Many of the early sociologists were also ministers. It is only since the advent of an isolated academic sociology that do-gooders have gotten a bad name. Gary Gunderson illustrates creative new approaches to public health originating from efforts of religious organizations. Using the sociological imagination, he shows how individual predicaments can reveal common patterns of need that can be addressed by a community.

I came out of the hunger movement. For the last 20 years I have worked, mostly as a layperson, with poor and hungry people at congregation and community levels. A lot of this experience has been at Oakhurst Baptist Church in Atlanta, the congregation that ordained me. Oakhurst is an odd little congregation on the edge of one of the poorest census tracts not just in Atlanta, but in all of Georgia. My personal experience of the role of a church in community has been formed there. More than 150,000 houses of worship now keep food on site for distribution. Nearly every community in the United States has an organized, coordinated system that networks congregations to make available food, clothing, and shelter. However, this has not in any way reversed the underlying plight of those on the margins, the poor.

As we engaged people who were hungry, we found that they had far more problems than could be answered by food. People with empty stomachs also lack most other survival resources and are caught in a web of defeat, despair, and brokenness that is nearly intractable. A great number of creative, smart, and tough-minded ministries have grown out of the movement against hunger. Cafe 458 in Atlanta began as a free cafe where hungry people could be served just as they might in another restaurant, instead of in the industrial style of the large downtown soup kitchen. The cafe setting was designed to encourage conversational interaction among the clients and volunteers. Not surprisingly, we learned an enormous amount in a hurry about the real needs and lives of the guests. The primary fact was the endless struggle with different addictions, in some cases multiple ones.

Collaborating with our little Baptist church, the managers converted a homeless shelter across the street from the cafe into a place for long-term stay for clients participating in a new rehabilitation ministry. The ministry showed early signs of successful rehabilitation not only of the addictions but also of other transitional complications such as housing and job placement. The key is the small, intimate scale and constant personal interaction among guests and volunteers. Healing happens one by one. This is a difficult model to lay over against the larger-scale hospital. It cuts to the heart of the problem with medical protocols and reminds us of the tremendous power of eye-to-eye personal relationship. When the ministry faced problems with its downtown location, the congregation agreed to move the whole program into the church building. They saw how important it had become not only to the men, but also to the congregation.

If you have ever been in a soup kitchen—as one eating or as one serving—you've noticed there is almost no difference between the two kinds of people, except for their temporary circumstances. A soup kitchen is not a simplistic reenactment of the sheep and the goats, the blessed and the damned. That may be the impression if all you know is what you see on the 45-second Thanksgiving news clip. Actually, some people are there because they need to eat and they know they can find food. Others come with another basic need, the need to serve, to be there for those in trouble. And sometimes, those roles reverse. In our uncertain economy some who never thought we would find our way into a soup kitchen, in fact, do. And some of us who have been there as clients find ourselves, not long after, helping someone else.

Wounded people know something about how to lead others. In my experience, you find leaders not in the ranks of the highly qualified, highly credentialed new and shiny experts. You find them among the wounded. This was confirmed when the Catholic Health Association did a major study of what characterized the best leaders, the managers of their most successful health care systems (Sanders, 1994). These are not soup kitchens; they are sometimes billion-dollar assets. The common factor among the successful leaders was that they had suffered some personal setback, some personal wound, and had moved through it. That factor was more consistent than management style, education, or credentials. Such leaders can be partners in building a healthy community.

If we had the chance to talk with each other, we would eventually move through the superficial chatter about our degrees, jobs, and kids, and we would find ourselves, at a deeper level, beginning to talk about our woundedness and brokenness. When we remain at the technical and shiny parts of our identities, we slide past each other without friction, like stainless steel balls. We do not engage and nothing is created. It is at the rough spots of our lives where

we form the bonds that allow us to be community. That bonding is what draws us to the soup kitchens even when we aren't hungry. That's part of what we hope for when we gather to talk about creating healthy communities.

THE CHURCH'S MISSION IN HEALTH CARE

I am director of the Interfaith Health Program at Emory University. Our mandate is to mobilize faith groups toward their full potential as agents of healing and wholeness. We originated at the Carter Center, under the leadership of President Carter and Dr. Bill Foege. We orient mostly toward public health threats and community responses.

The Interfaith Health Program is tantalized by two numbers:

1. At least 60 percent—many researchers would say up to 90 percent—of the years of life lost before age 65 result from factors that are preventable. At least two-thirds of suffering is premature and preventable!
2. At least 150 million U.S. citizens participate in some faith group—a church, synagogue, or mosque—all of which share a high priority on healthy living, wise choices, and alleviating and preventing suffering.

One thing we do at the Interfaith Health Program is to present religious denominations with new models for doing health care. The religious community is still an underachieving force in health, especially when you recognize health threats as inclusive as violence, substance abuse, and other behavior-linked risk factors. Many religious groups are not aware of some of the innovative approaches going on around the country. Others have not rethought their mission for hundreds of years. The strategic leadership gap is not so much a matter of envisioning but of remembering. We need to remember what is behind a church-related hospital: the basic commitments that precede the buildings and technologies.

Sister Mary Marie Ashton, who is a professional colleague, was the CEO of Fairview Hospital in Minneapolis when it was the largest hospital in the city. She also served as the state health director for 8 years before returning to guide the Sisters of Carondolet through the painful but liberating decision to sell the hospital and find a new mission—expressed through nine free community clinics scattered around the city in underserved neighborhoods. I asked her how the sisters were able to undertake such a dramatically different path. She says they came to the point where they remembered why they came to Minnesota in the first place. "When we remembered who we were, we knew where to go."

If a hospital is merely one more polished secular service agency, it has no power beyond increasingly bureaucratic technique. The specific phrases of its founding statements are important only to the extent that they encourage us to reengage the living God of today. For the power of God is not evidenced in what happened once long ago, but in our ability now to frame commitments for the future. If we remember who we are, we will know what we must become.

PUBLIC HEALTH AND RELIGION

People in all faith traditions have always understood that God wanted us to serve the sick and the poor. For most of recorded human history, however, "professionals" in both religion and health were essentially helpless before an overwhelming array of disease. At the time of Jesus, average life expectancy was around 40 years. As late as the 1700s, most philosophers thought it was the will of God that half of all children died before age 8. The most religion could hope for was mercy, comfort, and grief support amid capricious suffering. It just didn't dawn on us until about a hundred years ago that God had built into the system the possibility of preventing disease and injury—of changing the world.

The public health movement and the social gospel movement were born together, influenced and protected each other's early years, and must share credit for their joint accomplishments. Most public health departments emerged to deal with disease epidemics rooted in poor sanitation. Sanitation is one of those simple concepts that changes everything. It is a much more important contribution to longevity and quality of life than all the antibiotics put together. Average life expectancy is about two-thirds longer than

it was a hundred years ago. The largest part of that astonishing rise in life span occurred long before the pharmaceutical revolution. The notion that people could systematically study disease patterns, identify specific causes, and prevent the problems by community intervention was revolutionary.

In fairness, the public health pioneers weren't trying for a revolution; they just wanted people to take out the trash. Indeed, because we stand on this side of the revolution, it is easy to forget how recent it was and how much it changed. Until the later part of the 1800s, epidemic diseases such as cholera and tuberculosis were felt to be associated with moral failings of one kind or another. As scientists began in the mid 1800s to prove that epidemics were instead linked to environmental factors (especially sanitation and water), the focus turned to community efforts, to social choices and not just individual moral failings.

Through TB one can see nearly the whole cycle—from despair, to social action, to institutionalization, to overreliance on pharmacology, to today's renewed recognition of TB as a disease embedded in poverty and marginalization. Although TB was a leading cause of death until the early 1900s, it attracted little attention because it was thought to be hereditary. In 1865, it was proved to be contagious. In 1882, the tubercle bacillus was discovered (one of the first pathogenic organisms found); this revelation established the disease as a communicable and thus preventable disease. However, this discovery was resisted well into the 1890s, notably by physicians who regarded the disease as a nerve problem. The early stages of the public health response to TB were mobilized by laypeople and community organizing strategies built on religious leadership and congregational structures. By the turn of the 20th century, leadership began to be preempted by physicians, with women and clergy receding into the background.

The social activists fighting TB preceded the medical experts in ways we saw repeated in recent years when the gay community, awash with friends dying of AIDS, moved in advance of the credentialed technicians. The TB society lasted into the 1940s when the TB treatment was discovered and implemented, making complex social action seem unnecessary. In effect, pharmacology supplanted social action, a story that would be repeated in communities throughout the developed world and with other diseases.

The challenge of HIV has pressed hundreds of congregations to mobilize their strengths to minister to those in crisis among their own members and neighborhoods. In most cases, this has meant not hiring new staff but more effectively recruiting, training, and organizing volunteers. The volunteers do need special training to understand the course of the disease and how to help appropriately. Many of the same congregations also transfer these lessons to other kinds of chronic conditions in which people need not just a casserole and a prayer but months of smart assistance. The Robert Wood Johnson Foundation has recognized the powerful difference such volunteer caregivers make and has seeded partial funding for more than 1,100 volunteer caregiver networks around the United States, each involving 5 or 10 congregations. The funding goes mostly to provide a partial salary to a coordinator who makes sure volunteers are screened, trained, and well organized.

MOVING INTO THE COMMUNITY

The disciples of Jesus were not trained as musicians or youth directors. They were trained and commissioned as agents of healing and sent to communities. The closest we have to this model today is the congregational health minister, often called the parish nurse. There are now some 3,000 U.S. congregations with some variation on this theme. In this country, there are some 300,000 houses of worship. What if 1 in 5 had a trained health promoter mobilizing the congregation for health ministries in the surrounding neighborhoods?

The Interfaith Health Program is working with two clusters of congregations in severely underserved parts of Atlanta. We have assigned a part-time health coordinator to each cluster of 10 to 12 congregations of widely varied faith traditions. Interfaith Health Atlanta identifies health promoters in each congregation whom we train in basic health promotion and disease prevention strategies. These laypeople are usually without formal health training but are clearly identified as accepted natural helpers in their congrega-

tions. Operations are covered by a little funding from the Pew Charitable Trust. The training is provided by the Emory University School of Nursing, which hired an instructor with particular cultural skills.

People of faith can recognize the linkage between the immunization of a baby and the inbreaking of God's eternal hope for that same baby. The more we learn about the connections between health, wholeness, and spirituality, the more we are driven to a renewed appreciation for what can happen in a healthy congregation. The more we learn about the patterns and predictors of disease and injury, the more we appreciate the congregation as a place where the family, neighborhood, and community can and must be built.

Any of us who has ever served on a church committee must tremble at the challenge. It is nearly miraculous when we can agree on the stationery, much less become a place of healing and wholeness for the community. However, examples of this model are emerging across the country. When the big mainline congregations moved to the suburbs, leaving many neighborhoods without a name-brand religious presence, 200 churches loosely affiliated into the Christian Community Development Association. These churches are usually interracial and filled with people from all classes, and they take saving souls and healing broken bodies and neighborhoods with equal seriousness. Nearly every one has some kind of free medical clinic and health outreach. In Baltimore, Newark, and Huntsville, the Breath of Life Heart Body and Spirit organization identifies strong neighborhood-level leaders and trains them to do basic disease screening and health promotion activities, identifying what health services are available locally and how people can access them in real-life situations.

At Oakhurst, we had a vision: What if everyone within 10 blocks of our church were well fed every day, every pregnant woman received prenatal care, every elderly person had access to a doctor, every infant were immunized, everyone of working age received cancer screening and help with smoking or drugs? What if we supported Oakhurst Community Health Center so aggressively that everyone got the attention they needed when they needed it? Those things, all combined, would probably extend the lives of people in our neighborhood by an average of 10 years each!

THE CAUSES OF DEATH

At the Interfaith Health Program we have been heavily influenced by a study of what the actual causes of death are (see Box 20.1) (McGinnis and Foege, 1993). We are beginning to penetrate behind the misleading data about the medical causes of death to think clearly about the actual causes of death and disability. These findings are unsurprising—but must be deeply troubling to hospital leaders who recognize that their institutions have focused almost exclusively on medical pathologies. The *vast* preponderance of medical expenditures are devoted to treating conditions ultimately recorded on death certificates as the nation's leading killers. Only a small fraction of funding goes to prevent those factors that represent the determinants of death and disability.

INDIVIDUALISM AND HEALTH CARE

What strategy do we adopt to improve health? When we look at the causes of death, they certainly look like individual choices. Most hospitals are organized to serve individual sick people. Individual choice seems to play a central role in disease and injury risks. Want health? Don't smoke. Don't eat unhealthy things. Exercise. Don't drink much. Watch out for infections. Stay away from environmental problems. Stay away from guns. Be chaste or use a condom. Wear a seat belt. Don't do drugs. See your doctor for regular checkups. Bingo! There go half of the causes of premature death! All because people made better individual choices.

This idea of "health choices" dominates thinking among most health practitioners today. It emphasizes emotional and spiritual factors, and it suggests that we rationally choose our destiny, our health, our stress level, our cholesterol count, our heart rate, our body fat ratio, our flexibility. The wellness movement says we have great control of our individual health outcomes. Of course, this is not a new idea at all but the absolute core American myth of the self-sufficient and independent individual.

The great weakness with this individualized wellness approach is it fails to seriously consider the obvious fact that disease and injury fall predictably along lines of groups, not just individuals. Socioeconomic status as measured by education level is directly related to health. The most common diseases, including arthritis, hypertension, back pain, psychiatric disease, peptic ulcer disease, heart attack, diabetes, renal disease, chronic bronchitis, emphysema, epilepsy, and stroke, occur two to three times more commonly in people who have fewer than 12 years of education (25 percent of the U.S. population) than in people with more than 12 years (Pincus and Callahan, 1994). These differences remain significant when adjusted for age, gender, race, and smoking. The only exceptions among relatively common diseases are cancer, allergies, asthma, thyroid disease, and multiple sclerosis.

Why are some groups of people less healthy? One's personal health can be seen as the accumulation of individual life choices regarding various health risks. However, an individual is shaped in a social context. Health risks reflect group choices, or at the very least peer-influenced choices.

Novelist Thomas Pynchon says, "If they can get you to ask the wrong questions, then they don't have to worry about the answers." The effects of wrong questions are not neutral. Rather, they favor the existing patterns of power, privilege, and domination. Power uncontested is power served. We must dispense with a public science that hopes to advance health without even examining the evil embedded in our corporate, government, and intellectual systems.

Sociology is certainly the missing dialogue in the faith and health care movement today. We are informed primarily by individualistic disciplines and individualistic theologies. We should note that the emphasis on finding health within is most popular among those most comfortable with the status quo. This is true enough to be dangerous. We are so conditioned by the American myth of individual causes that we fail to look beyond it for other factors. When this failure of self-understanding is made by the average person it is understandable, almost forgivable, and even somewhat charming in its rugged individualism. However, it is an absolutely unforgivable lapse

Box 20.1

The Actual Top Ten Causes of Death in the United States

1. Tobacco. The overwhelmingly largest cause of death is tobacco, accounting for 400,000 deaths a year. Although we perform nearly 5,000 tobacco funerals a day, there is never a tobacco death certificate written; but 11 to 30 percent of cancer, 17 to 30 percent of cardiovascular deaths, 30 percent of lung disease deaths, 24 percent of pneumonia and influenza deaths, and 10 percent of infant deaths are tobacco linked.

2. Diet and Sedentary Activity. Diet and sedentary activity patterns account for 14 percent of deaths, just under a third of a million per year. This is quite tricky, because diet links to so many other risks. However, we know that 22 to 30 percent of cardiovascular deaths find their cause here, as do 30 percent of diabetes deaths and between 20 and 60 percent of fatal cancers. If you take the upper and lower boundaries of these diseases, you have a range between 309,000 and 582,000 deaths per year. Taking the lowest number accounts for 14 percent of deaths.

3. Alcohol. Misuse of alcohol can be held accountable for 100,000 or 5 percent of deaths a year, but this misstates on the low the side the full impact on the health of communities. Alcohol contributes to 60 to 90 percent of cirrhosis deaths; 40 to 50 percent of vehicle fatalities; 16 to 67 percent of home injuries, drownings, and fire and job injuries; and 3 to 5 percent of cancer deaths. Between 5 and 15 percent of all years of life lost before age 65 are lost to alcohol.

4. Infectious Agents. Infectious agents, not counting HIV (which shows up in factors 7 and 8), currently account for 90,000 deaths a year. This factor would have been dramatically different at the time of the founding of most hospital institutions, which usually predated the growth of preventive public health measures and widespread immunizations. Tuberculosis, for instance, which was the second leading cause of death in 1900, accounted for 1,810 deaths 90 years later. Microbial agents, especially in tuberculosis and HIV, are now resurgent and are likely to increase as factors of death in the future.

5. Toxic Agents. Toxic agents are among the most difficult and controversial to identify, with estimated deaths linked ranging from 57,000 to 108,000 in 1990. Toxic agents pose threats as occupational hazards, environmental pollutants, and food and water contaminants and as ingredients in commercial products. Cancer deaths attributable to synthetic chemicals range upward from 30,000, including 9,000 from asbestos alone. This area includes large nonfatal effects that can be very damaging, such as those that result from childhood exposure to lead, and large-scale environmental changes whose impact we are only now attempting to track and understand.

6. Firearms. Firearms caused more than 36,000 deaths in 1990, 51 percent of which were suicides. The risk of death by homicide experienced by an African American male is now 1 in 20, surpassing all other risk factors by a large margin—41 percent of deaths between ages 15 and 19. This is a rate of risk at least 80 times larger than that in any other industrialized nation. Caucasian risk of homicide is also 8 times higher than in any other nation.

7. Sexual Behavior. Unprotected sexual intercourse accounted for approximately 30,000 deaths in 1990, which included approximately 5,000 from excess infant mortality rates among those whose pregnancies were unintended, 4,000 from cervical cancer, and 1,600 from hepatitis B. HIV accounts for 21,000 of the deaths.

8. Illicit Drug Use. Approximately 3 million Americans have serious drug problems resulting in 20,000 annual deaths. Vital statistics reports indicate 9,000 deaths directly attributable to drugs, but this figure does not include those clearly but indirectly linked, such as accidents, homicides, infections from HIV, and hepatitis. The linkage between intravenous drug use and HIV is likely to increase this factor as a cause of death in coming years.

9. Motor Vehicles. Besides those already accounted for under alcohol and drug use, approximately 25,000 deaths result from motor vehicle accidents. This factor accounts for nearly 40 percent of deaths among those aged 15 to 24, although the rate is going down as firearm deaths go up.

10. Other Factors.   Lack of access to primary care is associated with increased risk of death from many causes, although the exact impact is difficult to quantify. The Carter Project estimated that lack of access to standard primary care, screening, and preventive interventions accounted for 7 percent of premature deaths and 15 percent of potential years of life lost before age 65, mainly because of infant deaths.

Source: Based on an article by Dr. Michael McGinnis and Dr. William Foege in the *Journal of the American Medical Association,* Volume 270, Number 18, 2207–2211, November 10, 1993.

---

of health science and moral perspective when the individualist myth is endorsed by such a key health center as a hospital administration.

Beyond Individualism—Links to Community, Stages of Coherence

The community is the stage on which we make our choices and play out our lives. The leading edge of public health thinking is exactly where I am urging you to look: at the behavioral and social roots of most of our health risks. Sociologist of health Aaron Antonovsky points to the key aspects of coherence in a community. Coherence means that life in community makes sense—and that the community works. Beyond simple individualism, the idea of social coherence has great relevance for health.

1. *Linkage versus isolation.* Exclusion or isolation is a prime health risk for the physically or emotionally disabled, the mentally handicapped, the homeless, the isolated elderly, and the stigmatized. Health depends on relationship, not just care; conversation, not just instruction. People are social and can be healthy only in active relationship to others.

2. *Information versus noise.* A healthy environment gives us clear messages, and the messages must contain content that has some degree of freedom of choice. It is clinically unhealthy to receive incoherent messages that demand or instruct without any chance to reject, adapt, or respond. This is a central problem of minority groups, immigrant or illegal workers, lower-class persons, illiterates or those in any sense deviant, and in many cases women. Drinking or doing drugs is a risk, but it may be the only

way someone knows to stop the pain. Just telling a person to quit doesn't help. Likewise, people may know they should buy chicken breasts or expensive low-fat cuts of meat but may be able to afford only less healthy food.

3. *Availability of resources.* Even if one makes sense of the paradoxes of life and formulates a healthy, coherent strategy for living, the plan depends on the resources to put it into action. "It is the environment, of one's past and one's present, that determines the degree of freedom available to the actor in carrying out a plan" (Antonovsky, 1994, p. 8).

4. *Responsiveness versus rejection.* A healthy environment is responsive and attentive. The issue is not only the environment's baseline attentiveness, but the actor's power to compel the community to listen and respond. Antonovsky argues that inability to compel a hearing is itself a health risk, because such insensitivity further devalues and fragments the identity of already hurting people. Many poor people report going to the emergency room, waiting (sometimes more than a day), and going home unexamined (Kozol, 1995).

MOVING BEYOND HOSPITAL WALLS

Community organizer John McKnight tells of examining the major reasons for admission to his local Chicago emergency room. His local community organization won access to the hospital but failed to notice any improvement in the health of the neighborhood. It turned out that the top seven causes for ER admissions were automobile accidents, interpersonal violence, other accidents, bronchial ailments, alcoholism, drug-related problems, and dog bites.

McKnight points out that "the medicalization of health had led them to believe that hospitals were appropriately addressing their health problems, but they discovered instead that the hospitals were dealing with many problems for which hospitals are always too late and which required treatment of another sort" (McKnight, 1993, p. 221).

Community Health Care

Instead of being a place for receiving incoming wounded, the hospital can become a base for sending healing out into the entire community. Rather than just being a place to bring people when they are sick, it can be a center for health from which expertise, understanding, and compassion flow into the surrounding communities.

The Church Health Center in Memphis is about as good as you can do as a freestanding clinic for the working poor. Dr. Scott Morris has served 15,000 people with efficiency, medical competence, and compassion that simply establishes the benchmark. This is no mere Band-Aid-and-pill ministry. It has dentists, exercise classes, nutritionists, pastoral counselors, and a fabulous referral network of unreimbursed specialists. This is wrapped in a rich moral integrity that is a force to be reckoned with in Memphis. Of course, there are other clinics that also offer free or radically sliding-scale services in many communities throughout the country. Most are expanding their ministries as more and more people fall outside the reach of commercialized health payment systems.

The Church Health Center has strong relationships with 120-plus churches in Memphis that provide dollars, doctors, volunteers, and resources. However, the healing activity has all happened at the center. The center can take care of only about 10 percent of the underserved people in the Memphis region. As a result, the center has built a $4 million facility for "hope and healing" that focuses on training the congregations of Memphis in ministries of wellness and health that can be done in their own neighborhoods. And the center is working with a few strategic congregations to move directly into high-risk neighborhoods where they can take on the causes of ill health. The Reverend Kenneth Robinson is one of the strong pastors; He is also a medical doctor who has led his congregation to purchase a decrepit housing project. There, he aims to engage directly the tangled problems that in his view obscure the glimpse of God's hope that he wants to shine brightly.

Prevention: The Revolutionary Movement

The root idea of public health is that diseases are predictable and can be modified by action at the community level. Risks can be identified, once you know to look for them: mosquitoes, dirty water, human and animal waste, dirty food preparation and meat processing, smoke, toxins, lack of ventilation, unbalanced diet, lack of trace minerals, rodents. Beginning with tuberculosis in 1882, specific pathogenic organisms have been identified, analyzed, responded to, attacked, isolated, and treated. Only eight decades later, beginning with smallpox, many diseases were actually eradicated from human experience entirely. Interventions are significant at the individual level, but they were truly revolutionary when applied to whole communities. The actual difference was made at the community level: communitywide trash collection, food inspection, and sewers.

As the HMOs are learning, most prevention strategies are not very effective when they are restricted to only one part of the population, much less when they are aimed at individuals. Prevention makes sense only when it includes the whole population.

The health sciences have forgotten almost as much as they have discovered. Rather than exploring how social patterns contribute to health, even the discipline of public health finds a way to ignore its own data about community-scale patterns and asks questions only about individuals. These end up, inevitably, focusing on individual behavior modification schemes, usually called health education or health promotion. Imagine the death rates today if we had focused on individual sanitation, burning our trash in the backyard, and had not followed the science to build the public sewers.

Effective health care delivery depends upon community. For example, interventions for smallpox or HIV require a very sophisticated technical infrastructure, which in turn relies on a social, political, and moral infrastructure. The more sophisticated the strategy, the more complex the social infrastructure and the greater the moral energy needed to steer the implementation. This is the lesson of public health.

However, this intellectual breakthrough has been obscured by later (and lesser) discoveries in the field of pharmacology, especially by antibiotics and immunization. More recent psychotropic, biomolecular, and gene-level interventions continue the trend toward the conflation of medicine with technology. Imaging breakthroughs that began with X-rays are rapidly allowing us literally to see diseases and abnormalities at a molecular level almost at conception, giving us a sense of transparency. It is misleading to speak of "health choices" or "self-knowledge" in this context, because we are more and more reliant on highly trained specialists who can barely speak to one another, let alone us. The mastery of disease is held by people we pay, not by ourselves. It is not surprising that many of us think of health as something we must purchase from experts. And it is not surprising that public health policy then devolves into the political art of getting everyone access to these expert services.

Ironically, just at the time we have all this advanced medical machinery, the social infrastructure has deteriorated. We have forgotten the lessons we learned from community health. With increases in poverty and worsening social conditions, TB—once thought eradicated in the United States—is making a comeback.

Our individualistic strategies do not serve us well. Theodore Pincus notes that we spend far more resources on changing individuals' cholesterol level than on their socioeconomic level. This is not just a failure of moral courage, but a collapse of good science. Follow good science to the root causes of disease and injury in your community, and you will find more than just a long list of sick individuals. You will find a lack of community—social disorganization, a social incoherence. When there is social coherence, the community hangs together—we care for each other in time of need. When there is social incoherence, we all hang separately—individuals are abandoned to their own devices.

We understand it when Willie Nelson sings, "We can see how all the pieces fit as we watch them come apart." Parish nurses see people in pieces every day. Far more than even hospital-based medical staff, parish nurses are immersed in communities that are in pieces.

Community

In the last 50 years, the productive life expectancy nearly everywhere in the world has been growing at an amazing rate. But while everyone has been standing amazed at the latest computer-driven stainless steel hospitals in the United States, the real revolution has been accomplished through mundane but consistent application of preventive care, mostly achieved by teaching people what they can do for themselves. Cheap interventions such as immunization extend far more lives than the high-cost machinery in hospitals.

These interventions may seem boring, but they extend lives all over the world where they are promoted. This is a fact so well known that we can barely keep our eyes open when we hear about it. So why is it that the things that should be so easy have turned out to be so very hard? We still find it beyond our reach to bring a clean well to every village. We haven't gotten the most rudimentary gift of modern medicine, immunization, to every child. Indeed, in U.S. urban areas we can't seem to immunize children literally within a few miles of the most modern medical equipment in history. We don't get prenatal care to many poor women in this country; these women often don't see a doctor until their water breaks, if then. As a result, we have the highest infant mortality rate of any modern industrialized nation. More mothers also die in childbirth in the United States than in any comparable nation. And we have the highest proportion of low-birth-weight babies in the Western world—a condition that leads to health and developmental problems that often cost a lifetime of services. Compared to sending people into outer space, solving these things should be easy.

Then why are these things so hard? The answer is simply that the things that look easy but are actually hard are those things that depend on community, especially community expressed over time in simple acts of mutual caring. This challenge pushes congregations to look beyond their own walls for the answers.

The East Dallas Community Church is on the front line of poverty and ill health in Dallas. They have stitched together a rich assortment of medical and social services with the help of hospitals all over the city. But the big problem is jobs, not germs. The pastor, Billy Lane, doesn't want more health staff in the congregation, but he envisions a trained volunteer "health promoter" in every housing project in the city. Why would someone volunteer? "The training will give people an edge for entry-level jobs in the health industries—the largest employer in the county." He sees the whole pattern of poverty, hopelessness, and poor health as an integrated reality that needs an equally coherent linked answer. He thinks like a sociologist, not a doctor.

The Model of the Expansive Community: Implementing the Sociological Imagination

At first we respond to individuals—but, as I learned through my experience with my mom's health care, the individual is a type, one of thousands. In her last years, because of a series of small strokes, Mom found it almost impossible to talk. I constantly tried to figure out a way to help her particular challenge. One day, I posted a short note to the Interfaith Health Program e-mail discussion group (www.ihpnet.org). I quickly discovered that Mom's problems were shared by thousands and thousands of others. Indeed, entire associations of professionals had become organized and had assembled a clearly thought-out set of tools, technologies, and support groups. Although she was my mom, she was also part of a larger *pattern* of need.

The congregation's strength is recognizing individuals in their particularity, but the congregation also has the capacity to respond to patterns of need. For instance, a particular opportunity to visit an individual in jail gradually results in the formation of a jail visitation committee as members meet other inmates and become familiar with their needs. A member with HIV calls forth a group that gradually becomes organized for long-term, not sporadic, assistance; a family with a Down syndrome son gradually awakens the attention of the congregation to the op-

portunity to create a group home for him and others like him. Through the lens of particular relationships, the congregation gradually sees others, some in the church, some not, with similar needs.

Children's Hospital in Dallas is part of a broad coalition of hospitals and religious groups that are working together with a special focus on advancing the health of little kids. (Health professionals refer to this group less romantically as 0–3.) Children's Hospital sees about 900 spina bifida cases each year, each of which is its own unique tragedy. Spina bifida is a birth defect of the spinal column that can result in permanent physical and mental disability. It turns out that most of these cases would be prevented if all mothers received plenty of folic acid during the early months of pregnancy. Folic acid is found in leafy green vegetables, whole grains, legumes, and nuts. Children's Hospital publishes lots of dietary information for young mothers, but all the brochures and advertisements have not helped. It's not exactly the mothers' fault unless she understands both the risk and the remedy: What the heck is folic acid, anyway?

If the health departments did not already know about churches, they would probably try to invent them. A church is a social structure with high credibility and access to women of childbearing age. This structure already cares tangibly about mothers and children and is there with practical assistance such as food and volunteer help. Congregations are perfect social structures to get folic acid into the diet of pregnant moms. Such a task could not be accomplished one mom at a time or (worse) through impersonal mass media. It takes a social thing filled with grandmothers, priests, volunteers, sisters, and, yes, a sense of ultimate purpose and meaning.

Our dream is that a critical mass of all 300,000 congregations in the United States help deliver important health knowledge such as the importance of getting folic acid in the diet of moms. That's not all the world needs, of course. But ask any of the parents of those 900 Dallas kids who currently have spina bifida, and they will say it would have made a world of difference.

The critical issue is seeing patterns and not just individuals. Over time, if you are really paying attention, you see important patterns among those individuals. It is not only efficient but compassionate to see patterns of situations and not just isolated individual predicaments.

Public Health Partners

I am continually intrigued by the potential convergence of thinking between the public health community and the religious health community. The interfaith community and the public health community have come together with a focus on prevention rather than just on treatment. In the United States, we pride ourselves on the doctrine of separation of church and state. But we need an integration of church and state in the arena of public service.

In every city we visited, we found it easy to include hospital personnel and public health agencies in serious, substantive planning about how the faith community could play a role in advancing the health status of the entire community. From the Centers for Disease Control to the American Public Health Association, the public health profession is turning toward the religious community with an appreciative and open mind.

The Strengths of Churches

What is the strength of the religious community? Each of us deeply desires a community that will love us and care for us, even when our economic value may not be obvious. Again, the lesson of the soup kitchen: We want to be part of such a place because we need to care and because we may need to be cared for. If we stay long enough, we know deeply that we will need both more than once. The seed of this kind of coherence is found in the spiritual life of a community—not just in the spiritual life of isolated individuals.

Congregations have the strength to:

- *Accompany*—they show up and are physically present.
- *Convene*—they gather people in big and small groups across interest lines.
- *Connect*—they form complex webs of exchange across which resources can be accessed, help can be offered, and knowledge can flow.

- *Frame,* Give Context, Tell Stories—they not only "educate" but learn and discuss.
- *Give Sanctuary*—they are physical places where things happen.
- *Bless*—they evaluate, judge, encourage.
- *Pray*—they mark the intersection between human and holy.
- *Persist*—they have a long time span, memory, and hope.

MONEY, PUBLIC HEALTH, AND RELIGION

For hospitals, consolidation is an ever increasing trend. Consolidation is not always a bad thing. It is primarily driven by the fact that services can be provided more inexpensively. However, managed care tends to sacrifice those services that are unlikely to be reimbursed for any of several reasons—perhaps because the people concerned are uninsured, or because the services are long-range and indirect. Yet these are the kinds of services most prominently mentioned in the founding statements of many religious hospitals. As these services disappear, we must ask: Who is going to provide them?

Priorities and Values

The emerging dialogue between hospitals and religious organizations must rearrange priorities. Many today are content to justify the linkage of faith and health on the grounds of mere efficiency. Sometimes consolidation is just a strategy for obtaining coveted congregational facilities as cheap service sites. If the discussion were just about how to do blood pressures and home care services, it would be a simple cost–benefit analysis. Just get the highest-skilled volunteers and the lowest-skilled employees to do everything possible. Then make it hard for people to get reimbursed for everything else to dampen demand. This is what today passes for managing care.

Much of what we need to do is reframe the conversation. Health language is more frequently used in connection with mercy than with justice, with services than with change. Public health and religious hospitals have justified their existence in terms of mercy, which is admirable but inadequate in both theological and scientific terms. *Mercy does not necessarily lead to justice—to changing the social conditions that make the need for mercy inevitable.*

It is not easy to utilize health language as a tool for talking about social responsibilities. But I am hard pressed to see how other languages for talking about social responsibilities and social change are much better. The American social discussion is too much about money and too little about life. Religion especially needs a vocabulary for public engagement that includes more than economic indicators. Money is only and always an intermediate good. What do we buy? What do we actually aspire to, hope for?

Many of the models I cite are difficult or impossible to turn into reimbursable opportunities. Their only recommendation is that they help people be healthier in a highly cost-effective way. That doesn't help you if you are trapped in a competitive corporate culture unbound by any sense of religious or moral obligation toward the underserved. Financial stewardship is a heavy responsibility. This article looks at cost-effectiveness in a way that may well threaten traditional institutional structures.

But We Don't Have Any Money

I have been with hundreds of leaders of health ministries based in or allied with religious groups in the last couple years. Many of them talk and act as if the religious community has few resources with which to work. For instance, despite the obvious benefit and mission impact, most parish nurses are still volunteers with approximately the status of church librarian. The reason: no money. This is continually pointed to as a barrier to new or expanded health activities.

It doesn't take long to look around the religious landscape and realize that this complaint is either disingenuous or ignorant. The fact is that 86 percent of all charitable giving flows through local churches. For comparison, only 8 percent is given by foundations. But more to our point, the religious community controls or owns more than 700 hospitals—perhaps 29 percent of the acute care beds in the United States. Granted, there are a variety of control structures and joint venture relationships that buffer most hospitals

from direct intervention by religious organizations. But as strong leadership by Cardinal Bernadin showed in Chicago, many of these institutions are at least potentially accountable to religious structures. Hospitals with religious origins are not independent; they have a history and a family and a memory. They share in a larger hope. But more than sharing, they were born to serve a larger hope.

Unlike religious hospitals, foundations have the freedom to select their goals, invest in innovation, and pioneer new fields of knowledge with unequaled flexibility and speed. They are not subject to the whims of political change, popular taste, or intellectual fashion. Unaffected by the constraints of the competitive environment surrounding religious hospitals, foundations have time to anticipate the future, the important freedom to fail, and the freedom to persist (Keenan, 1993).

Of course, not every foundation operates on the scale of Robert Wood Johnson with its upwards of $100 million a year to invest. However, local foundations with relatively modest assets ($5 to $10 million) can utilize the same freedoms to have a large local impact. We must remember that the dominant trend in philanthropy is matching funds and collaborative funding. If you sold your hospital for a net $40 million, that might generate $3 to $4 million a year in unencumbered funding available for health ministry. That funding would be likely to leverage similar matching grants from national foundations, if you did your programming creatively. This combined amount could be relied on to leverage another match from local congregations for health ministries of demonstrable community impact. Thus, your $4 million could leverage $12 to $16 million in program expenditures.

Hospitals accustomed to budgeting for MRI machines and cardiac surgeons may have lost touch with what $12 million can buy in terms of community-based health workers and activities. For beginners, few communities need a great deal of capital expenditures: the buildings are typically underutilized. Health workers range up to, not down to, RN-trained personnel. Many relevant programs utilize community organizing skills that are shockingly inexpensive to recruit. My point is simple: $12 million buys a great deal more in community health than it does inside the walls of the hospital, especially when you are free to persist and answerable only to your most mature faith and honest health science.

I know of hospitals and systems that have converted their stainless steel and concrete into foundations that demonstrate what can be done. The Kansas Health Foundation was born in this way. The Jewish Healthcare Foundation of Pittsburgh, the Vesper Society in Oakland, and Lutheran Hospital in St. Louis are other recent models.

The most profound critique of hospitals is that they are the wrong tool for the time. At the current time and, perhaps, for some years forward, religious hospitals have the choice of transferring their assets into liquid form and then, through the vehicle of a foundation, into support for the abundance of community health structures that are highly adapted to preventive health science and highly unlikely to be paid for any other way. The reality is that, in most cases, there are existing community organizations capable of expanding to fill many of the needs implied in community health strategies. The hospital must find a way to strengthen what exists and need not usually start from scratch. The tool most fitted for the transfer of resources is the philanthropic foundation.

I do not want to be understood as downplaying the importance of excellence in the hundreds of core functions performed by the best hospitals. Nor do I want to suggest that in every case religious hospitals should abandon their service areas. But I do want to offer those who cannot survive in this environment another way—I would say a preferable way—to serve their God-given mission of promoting health and wholeness and defending the interests of the marginal people God loves. For achieving health goals in your community, foundations can be an effective institutional alternative to the hospital structure.

Building Partnerships between Organizations

In the Interfaith Health Program research, we have discovered that institutional isolation is also a primary health risk in most communities. As we went from city to city, we knew that people of different faiths often work without learning from or collaborating with each other. This is true from soup kitchens to hospitals. People of the same faith traditions but from different ethnic groups are isolated, too. And people of all faiths tend to work in ignorance of their colleagues in secular settings or in different disciplines.

We can't each be involved in everything, but we do have to be connected to other institutions that are. This calls for collaborative creativity. Collaboration is hard work, demanding sensitive planning and analysis. Sharing is threatening for all of us, from 4-year-old kids to 40-year-old institutions. But it is the future, especially for hospitals.

WHAT IS COMMUNITY?

Those of us who follow Jesus know the words as we know our own names: "For I was hungry and you fed me, I was lonely and you visited me. . . ." Every religion has a similar central spiritual principle. Apparently it is obvious to anyone of any spiritual vision whatsoever that spirituality is about connections to other humans, not about learning something secret or difficult that would somehow separate you from people.

Bill Foege of the Carter Center tells of his breakthrough when he realized that the saying, "Some things have to be seen to be believed," is exactly wrong. In fact, you have to believe in order to see what you are looking at. Community requires that we believe we are connected. With eyes opened by belief in community, we can see the patterns of connections emerging everywhere.

I was recently in the Bay Area of California, and I had the chance to walk among the redwoods in the Muir National Forest. Redwoods may be the only trees that can compete with live oaks for grace and mystery. I had walked among them before, but I had never really seen them. That afternoon I found myself standing in the middle of a 40-foot circle of redwood trees, each of which was 10 to 13 feet in diameter. Even bending back, I couldn't see the top of them. So I lay down on the soft ground, and then I could see that the circle of trees converged almost out of sight up in the fog. They were touching one another—as if it were one tree.

The most important thing to understand about redwoods, and about communities, is how they replicate. Where does the next generation come from? Redwood trees don't usually spring from individual seeds; they spring from the root of the older trees. I was lying in the middle of what had once been an ancient redwood tree. The trees surrounding that circle were, in fact, the young ones. They reached 250 feet into the air, but they were the children. And they had sprung up from the roots of the mother tree where I was lying. I realized that it is nonsense to describe one redwood tree. Not only are they tangled together at the top; they are inseparable at the bottom, where their roots are deeply woven together.

Something like that is true in communities. It would not be terribly important to know how communities replicate if you lived 300 years. But if you live only 70 or 80 years, it becomes critical to understand how each generation passes on that which makes a community cohere, that which makes it hold together.

It's very important for us to understand that we too spring from the roots of those who preceded us. We are not held up by living soil like trees, but we are sustained by the coherence, the living meaning that we experience in our communities. That is a spiritual function, and it is one that is entrusted to all of us who resonate, who believe in God by whatever name we know God, by whatever way we know God.

Of course, we are not trees. The analogy breaks down when you realize that, unlike trees, we have the power to choose where we live—and indeed, many of us pull up and put down roots several times in a lifetime. But we are still not the isolated, independent, self-sufficient individuals that our dominant culture likes to tell us we are.

Beware of simplifying spirituality down to a list of mechanical tasks, of dumbing it down to one more currency in the bank of "social capital." It is now popular to talk about spirituality and healing, faith and health. But many are coming at this from very poorly nourished soil that reflects an individualistic model. One clue is that you'll find the books on the subject in the self-help section of the bookstore, as if spirituality was one more vitamin to use for self-improvement. You must resist this understanding of spirituality. In the same way that it makes no sense to talk about the life of a single redwood tree, it makes no sense to talk about private spirituality. Spiritual health lives in community, if it lives at all.

BIBLIOGRAPHY

Antonovsky, Aaron. *Health, Stress, and Coping.* San Francisco: Jossey-Bass, 1979.

Antonovsky, Aaron. *Unraveling the Mystery of Health: How People Manage Stress and Stay Well.* San Francisco: Jossey-Bass, 1987.

Antonovsky, Aaron. "A Sociological Critique of the 'Well-Being Movement.' " *Advances: The Journal of Mind–Body Health,* Volume 10 (1994), pp. 6–12.

McGinnis, Michael, and William Foege. "Actual Causes of Death in the United States." *Journal of the American Medical Association,* Volume 270, Number 18 (November 10, 1993), pp. 2207–2211.

Keenan, Terrance. *The Promise at Hand: Prospects for Foundation Leadership in the 1990s.* Princeton, NJ: Robert Wood Johnson Foundation, 1993.

Kozol, Jonathan. *Amazing Grace: The Lives of Children and the Conscience of a Nation.* New York: Crown Publishers, 1995.

McKnight, John. "Taking Charge of Health Care in a Chicago Neighborhood" in Richard Luecke, *A New Dawn in Guatemala.* Prospect Heights, IL: Waveland Press, 1993, pp. 219–227.

Pincus, Theodore, and Leigh F. Callahan. "What Explains the Association between Socioeconomic Status and Health: Primarily Access to Medical Care or Mind–Body Variables?" *Advances: The Journal of Mind–Body Health,* Volume 11 (1994), pp. 3–33.

Sanders, Susan. "Catholic Hospitals and Community Benefit Activities." *Health Progress* (January–February) 1994, p. 46.

21

Surviving as an Applied Sociologist

PAT SHEEHAN

Editors' Note: Pat Sheehan traces the trials and tribulations of trying to make a living as an applied sociologist. To borrow on an old saying: "With a Ph.D. in sociology and a dollar and a half, you can get a cup of coffee." Many think that once they have their degrees, their job will be handed to them. However, most will have to create their own careers.

Applied sociology certainly did not come to mind as I filled out my application for graduate school. In fact, I could not have told you what the term meant. All I knew was that sociology appealed to me as much in my 30s as it had when I was in high school, and when the opportunity arose for me to pursue a graduate degree in that field, I jumped at it. Applied sociology did not cross my mind as I plunged into my class work, prepared for comprehensive exams, or planned my doctoral dissertation, either. Sociologists did not do clinical work; everyone knew that. They stood at the front of classrooms explaining abstract theories to confused students, wrote abstruse papers that only other sociologists could understand, or crunched long strings of numbers in a research lab somewhere, probably for the government. That is what everyone did, and I would, too. There was no question.

I had nearly completed my Ph.D. before I realized, to my horror, that none of those activities appealed to me. I wanted to be independent, to throw tenure to the wind, to work in the real world with real people. In short, rather than teaching sociology at some budget-starved university, I wanted to open my own practice.

This was a dangerous decision. At the age of 47, many people are thinking about pensions and wishing they'd stuffed a little more money into their IRAs. Here I was casting aside all sociological protocol, not to mention any hope of having a secure retirement, in exchange for the opportunity to "apply" sociology rather than just "using" it. The result of my decision to work as a practitioner was that a diminutive but lucid understanding of the concept of applied sociology began to form in my mind. Comprehending exactly what I was getting myself into, unfortunately, was not so clear.

FINDING FRIENDS

The first dilemma I tackled, for example, was finding allies. Sociological practice was not a popular concept among the academic scholars that I knew. Every sociologist who had befriended me eschewed the idea of working with individuals or minuscule groups. They preferred sitting at scarred desks writing learned sentences, counseling clueless students, and getting paid to think, or at least look like they were thinking. None of those pastimes fitted me. I was not like them. If they symbolized sociologists, I represented frauds. Even more worrisome, I was a financial moron. I knew absolutely nothing about running a business. Hell, in the whole 30 years I'd had a bank account, I had never once been able to balance my checkbook. How did I expect to survive?

Despondent in my solitude, I began to seek other misfits like myself who could provide information on ways to apply sociology. My quest for guidance started at the school where I taught part time, but no self-respecting colleague (spelled No One) was willing to discuss private practice. I checked the school library; but because the sociologists in our department ordered the sociology books, to say that resources were sparse would be an understatement. Then one day I received an e-mail advertising classes in sociological practice that could be taken over the telephone. My prayer had been answered; I signed up immediately.

It was a good decision. Not only did the instructor provide pertinent information about practicing sociology, he introduced me to other sociological rebels who preferred practice to research. They gave me pointers about business and offered advice about social therapy; and, most important, they encouraged me to do what I so strongly desired yet feared to do: open my own practice.

ADVERTISING

My new contacts told me, among other things, to set specific goals; become known in the community; join the chamber of commerce; advertise (in the paper, in the phone book, on the airways, on billboards?); and, for God's sake, pick a name. Like most scholars, I had always been an excellent student, so I followed these instructions to the letter. I invented a catchy name (Learning Alternatives), took out ads in both local papers, joined the chamber of commerce, got a business phone, designed my own business cards and stationery, and placed an ad in the yellow pages. My funds, which had consisted of graduation money from my parents, were dwindling quickly, so my sign had to be a homemade job that I planted in the front yard right next to my petunias. The response was amazing. The sign had only been up for one day when some guy knocked on my door wanting to know if I made signs for a living. Offended, I shooed him away—a mistake I would not make today. After all, the bills have to be paid somehow.

THE FAIR

Deciding that I needed more training, I took another course over the telephone and was advised to do more advertising. It was now summer; my practice had been open for three months, I had not had one client, and the business was nearly broke. Because my new colleagues advised that advertising was essential to commercial success, I dipped into my sparse funds one more time and set up a booth at the local county fair, offering a free class as a prize. I even created a brochure that described poor communication and offered classes to help people improve their conversational skills. It took me two days to convince people to try their luck, but once I got the hang of marketing, I convinced over a hundred potential customers that they were idiots if they failed to take a chance on winning such a useful and valuable prize.

When the fair ended, I drew the names of the ten lucky winners, figuring that more winners would translate into more return customers, more word-of-mouth recommendations, or both. Because my office was small, I paid the high school $25.00 to rent a classroom. Then, picking up the phone, I dialed the first lucky contestant. When I told her who I was and why I was calling, she hung up on me. The second winner insisted that she had never applied for the class, and hung up on me. The third threatened to turn me in to the police if I harassed her again, and hung up on me. Thinking that winners would be more impressed with their prize if they were officially informed of their luck by mail, I drew three new names, sat down, and drafted a letter explaining to people what they had won, and when and where to collect it. On the night of the class, one person showed up. She was a real estate agent. She tried to sell me a house.

THE MEDIA

Thinking that I might benefit from a little more education, I took a third class. This time I was advised to get my name out in public any way I could: maybe get my picture in the paper, or even do a talk show on the radio. Always a resourceful person, I quickly found someone to speak in my behalf with the owner of the local radio/television station. He promised me a TV talk show if I provided my own sponsors and guests. While I was still in the process of negotiations with him, I received a call from the local newspaper wanting to write an article about me, and from the town beautification committee asking if I would have my picture taken with the mayor at a ribbon-cutting ceremony. I naturally agreed. To my delight, within a couple of days after my article and picture were featured in the paper, I received a call from a man who said he desperately needed my help. We set an appointment, and I spent the evening prior to our meeting wondering if it would be unprofessional for a sociological practitioner to frame her first dollar bill and hang it on the wall under her doctoral diploma.

Unfortunately, my concern was wasted. The guy showed up dirty, with uncombed hair and few teeth, asking me to help him get his wife back. It seemed that she had come into an inheritance after she left him and he had suddenly realized that he still loved her very much. We talked for more than an hour, and as he reached for his wallet at the end of the session, I told him to keep his money. He never came back.

TELEVISION

My practice had been open for four months, my graduation money was nearly gone, and I had not earned one cent. When my television show began and my face became familiar to the whole community, however, clients surely would flock to my door. Every Friday at noon from October to January, I offered educated insights into the social problems of our small community. My show was a call-in program and presented public and private service providers as guests. Topics spanned many issues, including spouse abuse, drug use, and home health. I knew a lot of people in town, so I had no problem finding presenters; but getting callers was harder, and through most of my programs the phone sat on the table beside me like an embarrassment. After I had quit the station, I learned that all of the organizations presented on my show had benefited from the public exposure they had enjoyed. I was not so lucky. The time and work did not bring one client to my door.

I was beginning to get calls, however. A few months after I put my sign out, I began hearing from parents who hoped I could help their children perform better at school. It took me a couple of weeks to figure out that the bright primary colors and the word *Learning* on my sign had led people to conclude that my company offered a revolutionary teaching method to improve students' grades.

COMMUNITY SERVICE AND THE JAIL

The one successful move I made was joining the local Substance Abuse Council. The council had members from various parts of the community, including businesspeople, county officers, and plain old everyday civilians. When our secretary, the county health nurse, noticed the high recidivism rate among drug and alcohol offenders, she began looking for someone to offer treatment to the inmates. Luckily for me, no one else wanted to spend 2 hours a week locked in the detention center with a bunch of convicts, so she asked me if I would do it. Sly businesswoman that I was, I agreed; and it was the money I netted from that job ($50 an hour, 2 hours a week) that paid my utility bills, bought office equipment, and generally kept my practice open.

It had always been my belief that prosperity brought responsibility. Innocent dolt that I was, it never occurred to me that extra cash could also bring grief. I loved my job at the jail, but I quickly came to hate the war that raged between the jailers and myself, a battle that centered on—well—stupid things. The biggest issue was time. Although I always arrived early, I was inevitably made to wait. It got so bad that I started thinking the sheriff had refused to hire anyone who could tell the big hand from the little one. Occasionally the jailers' excuses for these delays were rational (a new inmate who had to go through processing), but more often they bordered on the preposterous. It was not unusual, for instance, for me to be left sitting on a hard wooden bench in the lobby for half an hour before being dismissed with little more than a haughty nod from a snotty jailer. I still clearly remember the time that I cooled my heels for 30 minutes before being told class had been canceled because the women needed to be treated for head lice that night. And the most frustrating thing was, there was no recourse—because they didn't care if I quit. They didn't want me to come back. Bringing the inmates to the substance abuse class was just a lot of extra uncompensated labor as far as the jailers were concerned.

Another skirmish that frequently occurred between the jailers and me revolved around my popularity with the inmates, a situation that warrants some explanation. There were two male and two female jailers at night, whose personalities ranged from the "ignorant jerk" who got off on shooting pepper spray into the eyes of helpless inmates, to the genuinely nice man who would take sick inmates to the doctor on his days off. This wouldn't have been so bad if our sheriff hadn't come up with a foolproof plan for guaranteeing that the jackasses always worked together. When the nice jailers worked, they generally looked the other way when inmates crowded around me like adoring fans at the end of the evening. (No delaying tactic was too flimsy if it meant that an inmate was able to delay returning to his or her tiny, airless cell.) On nights when the mean jailers were on duty, however, the same tactics drew threats of harsh punishment, particularly the threat to send the inmates to lockdown if they didn't get moving.

Being locked down is the most dreaded form of sanction, because it means no smoking, no refreshments, and no phone. As hard as it is on the men, the punishment is much worse for the women, because the lockdown cell is situated where passersby can peek in through a tiny window in the door. Inmates are not allowed to cover the opening, so they cannot use the toilet or wash up without risking being seen by a large percentage of the jail population, most of whom are males. Even so, although my inmates were well aware of the horrors of lockdown, they were willing to take their chances if it meant staying with me and out of their cells a little longer. Although I always encouraged the inmates to cooperate with the facility's rules, the most hateful jailers still blamed me for not making them act obediently. They repaid this insult to their authority by keeping me waiting and jerking me around in general. For example, one night my guys kept the nastiest jailer waiting, and in turn he locked me in the library for a half hour before bringing in the women. When I realized what he was doing, I fought his attempt at control by ignoring the

situation, choosing to sit down and calmly read the first book I could get my hands on. When he realized that he couldn't scare me, since he had no power over me, he unlocked the door and brought in the females.

DRUG COURT

While I was in the process of taking classes and opening my business, someone recommended that I read the book *Reckoning* by Elliot Currie. I liked it so well that I bought another of Dr. Currie's books, *Crime and Punishment in America,* along with a book by David Anderson, *Sensible Justice.* These latter works offered options other than incarceration for drug offenders, including something called Drug Court. The Drug Court program appealed to me because it advocated frequent therapy, drug testing, and contact with the probation officer. Families benefited from the program, because Drug Court clients were ordered to work, pay child support, and fulfill the day-to-day responsibilities that most of us perform without being coerced. Best of all, there was tremendous opportunity for federal and other grants to support the program.

I thought that the Drug Court method would be perfect for sociological practice, and I envisioned myself as either a therapist or an administrator. Armed with stacks of brochures and loaded with columns of statistics that demonstrated high levels of success among Drug Court participants, I introduced information about the program to powerful people in my community, people who had the power to make it happen. The mayor, the sheriff, the chief of police, both circuit and superior court judges, and the County Council all listened to my spiel. When it was pointed out to me that there was no one to write the grant proposals, I even took money out of my business's meager checking account and paid for a class in grant writing. Although the council was moderately interested in saving money and receiving grants, the overall response of law enforcement officials was blatantly underwhelming. The local criminal justice system made large profits, which no one was willing to reduce, off the incarceration of drug offenders. For instance, the county paid the jail something like $25 per inmate per day. When their jails were overcrowded, other counties paid around $45 a day. If one added the revenues from fines and court costs to these figures, it became apparent why people in law enforcement would not be interested in reducing the number of detention center residents. Each year the jail was realizing a profit well in excess of $100.000.

TODAY

I have not tried any new strategies since the Drug Court fiasco, although someday I may. Today, I use my sociological knowledge and survive financially by teaching part time while working full time as an investigator for Adult Protective Services. Even though it isn't my own private enterprise, my job does use applied sociology to help ensure the safety of elderly and disabled adults in four of the largest and most sparsely populated counties in my state. My most difficult task is keeping people who are capable of living on their own, with a few in-home services from the state. out of nursing homes—because state budget cutbacks have eliminated a large portion of the needed home services. My job is stressful, pays $23,000 plus mileage annually, and cuts into my scholarly endeavors. Nevertheless, it is one of the most fulfilling jobs I have had, and I am exceptionally content to use my sociological expertise helping those who have no one else.

As to my business, it is still open. The sign still stands in my front yard, and people still ask me to teach their children. Occasionally potential clients will call; and if I have time, I call back and basically tell them to stop talking like idiots and act like human beings. Sad thing is, I figure that is pretty much the same advice their grandparents would give them, if their grandparents were not wasting away in nursing homes because there are no services to keep them at home.

Finally, I have decided that I do not have to teach uninterested students, write boring papers, or crunch lengthy numbers to appear as professional and scholarly as befits my degree. I spend my days applying and enhancing the sociology that I fell in love with so long ago, and making an adequate living doing it. Even more important, I am happy, sleep like a baby, and never dread going in to work. If that is not a successful way to live. I do not know what is.

22

The Sociologist as Artist

WILLIAM DU BOIS AND R. DEAN WRIGHT

Sociology should be about *inventing*. The sociologist as an artist invents new social forms. As a discipline we should be creating new resources, inventing programs, and designing demonstration projects. Applied sociology should serve as an incubator for new ideas and model programs.

We need a *new kind of sociology*. C. Wright Mills (1959) talked of the *Sociological Imagination:* the ability to integrate personal troubles and social issues. The true application of the sociological imagination is in inventing social resources individuals can bring to the situation to address personal troubles.

Ralph Waldo Emerson (1975/1844) wrote, "To believe your own thought, to believe that what is true for you in your private heart is true for all men, that is genius." As an artist, the sociologist asks, what social resources would be helpful to people experiencing the same problems that I am experiencing?

"The artist talks to himself out loud. If what he has to say is significant, others hear and are affected" (Carpenter, 1970). As an art, the application of sociology is no different in either substance or form.

APPLYING SOCIOLOGY

One has only to look at sociology in the early part of the 20th century to realize the applied character of most academicians in the field at that time. The University of Chicago, especially, fostered a perspective in tune with our perspective in this book. Sociology, the Chicago school contended and demonstrated, was first and foremost a discipline with the inherent aim of solving social problems and directly addressing social issues.

The earliest gurus of sociology stated over and over again that the major role of the discipline was "social amelioration," or improving social conditions. They took theory and method to the streets and worked to solve the major social problems of the day. The perfect example was Ernest Burgess. In the early 1900s he almost single-handedly carved out the disciplinary niche called family sociology while serving as the chair of the major committee on homelessness in the city of Chicago. While he and Robert Park (1921) were writing the first major introductory sociology textbook, the one that first synthesized the discipline, Burgess was working with his students to directly address the problem of homelessness in the city. Through their personal work and research, Park and Burgess guided a new generation of sociologists who took their ideas and created a viable, rich, and perhaps idealistic discipline that had and still has the potential to change the world.

The early Chicago school sociologists, including W. I. Thomas, Ernest Burgess, and even George Herbert Mead were all frequent visitors to Jane Addams's Hull House, a settlement house in a poor neighborhood designed to address the needs of the poor. They did not see this as a hobby or after-work charity, but as an integral part of their appointed mission as sociological professionals. They taught there. They took students there. And they led social action programs (Fritiz, 1989).

One tired old argument says that sociology and social work were once one, but that social work became the social action arm, whereas sociology evolved into a pure science in pursuit of knowledge. Jane Addams didn't see it that way. Neither did the early sociologists of the Chicago school. They saw sociology as intimately entwined with social action and as inevitably working to make the society and community a better place in which to live. To split sociology and social action negates the vision of sociology as a creative exploration of new social institutions and a new society.

W. E. B. Du Bois (1968) quit his faculty position and left sociology to found the NAACP because he could not be content merely lecturing about racial injustice while blacks were being lynched in the streets. In the truest of academic intent, the profession has an obligation to tie the academy and knowledge to the real world where it can make a difference in the lives of ordinary people. Today, we so often see the opposite: academicians accumulating worthless analysis of meaningless social activities and publishing the results for a small group of fellow academicians with no value to real people in the real world.

One must draw a contrast, as Ernest Becker did, between two different versions of sociology: one that would analyze (scientific) and the other that would change the world (humanistic/action-oriented). One is the narrow academic discipline that colors politely within the lines, seeking only journal articles, research grants, and tenure. This scientific stance was expressed in W. F. Ogburn's 1929 American Sociological Association presidential address: "Sociology is not interested in making the world a better place." Ogburn saw the discipline as a science that should limit itself to collecting facts and making theories.

The other sociology takes to the streets. It is the original sociology of Comte, Marx, Ward, and Small, and it is the sociology to which Lynd, Sorokin, C. Wright Mills, and Gouldner each invited us to return and reconnect to the real world. This humanistic/action image envisions sociology as a discipline concerned not just with what is, but with what ought to be. It is the idea of an applied academy involved in implementing the ideal society.

Academic sociology has responded to social problems by selling society on a traditional research agenda. Academic sociologists address any social problem by calling for more money to do research. Often both liberal and even many conservative politicians are happy to oblige. Action gets postponed. As the early sociologists understood so well, piling up more and more facts will never get us to a science of humanity. A perpetual agenda of "more research" means the business of making a better world can be delayed, perhaps forever.

Over time many scholars narrowed the focus of the field and concentrated more and more on less and less. A never ending array of smaller and smaller facts let us expand study to absurdity. In 1886, John Eaton leveled a criticism that should be repeated over and over again today: "Let the warning cry fill the air of scientific associations, from meeting to meeting, that science is our means, not our end" (quoted in Becker, 1968: p. 73).

One idea that has dominated the field is that we must first do the research and collect all the facts, and *then* we can get around to action. The ultimate truth we must face as a discipline is that all the facts will never be in. Ernest Becker (1968) gave us insight into this dilemma and the problems it creates for a discipline intent on making a better world:

> By lifting an activist humanitarianism to the detached scientific heights ... we have lifted it right out of the world of contemporary social problems. ... The humanistic criticism of social values—radical in intent—bogs down practically into a conservatism of method that is self-defeating ... Sociology would thus be in the business as a disinterested discipline for a long time, and life would go on—and right by it. This is exactly what is happening today. ... (p. 77)

Becker (1968) notes that Lester Ward, who invented the term *applied sociology,* saw

> that sociology was not a descriptive science in search of facts, and he understood better than we do today that facts by themselves can impede the progress of science. ... He held that ... scientific fact gathering represented a rudimentary stage in science. It was the job of sociology to transcend this stage, and take its place as a mature science, that is using, correlating, generalizing, synthesizing the work of the various

Box 22.1 ■ Understanding Human Situations and Needs

"Truck Stop" for Homeless Youth

WILLIAM DU BOIS

We must approach homeless youth where they live and design programs to meet their needs as they see them. The kids are on the street. We must accept that, if we are going be effective and possibly later help them make a new life. We must begin by meeting their needs and attracting them as we would a customer.

The "truck stop" is not located on the interstate; it's located downtown in an area where street kids already hang out. However, conceptually, it's a truck stop. It provides:

- a warm bowl of soup and a friendly face
- a place to sit, rest, and get off the road awhile
- road maps, directions, and advice on the road ahead
- an information network
- showers
- a laundromat
- a communication switchboard
- emergency beds
- a place that's open 24 hours a day, 365 days a year

The variety of programs that exist for homeless youth often are not working. Many kids actually prefer life on the street with all its danger and abuses to paternalistic programs that push them in directions they may not be ready to go. Guidelines for residential care are often strict, and a great many homeless kids would rather live on the streets than put up with their structure. We may debate the morality of this until kingdom come, but the fact remains that many young kids are on the streets with needs vastly unattended.

What type of program would work for these kids, meet their needs, and successfully draw them toward an eventual opportunity to get off the streets? When we interview the kids, we are often surprised at what they say their needs are. For instance, in Des Moines there is no place for a homeless kid to take a shower until 11 o'clock in the morning. Even if the youth wants to get a job, most jobs start well before that hour. Laundry also becomes a problem, as does emergency food. If we are going to deal effectively with kids, we must approach their needs from their standpoint and not ours. It is only then that we will be able to offer them services and convert them to a productive lifestyle.

Authoritarianism does not work when we are trying to meet the needs of throwaway kids on the streets. Many children left home precisely because of a restrictive environment. They are not going to submit to a new authoritarian structure. They value their new autonomy, complete with all its permissiveness and partying. The last thing they are going to do is trade their freedom for shelter. Yet they need help. The party bottoms out. Food becomes a problem. Medical care is needed. We must provide assistance in a way that is *accessible to their lifestyle*. We may eventually address the same needs as traditional counseling and treatment, but the *delivery* of these services needs to be packaged in a way that is compatible with the kids' needs, desires, and lifestyle. If we are going to *help*, then we must design programs to meet their needs, not our preferences.

---

disciplines. In Ward's view, sociology called for broader, deeper, keener, more synthetic intellectual powers than did the various ancillary disciplines. When Ross wanted to leave economics and become a sociologist, Ward encouraged him, saying he had a big enough mind for it. Needless to say, we are far from this view of sociology today; practically anyone who can come in off the street and master its techniques can pass as a sociologist—synthetic mental powers would even be a positive disadvantage in most of our graduate schools. (p. 71)

Unfortunately, today's graduate schools train students merely to relabel the world into new categories rather than to invent bold new solutions to social and organizational problems. Sociology should be about making the world better. Whitehead says, "The purpose of knowledge is to promote the art of living." We should be inventing effective social forms and creating social arrangements in which people flourish. However, instead of fostering synthesizing, creating, and inventing, most of what we learn in

I conceptualize a resource center closer to a truck stop than a traditional center. We could staff the "truck stop" with counselor/interns who would wait tables, cook food, and other duties. The most effective counseling takes place around a particular problem, at the point of crisis. The truck stop staff is available on the spot should needs arise. They become familiar to the kids, learning about their situations and lives, and may be sought for advice. Hanging out at the lunch counter can get you connected to community resources. It is known that you can always trade an hour of work for food, petty cash, and so on. The truck stop is also an information center.

Other agencies can periodically provide staff to work shifts at the truck stop. Perhaps, once a week, a child abuse counselor waits tables. The counselor should be indentified by wearing a button or such, but otherwise acts much like any other employee: waiting tables and serving food. The counselor then becomes known and is more likely to be approached by kids. The center should be overstaffed, with frequent breaks for employees so there is time to visit with the kids and perhaps discuss problems should the kids want. Waiting tables is normally a lower-status position. By having some professionals serve the kids, they become more accessible.

This idea is not without precedent. During the 1960s a midwestern university received a national mental health grant for psychiatrists interested in alcohol rehab to do their residency internships as bartenders. The logic was, "If you're going to treat alcoholics, you should go where the alcoholics are." The traditional role of the neighborhood bartender has always been to listen to personal problems and dispense psychological advice. We might as well put a professional in the role. This is similar to the truck stop idea. We go to where the homeless kids are and meet their needs. Staff is then available to provide advice and direction should the child desire it. Unless we respect their desires and they want our advice, counseling will be ineffective anyway.

Conceptual problem: How do you keep the truck stop from becoming a youth center? If it becomes just a youth center, a stigma may get to be attached to taking a shower or needing emergency food. Therefore, it doesn't have many pool tables, video games, and so on.

This is not a hangout but a place where people come, get their needs met, and then move on. As with most truck stops, there will be people who stop here regularly. The distinction in practice may be subtle, but maintaining the "truck stop" conception is crucial, both to prevent stigma from surrounding the needs of street kids and to avoid encouraging normal kids to leave home. The truck stop is not a perpetual youth hangout but provides maps, information, and resources.

It is also very important not to conceptualize it as a neighborhood café. We need to understand what a truck stop means to truckers. Normal travelers may drop into a truck stop on an erratic basis. However, despite the distance of their journeys, the truckers are regulars. It is a type of home away from home to them, complete with all the familiarity of being known.

graduate school takes us in the opposite direction: analyzing, dissecting, rationalizing. The schools train technicians, when what we need are artists.

OUTRAGEOUS IDEAS

The social artist invents real-life programs and structures. The finished product is in life, not on paper. What is written on paper is important. However, it is a means of getting us to action and not an end in itself. Thus, artistic statements may lack the precision of scientific statements. A useful map may appear at first glance vague and sketchy. We write to encourage the sociologist as coproducer to invent new programs and alternatives.

Robert Lynd wrote his classic book *Knowledge for What?* in 1939. He and his wife, Helen Lynd, were the preeminent researchers studying social class in the United States. They had devoted most of their life to this project, doing participant observation and

Box 22.2 ▪ Understanding Human Situations and Needs

Runaway Kids and Small Town Economic Development

WILLIAM DU BOIS

I have always thought there was a fit between the needs of street kids and the economic development needs of small towns. Perhaps a small town could get a grant to start a small business (such as a hamburger cafe) and employ homeless or near homeless kids. The whole town would then "adopt" the kids for the time they were there. Small towns are such that everyone would know who the new kids were, and would provide a sense of community. The trick would be getting some of the local churches to come on board in a truly Christian rather than a puritanical way.

The reality is that street kids are sexually active and also do drugs and alcohol. Come to think of it, they sound like normal high school kids.

Maybe that's all an impossible dream, but I think it might work in the right community. In some small towns everybody is in everybody's business. In others, everybody is so close that they actually tolerate each other's differences: live and let live.

If several towns had these economic development/ homeless grants, kids could migrate from one town to the next. There would be shelter, a job, and different education and training available. *One reality we have to acknowledge: Most of these kids will not be going home. We need to create resources so they can live.* We tend to design programs as if they have normal parents and their parents want them back. Most don't.

In Iowa, most runaway girls are pregnant. Most have been sexually abused. Most come from dysfunctional homes. Dean notes that studies in Los Angeles and New York found that about half of throwaway youths were gay and that their parents had disowned them upon their confessions, or that they had run away to escape the harassment and guilt that our society places on such children.

---

surveys in the midwestern community where they lived. As the Nazis moved across Europe, getting only muted response from German sociologists, Lynd wrote his book and asked the question, "What are we doing?" He put forth the striking proposal that social science should be serving human needs.

Robert Lynd ended *Knowledge for What?* with some "Outrageous Hypotheses." To illustrate the role of the sociologist as artist, let us present some outrageous ideas that we hope will stretch the reader's imagination.

Understanding Situations and Needs

We need to understand situations and then develop resources and programs that meet the needs of people in those situations. The sociologist studies a situation and then invents new resources that have the potential of being helpful and changing lives.

Dean's service learning work with the homeless ("Tramp Training") illustrates how understanding needs and situations can help sociologists create new programs, such as the Port of Entry program and the tutoring project for homeless children.

As artists we can imagine more possibilities. For example, as we study homeless kids, we learn that most children on the street aren't runaways; they are throwaways. They won't be going home. No one is really looking for them. They may have been in trouble with the law. Many have been sexually abused. They may have been in and out of juvenile placements where the average stay is 6 months. Most street kids prefer the streets to the conservative rules of shelters and treatment centers; these facilities expect them to be celibate, keep early curfews, not drink or do drugs, and conform to middle-class norms that the rule-making middle-class staff have constructed and the upper-middle-class board members have endorsed. Many of the boxes offer practical examples of what we mean by inventing resources people can use in their particular situations. We might design a "truck stop" where homeless kids can get off the road. Another idea would be for a small town to "adopt" a group of homeless kids. As Bill Wagner teaches us in

"Parenting without Controlling," the behavior of homeless kids "makes sense" to them. We must provide kids with resources useful in their struggles to create a more positive life.

William Foote Whyte's (1977) work with a restaurant in Chicago in the 1940s provides the classic example of the sociologist as an artist doing sociological research to understand a situation and then inventing a resource to improve the situation.

When a waitress would yell orders to the cooks, the cooks resented being ordered about by the lowest-status employee in the place. The cooks often had years of tenure, but a waitress might be the last person hired. The cooks also were male and the waitresses female, which at the time also represented a status differential. To solve the problem, Whyte's co-researcher Edith Lentz Hamilton noticed that Harding's Restaurant had invented "the spindle."

Box 22.3 ▪ Understanding Human Situations and Needs

Finding Someone to Love

WILLIAM DU BOIS

If a sociology student wants a million-dollar idea, here's one: Solve the problem of how singles can meet people. Economists now talk about the loneliness industry: singles ads, video dating, introduction services, singles bars. Entrepreneurs are making vast sums of money but aren't very effective at meeting people's needs.

When I was doing consulting with bars and nightclubs in northern California, a newspaper wanted to interview me about my work. They were planning to run a series of 6 to 12 articles on alternatives to bars where people could meet people in the Bay Area. The series never ran. They couldn't find enough places in the San Francisco area to write about. The one article that did run cited laundromats and one particular grocery store. This does not represent much advice.

It used to be that society provided ways to matchmake people. Church was a viable way to meet people. If that failed, every town had at least one person who felt it was their duty to play matchmaker for any available single. Nowadays, once people move past college age, potential ways to meet people diminish. Graduates accept a job in a new city and find themselves separated from friends who formerly provided a network for meeting people.

Some health clubs are emerging as potential meeting places, but few understand this as a major part of their business. Part of the secret is providing an atmosphere where women feel safe and unthreatened. Many women feel self-conscious working out around leering men, and many health clubs develop a reputation as "meat markets."

We might begin to imagine alternatives. Perhaps we should train matchmakers. The world could probably live with more matchmakers and fewer psychiatrists. Despite our supposed psychological and sociological knowledge, we know very little about who is specifically attracted to whom. Matchmaking is an art requiring knowledge and intuition. Chemistry between people is crucial. What kind of knowledge would be helpful to potential matchmakers? How can we develop such a knowledge base? What skills need to be developed? Perhaps we should imagine an Academy of Matchmaking.

Matchmakers could match potential marriage partners. They also could match mentors to at-risk youth, or children to surrogate grandparents in nursing homes. The idea could also be expanded even to choosing college roommates, thus decreasing dropout rates.

Finding someone to love is serious business. Many find themselves alone on Saturday night without any viable means for meeting someone. Perhaps we should invent a board game that people can play at large gatherings that introduces people to each other, creates self-disclosure, and affords the opportunity for what Lillian Rubin calls the "go away a little closer" dynamic of dating. Or one might imagine a Disneyland of Dating—a singles vacation complete with computer matchmaking, astrological and palmistry readings, and rides that mix and match, gradually rejecting some from your pool of eligibles and leading you toward someone suitable. Such a setting could be complete with participatory resources and openings for unanticipated synchronicity and magic to occur.

Box 22.4 ■ Inventing Solutions to Social Problems

Ideas Wanted!

NICHOLAS ALBERY

I define a social innovation or social invention as a new and imaginative way of tackling a social problem or improving the quality of life. Unlike a technological invention, it tends to be a new service, rather than a product or patentable process, and there tends to be no money in it.

The Institute for Social Inventions, of which I am chairman, collects visions, ideas, and projects. It was launched in 1985 with the aim of encouraging the innate inventiveness of the British public and collecting, researching, publicizing, and carrying out the best ideas.

Back in the 1950s Clavell Blount persuaded a member of Parliament to promote a debate on the topic of "Ideas into Action" and wrote a book with that title. As he wrote, "We have reached a point in our history where we are faced by a choice between two alternatives: Either we believe it would be best to leave our fate to a few 'master minds' who will decide just how the industrial and social life of this nation is to run, and who issue directives through chains of command, or every man and woman in the country should be encouraged to observe, tackle, and help to overcome those anomalies and inefficiencies of which he or she has firsthand knowledge."

The main incentive the institute has been able to offer so far has been dangling the bait of our annual competition, judged in June of each year, offering a minimum 1,000 pounds (approximately $1,700) in prizes and a variable amount of publicity. This competition is merely a lure to entice by the finger so that the rest of the body will follow. The institute then encourages the senders-in of ideas to take matters farther themselves, often giving hints on whom to approach and how. Some ideas the institute does take up itself. The institute has launched social inventions workshop programs in many state schools, and it promotes community counseling circles as a way of training large groups (and has published a book on this). It has helped a number of its own pet schemes get going, including a Natural Death Centre ("to improve the quality of dying" and to support those who are dying at home); an Adopt-a-Planet competition (in which school classes caretake a vandalized part of their local neighbourhood); a Hippocratic Oath for Scientists (signed by many Nobel Prize–winning scientists); a Universal Declaration of the Rights of Posterity; a rating scheme for gurus and spiritual masters; a rating scheme for advertisements; and Forum Theatres (to help resolve children's disputes).

With help from the Network for Social Change, the institute has also been active in eastern Europe, helping found the East Europe Constitution Design Forum, which brings together (at international symposia and by fax) the key constitution designers and politicians from eastern Europe and the ex–Soviet Union in an attempt to use constitutional and electoral models as a way of defusing some of the ethnic turmoil

---

Waitresses now wrote their orders down and clipped them onto a metal spindle, which spun around for the cooks to read. Most restaurants around the country still use the spindle today. The seemingly simple device is actually a quite sophisticated solution to the situation.

A sociologist might invent viable ways for singles to meet each other. Here again, we illustrate C. Wright Mills's sociological imagination. The sociologist as artist does research to understand a situation. However, he or she does not stop with research, but utilizes the understandings gained to invent new resources that help solve personal problems.

Inventing Solutions to Social Problems

We need novel new approaches to social programs. In the Canadian Yukon, Judge Barry Stuart works with Community Peacemaking Circles that treat crime as a symptom and sentencing as an occasion to treat underlying problems. Darrol Bussler and Mark Cary first tried this approach in the United States in Min-

resulting from the decolonization of the Soviet empire. The institute has published a timely book, *Can Civil Wars Be Avoided?*, which argues that local balance representation might be a suitable model for many of the emerging democracies (and for Northern Ireland). In this electoral system, parties are penalized and begin to lose seats they would otherwise have won if they fail to get a minimum number of votes in all areas of the country; this encourages them to appeal to all of the various ethnic groupings.

My personal preference is for projects at the neighborhood level, where there is still a human scale—with the aim of helping to restore this sense of scale to our overblown "giantist" societies, where most problems are insoluble (or at least beyond the reach of "ordinary" people) until the scale is reduced. It is more productive to concentrate on neighborhood schemes at this stage, until the Institute gains leverage as it becomes more weighty and established. It is dispiriting work trying to put pressure on government ministries, which routinely resist new ideas from outside.

George Fairweather, writing in the early 1970s, argued not only that our survival on earth was threatened as never before, but that revolution and nonviolent protest were unlikely to bring about the social transformations required. In his view, there needed to be organizations that could deal with problems before they became crises, and that could set up, test, compare, and evaluate small-scale innovative solutions before applying them more widely. He wrote, "A mechanism for social change that involves innovation, advocacy, and preparing the culture for the future needs to be created so that continuous problem solving can occur. Experimental social innovation transcends revolution, because it creates continuous problem-solving social change."

Rather than an obsession with one particular scheme, the ideal social inventor has a track record of successful projects, with plenty of ideas for more. You will, I hope, find at least a few ideas that appeal to you as being not only new and imaginative but also feasible. Anything you can do to help implement them within your profession or sphere of competence, please do. Some of the ideas are evidently not feasible as they stand but have been included for their provocation value. The trick is not to demonstrate your critical faculties by picking holes in the ideas but, as in brainstorming, to prove your ingenuity by imagining an improvement or an entirely revamped scheme that would work.

To submit entries to the institute's £1,000 annual contest for imaginative ideas or to subscribe to the Institute for Social Inventions, write to us at: 20 Heber Road, London NW2 6AA, UK.

Global Ideas Bank home page is at http://www.globalideasbank.org.

Contact: rhino@dial.pipex.com.

nesota ("Coming Full Circle: A County–Community Restorative Justice Partnership"). This invention is spreading from community to community as it captures the imagination of courts that have been seeking solutions.

Rather than just waiting until after crime has happened, peacemaking circles get proactive. One Minnesota circle was meeting on a teenage drug case. The conversation deteriorated into "kids these days," but then it got around to talking about latchkey kids and the lack of after-school care. Before the conversation was over, the group had decided to create a day-care center and an after-school program. The drug crime became the occasion to look at root causes and invent new prevention programs. As the local Department of Corrections head commented admiringly, she had never dreamed criminal justice would take her on such an adventure.

In his 1981 presidential address to the American Sociological Association, William Foote Whyte called for social inventions for solving human problems. He said a social invention might be a new element in an

Box 22.5 ■ Inventing Solutions to Social Problems

Making Bureaucracy Pay for Delays

NICHOLAS ALBERY

British bureaucracy sometimes rivals Third World bureaucracy for delay, rudeness, and complacency. The London passport office took 6 months to renew my passport, including losing my application form after cashing my check. It took patience and a phone with automatic repeat dialing for me to be able to get through to them. Their advertised numbers were and no doubt still are almost continuously engaged. Even so, phoning seems to work better than letters: They cheerfully admitted to me that it was taking them 3 weeks even to open mail, let alone deal with it.

When my passport finally arrived, I sent them an invoice for a modest £15 for my time for the estimated 3 hours I had spent chasing them up by phone and letter, and asked for a further £4.53 for my material costs, including phone bill and stamps. Before the month was up I received a check for the full amount as "reimbursement for the difficulties you incurred in obtaining a passport" and as an "ex-gratia payment in full and final settlement."

I advise anyone else who has been made to wait overlong by bureaucracy to charge for their time. The paymasters for these organizations must be made to realize that allowing their services to be run on minimum budgets so that they are then overwhelmed by demand is not acceptable. A change of attitude is also required. As Stuart Conger puts it in "Social Inventions" (Saskatchewan Newstart), social agencies, like businesses, "must proclaim the customer king." The emphasis must be on building the self-image of clients rather than humiliating them, and the orientation must be toward pleasure rather than puritanism. Every government department and social services agency needs a unit solely concerned with trying out new and improved ways of delivering their services to the public.

---

organizational structure, a new procedure, a new policy, or a new role (Whyte, 1981). In England, the Institute for Social Inventions actually gives cash prizes each year for the best new social invention.

Perhaps we need to have an annual Inventors' Fair, as Bill Du Bois and Gary David tried to organize at the 1999 Midwest Sociological Society Meetings. Professionals could outline new existing social inventions in poster exhibits, and students could present ideas for new solutions to social and organizational problems. Policy makers and organizational leaders could be invited as judges and could also shop the Inventors' Fair for new ideas to take back to their own problems.

Opportunities for invention abound. For example, violence and the public response to violence have become epidemic in the United States. We need effective new programs rather than political knee-jerk reactions and collective tantrums of vengeance. Utilizing what we know so far from research and theoretical insights, we need to invent programs, tinker with them to make them better, and evaluate their successfulness.

As Bill Wagner says, "We need to design programs that kids run to instead of from." We are competing with the pimps who nurture, buy clothes, and court kids. We are competing with gangs that protect kids, befriend them, are there for them, and even understand, comfort, and identify with those running from child abuse or alcoholic parents. We are competing with bars and the glamour of drugs and alcohol. "Just say no" doesn't work. We need a variety of attractive alternatives kids can say "yes" to. What would improve the odds that any one person might make it? What resources would be helpful to people in their personal struggles?

Psychologist Carl Rogers says, "Violence is the last resort of a powerless person." Violence occurs when a person is out of resources and sees no alternatives. As Hal Pepinsky argues in his peacemaking approach to crime, prisons must become healing centers if we are ever to break the cycle of violence. If prisons are only places where society extracts revenge, then those most broken will not return to society whole.

The way people get off drugs is that they get a "life transplant." The Alcoholics Anonymous party lingo is that you get "new playpens and new play pals." A similar thing happens with crime. Perhaps what we really need are *Human Recycling Centers*. An immediate question comes to mind: What would a Human Recycling Center look like? We are reminded of a young woman we know whose sister is a stripper, drug addict, thief, and sometime prostitute. She is in and out of jail, treatment programs, and even prison. What resources would help her turn her life around? This is a call for invention.

A New Haven, Connecticut, project teaches prostitutes to be feminists. The idea is to develop self-esteem so as to keep women from being used by pimps. In San Francisco, a group of former prostitutes have formed Hooker U. They have purchased an old motel where women can live safe from their pimps, and they are retraining ex-hookers for jobs in the travel industry in conjunction with a local community college.

Other problems need solutions. What would work with sex offenders? The common wisdom is that nothing will change them. We have simply given up and accepted this as fact. This is an outrage. We spend millions of dollars and get nothing for our investment. Rather than giving up, we need to be exploring new programs. What would work? This is an area ripe for social invention.

We have also given up on sociopaths. In fact, the origin of the term *sociopath* is interesting. The same people were originally called "psychopaths." However, this term might suggest that these people could be helped by a psychologist. If you are a mental health worker, a psychopath can really mess up your shift by giving you a black eye or leaving blood on your clothes. Even if small, psychopaths have learned that most people would rather avoid fights, so bullying is effective. If it takes urinating on the walls to get your attention, so be it. They will do almost anything to win by intimidation. Mental health professionals didn't want to have to deal with such people. They redefined them as "sociopaths." The clinical diagnosis is that these persons have not been properly socialized, have failed to internalize a conscience, and nothing can be done to help them. You can actually

Box 22.6 ■ Solving Social Problems

Third Class of Substances: Legal, Illegal, Tolerated

WILLIAM DU BOIS

I think we should have a third class of substances. There are legal substances and illegal substances. I think we should also have "tolerated substances." These would be legal to use (and manufacture) but illegal to promote in any manner.

I would put cigarettes in this category. They would be sold in plain generic paper wrappers with the name in standardized lettering. Advertising or any effort to promote sales would be strictly forbidden. It would also be illegal to organize any kind of word-of-mouth campaign to encourage use.

Marijuana might also be placed in this third category.

To make this effective, we must also pass a law that says that companies that own "tolerated substances" cannot own another company or be owned by any other company. With interlocking ownership, companies could find ways to skirt the law and promote their tolerated substances. For example, currently in the United States cigarette advertising on television is forbidden. However, interlocking ownership allows companies to plant sexy stars in movies smoking cigarettes. Even if these product appearances are not directly paid for, interlocking ownership gives a company leverage to threaten withdrawing their financial support.

Winner, Crime Category, 1999 contest of the Institute for Social Inventions. From Institute's annual book, *Social Dreams and Technological Nightmares* (1999, p. 86).

be so crazy you get kicked out of a mental institution. Thus, those who the general public would certainly say are the most "crazy" get defined as sociopaths and go to prison and not a mental institution. We might imagine a program where winning by intimidation was not effective. Streetwise ex-boxers or football players with experience in not overreacting to physical blows might be taught psychology and counseling skills. We could establish a short work week so these special therapists would have time to regenerate after the rigor of working with sociopaths.

Box 22.7 ■ Solving Social Problems

Welfare Reform

WILLIAM DU BOIS

To realistically get off of welfare and out of poverty, people need several things:

- *Day care:* Without free or cheap day care, going to work doesn't pay for women with large families.
- *Medical insurance:* Gambling on your own health to take a low-wage job without medical insurance is one thing. Risking your children to leave behind the medical benefits of being on welfare is another.
- *Training and education:* Welfare moms need viable skills that will get them good-paying jobs.
- *Jobs:* All the training in the world doesn't matter if there are no jobs near where you live. We must create jobs where necessary.
- *Transportation:* Public transportation is not viable in most areas. Taking the kids to day care by bus and then transferring to a different bus to get to work can be difficult to impossible. Schedules for buses in most cities preclude the possibility of using public transportation. The buses simply don't run early or late enough.

Maybe we need to encourage people to start their own businesses. Perhaps we need a whole new variety of entrepreneurship for inner-city and isolated rural areas. What kinds of resources would be helpful for starting businesses?

Some of the businesses could be day care centers. Former Texas Governor Ann Richards made an interesting comment, noting there are two simple-minded approaches to child care: Critics say middle-class women need to stay home and take care of their children rather than go to work. Simultaneously, they say lower-class women need to get off welfare and go to work rather than staying home with their children. Of course, if middle-class women stayed home, they would need welfare. If welfare mothers worked, they would have latchkey kids.

We need to reflect on solutions to day care. Many politicians suggest tax deductions for day-care expenses. But the poor don't think that way. A tax break in the distant future is meaningless when you don't have enough money and are struggling to make ends meet today. We need to invent more viable options to finance and improve day care.

Perhaps we could create a system in which you had to learn positive ways to manipulate.

We also need inventive antipoverty programs. Most welfare reform was bad art. What would humanistic welfare reform look like? As a nation we have chosen to try to punish the poor off welfare. We use rewards and incentives such as tax breaks to motivate the rich, but punishments to motivate the poor. We need to invent incentives for both. Some of the programs for the rich aren't very inventive and border on out-and-out theft by the rich. Nevertheless, the idea of incentives is basically good. Everything we know from social research says that rewards work, while punishments tend to be expensive and ineffective. A rewards framework should be used to invent programs for the poor as well as the rich. If it works well in one place, why can't it work in other places? We need to give it a try.

Perhaps we could deal with racial problems on campus by having students go on mock interracial lunch dates and gather afterwards to discuss what happened and community reactions. Or a student might shadow another to learn what it is like to be a minority in their community—for example, to see how blacks are followed as "potential shoplifters" when they enter many stores.

An applied sociologist might invent a board game to teach how prejudice, social class, and poverty work. It could be called Opportunities. "Middle-class" players would get to throw two dice each turn, whereas "lower-class" participants would get only one. A similar game, called Archie Bunker's Neighborhood, is designed to develop racial awareness among participants. Advantage is given to "white" developers, rules are enforced against "black" developers, and ultimately "minorities" experience considerable frustration as they

Box 22.8 ■ **Solving Social Problems**

Affirmative Action—A Solution

WILLIAM DU BOIS

The concept of affirmative action begins with the logic that you can't have a fair race if one group gets a lead while the other is being held at the starting gate. You must do something to promote the position of the minority group that is so far behind.

The city of Dubuque, Iowa, once tried to increase diversity. A new factory would locate in their town if they could provide the specialized, skilled labor. At the same time a group of laid-off skilled black professionals agreed to relocate. The city advertised to attract only minority workers. This was during an economic crisis when local workers were being laid off and farmers were losing their farms. Racial divisions erupted. The town found itself on national talk shows nightly, and the Ku Klux Klan even decided to hold a national gathering in Dubuque because it perceived such a favorable climate.

Bringing the new minority residents to town would actually have benefited everyone. Although whites might not have been employed at those particular jobs, the new inflow of money would have benefited the entire local economy, creating more jobs in other businesses. In reality, the jobs were so specialized that few locals would have been qualified if they had applied. However, the racial quota infuriated local residents.

Affirmative action is tricky territory. It is under attack from nonminority groups who feel that it discriminates against them and creates a new class of losers. What should have happened?

To invent a solution, we need a little perspective. Another example might make this situation more clear. In churches, single people are treated as a minority group. Everything is designed for families. A singles group may form, but it is an extra tack-on. Many singles just want to be part of the church; they don't want to

have to join an extra group, nor do they want to label themselves as "single."

Create a win–win situation. The solution is to *identify the needs* of the minority group and then *design programs that respond to those needs*. Don't stigmatize the minority group by specifically limiting a program to them. Don't exclude those in the majority group with similar needs or skills from also participating. Dubuque should have allowed the few whites who were qualified also to apply. Church programs for singles should meet their needs—for example, create a place to go on Thanksgiving—but not stigmatize them as lonely or losers or exclude someone whose spouse is absent for the holiday. Singles might organize to feed the homeless. They enjoy doing something together that helps others rather than just feeling like needy singles without a place to go. Most family members wouldn't want to do something on Thanksgiving or Christmas; they want to spend time with their families. This is precisely the point. However, if they found themselves alone with nothing to do, they could participate. The singles who do want to meet someone will have more success in the context of service than just staring at each other in a meat market.

The basic idea is a different version of affirmative action: Study and identify the needs of the minority group and then design programs to meet those needs, but do not exclude others who also might be benefited by the program.

A similar strategy could be employed with at-risk kids. We should spend money on programs addressing identified needs rather than devoting most of the resources and energy to identifying and tracking who is labeled "at risk."

---

find they have to lie and cheat to become successful . . . just as many have done.

Criminal opportunities could be presented in such a game, complete with risks of going to jail. A sociology class might adopt inventing this game as a class project. Students could bring situations from their own lives as predicaments to include in the

game. The examples could go on and on. The reader might use her or his imagination and invent new ways to deal with the topic. Or perhaps an upper-division sociology class could invent the game and try it out in introductory sociology classes to teach about prejudice or social class. They could then use the experience to revise the game to make it even better.

Box 22.9 ■ Solving Organizational Problems

Getting Involved at Work

WILLIAM DU BOIS

The Oneida Colony in 19th-century New York practiced group marriage. In theory, everyone was married to everyone else. In practice, however, not everyone wanted to have sexual relations with everyone. How could one reject another's advances without leaving both people feeling terrible? In a community that worked closely together, unwelcome advances as well as rejections might destroy cooperation. Oneida solved this problem by having a go-between inquire about the welcomeness of advances.

I propose that we do a similar thing when someone wants to get involved with someone else in the workplace. Despite all the prohibitions about getting romantically involved at work, the simple fact is that people do. Especially when people work closely together on projects, many become attracted to each other and get involved. Having a go-between formally keep track of the relationship protects both parties from the subtleties of sexual harassment.

Rejections could be noted. If advances persisted, there would be someone already aware of the situation who could intervene. Similarly, involvements could be noted: Should a relationship fail, there would be someone who could track the progress, offer counseling if needed, and make sure reprisals did not occur. The company would face less risk of legal liability should problems arise. The individuals themselves would be able to traverse a potentially dangerous situation with both being able to save face—the hallmark of the old-time conception of etiquette.

From the annual book of the Institute for Social Inventions, *Social Dreams and Technological Nightmares* (1999, p. 60).

The need for inventors is everywhere. Government vouchers for day care might spawn a whole new cottage industry of small businesses. If we are really interested in stopping drunk driving, then maybe we need to fund a trolley to take people bar hopping. For such a plan to be successful, we would need to take the stigma off it (not treat it only as a vehicle for people too drunk to drive) and make it fun.

A recent television newscast asked what the police were going to do to stop drunk driving. In reality, the police have little control over drunk driving. If we are honest about it, the approach of our whole criminal justice system is fairly impotent; the root causes of crime are unresponsive to the remedies under its canopy. The then police chief of Minneapolis Tony Bouza gave the City Council back the extra money that they proposed to spend on enforcement, advising them to spend it instead on eradicating the social causes of crime. How might we invest? What might we invent?

Solving Organizational Problems

The sociologist as artist can find plenty of problems in organizations that call for creative solutions. Absenteeism, worker turnover, organizational communication, employee theft, sabotage, labor conflicts, poor motivation and morale, low performance—these are just a few of the opportunities that may invite sociological invention.

These problems often call for the same variety of solutions: creating a better work environment in which employees are appreciated, empowered, and rewarded. Synergy calls for inventing win–win solutions, both between labor and management and between the individual and the organization. As Paul Rossler and Ken Kiser show in their article "Why Organizational Change Fails," change takes time and ample commitment. We spend most of our waking lives in organizations. It is essential that we create organizations were people can flourish.

Nursing Home Staff Absenteeism and Turnover. Many nursing homes experience absenteeism and high worker turnover. They are depressing institutions, and there are not many things that one can do to make them exciting places in which to work—but here are some ideas. Ask local groups to become the backbone of regular games. Develop a group of high school volunteers to become mentors to residents who are experiencing memory loss. Wouldn't that be unique—*youths mentoring adults?*

A top-ranking executive with a large nursing home chain told us recently that they have so much trouble recruiting and retaining staff that they anticipate closing nursing homes in many rural areas during the next 20 years. This is nonsense! We are familiar with the politics of this organization. Staff are concerned but often unempowered. Turnover exists because of an authoritarian management style, a feeling that you can't change the organization, and a lack of resources. Management needs to create an organization that respects people and gets staff involved. One employee idea acted upon is probably worth thousands of dollars in motivational speakers.

Quality of life could also be improved for the residents. Perhaps local churches could adopt a particular nursing home. Maybe residents could be given a choice about meal selections. Being able to control what you eat is a primary freedom. Perhaps local judges might sentence nonviolent offenders to community service in the nursing home: For instance, you might be "sentenced" to play the piano or use some other talent. Nursing homes are the settings for the last years of life of many residents. *Nursing homes should be a celebration of life.* Now that is a novel concept. What could we do to implement it?

Keeping Residents in State.   We know of one social researcher whose state government gave him the assignment to improve the retention of residents in the state. He ended up simply selling them on a traditional research agenda. That is too bad, because one can imagine the possibilities. Bill once put together a brochure for business recruitment in Bloomfield, Iowa, captioned "An Opportunity to Participate in Your Own Life." The best rewards are participation, appreciation, belonging, love, friendship, meaning, and the opportunity to be a star—that is, to make a difference, to be somebody. These are exactly the motivators that would get someone to stay in, or return to, a state. Small business grants, an incubator for new ideas, a marriage matchmaking service are just some of the first ideas that come to mind for keeping residents in state. A whole nation was settled by the Homestead Act; perhaps dying communities could actually give away land or even vacant houses with the understanding that someone has to live there for a given length of time.

Student Retention.   Innovative ideas can also be invented to improve student retention. Colleges have

Box 22.10 ■ Solving Organizational Problems

The Nursing Home
R. DEAN WRIGHT

My mother is in a nursing home, and has been for almost 5 years. She resides in a city of 3,100, the community where I was raised. She has remained there because of a sociological principle: People there know her; she has lived in that community for most of her adult life. My cousin is the social worker, and a person with whom I went to grade school is one of the head nurses. Informal social mechanisms are routinely at work.

When my mother first entered the nursing home, it was owned and managed by locals. I felt comfortable; locals are user friendly. A few years ago the property was purchased by the largest nursing home owners in the country—they own more than 800 such facilities. I quaked: impersonal, business-oriented, noncaring, capitalist....

Guess what? Things have been very good. The workers in the local facility are the same people who reside in the community. The business has made many changes, including architecturally rebuilding to make the nursing home more user friendly. New programming involves patients in highly interactive activities instead of leaving them staring into a supersized television screen. There is better coordination of staff, more training, and the demand for professionalism. In some instances, even big business has come to appreciate sociology and its principles.

had to invent many new programs during recent years to keep their students coming back. Finding one new friend might make the difference between staying or dropping out. A school could build more hangout nooks where friendships might spontaneously occur, as Bill suggests in his article on social architecture. Programs in which juniors and seniors mentor incoming students have been successful at some schools. Some large schools have experimented with having freshmen enroll in at least three classes together so they become familiar to one another. This only scratches the surface. We could get truly inventive. The more we understand demographic and social trends, the more realistic a social invention will become, and the greater will be its chances of enduring and making a real difference in the lives of people.

Ministerial Retention.   Most religious denominations today have a problem attracting enough ministers. Several factors conspire to create the problem. Fewer young people are electing a religious vocation today. More people are now entering seminary in their later years as second careers, meaning that they spend fewer years in the ministry. There is also a major problem with ministerial retention.

As Bill argues in his group home article, juvenile delinquents need to be able to get offstage and out of the public eye; like all human beings, they need a backstage region. So do ministers. We know ministers who drive 30 miles to the next county to buy their beer or wine. Some hesitate to go to the grocery shop in their own neighborhood, because if they do they must be "in role." In short, one of the ways to keep people in the ministry is to allow a minister to be a person.

Sociologists refer to this concept as "role distance." Ministers certainly need to perform all the tasks and duties of the role, but they also need to be able to take the role on and off like a costume. The idea of role models is a faulty concept: It demands that someone be perfect. But underneath our costumes, we are not perfect—we are fragile human beings with blessings and faults, struggling the best we can with our situations. A human being who is trying to be a good person both in and out of role is the best model that we could want. Congregations who want to hire "role models" should purchase cardboard cutouts of characters from television shows and place them around the chapel. Real life demands something better. In today's culture, ministerial roles in which people can't be themselves will be hard to fill for long. More and more people decline such a vocation.

In another approach, many denominations are doing more to encourage lay participation. This is true even in the Catholic Church, in which many things previously reserved only for priests are now shared. Some of this has to do with an emerging phi-losophy of inclusiveness, but much has to do with the growing scarcity of ministers. The Methodists refer to this approach as mutuality in ministry—even sermons are sometimes being delivered by laity. What roles would make more sense to be done by laypeople so the minister could be freed up for other tasks? Each congregation needs to design its own answers to take into account its minister's unique goals, talents, and desires.

There are only two things that a minister must do to keep the congregation going (besides the Sunday service): marrying and burying. The phrase that ministers use for these functions is "paying the rent." However, most people got into the ministry to serve God, to help and to make a difference. What if churches really implemented Christian values such as charity and forgiveness? What if each church became a relevant force for addressing social problems and getting things done? What if there was a spirit of joy in church?

Perhaps we need to make ministry fun. Now there is a novel idea! In previous generations, self-sacrifice and self-denial were commonly shouldered destinies. In the United States today, everyone has the cultural shared meaning that people should be happy. We will have to make ministry a win–win situation both for the church and for the person who is the minister. In what ways could we make ministry fun? Such an approach might be contagious; church might be fun, and more people might even attend.

Closely related to the issue of the declining number of ministers is a decline in membership numbers. One major approach to this issue is to invent programs that have the potential of attracting new participants. These programs could be based on an understanding of demographic trends—working mothers and communities of young people. Today, more and more families like to spend quality time together on Sunday morning. Family time means less time to do traditional religious things at the customary hours. We could develop evening rather than traditional day activities. Some churches have added an alternative Saturday evening service and made their institutions more user friendly. The result: larger attendance patterns on Saturday and diminished activities on Sunday. The more sociologically informed decision making becomes, the more successful will be the outcomes.

Improving Grades. The next time parents approach Pat Sheehan to tutor their children after seeing her "Learning Alternatives" sign, perhaps she might want to try the approach Bill proposes on the next page to improve the grades of a college sorority in danger of losing its charter.

APPLYING SIGNIFICANT RESEARCH FINDINGS

Much of the fundamental sociological research has been done. Rather than further categorization and record keeping, we need to apply what we know.

For example, research shows clearly that the most prejudiced people have had little or no interaction with the people toward whom they are prejudiced. If you live in isolation, it is possible to believe all sorts of preposterous things about the group you are prejudiced against. If you get to know the people as human beings, you know better. When the Supreme Court made its landmark 1954 decision abolishing school segregation, it relied in part on this sociological research finding. The applied sociologist could invent all sorts of ways to apply this. We could get people working together across racial lines on a common purpose or even even against a common enemy.

Another research finding shows that five is the ideal group size. People in five-person groups like each other better, enjoy the task more, and perform better than those in groups of three, four, six, seven, eight, or nine or more people. Sometimes, of course, five is too many people for a particular task. Sometimes you need a team larger than five to adequately represent all contingents. However, all other things being equal, it makes sense to use this finding.

An invention can start from the smallest research finding. In his social architecture article, Bill tells how he started with Homans's Liking Principle, which states that proximity leads to interaction, repeated interaction, liking, and friendships. He consistently applied this simple finding to create a whole atmosphere. Inventors proceed like this. You can start anywhere. Take a research finding. Apply it consistently. See where it leads. You might be surprised.

APPLYING MEANINGFUL THEORETICAL INSIGHTS

So much of what we know about living is fundamental. Writer Henry Miller noted the classic line that we need to "remember to remember." It is simply amazing that we seldom remember errors and successes from our past. You would think that at some time in the future we would realize, for instance, that smaller schools are much more functional and better places in which to be students and teachers than large, formal, anomic structures. Closer, personal space makes social things happen. Larger, formal space retards social things. Since the classic writings of Georg Simmel (1964) in the late 19th century, we have known that elementary fact. Yet we build schools in our suburbs that try to educate two or three thousand students and then scratch our heads in amazement when bad things happen. When will we ever learn from our past and realize that we can be better than we are?

Take time to make a notebook of meaningful theoretical insights. What's important to remember to remember? Include your favorite things. What have you learned in school so far?

Whenever we are consulting, there always comes a point when we really wonder whether we really know anything. Perhaps we've just conned the people (and ourselves). Now that we've got their attention and they're listening to us, what are we going to do? But we can relax. We really did learn something in school. You can trust the research findings and the theoretical insights. Imagine from them. We are operating from a firm base. How can you apply them? Imagine new alternatives and implications. We don't have to prove we are knowledgeable experts by being overly complex. Social inventions can start from the most elementary premises and go from there. Let your mind wander. See where your thoughts might lead. You never know where an idea will take you until you give your mind the chance to consider the impossible.

Differential Association

From a simple, commonsense theory can come radical implications for inventing new programs. Differential association is the elementary idea that you

Box 22.11 ■ Thinking Sociologically—Inventing Solutions

Sorority Grade Improvement

WILLIAM DU BOIS

A student who'd just become president of her sorority came to me after a social psychology class asking how to improve her sorority sisters' grades. The sorority was going to be kicked off campus if their cumulative grade point average didn't improve a tenth of a point. I gave her the following suggestions. I have no idea whether she followed them or what happened. Shamefully enough, I have even forgotten her name. However, since that time, I have routinely given these suggestions to my applied sociology classes.

THE PROBLEM: THINKING SOCIOLOGICALLY

Unfortunately, most sociology students' knee-jerk reaction to the problem of raising a group's grades is usually authoritarian and not very sociological. The first suggestion is often a mandatory study hall. The problem with such an idea is that forcing people just doesn't work. Getting people to the study hall and then making them study is going to be hard. Implementing such confines is probably going to require more authority than a sorority president actually has. Future membership recruitment for the sorority might also suffer from such heavy-handed techniques. Instead, an effective strategy would have to make studying fun, or at least use influence rather than force to get people interested in studying. Perhaps study sessions could be scheduled with a male fraternity.

There are also other strategies that can be used to raise a sorority's grade point average. One-tenth of a point is not much. We should examine the politics of how grades are given and why. Knowing how to study is certainly important, as is knowing what to study. A sorority could certainly introduce classes on study skills. However, this is all very traditional and not very exciting. The university offers classes on *study skills*. What is needed is a new *delivery* system.

Thinking sociologically, we could come up with strategies such as the following.

Making Learning Fun, Matching People

- Study sessions: Match with male fraternity; perhaps have sessions for particular classes or subjects.
- Peer tutors (cross-gender).
- Peer tutors/mentors (sorority members who are really interested in a subject).
- Jeopardy-type games with male fraternity on test items (with neat, creative prizes); or maybe a dating game with test-type questions, or . . . ?

Sharing Information

- Best classes
- Best instructors
- Whom to avoid

Creating New Shared Meanings

- "It's neat to be interested in something."
- "Being smart doesn't make you a nerd."
- Change shared meaning that "Girls shouldn't be smart."
- "It's OK to ask for help in class." Whoever asks the most, learns the most.
- "It's OK to ask for help from other sorority members." We are here to help you. People like helping. It's OK to be vulnerable. It's OK to ask.
- "It's OK to fail." This shared understanding needs to be promoted to remove the stigma of making mistakes. People will be more likely to ask for help, identify problems, admit weaknesses. Failing needs to be non-punitive. Separate the person from the behavior; non-judgmental feedback

Posting a List of Who Needs Help at the Sorority

- List is published so everyone knows who needs help and can offer.
- There are two ways to be on the list. (1) All receiving midterm slips or on probation are on it, with

learn your behavior from the people with whom you associate. This idea is usually used to explain delinquency: People who hang out with delinquents learn delinquent behaviors. It also explains other behaviors: People who hang out around doctors learn doc-

tor behaviors; people who hang out around lawyers learn lawyer behaviors. Human beings reinforce other human beings and feel most comfortable with others who reinforce their behavior (Sutherland, 1947).

classes they need help in identified; or (2) people needing help in certain classes can voluntarily place their names on the list.

- This is not a stigmatized list. One of the changes in shared meanings that needs to occur is a shared understanding that "everyone needs help"— some in different things, some at different times.

Creating a Culture of Interest

- Get people turned on to things they are interested in and excited about.
- Match people interested in subject to sorority mentors majoring in that area
- Offering how-to-study tips.

Creating a Climate of Concern

- Get help when relationships fail: A lost lover can ruin a semester's grade; people need to be aware of this.
- Get help for problems: Coping with personal problems can lower your grade point average. Consider dropping classes to a minimum during traumas.
- Try to help; don't just let others drown.

Presentation of Self

- Packaging term papers: Use laser printer, spiral binding, attractive cover.
- Teachers are people. Even if a paper isn't good, they are influenced by presentation; they are subject to the same influences as others.
- Get to know teachers, ask for help, express interest. Go to their office because you are interested in learning. Do it during the first two-thirds of the semester—that's when nobody comes to see them, and they have time. Be sincere. Your question must be about something you actually are interested in. It must be genuine. Faculty will remember this.

Tricks of the Trade

- Take 12 hours each semester rather than 15. That makes it easier to get better grades while still qualifying for student aid.
- Register initially for 15 or 18 hours, then drop the least interesting classes.
- Smile, nod, respond. Studies show teachers concentrate on the side of the class that is "paying attention."
- Sit in the front and relate to the teacher as a person.
- Drop classes that meet at times of day you don't like. If you are not a morning person, don't sign up for an early-morning class: You won't go that often, despite your resolutions. Delay taking the class for a semester until you can get into it at a better time.
- Take classes with friends. This gives you a reason to show up: If nothing else, it is a time to see your friends. Share rides; that will get you up and going. You also will have someone to get notes from and to study with.

Organizational Dynamics and Bureaucratic Sophistication

- The sorority itself needs to pay attention to drop dates. Make sure everybody drops that needs to. Make it a sororitywide campaign, perhaps going door to door.
- Encourage taking incompletes via a campaign at end of semester by mentors; again, go door to door.

Changing the Culture: Reward Learning

- Parties/rewards if whole sorority gets a certain test score/grade point/final grade.
- Contests, prizes. (Paying for grades works, despite the fact that we don't like it.)
- Rewards for improvement.

This is why we should never *force* delinquent youth and criminal adults to return to their home community and peers following incarceration. We do and then are amazed at the consequences. We do just the opposite of what differential association suggests

we should do. We take "bad" kids and surround them with other bad kids. We send kids using drugs to drug classes, where they make more drug connections. We send shoplifters to shoplifter classes, where merchants recount the horrors of shoplifting—*but* where

Box 22.12 ■ Applying Significant Research Findings

Parental Home Ownership and Juvenile Delinquency

WILLIAM DU BOIS

Oddly enough, one of the most significant factors Clifford Shaw and Henry McKay (1938, 1969) found related to low delinquency was *parental home ownership*. If the parents owned their own home, it significantly decreased their child's chances of becoming a delinquent. Even if a family lived in a a dilapidated neighborhood in a run-down house, home ownership lowered delinquency.

We might ask why this is so. Several factors seem to be involved. If parents own their own home, they have a commitment to the neighborhood. They can't just pick up and leave. They have an investment in the future of the neighborhood. Transitional neighborhoods have high crime rates. When people come and go they don't get involved; they move on rather than change things, and they have no real stake in the area. Home ownership provides roots and a sense of belonging.

Interestingly, Shaw and McKay's research was on the books at the time of the establishment of the notorious East St. Louis housing projects that residents burned to the ground. Many questioned why; cries of "ungrateful" emerged. Public outrage was so great even among liberals that this one event contributed significantly to a decrease in federal funding to the inner city. But we must understand what the residents were doing. These were "the man's" apartments—they represented the social worker, the system. When people raised a torch, no one lifted a hand to stop them. When graffiti filled the walls, no one expected anything different. All the tenants experienced rage at their living conditions. Yet Shaw and McKay's research on home ownership existed before the housing projects were set up. If we had taken their insight seriously, we could have provided ownership. If we're going to *give* people housing, then why not let them buy into it? They could establish equity and actually sell that equity to others as you would a condominium. Even if the payments were only $50 a month, this would establish a sense of commitment, ownership, and investment. Then the East St. Louis housing projects would have turned out quite differently. If someone had started to paint graffiti it would have been on "our walls." And no one would have allowed people to burn "our homes" to the ground. This social invention would have had the added bonus of decreasing delinquency in the community.

---

the kids also learn from other kids new shoplifting tricks and which stores are better targets. Or we send all the bad people in the state to a prison, where they associate and become even more criminal. When will we ever learn?

The never mentioned implication of differential association theory is that we should try to get the "bad" kid to hang out with "good" kids. Teen Court is an interesting program in which we have learned to do just that. With the crack of a gavel, kids go from being part of the problem to being part of the solution. Youth sentence other youth. Sentences are pretty traditional but also include having to serve on future teen court juries. Since most of the teen court jurors are volunteer kids who are doing it for fun, we have "bad" kids sentenced to hang out with "good" kids. The program also provides empowerment and meaning and lowers delinquency (Godwin, 1996).

EXPERIMENTS OR EXPLORATIONS?

In the scientific dream, we strive to get to a God-like place where we would know everything, see all the variables, and comprehend how everything works. Welcome to Central Control: All causal relationships are neatly drawn out on the blackboard. But, as philosopher David Hume noted, when we think we have all the causes and angles figured out, it is time to return to reality and play a game of billiards. Even with total institutions such as prisons, mental institutions, and perhaps cruise ships, control is far from total. There are always unanticipated consequences as human beings strive to regain some power over their situations. We must recognize the impracticality of a predictive social science. For example, we can never predict exactly which students will bring guns to school and go on a killing rampage. It is like looking for a needle in a haystack. And humanity is a very large haystack with few needles.

Another trouble with the scientific model is that it assumes we must first get *control* in order to manipulate. A value-free version of sociology can be used for fair or foul: Political pollsters, market researchers, and jury consultants may sell their soul to the highest bidder as they try to manipulate us for their masters' ends. Such an approach threatens human freedom and dignity. We must remember the old distinction between white magic and black magic. Indeed, the whole Western definition of power is equal to black magic: the power to control and compel others against their will. We must be suspicious of a control-happy sociology that seeks to perfect "the art of enslaving" (Becker, 1968).

Our scientific quest for prediction, control, and certainty would eliminate free will and render others powerless. If we opt for human beings as ends and not just as means, we introduce indeterminancy into the world. If you allow others freedom, it means you can't determine the outcome. Freedom means ultimately the ability to do something that others may not want you to do. If people do only what others want them to do, then their freedom is hypothetical

and not tested. If we respect people as important, then at some point we trust them and refuse to manipulate. This takes a strong person. This is Bill Wagner's approach to parenting.

Research should empower. Rather than manipulating people who have no idea they are even being studied, we should ask people what they need. This was the focus of Corey Dolgon in the janitor's strike, William Foote Whyte with the hotel, and Bernie Jones with public housing design.

The benefit of science is that it provides a map that manages and organizes information. It is not enough to discredit scientific sociology. We need a map to take its place. In Chapter 1, Bill Du Bois provided a framework in which we can do applied sociology. For instance, we can seed resources into the school and community environment that make it less likely that it will foster alienated students who turn to violence. We can create meaningful roles, community, and resources that nurture and empower people.

Bernie Jones quoted Winston Churchill: "We shape our buildings, and then they shape us." It is one of the crucial insights about culture as well as architecture. William Blake said, "You become what

---

Box 22.13 ■ Applying Meaningful Theoretical Insights

Community and Crime

WILLIAM DU BOIS

Tom Wicker of the *New York Times* once did a television special on crime and delinquency. He showed all the fancy things people were doing to try to make their neighborhoods safe: walls and gates around their properties, high-tech surveillance, guards, security firms, fancy locks. In each case all the security wasn't really working: People still didn't feel safe from crime. Then Wicker compared two bordering neighborhoods in Philadelphia. Both neighborhoods were lower-class Italian. Yet one neighborhood had a high crime rate and the other maintained a low crime rate. The difference was that the neighborhood with the low crime rate had a high sense of community. This turns out to be one of the most significant factors in lowering crime and delinquency.

Good neighbors keep you safe. If no one knows you, someone may be over to your house at 2 A.M. in the morning with a U-Haul truck and the neighbors will just think: "Gee, that person's moving out. Never did know who they were." But if you live in a community and they see someone moving your things, they may say, "There's a light on over there, and I know they're at her mother's this weekend." To turn a Frost quote upside down: "Good neighbors make good fences." This is a real community watch program.

Implications: Community building is effective crime prevention. Everything we can do to create community will have the added benefit of reducing crime.

BOX 22.14 ■ Applying Meaningful Theoretical Insights

What If the University Really Cared about Social Problems?

WILLIAM DU BOIS

For the university to be fundamentally relevant to social and organizational problems, we need to reexamine our basic framework for knowledge and reconceptualize the role of the university.

THE NATURE OF KNOWLEDGE—A NEW EPISTEMOLOGY

The university typically reacts to social problems by selling society on an academic agenda: more research. As the early sociologists knew so well, more research means action delayed. The dilemma of the social sciences is that all the facts will never be in. Teasing out the truth in an inductive analysis may never bring us to action.

As scholars from Aristotle to Dewey have understood, a science of community is by its very nature political. An applied academy is involved in implementing the ideal society. Social science is by its very nature a utopian science. It requires an interdisciplinary synthesis. To avoid value relativity, the social sciences must be firmly focused on human well-being—this should be our referent. This is the solution of Aristotle, Kant, Comte, Lynd, Mills, Fromm, Maslow, and Becker. It also echoes the pragmaticism of James and Dewey. Social science should be about designing institutions that meet human needs. This means a true partnership with business and government, but not in the academic image.

RE-VISIONING THE UNIVERSITY

We need to reconceptualize the university with specific attention to the following:

Whom We Hire, How We Give Tenure. If traditional research and publications are the ultimate pedigree, faculty may have neither the skills nor the time for viable community service or for implementing solutions to societal problems.

What Counts as Knowledge. We all know that data gathering and analysis is only one kind of sociology. Yet somehow this has become virtually the only standard for evaluating and credentialing Ph.D. candidates.

Dissertations and theses should be demonstration projects in which sociology students invent, implement, and then evaluate a program, organization, or other social invention. This kind of work should count as a significant contribution to knowledge.

Publications versus Significant Community Contributions: We need to develop alternative ways social

you behold." Edmund Carpenter (1970) extended it to society: *They Became What They Beheld.* We create our environments and thereafter they influence us. Then what kind of an environment do we want to create? Bad magic seeks a deterministic environment. Bad magic leaves people passive, controlled, fearful, and without identity. Good magic creates resources people can use in their individual dramas to further themselves.

We don't need more experiments. We need explorations. We must be artists creating new social forms. Otherwise sociology is just armchair curiosity, or it is research findings that others may use for fair or foul purposes. The model of the physical sciences does not fit the social sciences. We need a spirit of play and exploration, discovering new alternatives. We must tinker with our explorations, redirecting and revising them until they work. We cannot afford a failed human experiment.

AN INVENTORS' FAIR

Research methods too often hover between being quantitative or being qualitative. There is a third force in sociology. It is action sociology. Applying research findings and theoretical insights, sociology could become the major incubator for new projects—an inventors' fair.

For the most part, the only people imagining new solutions are those on the political right. Their at-

inventors can be given credit, document accomplishments, and be granted credibility.

Proportionate Full-Time Pay for Part-Time People. Faculty should be allowed to buy out of teaching for community service. Practitioners in the community should be recruited as adjuncts and paid proportionately to full-time faculty. This encourages a two-way street where both the academy and the community gain expertise. If adjunct faculty were paid in proportion to full-time, then people could move back and forth between academia and the community with some fluidity. People could afford to have a permanent foot in both worlds.

In fact, this approach might make it difficult to distinguish who were faculty (also working in the community) and who were community practitioners (also teaching at the university). A true cooperative effort would exist between the university and the community.

Consulting in the Community.   Consulting should not be viewed as a distraction from teaching and intrusion upon research. Consulting is a complementary activity lending expertise for the betterment of the local community and validating the relevance of knowledge.

Seeding Cottage Industries.   Rather than bickering over the proprietary ownership of ideas, patents, and inventions, the university in a service/information economy should strive to seed ideas, generate opportunities, and spawn cottage industries in a synergistic style, thus growing a larger community pie. If a faculty member creates a new enterprise that employs people in the community, everybody wins.

Service Learning and Service Programs.   In the old hierarchy of science as the truth (rather than for the public good), service programs have been seen as "beneath" universities and relegated to community colleges. Service programs should become fundamental components of education. A full-time semester or longer service internship might be an interesting model.

An Incubator for Social Inventions.   The university must train artists rather than technicians. We need to invent, not just inform. The university should create new resources in the community. Businesses, agencies, and people should bring their problems to an Applied Institute for invention and implementation. The university should be a center for demonstration projects.

---

tempts often take the form of trying to outlaw the symptom. But you can't just force your way out of most problems. At best, such naive strategies drive behavior underground. At worse, they pour kerosene on the brush fires of society while adding insult to injury.

In our experience, most sociologists also have very little imagination. When asked to invent, most students vary between the authoritarian and the individualistic: They reach for new legislation—"There ought to be a law"—or they revert to a psychological mind-set that blames and tries to fix the individual. It is as if we have learned sociology, but we don't know it. We are used to coloring between the lines, or doing "normal science." We are not trained to think outside the lines and invent creative new solutions. Indeed, if

sociologists truly knew about creating and implementing new social structures, you would expect sociology departments to be run in innovative ways—in ways quite different from those prevailing in other departments. Such is hardly the case.

What could we invent? We know of one university that gets grants for millions of dollars a year to study rural mental health in the region. For that kind of money, we could *fix* the rural mental health of the region. Imagine the resources that could be generated from that kind of money with creative applications of sociology! Universities are intent on training researchers. We would encourage artists.

In our classes, we have students make a notebook of the significant research findings and meaningful theoretical insights they have learned. What is worth remembering? From research findings and meaningful insights, they are to create a project: Invent something new. Such should become the task of all sociologists.

ACTIVE DRAMATURGY

Shakespeare wrote, "All the world's a stage, and all the men and women merely players." Society is a large adult game of pretend. How do we stage a meaningful drama?

We all need meaningful roles that involve us in a larger purpose. Everybody needs to be somebody. The most significant fact about human behavior is that human beings act with purpose. We are a product of aims and pulls as well as pushes. We need meaning to make sense of our lives. We need to be a significant actor in a meaningful drama; to be part of something important; to feel that what we do matters. As Ernest Becker wrote, " 'Higher' esthetics is precisely that; it calls more of [the human] spirit into play." Contrast, if you will, the bright-eyed 3-year-old with the well-schooled 8-year-old who has learned to sit in straight rows, raise a hand to go to the bathroom, and stare vacantly into space; or with the grown worker who becomes again a childish prankster upon walking in the factory gate. We suck the life out of the school child and the factory worker, and then we worry about motivating them.

By trying to make everything controlled and predictable, we have taken the awe and wonder, the magic and mystery out of everyday life. We have created a passive, shallow society in which love and meaning do not flourish. We must be active participants in our own lives rather than merely after-work consumers. We need an active dramaturgy to better stage the dream on earth.

To review, culture is:

The script, the plot: shared meanings

The roles

The stage directions: norms, rules, and policies

The stage, props, costumes: the material culture

The ethos: the spirit of the culture (general feeling or mood)

In his article on the sociology of architecture, Bill shows how to utilize the physical stage to influence behavior. His article "Transforming Community Attitudes and Morale" demonstrates one way to change the ethos of a community. Des Connor's work on positive citizen participation helps companies create a spirit of cooperation. Sidney Jourard asks us to examine our cultural myths of marriage and to construct a better model. Larry Miller's strategy for organizations concerns their vision and purpose. Marty Miller creates a new shared meaning surrounding sport.

Shared Meanings

Culture is a set of shared meanings. It is shared understandings, definitions of the situation, visions, values, beliefs, myths, folklore and stories. Who are we? And what are we doing? Shared meanings are what sociologist Max Weber called the "webs of our significance."

Shere Hite wrote in *Women and Love: A Cultural Revolution in Progress* that women are changing the script for love. Culture is a story, a plot. The role of woman has changed dramatically. "I love you" used to mean "I can't wait to get barefoot and pregnant." A woman would stay home and take care of the house and the kids. She would take her husband's identity and his goals, and even his name. He'd work and take out the garbage. "I love you" doesn't mean that anymore. We are opening a brand-new story—literally a cultural revolution is in progress. In some ways, none of us knows now just what the story will be.

What would a nonsexist relationship be like—in which people treated each other as fully human? What would a nonsexist romance look like? We don't have any scripts. The sociologist as artist might want to write a song or novel or a play. We are all experimenting with our lives, but we also need common maps and shared understandings to which we can refer when we get confused or lost.

Feminist Gloria Steinem (1983) made the distinction between "eroticism" and "pornography." Pornography is the abuse of power. What would nonsexist eroticism look like?

We might note how the role of woman has changed and is changing. Elizabeth Talbott, a 15-year-old, writes a view of our girl-killing society. She reminds us of Virginia Woolf's line: "A feminist is any woman who tells the truth about her life."

As Rebecca West said in 1913: "I myself have never been able to find out precisely what a feminist is. I only know that people call me a feminist whenever I express sentiments that differentiate me from a doormat."

Definitions of the Situation

By creating new definitions, the women's movement gave voice to private feelings that previously may not have been recognized or articulated, and surely were not acted upon. This is a classic example of the sociological imagination: creating shared understandings that people can then use to interpret their private experiences.

New shared meanings provide ways of recognizing our feelings, organizing our understandings, and creating vocabularies for justifying our behavior. For instance, with the rhetoric of "self-fulfillment," a whole generation rejected self-denial. "Personal happiness" became a legitimate rhetoric of motive. As Theodore Roszak (1981) noted, the new personhood movement did not affect just college students; it spread throughout the culture. Construction workers walked off the job, demanding to be treated like people. Even Grandma and Grandpa wanted to have lives rather than just being "Grandma" and "Grandpa."

Similarly new definitions of the situation changed our treatment of insanity years ago. Redefining bizarre behavior as a "mental illness" rather than blaming "possession by the devil" or "witchcraft" or defining the person as "the village idiot" led to a difference in how we responded to the situation. Thomas Szasz (1974) has argued that we need to redefine the situation further as "problems in living," thus calling for help from financial managers, friends, new opportunities, and perhaps legal representation rather than hospitals, psychiatrists, and pills. The sociologist as inventor might create new vocabularies of motive.

In the article on social architecture, Bill shows how a nursing station might be redefined as a gen-

Box 22.15 ■ Example of a Social Invention

An Etiquette Book for Dating

WILLIAM DU BOIS

As a high school graduation present, my great-aunt gave me an etiquette book. I was never so insulted in my life. It took me a long time to understand what she had intended. In her generation, growing up at the end of the 19th century, etiquette was a collection of practical suggestions for successfully traversing situations.

Today, when it comes to dating, that popular body of collective wisdom and folklore does not exist. The rules have changed, and both men and women don't know how to act. We need a good book of practical advice for negotiating situations. Returning to the old rules and games, as proposed in a ridiculous recent book, won't work. Sidney Jourard points out in his article "Marriage Is for Life" that honest dialogue is critical for healthy relationships. As long as men and women play games with each other, we are setting up problems. As critic Warren Farrell says so well, "Sex-role training is divorce training." Rather than games, people need practical guidelines for creating win–win situations. Someone should write an etiquette book of emerging shared understandings for negotiating interpersonal situations.

---

eral store. Perhaps nursing homes could be redefined as places of life celebration rather than as places where you do meaningless diversions as you wait to die.

We might create a new definition of the situation or shared understanding and make greed socially illegitimate. How would you institute such cultural change? How could we create worker cooperatives such as Frank Lindenfeld recommends, with pay differential ratios of 1 to 6 between the lowest- and the highest-paid employees, rather than 1 to 300?

Roles

By the time they reach high school, most students are relegated to the sidelines. There is more room for participation in the parking lot than in the gym. But everyone needs to be someone. People need to feel

Box 22.16 ■ Artist's Toolbox: Overcoming a Girl-Killing Culture

Hello, My Name Is Inigo Montoya

ELIZABETH TALBERT

I used to play with the neighbor boy. We acted out great scenes from movies we had seen. We would take turns playing the heroes and the villains. Sometimes, there was no hero, just a simple, "Paint the fence . . . Paint the house . . . Wax on, wax off," from *Karate Kid*. But one of my favorite scenes to act out again and again was the powerful one from *The Princess Bride* where Inigo Montoya is almost slain by the villain who killed Inigo's father. Inigo, determined to fulfill his life's aspiration, fights the pain, gets up, and repeats this same line over and over again: "Hello, my name is Inigo Montoya. You killed my father. Prepare to die." They then go into a dramatic fencing arrangement. I loved every second of this game; my Spanish accent was good, and I felt at that moment that I was Inigo Montoya. That's the great thing about imagination. The worst thing about imagination and that type of self-confidence is that you can lose them. And when you lose those two things, it is a great challenge to accept the loss and try to either recover them or move on with your life.

About seventh grade, I stopped playing the "Inigo Montoya" game with my friend. I still wanted to be characters in movies and books, but I resigned myself to the insubstantial feminine roles. Inigo, Lancelot, D'Artagnan, and Robin Hood stepped back to let Buttercup, Guinevere, D'Artagnan's girlfriend (I think her name is Constance), and Maid Marian replace them in my mind. (Give me a break: Buttercup? The name says it all!) My pretend magic potions and imagination soon made way for lipstick and multiple issues of *Seventeen*. Now, one of the prime challenges in my life is to try to regain the self-assurance I once possessed. It's a challenge to oust the stereotypical feminine role from myself.

Recently, I've found a whole new group of characters from my books and movies. This category isn't as evident as the others, but it's still there. It includes the women characters who could fence if they put their minds to it. They're the characters who are dead-determined and who understand themselves. Good role models, eh? I found Anne Shirley, and I read about Morgan Le Fay. I read *Gone with the Wind* and knew Scarlett fit right into my category.

And then there's me, Elizabeth. I think there must have been some cave-in on my inner self. Now I'm waking up from the coma produced by it. I hope. It's painful for me to see young women giving into the temptation of just being Buttercup, some "superior" person's girlfriend. So, like Inigo, I have been hit in the stomach with a dagger, but I refuse to give up my fight. My self is much too important a thing to surrender to a wound, no matter how deep.

The greatest challenge of all would be taking on society. I'll start my campaign by setting the latest *Seventeen* on my rocking chair. I will stare at the half-starved model on the front and, not necessarily speaking to her, but to girl-killing society as a whole, including everyone surrendered to it, I will say a simple sentence. "Hello. My name is Elizabeth Talbert. You killed my dreams, my spirit, and my self-acquaintance. Prepare to die." Then, delivering a defiant swipe at the magazine with my conjured sword, I will say, "Hello. My name is Elizabeth Talbert. You have killed countless spirits. You killed part of mine. Prepare to die." When the magazine is at its point of surrender, I will say, "Hello, my name is Elizabeth Talbert. You shall not kill me. I shall never die from your infliction."

Then the curtain will close on that scene. Maybe someday, I will again say playfully to the neighbor boy, "Hello, my name is Inigo Montoya. You killed my father. Prepare to die." But, for now, I believe my truest line is, "Hello. My name is Elizabeth Talbert."

Elizabeth Talbert played volleyball for Marty Miller when she was 12. At 15 she wrote this essay; it was published in *New Moon* (September/October 1998). Reprinted, with permission, from *New Moon*®: The Magazine for Girls and Their Dreams. Copyright © New Moon Publishing, Duluth, MN, www.newmoon.org.

that what they do matters. We need to create meaningful roles and to provide opportunities for participation in a meaningful drama.

When Des Moines was without running water for nearly a month during the Great Flood of 1993, crime was way down. Everyone worked together for a higher purpose. Rather than looting abandoned houses, gang members worked side by side with others to sandbag the river. Social distinctions melted away as a common need was recognized.

We need opportunities to be a star. Falling in love is certainly such an opportunity. So is having someone important to do something for, whether it is a lover, an elderly person in need, or someone seeking a mentor. We need to train more matchmakers and fewer counselors.

Being a peer tutor or a peer counselor may or may not reduce the delinquency rate for the person tutored or counseled. It probably will reduce the delinquency rate of the peer tutor or counselor. Motivation is a reason to get up in the morning and a reason to stay up. It is being interested in someone or something. For years we have tried to get a friend of ours in Des Moines to keep his inner-city radio station on the air all night on weekends. It would give one or two kids an opportunity to be a star—they would spend all week planning for their DJ stint and would probably stay out of trouble.

Staging Meaningful Dramas

Sociology has been far too conservative, coloring between the lines when it comes to thinking of what sociologists can do. We need to be bold and outrageous. A sociologist could design a convention hotel that creates a sense of community, provides nooks and crannies where old friends could congregate, and also promotes mixing so people will be more likely to meet the right contacts. Perhaps a sociologist could create a miniature golf course complete with a clubhouse designed to be a teen hangout. Or we could design a singles apartment complex where young professionals new to the area could find friends and potential partners, all in an atmosphere that respected their privacy and their lives. We could create a lovers' retreat where couples could rekindle relationships.

Perhaps a sociologist could invent a youth volleyball program as Marty Miller did, or invite citizen participation in the planning of public projects run by large corporations as Des Connor does. Maybe you will set up a booth at the county fair, like Pat Sheehan, peddling your skills to an audience that doesn't quite know what sociology is. Maybe, like Dean, you will take youth to the streets to meet the homeless and will return to invent more realistic programs.

We need to create resources that stimulate others to come up with their own meanings. This is a diverse country. Social planning should not be prescriptive. It needs to provide resources people can use for their own purposes in their personal dramas.

Alienation is what happens when a system of meaning does not make sense. You have the feeling no one cares and you don't feel you belong. No one really gives a damn what you are going to do with the rest of your life; they are too busy making a name or a place for themselves. Across the United States there are communities where teenage suicide is epidemic. Why are so many choosing not even to play the game? How can it be that walking into high school and killing your classmates and yourself make sense?

Our culture built on rationality, marketplace goals, and technological gimmicks has abandoned feelings and the deeper yearnings of the human spirit. It is a sterile culture with few opportunities for legitimate innovation. So many today seem to connect to mystery and wonder only in the form of the macabre. It is shock politics seeking to rekindle some sense of magic in a world gone deaf and numb to meaning. Becker (1968) shows that evil is a complex response to the coercion of the human spirit and a shallowness of meanings. Evil results from powerlessness and lack of meaning. Without realistic hope, all sorts of negative behaviors occur. We need to create society as an active drama in which we can participate rather than be alienated.

THE SPIRIT OF ART

Go into any shopping center in any community and the shops have the same names and the people who work in them wear the same uniforms. The diversity

Box 22.17 ■ **Artist's Toolbox: The Need for Meaning**

Society as Drama

WILLIAM DU BOIS

Life is a drama. People need meaningful roles to feel important. We need to feel that we matter and can make a difference in a meaningful drama. Successful corporations find ways for their employees to be stars. Creating such opportunities is even more critical for youth. The gang provides a way for stardom and meaning. We must find healthy ways to be somebody.

Suburban delinquency as well as inner-city delinquency is explainable by a sterility of available meanings. Increasingly, there are fewer and fewer resources for teenagers. By high school only the very best participate in sports and other school activities. Some towns now ban youth from driving around the loop. Architects are hired to eliminate places where young people might congregate at shopping malls and even in parks.

Relegating youth to the sidelines is not only ineffective but dangerous. They soon learn that there's more heroism and drama in putting on gang colors and strutting down the street than in learning to say "Do you want fries with that, Ma'am?" Youth want to make a difference. They seek meaningful opportunities to participate in their own lives. An active dramaturgy suggests we need to design settings where youth can stage positive, meaningful dramas.

The main complaint among youth in every city, large or small, is: "There's nothing to do." One idea might be to create a youth bar designed consciously as a stage for meaningful interaction. Counselors could help wait tables and thus become familiar and be on the spot at the point of crisis. Leaders from different groups could be hired and trained in conflict resolution, self-esteem, and the art of making everyone a star. Staff would seek to match youth with similar interests to get people involved and interested. The club could become living theater, where people would bring ideas for promotions or events and a promotion person would help create them.

A youth club can't be second rate. It is competing against gangs, private beer parties, and adult bars for those with fake IDs. A youth club must be state of the art. It has to be exciting. People need a sense of ownership. Creating a club as living theater offers kids the opportunity to create meaningful roles and provides resources where people can stage their real-life dramas in an more effective fashion.

---

of little stores and unique shops has been ground into a standardized reality. George Ritzer has called this the "McDonaldization of America." It is an eroding of all depth and subtleties. People, moods, feelings are stuffed into preset molds.

We have mass-produced a common-denominator reality. The lowest common denominator has something for everybody, but it doesn't really satisfy anybody. There is little room for true participation. It is small wonder we produce alienated youth, alienated workers, and alienated customers.

We see something similar in most fields of artistic endeavor. A few large corporations own most of the movie and television industry, the music industry, art publishing houses, and bookstores. It is hard for something new to make it. Everything must fit the common mold of what some market researcher has decided sells. Products are addressed to the hypothetical consumer. Art becomes a mere commodity.

The reason art thrives in the first place—the reason for the surprise hit television show, the "sleeper" movie, or the first novel everyone reads—is that it strikes a chord in people. When something new manages to break the mold, market research declares it in fashion and scurries about mass-producing clones. However, art is always new. It brings us back to fresh experience. That is why the original touches us in the first place. As copies become but clichés blending into the environment, they lose their ability to move us. Even the song that was originally an artistic breakthrough becomes a parody of itself as it gets played over and over and is appropriated to sell cars, mouthwash, and real estate. The richness and substance that might inspire is gone.

BOX 22.18 ■ Staging Diversity in Society

Television Scheduling

WILLIAM DU BOIS

By scheduling television programs as if they were in a high school wrestling meet, TV execs have created a situation in which everyone loses: shows, networks, and the viewers.

How many times have you turned on the television and found nothing on? Or how many times have you checked the TV schedule and found three things you'd like to watch all scheduled at the same time? TV programs are scheduled by the networks for one reason only: ratings. And while the networks are struggling over a particular time slot, they are losing the war. They have forgotten the viewer. In their battle over consumers, we lose—and, ultimately, so do they.

It is a wrestling-meet approach. In a wrestling meet, coaches try to win every match by putting their best wrestlers up against the other teams' best (and the worst against the worst). TV executives do the same; they try to win every time slot.

I remember the first time it happened. The networks took my three favorite shows and scheduled them head to head: *Murder She Wrote, Family Ties,* and *Spencer for Hire.* Forced to choose, I watched *Family Ties,* which promptly went off the air the next year. *Spencer for Hire* quickly followed, a victim of the ratings wars; and I never quite got interested in *Murder She Wrote* again. I found myself scanning the Fox network on Sunday evenings.

The percentage of television sets tuned to the networks is down. Part of the reason is of course cable, but some of it is the networks' insistence that they're the only game in town; rather than court viewers, they force them to choose as they draw a bead on the competition in a gunfight at high noon—or, more aptly, at 8 P.M. Sunday night. Many times there is nothing to watch. Many people switch off the TV. The big winner is video rentals.

The alternative is a "market segments" approach. You arrange the schedule so there is always something on for everybody. This way everyone wins, including advertisers and networks.

We are actually living in an anti-art culture. We see art as a diversion, not as a fundamental way of organizing our society. The marketplace seeks to capitalize on the art product, but it does not value the artistic process. The larger culture wants confirmation of its prevailing clichés, not invitation to new perceptions.

Even in our culture, however, magic has not completely disappeared. Utopian visions seem to reopen the childlike eyes of awe and wonder in all of us from time to time. It may be the insight of the poet who touches us in a way we had almost forgotten. There are times when life seems more a miracle than the cause-and-effect phenomenon of science. Children are born, and life awakens itself with fresh possibilities. People we loved die, and life again becomes a fragile construction on this side of the veil. Our lives change, and who we thought we were also changes. We fall in love, and the world is transformed down to our very perceptions. We undergo a career change or a divorce or a cross-country move; and the world seems so different until we manage to snap it back in place. Or we go through profound changes that shake us to our very roots, and yet the rest of the world seems untouched. The larger reality is there only to capitalize on our experience by selling us wedding rings, coffins, and souvenirs.

We need a society that respects and enhances private experience and helps us better live the dream. We cannot afford a society where love is banished backstage. We need to provide people with resources to better live their lives. Art provides direct inspiration, reconnecting us to our most fundamental longings. Artists invent ways to answer human needs. They teach us how to be more ourselves. They show us how to love more. To better stage the dream. We need to create better relationships, organizations, and communities; we need to shape a healthy society. We are moving with social forces, other people's dramas, and the very hand of life itself.

Box 22.19 ▪ The Artist's Toolbox

Participatory Resources

WILLIAM DU BOIS

Participatory resources are addressed to the coproducer rather than the consumer. They range from the micro to the macro:

1. In a nightclub consultation, I made a DJ stand function as a voting booth. Similarly, a jukebox can function as a voting booth where people can debate and settle on a collective mood, usually without ever being conscious of such a dynamic. Both allow and encourage people to participate rather than being merely passive consumers of an environment.

2. An annual horse-drawn tour of the Christmas lights involved people in a small community recovering from the first major bank closing in the Midwest. Some of the dynamics surrounding this participatory resource could have been predicted: romantic couples, sing-alongs, family/company outings, drinking parties, entrepreneurs making their own horse-drawn rigs, houses getting decorated, a spontaneous community cleanup, witnessing your community and taking a look at your life/town, tourists, increased business, and so forth. Other outcomes would have never been anticipated: the distance some would travel to ride, the loyalty of seniors even on the coldest nights, free publicity from the area TV station, its use in the TV station's on-air Christmas greeting, and a young couple's decision to get married on the tour.

3. The Bloomfield Christmas Elf giveaway program creatively applied B. F. Skinner's research findings showing the best rewards are spontaneous, on-the-spot, and tied to a behavior.

4. Bill Veeck was general manager of the Cleveland Indians baseball team when they set an attendance record that lasted more than three decades. He said the secret of a good promotion is "incongruence," that is, something that just doesn't fit. "You could give

10,000 people an ice-cream sandwich or give one person 10,000 ice-cream sandwiches." With the latter, people were forced to do something before the ice cream melted. They organized lines tossing and distributing them throughout the stadium. The entire crowd became involved. The incongruence presented a problem that had to be solved. It demanded participation.

5. On a macro level, the EPA sells "pollution credits." They put a cap on the total amount of pollution in an area and then allot so many credits per company. Over time, the total is gradually reduced. In the meantime, companies that pollute under their share of pollution credits can sell their excess to other companies who are over the limit. Rather than just punishing negative polluting behavior, this sets up an interesting dynamic in which nonpolluting behavior is rewarded and companies have a positive incentive to get below their quota.

6. A more controversial example: The Clinton administration's health care plan was a wonderful example of a participatory resource. The plan itself had wonderful participatory dynamics, if people would have only played. It set up a new game with some loose rules and room for all sorts of interesting dynamics to evolve. Some of the most interesting would have been around home health care, prevention, and health care delivery in inner-city and rural areas. Incentives would have been there for innovative artists to invent new things. Unfortunately, insurance companies opted to wage a propaganda war to disguise their greed, and most Americans never learned the truth about what the plan looked like. Note what the plan did: It set the frame (the loose rules of the game and incentives) and then would have allowed the rest to evolve through a participatory process. This could have been a model for what the ideal social resource would look like in a humanistic society.

Artists testify that they are but a channel through which the magic passes: "It comes through me, not from me." Science looks for techniques, but the artist looks for inspiration. The artist invites us to life. The artist awakens childlike awe and wonder. Art puts us back in touch. It is innocence and beauty. It is explo-

ration and connectedness—depth and wholeness of experience that calls us to our soul.

The spirit of art is about love. True art puts you in touch with a larger power—pick a word: creativity, the muse, God, the life force—through which the spirit is expressed. It makes you feel alive. It whets your appetite, brings you back to you. It awakens creativity and a reverence for life. It invites us to a larger depth of spirit. As one author wrote, "The function of poetry is to invoke the muse" (Graves, 1952, p. 7). Art puts us in contact with the same feelings the artist felt. And very often those feelings have just been dormant; you didn't even know you had them.

Artists as painters, potters, or sculptors must master their medium. They must learn the subtleties and nuances of how to work with oils, acrylics, clay, or bronze. So must the sociologist as artist learn his or her media. The sociologist's tool box contains significant research findings, meaningful theoretical insights, and the very elements of culture itself.

The Reverend Gary Davis, who invented many popular guitar styles, used to say, "You be too perfect and the mistake done already been made." This comment reminds us of the T-shirt Marty Miller wears as a coach the first day of practice. If you make a mistake, it gives you a chance to discover something new. That is certainly true of playing the guitar: You find a sound you didn't even know you could make, and you wonder, How did I do that? We watched a friend painting. She does the same thing: lay in color and then correct it. Most inventions are serendipity. We need a spirit of play and exploration.

PARTICIPATORY RESOURCES

Participatory resources are social inventions that empower the person. Bill Du Bois coined the term *participatory resources* to include any program, rule/policy, social form, or shared understanding a sociologist might invent that people can use in their own purposes and meanings or can utilize in their personal struggles and troubles.

Some examples might include:

1. A new rule or policy that creates a dynamic such that when people work the system, positive behaviors emerge.
2. A new social invention or form that solves a social problem, such as a way to arrange court-ordered visitation of children without jeopardizing a battered woman's safety.
3. A shared understanding in an organization or community that promotes creativity and innovation.

4. A social arrangement that creates a synergistic win–win situation.
5. A physical design or prop that encourages participation and which actors can utilize in their own dramas.
6. Inventive solutions to social problems, resources that help create community, empowerment, and meaning.
7. A new program such as restorative justice, which empowers and meets the needs of all participants.
8. Any newly invented aspect of culture that individuals can use to create more meaningful lives.

Participatory resources are vague and sketchy. They loosely frame a situation, leaving room for participants to fill in the details. Participatory resources are resources artistic sociologists can invent that people can utilize for their own purposes.

To clarify more: McLuhan talks of hot and cold mediums. Hot mediums are detailed and defined. Scientific and bureaucratic planning is that way; so are canned environments such as fast-food restaurants. Everything has been scripted and planned. Cold mediums, on the other hand, are imprecise and fuzzy. Participatory resources are cold mediums. They frame a situation but demand that the details be filled in by the participant.

Of course, a new invention may not necessarily change things for the better. We need to pay attention to how it might be used. This is the problem of the artist. Like any architect, we must anticipate potential uses and unintended consequences. Some tools lend themselves better to some things than others.

THE SOCIAL CHANGE ARTIST AS MAGICIAN

A true applied sociology is involved in action research. As Kurt Lewin says, "The best way to understand something is to try and change it."

For example, how might a sociologist create community in a neighborhood? In many ways, a friendly neighborhood is a self-fulfilling prophecy. But how do you change it? The article "Transforming Community Attitudes and Morale" offers one way. We should be training social change artists.

Sometimes it takes a magician. In his classic article on creating successful programs to reduce delinquency, Marty Beyer (1991) wrote:

> *The best juvenile programs start with a visionary leader, a wizard. One of the strengths of the wizards who operate effective adolescent programs is that they acknowledge that the goal of treatment is to change values. . . . Changes in behavior and values are only possible if young people can integrate their past with their new selves. Wizards whose residential or day treatment programs achieve enduring change in participants train staff to invest a substantial amount of their time enabling people to accept new values without rejecting their origins.*
>
> *Wizards are the ultimate motivators. They are not bound by training or habit to one approach. They do what works. Their programs are driven by the needs of the young people. (p. 174)*

Success is more than just finding a charismatic leader. It means inventing social resources. It is at that intersection of sociological knowledge, personal lives, and fate that seems like a calling—where people change. The research on successful aftercare shows that social support and job placement are critical. In practical terms, we are talking about getting a new life. The key for these young people is getting involved with someone or with something. Just as with falling in love, it may be simple to diagram on the blackboard, but it is easier said than done. When it happens it is true magic.

How does it happen that someone changes? William Foote Whyte (1982) tells the following story:

> *When I was beginning a study of the remarkable shift from conflict to cooperation in the Inland Steel Container Company, one day I confessed over the telephone to a vice-president of the parent corporation that I was having difficulty in figuring out the change. He commented, "Yes, that did puzzle me for a long time, but I have finally figured it out." In eager anticipation, I asked for the answer. His reply: "They learned to trust each other." For a moment I sat speechless, waiting for something else to come out of the receiver, but that was all there was. I drew a deep breath and said, "Well, I guess you're right, but how did they learn to trust each other?" The vice-president laughed and said, "You're the sociologist. It is up to you to figure that out." That is the challenge for sociologists.*

> *. . . We are rarely able to change behavior simply by telling people that they should change their attitudes. Attitudes, beliefs, and values do indeed change as people, in grappling with persistent social problems, devise creative ways of restructuring their activities. . . . In studying the social inventions that enable people to bring about such changes, we can build a more useful applied sociology. (p. 13)*

How do we train sociologists in the art of meaningful organizational intervention? As Rossler and Kiser show in "Why Organizational Change Fails," real organizational change is hard and takes time. Much of what passes for organizational consulting are dog and pony shows that create a sensation but leave the organization fundamentally unchanged.

Humanistic power involves inviting, courting, setting the stage, creating resources. There is a theatrical term to describe what the director does: *mise en scène.* The phrase means "to put in the scene." After we write the script, create the roles, make the costumes, set the stage, assemble the cast, and provide the props, something must still happen to breathe life into the play. The director doesn't *make* it happen. It is more a matter of setting the stage, enthusing the participants, and allowing the magic to show up. This is an interesting metaphor.

Neil Smelser's (1962) theory of collective behavior could be recast as a method of staging a "happening." For collective behavior to occur, there must be several recipe ingredients: structural conduciveness, structural strain, mobilization for action (available resources), and generalizing beliefs (which provide the definition of the situation). Finally, there must be a precipitating factor—a spark—to ignite the other ingredients. How does the sociologist act as a catalyst to make something happen? Social change artists basically assemble the ingredients and then wait for a precipitating factor to ignite the magic. They may also act to help create the chemistry to ignite the spark. One of the most frustrating things as an applied sociologist is knowing that you have the combination to unlock a problem, but not being allowed to turn the key.

In the legend the magician moved with the grain and purpose of life. We are offering up a resource that people can use. Some of it is waiting for the right time and place. Sometimes you get confirmations: You know that this is going to work, and things start falling into place. And sometimes, no matter how hard you work, it just doesn't happen. Whether we are religious or not, we must all admit that the hand of life is moving through our lives. There are social events and forces moving beyond us. Social change as art is beyond cause and effect. No technique will suffice. Magic is empowering people.

INVENTING THE IDEAL SOCIETY

The early sociologists felt that sociology should be a science in the service of human needs. We agree. We should start with a basic sociological understanding: Societies and organizations that don't meet human needs have all sorts of problems.

This doesn't mean a good society will not have deviance. Deviance performs essential functions, including showing us where the boundaries are and demonstrating the individuation process whereby juveniles break away from their parents and establish their own identities. It does mean that synergistic societies that meet both societal and individual needs will have fewer social problems.

The exact enumeration of human needs is not important. A list of needs might include security, meaning, love, recognition, and even fun. Psychologist Abraham Maslow talked of "being motivators" (b needs) and "deficiency motivators"(d needs). D needs are the basic needs for survival, including food, shelter, and clothing. They operate as pushes—we try to avoid deficiencies. The b needs include self-esteem, meaning, and love. They are pulls: We are drawn toward them. Sociologist W. I. Thomas spoke of the Four Wishes: security, new experience, response, recognition. (Response is the realm of intimacy: people responding to you and caring.) People in conflict resolution are also realizing that we need to pay attention to human needs (Burton, 1990a, 1990b). Peacemaking is more than avoiding war.

Architect Ken Kern once wrote, "It would be easy to build homes if people just knew how to live." What audacity. It is as if a tailor had said, "It would be easy to make clothes if people just had the right kind of bodies." Unfortunately, the same kind of logic often takes place in society: "It would be easy to build society if people would just follow the rules and con-

Box 22.20 ■ The Artist's Toolbox

The Power of Belief

R. DEAN WRIGHT

People sometimes have to believe in magicians. Without a common belief about the power of magic, there could be no change. Several years ago there was a movie titled *The Dragon Slayer*. In one scene the apprentice talks with the old wizard, the dragon slayer. The student asks his master why there are so few slayers of dragons today. The sage tells his apprentice that once there were many dragon slayers, but people stopped believing in them and today there is only one dragon and one dragon slayer—and "When I slay the dragon, there will no longer be dragons to slay and no longer be a dragon slayer." He confides that he is the last and that there will be no need for the apprentice, because people will no longer believe in dragons or dragon slayers. Similarly, people who believe in magic work together and make things happen and change in society. Once people stop believing that they and their leaders can make a change, there will be no change. Believing is a powerful thing. Whether we call it magic or skill, it has the power to create a better world for everyone. Belief changes our world down to our very perceptions.

Whatever people believe in, is what lives. The opposite of "Seeing is believing" is true. You have to believe in it to see it. We are the creators of culture and reality.

---

form." We must learn that social arrangements, social forms, and institutions should function for the person; we must not just attempt to mold the person for society. The social forces that the early sociologists talked about are human needs and purposes. We must take them into account. Society needs to provide a series of resources to meet basic human needs.

Following Ernest Becker, we recommend several ideals for the good society:

- Buber's "I and Thou" is the model for the ideal relationship. This is the model of relationship Sidney Jourard talks about in "Marriage Is for Life." You and I are equally important, and I feel your needs just as if they were my own. It is the "Golden Rule." You are not an object for manipulation (an "it"), you are a "thou."

- Self-esteem (a subjective feeling of well-being) should be the basic mandate for the social sciences. What is good? In an effective society, people will experience a feeling of well-being. Social institutions must answer human needs.

How we develop self-esteem is not just a psychological issue. We need to create a social context in which the person can flourish. For a while, psychology talked about the "human potential." We must come to realize the truth of Charles Cooley's: "The individual and the group are but two sides of the same coin." Self-fulfillment takes place best in the context of a community in which you are known, have real friends, and enjoy social support. Community is not a matter of being stuffed into community as we might feel at a family reunion—it is not conformity. It is an environment in which you have neighbors and can also be yourself.

Democracy is a paradox, as C. Wright Mills (1959) noted: a group that values individuality. Yet everything we know from small group research says that groups tend to stamp out individuality. How do we teach people to be individuals in the face of the group? How do we create a society that allows and enhances freedom and exploration and still remains a society?

How would we teach respect? How do we make it OK for people to be different? This gets at the very crux of our social need to conform, and to fit into the group. We should create inventive programs to deal with schoolyard hazing, teasing, taunting, and tormenting. We should not just wait until a child becomes a bully. We might address all mocking of difference (inferiority, superiority, overcompensation). How do we create a group that supports individuality? It is a valid research question for exploration and invention.

The clear implication of Hal Pepinsky's "Safety from Personal Violence" is that we need to promote empathy. Can people learn empathy? By definition, it seems that true sociopaths cannot be taught empathy. The best we can hope for is to turn them into technicians who learn to follow the rules for their enlightened self-interest. But isn't that what we all do? Furthermore, empathy may just be dormant in many people mistakenly labeled sociopaths. What kind of program could we invent for sociopaths? You may not be able to teach empathy, but it can be recognized, developed, and nurtured.

How do we promote love? Nothing is harder, but nothing is more essential. How do we create community? How do we create relationships that enlighten and empower people? This is the calling of the true sociologist as artist.

Humanizing Bureaucracy

We tried to find someone to write an article on humanizing bureaucracy. Most people laughed: they thought it was a contradiction in terms. Yet most people spend most of their waking hours in large organizations that care little about them. We need to humanize the workplace.

When it comes to humanizing bureaucracy, we need to get fundamental. A bureaucracy has four elements:

> written—the nature of writing
> rational—thinking and planning
> rules—dynamics of rules and policies
> roles—division of labor, ritualized rule following

Darrol Bussler and Mark Carey worry about their peacemaking circle becoming institutionalized. *Institutionalized* is simply a fancy sociological way of saying patterned and routine. The trick is to hold expectations lightly; to remain conscious and notice when we are moving something to the level of a norm (where violations of expectations receive sanctions), and thus to prevent things from hardening. As a Spanish proverb says, "Habits first are cobwebs, then they are cables."

Sidney Jourard recognizes a similar dynamic in marriages: Holding expectations lightly keeps an image of marriage from taking on a life of its own and dominating your interaction with another human being. Jourard recommends that we move beyond masks and meet each other in constant dialogue. Bill Wagner takes the same approach to parenting. It is not that the parent refuses to be a parent when needed. It is not that you play the role of friend. It is having role distance so that you can drop the parent mask and also be a human being. We must be con-

Box 22.21 ■ The Artist's Toolbox

The Nature of Rewards and Punishments

WILLIAM DU BOIS

As behavioral scientists, we probably know more about rewards and punishments than anything else. Rules and policies are inherently involved with rewards and punishments—or what sociologists call sanctions.

1. *Rewards are more effective than punishments.* All research suggests rewards work for a long time while punishments are relatively ineffective. Even B. F. Skinner's work on rats demonstrates this to be true. If rewards work better than punishments for rats, they certainly work better for human beings.

2. *Rewards are more efficient than punishments.* Punishments are much more expensive.

3. *Punishments create behavioral pollution.* Punishments are accompanied by unanticipated and often unwanted side effects; punishments are nonspecific.

4. *When a reward becomes a right, it no longer functions as a reward.* When a reward becomes institutionalized or expected, it no longer works as a reward. The first manager who ever gave away a Christmas turkey had found a spontaneous way to reward employees. By the next year and the next year, however, the turkey had become expected—seen as part of the job benefits and viewed as a right. Similarly, Christmas bonuses probably worked well when they were an unexpected surprise. Now many employees put their bonuses on their MasterCard right after Thanksgiving. Even a small decrease in the expected bonus would cause severe financial strain. The bonuses no longer function as rewards but are rights.

To be effective, rewards need to be spontaneous, on-the-spot, and tied to a behavior. We must stay forever creative in establishing rewards. Once a reward becomes institutionalized, it's no longer a reward.

5. *When a punishment becomes a way of life, it no longer functions as a punishment.* When a punishment becomes routine, expected, a part of normal life,

it no longer functions as a punishment. Youths who are sent to high school detention the first time worry about it; they miss the bus; they fear what will happen. The youth who frequently gets sentenced to detention learns to do time: He or she makes friends, finds ways to pass the time, and perhaps even discovers new things to do on the way home. When punishment is normal, it just becomes part of the everyday landscape and losses its reinforcement value.

6. *Punishments are informational,* providing feedback concerning the extent of unacceptability. When a punishment exceeds its reinforcement value, the excess becomes something else.

7. *Rewards and punishments are not additive.* Subtracting a reward is not the same thing as a punishment. Removing a punishment is not the same thing as a reward. Fear and attraction are different realms. There is a difference in kind between winning a trip to Hawaii and finding out your father is not dying. Learning you did not win this week's lottery drawing isn't comparable to finding out someone stole your wallet. The whole realms of rewards and punishments are totally different theaters. One is not just a positive and the other a negative. They involve different experiences, different emotions, different dynamics, and different players.

This is too often misunderstood. Maslow probably can be seen as a footnote to Skinner in distinguishing between "b" and "d" motivations. The b or being motivations are pulls. We are attracted to them; we desire them. With d or deficiency motivations, we are pushed away from them; we seek to escape.

8. *The best rewards* are participation (empowerment, ownership); appreciation (praise must be genuine); belonging (the best of the "team" and community concepts); interpersonal rewards (friendship, love, liking, positive interaction); meaning (motivation is meaning).

scious of the natural tendency of ideas to become rigid and reified. Ideas are necessary to express our thoughts, but patterns of thinking can also turn to concrete and prevent us from seeing.

In primary roles such as marriage and parenting, we are supposed to be close to others. In secondary roles, we don't want to invest such time. Secondary roles are designed for efficiency. That is the very

Box 22.22 ■ The Artist's Toolbox

Community and Empathy

WILLIAM DU BOIS

The community of the research that finds a sense of community related to low crime rates is not just the community of strong norms and conformity. Nor is it merely community organizations that interrelate and network together. That may be a symptom of community, but it is not how we got there.

Community is feeling responsible for each other. It's not just a matter of having strong community norms. It's more than just correcting other people's children. It's being there for them. It's not a matter of people who don't mind their own business and get in each other's business. It's that people feel responsible for each other. And take responsibility for one another. Low crime societies don't just abandon individuals to their own devices.

It's not the community of intolerance and conformity where you are stuffed into community. It's not something that is just tacked on through a neighborhood watch. It's not a matter of just having interrelating agencies solve the problem for us. Relegating it to agencies and professionals is really a true confession of the lack of community.

Community is that feeling of "we" that is missing so much in America. It's knowing your neighbors. It's caring about your neighbors. It's responding to your neighbor's needs. Community is helping with a pole barn raising if your neighbor's barn burns down. It's helping sandbag to protect from the flood. It's bringing over food when your neighbor's crops have been decimated. It's taking in your neighbor's kids when they are sick or need to be fed or clothed. Community is looking out for one another.

That's what community means and that's the community that translates into low crime rates.

---

reason they came into existence. We are not looking for a relationship at the checkout counter at the grocery store; we want milk or margarine or cigarettes. And yet we often feel diminished when a clerk parrots some singsong phrase that the corporate office has prescribed. Whatever chance there was for even a fleeting human exchange has been preempted. We

need a healthy amount of role distance. We must notice how bureaucracy goes together. It is really quite subtle. Bureaucracy is a system of secondary roles designed for a purpose. Social designers need to pay particular attention. We must be careful how we rehearse our parts. Sidney Jourard argues that even when you are playing a role, it is essential to be transparently yourself and let others see who you are. Otherwise, roles can destroy our humanity and cast us as strangers even to ourselves.

Bureaucracy is also rational planning. Rational, scientific planning means all the details must be scripted in advance. Obviously, we wouldn't be able to plan a *good party* that way. There would be no room for anything to happen. There would be no room for participation. Successful planning may mean simply assembling ingredients and allowing people to use them for their own purposes and dramas. It is similar to the magician's version of Smelser's (1962) theory of collective behavior: assembling ingredients and waiting for a spark.

We need a way of planning in which thinking doesn't replace living. This requires a way of talking about the world that organizes our understandings but doesn't prevent spontaneity and newness. We need a way of creating an organization that gives us a sense of direction and puts people together in an organized fashion, but does not cripple the human spirit.

It is interesting to note the organizational consulting going on with religious organizations. Organizational development models are being taken straight from secular bureaucratic organizations and pasted onto churches, religious service organizations, and even monasteries. This provides an excellent illustration of the aspects of scientific bureaucracy that render even the last vestiges of "the sacred" predictable and routine. It also highlights the need for inventing new forms of organization. We need new models of organizations that are quite different from the rational, scientific bureaucracy if we are to transform the world.

Max Weber wrote that bureaucracies were originally a way to routinize charisma. Rather than risk the precariousness of societal change following the death of a charismatic leader, a bureaucracy was introduced as a way of making charisma routine. It is interesting to look up the word *charisma* in the dictionary. It means literally "a gift of grace." With a rigid structure of rational planning, we eliminate spaces where magic, charisma, and grace can occur and influence the planning and shape of the organization. Vision is something you can gain by climbing to the mountain-top for inspiration, but once you come down from the mountaintop, everything is done by procedure. In a scientific process, intuition is allowed in only during hypothesis formation. By regimenting behavior, we may outlaw potential abuses, but we also repress creativity, positive innovation, and expression. We prevent anything new from happening. Magic cannot intrude. There is no way for grace to make a difference in the daily functioning of most organizations.

By trying to eliminate the capriciousness of charisma, we also prevent the spirit from intruding. How could we structure organizations and leave room for the movement of the spirit in the organization? It means a different way of planning, thinking, and organizing. How could we design an organizational structure that sets the stage for miracles?

Rules and Policies

As Maslow noted, "If the only tool we have is a hammer, we tend to treat everything as a nail." If the only tools we have for social design are rules, then we tend to treat everything as a problem for legislation.

Georg Simmel felt that sociologists should study the fundamental social forms—the tools we use in constructing the social world. We need to understand that different social forms have different characteristics and dynamics. Tools lend themselves to some tasks but are not as appropriate for others. We need to understand what a social form can do and what are its limitations.

No social form is more important to understand than rules and policies. Just as where architects place the walls influences human behavior, so does where we draw the lines of the world. How and where we create rules and policies makes all the difference.

There is a Lao Tzu saying: "You should rule a nation like you fry a small fish—with the least possible turning." Such a laissez-faire approach is popular in management theory today. Less structure is seen as

better. Actually, this is just one side of the coin. The other side of the same coin is that whenever we have a problem, we reach for legislation: There ought to be a law. We have an all-or-nothing approach to rules and policies. However, flipping the coin from one side to the other is not effective. What we need is a whole new framework. We need to understand what rules can do and what they cannot. We need to design better structures.

Outlawing something doesn't necessarily eliminate it. It may just drive it underground. Drawing a line also means that you must police that line. Without enforcement a line doesn't really exist. Witness the quaint antique laws still officially on the books that haven't been paid attention to in years. There is also always a lot of activity around a boundary: There is a natural tendency to test the limits to determine exactly where the line is. Can you drive 5 mph over the speed limit, or 10, or 15? It takes someone crossing the line and getting arrested in order for the rest of us to know exactly how fast is too fast. The value of punishment is feedback: It is informational; you are over the line, and it won't be permitted. Feedback needs to be just loud enough to convey this information. Too great a punishment can create unanticipated side effects. We need just enough volume to get someone's attention, but not so much that we incapacitate them or turn them into perpetual criminals. The sociological insight must be that you can force someone to do something, but not without consequences.

Despite the lawyers' dream, writing a rule down on paper and making it law doesn't mean that behavior will follow. Saying doesn't make it so. And even if the behavior does follow, it doesn't mean the situation will turn out the way we planned. Rule making can take us only so far. We must understand the dynamics of human behavior Rules are essentially resources that we offer to people that they will use for their own purposes.

THE SOCIOLOGICAL CONSCIOUSNESS

We are used to thinking in individualistic terms. We blame individuals for their problems and assign them total responsibility for fixing them. The layperson's idea is that sociologists think "society did it." Such a

BOX 22.23 ▪ The Artist's Toolbox

The Art of Rules and Policies

WILLIAM DU BOIS

Do rules accomplish what you want? Or do they just sit there, ignored?

We need to understand what rules can do. And what rules can't do. Just writing something down on paper doesn't make it so. Human actors will always take rules with a grain of salt and manipulate them for their own purposes. We need to understand the fundamental dynamics of rules and policies.

PEOPLE WILL ALWAYS WORK THE SYSTEM

Either we can bemoan this fact—to no avail—or we can design rules and policies with this dynamic in mind. Everyone works the system. The governor does. Lawyers do. Factory workers do. When we make a law, the first thing people do is decide how to get around it or hope to integrate it in a way they can live with. When you design rules and policies, you are really offering up a resource people are going to utilize for their own purposes.

THE SPIRIT OF THE LAW

In political circles, we may debate the appropriateness of the spirit and the letter of the law. But for organizations, policies must be designed for only one reason: to accomplish the purpose for which they were intended. We are interested in the spirit and not the letter of the law. Indeed, no organization functions by the exact letter of its rules and policies. If you don't know someone in an organization willing to cut through red tape, you have to go through channels and nothing gets done. When organizations such as the Postal Service prohibit strikes, workers organize work slowdowns. They do so by following the letter of the law. Following the letter of the law brings their organization to a grinding halt.

BUREAUCRACY IS THE ART OF WRITING

Bureaucracy, according to Max Weber, is a set of written, rational rules. Being able to write effectively to convey the spirit of the policy is essential. Legal jargon is the opposite of effective writing. Good writing conveys what is meant and what isn't. Use understandable language.

FORMAL AND INFORMAL NORMS

The difference between formal and informal norms, or rules, is usually whether something is written down or simply an oral understanding. Rules and policies should be designed to accomplish your purpose. This often means setting a line of formal policy quite different from what you actually want to accomplish. We need to be aware of where the development of *informal shared understandings* will draw the line.

For example, often signs at highway rest areas warn, "No Overnight Camping." Does that mean you can't pull off the highway and sleep if you are tired?

---

version of sociology deserves to have fallen into disrepute with policy makers and the general public. Blaming everything on social causes and freeing the individual from any responsibility is simplistic and just plain wrong. We need to teach people what sociology is. It is inventing resources that people can use in their individual struggles. Behavior takes place in a context. We can seed resources into the environment to increase the probability that certain behaviors will occur.

Sociology is a probability model. When Bill was working with the Bloomfield Chamber of Commerce, he found some store owners whose general attitude was that "if someone wants to buy something, they will." Thus, they considered signs, advertising, window displays, and promotions to be a waste of money. They failed to understand probabilities. Some investments are clearly a waste of money. Others increase the likelihood that someone will buy something.

Probability is a step at a time, a nickel-and-dime approach. How do you get one person to spend one more dollar? How do you increase the likelihood that people will look in the store window? How do you increase the probability that they will enter the store? How do you get one person to stay 5

No. The informal shared understanding is that you can sleep as long as you don't create a nuisance. The formal standard is invoked only if someone violates the informal understanding.

WORST-CASE SCENARIOS

Boards of Directors often sit around worrying about what could possibly go wrong and legislate on that basis. Many governments legislate to keep the past from ever happening again. Instead, we should design rules and policies for normal, everyday interaction. When worst cases arise, deal with them as exceptions. If you create rules and policies for worst-case scenarios, you design bad rules and policies.

FEW WILL OBEY UNREASONABLE LAWS

In my hometown, a certain park has a 5-mph speed limit. A 20-mph might have been obeyed, but 5 mph means nothing. People pay no attention. Every time you make a law that you know most people won't obey, you are setting up a danger of discrimination, because you know police can decide to enforce the law at will against whomever they choose. You turn the law or regulation into a joke, as in the FBI warning against copying videotapes.

Furthermore, needs will always dominate. People will try to get their needs met. Outlawing them will not prove effective. You might make eating illegal, but that doesn't mean people won't eat.

THE LIMITS OF LEGISLATION: WHEN TO MAKE A RULE, WHEN TO TALK, WHEN TO DO NOTHING

We have developed a cultural reflex of picking up the pen whenever somethings bothers us: "There ought to be a law." We must discover McLuhan's idea that writing itself is a medium—a cultural invention that is not a neutral container for our ideas. The medium is the message. Ideas take on new content from their container. Writing adds new seriousness and a new dimension to ideas. Consider how seriously the average employee takes "being written up" as opposed to a verbal reprimand.

We must understand the limits of what we can accomplish with rules. Our first tendency is not to talk or confront someone face-to-face. Instead, we dash to the office and write a memo or issue a new rule or policy. Problems can often be dealt with more effectively at the lowest level of structure possible. Many policies are issued with only one person in mind. There are times to make a rule, times to write a memo, times to say something in person, and times when the problem will simply work itself out if you do nothing.

There are also times when jumping to a higher level of abstraction and making a rule will give you legitimacy and alleviate problems. Rules are resources people can bring to the situation and use for their own purposes.

more minutes looking around? We are playing with probabilities.

This is the way that geology works. Mountains are formed an inch at a time as sediment is laid down year after year. Across geological time mountain ranges form, and also erode by this same process. It doesn't take much. Unfortunately, human weight gain also works the same way.

We can take a similar approach to crime. How do we make it less likely that a person will turn to crime? How do we create an opportunity that increases the probability that even one person will change their life

for a night? For a week? For a year? We need to create resources that enable people to be good; that increase the likelihood of people's making the right choices.

This is really the sociological consciousness: taking a situational approach to increase the probability of an action. How do we get one customer to stay 5 minutes longer exploring our merchandise? Similarly, you can improve student retention at colleges by getting one more freshman student to make one more friend or get involved in one more activity. You look at the situation and create resources viable for people in that situation.

SYNERGY: MAKING THE GOOD SOCIETY

Sociologists need to be artists inventing new solutions to problems and creating societies and organizations where people flourish. We must create a win–win situation between individuals, between the individual and the organization, and between the individual and society. Synergy must be our evaluative criteria for any design or program. If there are still losers, we need to return to the drawing board.

Beyond Pluralism: Making Values Matter

One cliché has it that sociologists should begin by confessing their values at the onset of research. According to this view, values are only a matter of stating one's biases. True values—points of origination and direction—are missing in this schema.

We are into a conversation about what kind of a world we want to make. We must expect more than just a cold war standoff or peaceful coexistence between values. This kind of standoff works only when we're on other sides of the wall.

There is no accounting for tastes. People don't need to agree on liking broccoli, liver 'n' onions, or sweet potatoes. Values are a different matter. San Francisco, known as the prototype of pluralism and tolerance, erupted when homeless Vietnamese were found eating stray dogs in Golden Gate Park. In Vietnam eating dogs was normal. However, value relativity means nothing when we are debating eating the family pet. It is not just a matter of different tastes. *Beyond pluralism, we must begin the hard conversation about values—about the world we share and the world we would make.*

As Bill Wagner shows so persuasively in his article on parenting, we are in a postmodern world: We have learned that values are constructed. We must determine what to construct. "Human nature" is a self-fulfilling prophecy. Are people good or are they bad? A lot depends on what you expect and how you treat people. What values are important? What should we make? Robert Henri (1923) says in *The Art Spirit,*

> The study of art is the study of the relative value of things. The factors of art cannot be used constructively until their relative values are known. Unstable governments, like unstable works of art, are such as they are because values have not been appreciated. (p. 27)

Synergy: A Synthesis and Shared Meaning for Sociology

What is the good society? Synergy needs to become our evaluative criteria. We need to create a new shared understanding: In the long run, a win–win situation is the only thing that is practical. Greed is merely expedient and will result in all kinds of eventual problems. Synergy demands a higher-level understanding. Synergy is increasing the size of the pie rather than fighting over shares of the pie.

We must realize that there is no place to run. We are all in this together. Losers are dangerous. They are always waiting for next season to get even. They will murder you. They will rape you. No matter how high you build your house on the hill, they will break in. They will mug you. They will carjack your Lexus. You can treat your employees unfairly. They may not have the power to walk out on strike, but there are other consequences: sabotage, employee theft, alienation, lack of motivation, absenteeism, worker turnover. It was psychologist Erich Fromm who summarized the key sociological insight: You can do anything to people, but you can't do it without consequences.

It is amazing how, as a people, we came to a cult of greed. Talking with a university administrator in California not long ago, we realized that the new breed of millionaires and billionaires created by our technology-crazed society are almost totally individualistic and see the world in individualistic terms. The administrator related how these new possessors of wealth refuse to give their money to social causes: "I made it, and if they wanted to they could too" is their response. Even the old capitalists socialized their children into philanthropy. They set up foundations, and when their children reached majority they were forced to decide which worthy causes would annually receive money Although the old-line wealthy made money in sometimes unscrupulous ways, they also had a sense of charity. That is not true today. The new wealthy have no history of social conscience and are not giving their wealth back to those from whom they made their fortune. This pattern becomes more and more sharply defined as time passes. Charities are starting to suffer for lack of money, yet this is the era of fast wealth and extravagant personal spending.

Ernest Becker writes that the problem for August Comte and the early sociologists "was how to get social interest to predominate over selfish private interest." If we synthesize what we have learned during the first 150 years of sociology, we find that our research and experience "shows exactly what Comte had wanted: the fullest possible correlates of the dependence of private troubles on social issues."

> *Recurrent evils like sadism, militant hate, competitive greed, narrow pride, calculating self-interest that takes a nonchalant view of others' lives . . .* all stem from constrictions on behavior and from shallowness of meanings; *and these could be laid in the lap of society, specifically in the nature and type of education to which it submits its young; and to the kinds of choices and cognition which its institutions encourage and permit. Man could only be ethical if he was strong, and he could only be strong if he was given fullest possible cognition, and responsible control over his own powers. The only possible ethics was one which took man as a center, and which provided him with the conditions that permitted him to try to be moral.*
>
> *The antidote to evil was not to impose a crushing sense of supernatural sanction, or unthinking obligation or automatic beliefs of any kind—no matter how "cheerful" they seem. For the first time in history it had become transparently clear that the real antidote to evil in society was to supply the possibility of depth and wholeness of experience. Evil was a problem of esthetics. . . . It had never been so well understood that goodness and human nature were potentially synonymous terms; and evil was a complex reflex of the coercion of human powers. (Becker, 1968. pp. 325–326)*

Becker notes that the ideal for overcoming alienation is to "try to achieve maximum individuality within maximum community" (1968, p. 251). This formula is nothing other than synergy. It should be how we evaluate social inventions.

Synergy and Its Pretenders

It is important to understand what synergy is and what it is not. There are many possible pretenders.

We need to be very careful about making synergy into a norm. Synergy is not a matter of forced conformity. Synergy can't just be legislated. People cannot just be stuffed into consensus. It is not "Thou shalt get along" or enforced cooperation.

Nor is synergy a laissez-faire approach. It is not pluralism. Synergy boldly gets us involved. Synergy bridges new territory to address what are basic human needs and to forge new agreements on values. What is important? What matters? What kind of world should we make?

Synergy is not just a good trade. Synergy is not just wandering around looking for a bargain or good deal. This is not just an economic exchange between separate individuals. Synergy transforms both me and you; who we are and who we will become. It transforms the self and the other; the individual and the community.

Synergy is not just matchmaking. There is a popular psychological version of synergy floating around. Popular writer Stephen Covey speaks eloquently about the need for win–win situations. Covey's genius is that he understands that synergy is a matter of commitment. However, to understand synergy only as a dynamic between individual actors profoundly misunderstands and trivializes its societal impact. It is not just a matter of putting the right people together or finding the right match.

Synergy is a matter of inventing. It is inventing new resources that individual actors can then utilize in their interactions. It is creating new social forms from which the community and the individual both benefit. It is inventing social arrangements that align organizational goals and individual interests.

We also must be careful about compromise. You may compromise on wants, but you can never effectively compromise on needs. Synergy is a commitment not to settle for anything less than win–win solutions. Often it does not seem possible. However, once we absolutely commit to synergy as the only possible path, new options magically appear. Synergy brings something new into life. Synergy is ultimately about discovering, creating, and inventing. It begins the work of sociology as art.

To Make a Better World

To the sociologists who have come before us, we need to say, "Thank you for your research findings, facts, and theoretical insights; now we are going to apply them."

Graduate schools encourage students to stuff the library with meaningless trivia disguised as Ph.D. dissertations and masters' theses. Can you imagine what would happen if instead we were encouraging these people to create new projects in the community?

With scientific/academic sociology, the final product is the research paper, article, or theoretical insight. The final product of an applied sociology is the invention itself: the day-care center, the homeless youth shelter, the new rule or policy, the new organization. Theories, papers, and insights are means, not goals.

What if graduate students were inventing new things and then taking their dissertation committees for a tour? At South Dakota State University, for example, there are 40 Ph.D. students. What if there were 40 Ph.D. students trying to invent new projects in the community? Even a 90 percent failure rate would still mean four successful projects. Sociology departments across the nation could make a better world.

REFERENCES

Becker, Ernest. *The Structure of Evil*. New York: Free Press, 1968.

Beyer, Marty. "First, You Find a Wizard." *Corrections Today,* April 1991, pp. 166, 172–174.

Burton, John. *Conflict: Human Needs Theory*. New York: St. Martin's Press, 1990a.

Burton, John. *Conflict: Resolution and Prevention*. New York: St. Martin's Press, 1990b.

Carpenter, Edmund. *They Became What They Beheld*. New York: Outerbridge and Dienstfrey, 1970.

Du Bois, W. E. B. *The Autobiography of W. E. B. Dubois: A Soliloquy on Viewing My Life from the Last Decade of Its First Century*. New York: International Publishers, 1968.

Emerson, Ralph Waldo. "On Self-Reliance," in *Self-Reliance,* edited and with photography by Gene Dekovic. New York: Funk & Wagnalls, 1975. (Original publication 1844.)

Fritiz, Jan M. "The History of Clinical Sociology." *Sociological Practice,* 1989, pp. 72–95.

Godwin, Tracy M. *A Guide for Implementing Teen Court Programs*. Washington, D.C.: Office of Justice Programs, Office of Juvenile Justice and Delinquency Prevention, 1996

Graves, Robert. *The White Goddess: A Historical Grammar of Poetic Myth*. New York: Creative Age Press, 1948.

Henri, Robert. *The Art Spirit*. New York: J. B. Lippincott Company, 1923.

Mills, C. Wright. *The Sociological Imagination*. New York: Grove Press, 1959.

Park, Robert E., and Ernest W. Burgess. *Introduction to the Science of Sociology*. Chicago: University of Chicago Press, 1921. See especially pages 42–44.

Roszak, Theodore. Speech at Sonoma Institute, Bodega Bay, Calif., 1981.

Shaw, Clifford, and Henry D. McKay. *Brothers in Crime*. Chicago: University of Chicago Press, 1938.

Shaw, Clifford, and Henry D. McKay. *Juvenile Delinquency and Urban Areas*. Chicago: University of Chicago Press; 1969.

Simmel, Georg. *The Sociology of Georg Simmel,* translated, edited, and with an introduction by Kurt H. Wolff. Glencoe, Ill.: Free Press of Glencoe, 1964.

Smelser, Neil J. *Theory of Collective Behavior*. New York: Free Press, 1962.

Steinem, Gloria, "Erotica vs. Pornography," in *Outrageous Acts and Everyday Rebellions*. New York: New American Library, 1983, pp. 219–230.

Sutherland, Edwin H. *Criminology*. Philadelphia: J. B. Lippincott, 1947, pp. 6–8.

Szasz, Thomas, *The Myth of Mental Illness: Foundations of a Theory of Personal Conduct*. Rev. ed. New York, Harper & Row, 1974.

Whyte, William Foote. *Human Relations in the Restaurant Industry*. New York: Arno Press, 1977. (Original publication 1948.)

Whyte, William Foote. "Social Inventions for Solving Human Problems." *American Sociological Review,* Volume 47, 1982, pp. 1–13.